FRONTIERS
OF FEAR

D1453845

FRONTIERS
OF FEAR

IMMIGRATION AND
INSECURITY IN THE
UNITED STATES
AND EUROPE

ARIANE CHEBEL D'APPOLLONIA

CORNELL UNIVERSITY PRESS
Ithaca and London

First published 2012 by Cornell University Press
First printing, Cornell Paperbacks, 2012

Printed in the United States of America

Library of Congress Cataloging-in-Publication Data

Chebel d'Appollonia, Ariane.
  Frontiers of fear : immigration and insecurity in the United States and Europe / Ariane Chebel d'Appollonia.
    p. cm.
  Includes bibliographical references and index.
  ISBN 978-0-8014-5068-6 (cloth : alk. paper) —
  ISBN 978-0-8014-7774-4 (pbk. : alk. paper)
  1. United States—Emigration and immigration—Government policy.   2. Europe—Emigration and immigration—Government policy.   3. Border security—United States.   4. Border security—Europe.   5. National security—United States.   6. National security—Europe.   I. Title.
  JV6483.C457 2012
  325.73—dc23   2011037719

Cornell University Press strives to use environmentally responsible suppliers and materials to the fullest extent possible in the publishing of its books. Such materials include vegetable-based, low-VOC inks and acid-free papers that are recycled, totally chlorine-free, or partly composed of nonwood fibers. For further information, visit our website at www.cornellpress.cornell.edu.

Cloth printing   10 9 8 7 6 5 4 3 2 1
Paperback printing 10 9 8 7 6 5 4 3 2 1

For Simon, with whom I like "dancing in the moonlight"

Contents

FIGURES AND TABLES

Figures

Tables

ACKNOWLEDGMENTS

The origin of this book dates back to 2004—although I was not aware of it at the time—when I boarded a plane for Pittsburgh to become the first research fellow at the Ford Institute at the University of Pittsburgh. At that time my immediate concerns were to be allowed to travel with my cat, Lola, in cabin, to find a place to live, and to finish preparing my courses for the semester. I did actually find a house (I even married its owner), I enjoyed teaching again in the United States, and I spent a fortune on air tickets for Lola as the initial trip turned into a long journey leading to a new life—and this book. I completed it the day Osama bin Laden was killed. Given the mission and the structure of al-Qaeda, I suspect that he will loom as large a symbolic figure in death as he did alive.

When I started this project, there was already a vast literature on immigration issues, as well as on the impact of 9/11 and the subsequent development of counterterrorist legislation. However, most studies either focused on some particular aspects of immigration policies or addressed security issues as mostly unrelated to a more global context. They provided useful but patchy insights, instead of exploring why and how immigration policies were becoming more intrinsically linked to patterns of democratic development and the enhancement of security. My conviction was that the critical linkage between these dimensions was both a source of, and symptomatic of, some of the most salient and urgent problems facing both Europe and the United States today. This book is thus comprehensive in character. It is intended to provide a systematic and critical evaluation of the immigration-security nexus. That nexus is defined as the implementation of restrictive immigration measures intended to fight terrorism, while counterterrorism is used as a way to manage migration flows and control minorities. My goal is to show how and why the excesses of securitization have been detrimental to both migrants and immigration policies, generating in turn further insecurity both in the United States and in Europe.

I believe that a transatlantic comparison is crucial for at least two reasons. First, the United States and European countries face similar immigration and security challenges, and they have implemented policies that share common features, such as the emphasis on border controls, the framing of immigration as a terrorist issue (even before 9/11), and the reappraisal of state sovereignty to the detriment of civil liberties and human rights. Second, they all have to deal with the controversial and mostly unexpected outcomes of securitization, such as increasing illegal immigration and "homegrown" terrorism. On both continents, I argue, the search for greater security has both created more insecurity and degraded democracy, as surveillance, profiling, rendition, and the use of military courts have enhanced the prospects for the recruitment of a generation of domestically born terrorists.

I am very grateful for the financial and logistic support provided by the following institutions: the Ford Foundation; the Carnegie Corporation of New York; the Graduate School of Public and International Affairs and the European Union Center of Excellence at Pittsburgh University (where I was located in 2006 as a Fulbright Transatlantic Fellow); the Department of Political Science and the Graduate School at Northwestern University (where I was the Roberta Buffet Visiting Chaired Professor in 2005); and the CEVIPOF at Sciences-Po (Paris).

I would like to acknowledge the useful comments I received from workshop participants at Johns Hopkins University, New York University, Harvard University, Northwestern University, Princeton University, the University of Pittsburgh, Boston University, the University of Warwick, Florida International University, Sciences-Po (Paris), the European University Institute, and at meetings of the American Political Science Association, the International Studies Association, and the Council of European Studies.

I also very much benefited from the expertise of individuals who participated in the ISI Immigration Research Network that I co-directed with Simon Reich: Ilya Prizel, Didier Bigo, H. Richard Friman, Francisco Javier Moreno Fuentes, Patrick Ireland, John Tirman, Zsolt Nyiri, Lynnelyn D. Long, Carol Bohmer, Jan Willem Duyvendak, Frank D. Bean, and Susan K. Brown.

I wish to extend my deepest gratitude to friends and colleagues who provided me intellectual and moral support: Vivien Schmidt, Jolyon Howorth, Wendy Kates, Martin Schain, Michael Hanchard, Michael Loriaux, William Keller, Louis W. Pauly, Patrick Le Galès, Elspeth Guild, Kate Rothko, and Richard Ned Lebow. They all have made my work and my life in the United States much easier. I am also much grateful to my colleagues from the School of Public Affairs and Administration and the Division of Global Affairs at Rutgers University, who facilitated my migration to New Jersey.

I would also like to thank my students on both sides of the Atlantic, who forced me to focus on key questions—and sometimes to provide answers. I discussed with them most of the issues addressed in this book, and their reactions encouraged me to complete this work.

Comments and criticisms from two anonymous reviewers helped me to revise the earliest version of the manuscript, for which I am grateful. Herman Schwartz, with the approval of Peter Andreas, rightly believed that the initial proposed title sounded like a "boring shopping list" and suggested the current one. At Cornell University Press, Roger M. Haydon was exceptionally supportive. I gave him many reasons to run away (such as a first draft of five hundred pages, single spaced), but he never departed from his (British) poise in the face of my (French) transgressions. I could not have written this book without his guidance, incisive criticisms, and resilient confidence.

Over the years, I have been fortunate to have friends and relatives who helped me to get through life's painful events while sharing my happiness in the brightest moments. I am especially grateful to Julie, Lorène, Marc, Isabelle, Charles, Yacine (who left the boys' band too soon), and Simon Reich, my loving husband and best friend. This book is dedicated to him with my love and greatest admiration. Because he had faith in my ability to write this book, I did it—thanks to his intellectual support and his affection. Because he has a unique talent for combining high moral standards and joie de vivre, I feel lucky to owe him so much.

We are both immigrants, and children and grandchildren of immigrants. Like our ancestors, we had to adapt to a new country and to adjust to a new way of life. Unlike them, we did it by choice. In memory of them, we appreciate our fate.

ARIANE CHEBEL D'APPOLLONIA

FRONTIERS
OF FEAR

Introduction

The Immigration-Security Nexus

> The only fence against the world is a thorough knowledge of it.
>
> John Locke

In the immediate aftermath of the terrorist attacks of September 11, 2001, the U.S. government instituted a series of emergency measures designed to seal U.S. borders, grounded all aircraft flying, and imposed a lockdown on networks of transportation. Once it was revealed that the nineteen hijackers were foreigners, critics of the supposedly lax immigration system argued that the government should use all means available to protect the nation's security, notably by enhancing and enlarging the border security functions of the Immigration and Naturalization Service (INS). Within a week, the Immigration and Nationality Act was adopted. Under the new rule, the INS was allowed to detain any alien for forty-eight hours without charge and to extend detention for an additional period in the event of an "emergency or other extraordinary circumstance."[1] So began a series of reforms as the first step toward the implementation of harsher immigration restrictions supposedly designed to strengthen security.

In Europe the same process ensued, reinforcing the security logic of immigration: "Because any migrant may be a terrorist and because so many migrants come illegally, any measure restricting illegal immigration would be an effective anti-terrorist measure."[2] The measures adopted by the Council of the European Union on September 20, 2001, led to the "immediate strengthening of surveillance measures under article 2.3 of the Schengen Convention," with "utmost vigilance" in the issuing of residence permits and a "more systematic checking of identity papers."[3] A week later, the Justice and Home Affairs Council meeting encouraged EU member states to refuse the admission of non-European nationals (or third-country nationals, TCNs) for security reasons, including cases of economic immigration, family reunification, student visas, and long-term residency. Similarly, the Council Common Position on combating terrorism adopted in December 2001 provided for "appropriate measures" to be taken "before granting refugee status," to ensure that an asylum seeker has not planned, facilitated, or participated in terrorist activities.[4]

Over the next several years, the bombings in Madrid (March 11, 2004) and London (July 7, 2005) consolidated the policy linkage between immigration and security. Tony Blair's reaction immediately after the London bombings, for example, was symptomatic of the growing assumption that immigrants posed a security threat. He condemned immigrants who refused to "share and support the values that sustain the British way of life" and "have a rudimentary grasp of the English language." Thus, in the United Kingdom, as well as elsewhere in the European Union and in the United States, the common trend was to implement restrictive immigration measures allegedly designed to fight terrorism, while counterterrorism policies were used as a way to regulate the flow of immigrants and asylum seekers and to enhance the surveillance of minority groups already established in Western societies. The effect of these measures was to fortify existing negative perceptions of immigrants that subsequently legitimized and reinforced prevailing policies.

It was then commonly believed that immigrants as a group posed a security threat because they—as a group—were more likely than nationals to commit terrorist attacks. On September 1, 2005, however, Al Jazeera aired a suicide video recorded by Mohammad Sidique Khan, the leader of the London bombers. In this video, Khan declared he was a "soldier defending Islam" who was "avenging his Muslim brothers and sisters." Even more disturbing than his fanaticism to many was his broad Yorkshire accent. Indeed, three members of the "7 July Group"—Khan, Shehzad Tanweer, and Hasib Hussain—had been born and brought up in Britain and were by common standards well integrated into British society. A fourth bomber, Germaine Lindsay, was a British national who had been born in Jamaica. In Spain, of the twenty-eight suspects in the Madrid bombings, nine were Spaniards.

In fact, none of the terrorists who committed these bombings were asylum seekers or refugees. Yet European countries continued the same pattern: adopting new restrictive measures allowing them to revoke or refuse refugee or asylum status to an applicant when there were "reasonable grounds for regarding him or her as a danger to the security of the Member State in which he or she is present."[5] To compound the problem further, although all the 9/11 hijackers were foreigners, none were immigrants.[6] They were aliens admitted on temporary visas. Eighteen received B1/B2 visas for tourist and business purposes, including Saudi nationals who received visas in their country through the "Visa Express" program. French-born Zacarias Moussaoui entered the country using the visa waiver program. Marwan al-Shehhi and Mohamed Atta gained admission as tourists and entered into training at a flight school in Florida. The 9/11 Commission subsequently revealed that the perpetrators of the September 11 attacks entered the United States a total of thirty-three times using either tourist or student visas, like most aliens in the United States. The subsequent congressional joint inquiry into the events of September 11 asserted that better intelligence—not just different immigration laws—would have prevented the attacks.[7] Yet, regardless, further restrictive immigration measures were introduced targeting legal immigrants, asylum seekers, and illegal immigrants—all defined as security threats.

Nothing could interrupt the momentum toward this new focus on immigrants as a security threat, despite strong evidence that the linkage between immigration, internal security, border controls, and "homegrown" terrorism was more complex than initially anticipated. The conflation of the notions of "terrorist" and "immigrant" relied upon the belief that the attacks of September 11 were "unprecedented," marking the birth of a new age alternatively labeled as "global terrorism," "hyper-terrorism," or "mega-terrorism."[8] Indeed, a consensus emerged about the rise in global insecurity in which this network of issues expanded—to incorporate immigration, terrorism, *and* organized crime. This expanded public concern in turn required further "new measures heightening the level of security."[9] Popularized by the media, this security mantra justified an expansive use of the label "terrorism" and with it the profiling of immigrants.

These changes had two effects: First, terrorism was portrayed as a threat not only to people's lives but also to their values, freedom, and economic and social welfare,[10] justifying exceptional responses, outside the realm of normal democratic politics.[11] The definition of security was therefore expanded into many facets of economic, political, and social life.[12] Second, the category constituting the "others"—those outside the mainstream of society who were considered to pose a security threat—was also broadened. Today it includes all those who threaten—or are perceived to threaten—national unity and civil security. The categories of foreigners, immigrants, and suspicious minorities have been increasingly conflated—irrespective of their actual status—because "the impossibility of knowing where and against whom to fight back had led to increasing unease about the identity and the location of the enemy. Consequently, suspicions have been generated towards anyone who seems to share characteristics associated with the perpetrators of violence."[13] Guilt by association, treating all people who potentially look like the enemy as an actual threat, now predominates.

A "worst-case scenario" approach, treating everyone in these categories as potential enemies, has now informed U.S. and European immigration policies for a decade. The guiding principle has been, as a former head of counterterrorism at the CIA put it, "to shake the trees and hope that something will fall out."[14] Western democracies have spent a lot of energy and resources shaking those trees. The results, however, have been highly controversial. Experts and policymakers favoring the securitization of immigration in the United States claim that enhanced border controls limit the number of illegal immigrants and provide more security. They also argue that there is a correlation between immigration and insecurity, and therefore between immigration and terrorism. The security requirements they advocate discriminate against immigrants and their children (irrespective of their status) and more precisely Muslim foreigners and Muslim nationals, according to the logic of "preemptive suspicion." But they are convinced that the fight against terrorism requires a certain degree of infringement on civil liberties and human rights in favor of security needs: that racial profiling and other discriminatory practices are justified as a "lesser evil." Opponents point out that the strengthening of border controls actually increases the number of illegal immigrants. They argue that criminality among immigrants is a complicated issue, and the connection to terrorism is less evident than is popularly believed. These critics of the misuse of counterterrorist measures provide evidence that this securitization of immigration is detrimental to the integration of minorities and thus makes Western societies more vulnerable to terrorism and other forms of insecurity by fueling exclusion, frustration, resentment, and ultimately radicalization. Indeed, they contend that the fight against the ever-expanding definition of security threats has too often been used as an excuse to compromise human rights and civil liberties, as illustrated by military trials without due process, secret detentions, detentions without charge or trial, expedited removal processes, extrajudicial prosecutions, the use of secret evidence, and the invasion of privacy. They also contend that the current process of securitization reflects a more fundamental trend infecting key features of liberal democracy, such as the balance of power between branches of government, openness of the government, and democratic accountability. Policies based upon a "model of an unending war" thus are seen to seriously damage the sustainability of democratic governance.

This analysis points to two key questions that I address in this book: First, has the securitization of immigration issues actually contributed to the enhancement of internal security? Second, has the use of counterterrorist measures helped to solve the problems commonly related to immigration, such as the increasing number of illegal immigrants, the resilience of ethnic tensions that sometimes fuels civil unrest, and the emergence of homegrown radicalization? In answering these questions, I evaluate the *actual outcomes* of these measures according to the *stated objectives* of the proponents of restrictionist policy reforms that now dominate in Europe and America. I examine the main assumptions that inform the political agenda, analyze the implementation process, and evaluate the effectiveness of policies in terms of their stated goals.[15] Have these policies succeeded or failed?[16]

I argue that the securitization of immigration has proven ineffective in achieving its prescribed goals. Worse, in fact, the policies that have been introduced have aggravated the problems that they were supposed to address. The excesses of securitization have been detrimental to both immigration and counterterrorist policies, generating not less but greater insecurity. They have also seriously damaged the delicate balance between the need to control security threats on the one hand, and the respect for civil liberties and human rights on the other. As a result, security policies have led to less security and less democracy—not more. As I outline in the pages that follow, a vicious circle had been set in motion: Immigrants and native minorities have been reclassified as potential terrorists; therefore they have had to be watched and, where necessary, deprived of civil liberties through new security measures. This has created an environment in which radicalism among a small fragment of minority communities, whether domestic or foreign born, has festered—leading to more distrust and the introduction of more security measures. The circle is complete.

In part 1 of this book, I examine the most common assertions about immigration and security that gained currency before the events of 9/11 and have since constituted the dominant anti-immigrant narrative in both the United States and Europe. Critics commonly assert that minority groups and newcomers are more "different" than previous waves of immigrants, refusing to assimilate and preferring to form ethnic enclaves. Thus, they constitute an ethno-cultural threat by damaging the national identity of host societies and, therefore, social cohesion and internal security. These critics argue that the events of 9/11 and the subsequent terrorist attacks in Europe have confirmed the relationship between immigration and terrorism, and they endorse emergency measures designed to address unprecedented threats to national security. They claim that counterterrorist policies should focus on

border controls, and restrictive immigration policies should prevent terrorism. Accordingly, policies based on blurring the distinction between immigration controls and antiterrorism should enhance the prospects of addressing
the urgent problems raised by both immigration and terrorism. These assertions have framed restrictionist measures designed to protect national identity,
state sovereignty, and public safety.

Against this background, I examine the main rationale that has inspired
and legitimized the framing of immigration as a security issue. That is, how
do we explain why immigrants are perceived as a security threat? I argue
that this perception is mainly the result of a historical, social, and political
construction. In chapter 1, I examine the rhetoric of "invasion" by analyzing the problems raised by the definition, categorization, and perceptions
of immigrants on both sides of the Atlantic. Given the breathtaking impact
of the terrorist attacks, first in the United States and later in Europe, the
tendency for a heightened suspicion toward immigrants (broadly defined)
was quite predictable. These events, however, did not initiate the practice
of scapegoating; and although the threat has been described since then as
unprecedented, conflating the notions of immigrant and terrorist was made
easier by preexisting prejudice. I demonstrate that the current framing of
immigration as a terrorist threat employs traditional rhetorical arguments
dating from the late nineteenth century. Each prior wave of immigration to
Europe and the United States raised similar objections to successive waves of
newcomers who were accused of being too numerous, too dissimilar from
natives, too criminal in their behavior, and too alien from national traditions.

I argue that the current debate about the (in)ability or (un)willingness
of new immigrants and particular minority groups to integrate is based on
historical amnesia. Previous immigrants suffered from similar prejudice, and
their integration was the result of a long, difficult, and often painful process.
Yet newcomers are today contrasted with previous immigrants in order to
celebrate the successful integration of old groups and to justify the exclusion
of new ones. Identifying the historical consistency of migrant phobia thus
provides useful insights about of the linkage between immigrants and the
various personifications of "criminality" (from delinquents to terrorists). It
undermines attempts to assert the uniqueness of the post-9/11 era and suggests that, to some extent, history does repeat itself.

Yet there is strong evidence that the current securitization of immigration
goes beyond prior manifestation of exclusion and discrimination. The novelty
of the present situation relates neither to the high level of xenophobia nor the
nature of nativist reactions. It is, rather, the result of a combination of actual
threats and the overestimation of symbolic threats with the underestimation

of actual migrant integration. Relying on recent research in the field of social identity theory, I demonstrate that the negative perception of immigrants (irrespective of their status) stems from dramatic misperceptions of both the size and nature of immigrant populations. In doing so, I do not deny that socioeconomic factors are important determinants of attitudes toward immigrants. Yet concerns about the ethno-cultural composition of minority groups strongly reinforce these economic concerns, together with more-existential fears (about national homogeneity, the loss of certain values, or ways of life). Aggravating the problem, this "clash of misperceptions" works both ways. It fuels migrant phobia and, consequently, immigrants' sense of alienation and resentment. We thus face a new constellation of security issues generated by the backlash effects of suspicion and discrimination against particular minority groups—in contrast to previous anti-immigrant moments.

In chapter 2, I critically evaluate U.S. and European policies by arguing that 9/11 did not constitute a dramatic departure from either the U.S. or the European prior stance on the immigration-terrorism nexus. It marked, rather, an intensification of prior policies. I argue that the securitization of immigration policies is the product of a long-term process dating from the mid-1980s. Indeed, by the 1990s, the militarization of border controls, coupled with the reclassification of a wide range of activities as national security problems (such as drug trafficking, illegal immigration, and migrant delinquency), reinforced this trend. The terrorist attacks of September 2001 were therefore perceived as a watershed, opening a radically new era and justifying emergency rules to cope with unprecedented challenges. Yet neither the United States nor European countries dramatically changed their policy options in the aftermath of 9/11. Rather, they simply strengthened existing measures or implemented reforms. Interestingly, the "new" threats were not perceived as an incentive for policy innovation, but rather as the a posteriori legitimation of previous, failed policies. Such a reflexive tendency to do "more of the same" raises serious concerns about the relevance of both the premises and stated objectives of current immigration policies.

In chapter 3, I describe the "security packages" adopted in the aftermath of 9/11. Both the U.S. and European governments subscribed to the "emergency times" doctrine and thus adopted "exceptional" measures designed to enhance homeland security. The "war on terror" additionally included extraterritorial actions (such as the military interventions in Afghanistan and Iraq), as well as new regulations targeting some nationalities and/or categories (such as illegal immigrants and asylum seekers). The resulting increasing volume of counterterrorist activity, combined with the multiplication of immigration and asylum initiatives, illustrates how Western governments have been able to expand their realm of action despite the emergence of new global and domestic pressures. In tandem, these security concerns allowed the U.S. and European governments to circumvent both constitutional rules and international conventions.

The central puzzle addressed in part 2 is how and why security policies have resulted in a "security escalation" that, paradoxically, has enhanced insecurity by generating new threats (either actual or perceived). I argue that Western governments not only have failed to achieve their goals but have created new problems that fuel a security-insecurity spiral. In this section I explore how the securitization of immigration policies has aggravated the objective conditions and subjective perception affecting both immigrants and nationals of foreign origin, without providing more "safety" from either domestic or foreign threats. I emphasize three interlocking processes that fuel the *dynamics of policy failure*. First, in chapter 4, I address the spiral effect of policy failure relating to border controls. Comparable to events before 2001, when enhanced border controls increased the number of illegal immigrants and boosted the development of smuggling networks, there is strong evidence that post-9/11 policies have neither limited the number of illegal immigrants in the United States and Europe nor provided more security. I provide evidence that security-related immigration policies have undermined the ability of Western governments to bring border flows under control in two ways: by increasing the number of illegal immigrants who stay out of the reach of security controls, and by diverting scarce resources away from more-pressing security priorities. Tighter controls have produced more demand for the service of smugglers. More illicit activity has therefore increased a pervasive sense of insecurity that in turn fuels both anxieties about immigration and concerns about the ability of the state to control borders and protect the homeland.

Second, I analyze the security/insecurity escalation by which a (real or perceived) sense of insecurity leads to the implementation of further security measures. In chapter 5, I demonstrate that the overgeneralized characterization of terrorism tends to disconnect the perception of threat from the real level of insecurity. The increasing volume of counterterrorism activity has led to the proliferation of multilevel bureaucratic agencies on both sides of the Atlantic that suffer from similar flaws: they are hampered by a vague catchall definition of terrorism and a subsequent expansion of policies to tackle security-related issues that are not related to terrorism. They have created more problems than they have solved, notably in terms of operational capacity and institutional cohesiveness. This multiplication of agencies has damaged the credibility of those authorities involved in the war on terror, undermining governmental legitimacy because continued insecurity is interpreted as a sign of incapacity and fuels an enhanced sense of insecurity. As a result, the security-insecurity escalation creates new fears, raises the level of suspicion, and justifies more discriminatory measures against targeted sectors of society.

A third policy failure is in the realm of integration policy, where securitization—combined with socioeconomic exclusion, alienation, and resentment—has facilitated, not impaired, terrorist recruitment. In chapter 6, I examine the emergence of the concept of the "enemy inside." Belonging to a particular ethnic group or religious community has become, in itself, a security threat. The category of the "others" has therefore continued to expand: today it includes all those who not only threaten but also are perceived as threatening national unity and public security. A "law and order" approach has informed inclusive practices (such as an access to citizenship and a process of cultural assimilation) that may, paradoxically, have exclusionary effects. Both immigrants and nationals of foreign origin who attempt to conform to the normative demands of host societies face a growing rejection by natives. They also feel unfairly targeted by security measures that obscure the structural sources of socioeconomic inequalities and discrimination. While integration has therefore become increasingly difficult to achieve, a sense of alienation cultivates resentment and, sometimes, overt hostility toward host societies. It has fueled the anti-Western agenda of the supporters of radicalism and, ultimately, made terrorist recruitment easier. In the long run, both the United States and Europe may therefore achieve a tragic self-fulfilling prophecy as the current securitization of integration policies encourages practices and discourses that actually create a permissive environment of violence.

How can we explain these policy outcomes? Why is there such an evident gap between the goals of American and European policymakers and the actual outcomes of their policies? How do we explain why states persist in implementing policies that repeatedly prove inadequate? In part 3, I suggest that the answer relates to the persistence of "push factors" motivating people to emigrate; the inability to address the major "pull factors"; and bureaucratic inertia and proliferation. Chapter 7 therefore examines the West's inadequate attention to a key push factor, overseas development aid, despite its securitization with the goal of supporting "allies" in the war on terror. Western countries have increased their development aid in trying to respond to growing inequities between the North and South. I provide evidence, however, that neither the United States nor the European Union has effectively addressed this gap with their limited and targeted approach based on security concerns.

Such an emphasis on security concerns does not alleviate poverty; rather, it increases insecurity.

In chapter 8, I provide evidence that Western states do not adequately address the major "pull factors" of immigration either. The issue of employer sanctions, for example, illustrates the tension between the need to address labor shortages in some sectors and the goal of curbing the number of illegal immigrants, who persist as a source of cheap labor. Yet the inability of the U.S. and European governments to control their borders leads to the adoption of further restrictive measures. These in turn increase the number of illegal workers—without addressing the issue of the recruitment of foreign labor. Rather, both the adoption of restrictive measures and the negative outcomes of these measures provide political opportunities as fringe-party politicians criticize foreigners and promise to enhance border security, dividing the economy between employers dependent on illegal labor and those who are not.

In my conclusion, I examine the actual effects of the tradeoff between civil rights and public security. As one U.S. official noted, "after 9/11, the gloves come off."[17] In the same vein, Tony Blair, when prime minister, announced that "the rules of the game have changed."[18] So who have actually been the winners and the losers? In short, I argue that we have all lost, in terms of both the preservation of civil liberties and the enhancement of public security. Both have eroded.

First, I examine the common assumptions that justify a "lesser evil" position, such as the idea that sacrificing the rights of the "others" will protect "us." I argue that the distinction between "us" and "them" is morally hazardous, in part because the definition of the "others" keeps expanding: the number of "collateral victims" is increasing because of the conflation of legal and illegal status. On both sides of the Atlantic, current policies also infringe upon the rights of citizens as much as those of noncitizens. Citizenship does not itself prevent discrimination or the infringement of fundamental rights. The United Kingdom, for example, has persistently refused to sign the Fourth Protocol to the European Convention on Human Rights prohibiting the expulsion of its own citizens. In various countries, provisions allowing authorities to withdraw citizenship have been extended. Some of these provisions allow deprivation of citizenship if it is conducive to the public good.[19] Others refer to equally vague notions such as the protection of "vital national interests" or "public security." Terrorism has always posed a threat to liberal democracies, and counterterrorism has always raised questions about the actual capacity of democracies to limit—or prevent—the use of violence.[20] Civil liberties have often been subverted in the context of war. Yet, by linking immigration and terrorism, Western governments have taken extraordinary measures that may undermine the long-term viability of these liberties.

Second, the trading of *their* liberties for *our* security has made us less, not more, secure.[21] The prolonged effects of securitization affect key features of liberal democracies, such as legal and judicial review, governance transparency, and public accountability. These trends fuel a democratic disenchantment, as illustrated by the increasing level of political distrust at home and a negative image of Western democracies abroad. While the new U.S. administration has recognized aspects of this problem, its activities to date—and those it has promised to implement—are largely symbolic and do not address the root causes of the problems I identify. Europeans, perhaps in contrast, have generally failed to recognize the need to restore these civil liberties and human rights. They have instead reacted in two ways: a "retreat from multiculturalism" and a tougher policing of the loyalty of the "others"—enhancing, not breaking, the security/insecurity cycle. It is this theme that I return to in the concluding pages of the book.

● ● ● PART I

The Framing of Immigration as a Security Issue

Why has immigration increasingly become a matter of security? One common answer relates to the long-standing concerns about national identity, criminality, and economic interests associated with immigration on both sides of the Atlantic. From this perspective, anti-immigrant hostility is fueled—if not legitimized—by the belief that immigrants pose a socioeconomic and ethno-cultural threat to Western societies. Supporters of restrictive immigration policies argue, for example, that immigrants take jobs from native workers,[1] reduce their wages,[2] and consume more social benefits than they contribute by paying taxes.[3] These assumptions, commonly asserted by scholars and politicians, are shared by an increasing number of people on both sides of the Atlantic. According to a survey conducted in 2006 by the Pew Research Center, a nonpartisan think tank, about 52 percent of U.S. respondents (up from 38 percent in 2000) believed that "immigrants are a burden to the country," taking jobs and housing, and creating strains on the health care system.[4] In Europe, 52 percent of respondents (up to 84 percent in Slovakia, and 76 percent in Latvia) said that immigrants did not contribute to their respective countries.[5]

Immigrants are also regarded as threatening national identity and societal cohesion, especially the newcomers whose perceived ethnic distinctiveness challenges the assimilative capacity of the host societies.[6] A plurality of Americans (44 percent) believe today's immigrants are less willing to adapt to the American way of life compared with those who came in the early 1990s. This opinion applies to immigrants from Asian countries (49 percent viewed them as less willing to adapt) and Latin American countries (45 percent).[7] In Europe, the belief that newcomers pose a threat to the ethno-cultural homogeneity of host societies is equally widespread and relies on a construction of immigrants as irredeemably "other" because they supposedly maintain their culture and religious heritage to the detriment of any form of integration.[8] At the EU level, findings of a 2003 European Social Survey revealed that 58 percent of Europeans perceived immigrants as posing a "collective ethnic threat," and 60 percent expressed the belief that "there are limits to multicultural society."[9] Since then, anti-immigrant sentiment based predominantly on perceived threats to values and culture has become widespread in Europe. In Great Britain, for example, the belief that immigration has damaged and diluted British culture over the recent years was shared by 58 percent of British respondents in a 2008 survey.[10] Most Europeans expressed particular concerns about Muslims—both foreign and native born. In Italy, for example, 67.9 percent of Italians in 2007 believed that Muslims had little intention of becoming integrated.[11]

Western governments and public opinion often link immigration to higher levels of criminality—both in terms of illegal border crossing and delinquency. Fears raised by the arrival of ethnic others thus coalesce around concerns about the potentially disruptive presence of minority groups who are suspected of having higher crime rates than natives. In the United States, concerns about immigration-related crime reemerged as a prominent policy issue during the 1990s, as illustrated by the passage of laws (such as the 1994 Violent Crime Control and Law Enforcement Act and the 1996 Anti-Terrorism and Effective Death Penalty Act) aimed at controlling illegal immigration and related crime. The use of national origin as a proxy for evidence of potential criminality led various European states to reform their criminal code and/or their immigration regime, such as Greece with the adoption of the Law 1975/1991. This law stated in its preamble that "suddenly Greece became full of foreigners, who by illegally entering, staying and working in the country create enormous social problems; and at the same time they try to solve their inevitable problems by resorting to crime such as drug trafficking, robbery and theft."[12]

Finally, some politicians, elements of the media and public opinion, and several academic experts argue that immigration poses a threat to state sovereignty. This claim is linked to the multiplication of international and domestic constraints such as globalized market forces and human rights instruments that undermine the sovereignty of the nation-states, as well as the subsequent emergence of various actors (such as international and domestic nonstate actors) who influence the policymaking process.[13] In the field of the new global political economy, some scholars argue that globalization challenges the territoriality of the state, and more important its capacity to manage the movement of people across borders.[14] Through the globalization of technology, they contend, networks connect migrants with receiving countries and encourage immigration—from "mail-order brides" to prearranged employment. Globalization also enhances the development of a major pro-migrant international business sector (involving travel agents, bankers, lawyers, recruiters, and people smugglers), while multinational corporations address the restrictive national immigration policies by imposing an elastic supply of labor. States have to deal not only with domestic and international nonstate actors but also with transnational actors who gain an increasing influence on outcomes in international politics. In the field of social movement theory, some authors emphasize the impact of an emergent "world society" on an international environmental regime, or its influence on the creation of social development policy. Others emphasize the emergence of a global transnational civil society in which social movements together constitute a basis for an alternative world order.[15] Thus, taken together, economic, legal, and political globalization reduces the autonomy of the states. Facing the challenge to "reconcile the conflicting requirements of border-free economies and border controls to keep immigrants out," states are constrained by international forces and regulations. The state itself "has been transformed by the growth of a global economic system and other transnational processes."[16]

These concerns about the negative effect of immigration—on economic prosperity, national identity, social order, and state sovereignty—predated 9/11 and the terrorist attacks in Europe. Yet those events have turned these *concerns* into immigrant-related security *fears*. As a result, implicit associations between immigration and insecurity are now deeply ingrained. Indeed, both immigration and terrorism pose similar challenges to the management of border crossing, as well as the ability of states to provide safety and prosperity to their citizens. Like immigration, terrorism is often depicted as the "dark side of globalization"; and when bombings are perpetrated in the name of an extremist anti-Western ideology, terrorism is also a "threat to national identity"— actually more lethal than any forms of multiculturalism. It follows from this that the fight against terrorism should include immigration measures and, conversely, restrictive immigration policies should tackle the issues related to terrorism. This perspective assumes logically that the link between immigration and terrorism is obvious: immigrants are foreigners and pose a threat; terrorists are foreigners and pose a threat as well; thus any immigrant may be a terrorist, and consequently the best way to prevent terrorism is to be tough in dealing with immigrants. This "worst-case scenario" approach justifies a catchall strategy that has been the foundation of U.S. and European immigration policies for the last decade.

At first glance, this inferential linkage between immigration and terrorism is appealing. Terrorism undeniably constitutes a long-term threat. The events of 9/11 were followed by the Madrid and the London bombings, in addition to a significant number of failed plots—from the attempted bombing near the Glasgow airport in July 2007 to the narrowly avoided one at Times Square in New York City in May 2010. There is also evidence of a global crisis of immigration controls: the more that states manage immigration, the less successful they appear to be, as illustrated by the increasing number of illegal immigrants on both sides of the Atlantic.[17] This crisis fuels alarmism about the integrity of the *external* borders and therefore raises further concerns about *internal* security. This sense of vulnerability, in turn, generates fear and hostility—the two main components of "migration phobia," which according to the political scientist Mikhail A. Alexseev "implies that uncertainty about the causes of real-world developments and exaggeration of their implications are precisely the perceptual mechanisms that make people threatened—whether these developments actually warrant caution or not."[18]

Yet the assumed immigration-terrorism linkage suffers from many flaws, addressed in the following chapters. Let us consider the first part of the immigration-insecurity equation, the one that assumes current immigrants pose a threat because they are too numerous and are more distinct than prior waves of immigrants. A closer examination of this "rhetoric of invasion" reveals that the dangers associated with immigration are greatly exaggerated. Three key aspects framing the perception of immigrants as "enemies" deserve particular attention: questionable data, historical amnesia, and a subsequent clash of misperceptions. The current immigration-insecurity nexus is characterized by two interrelated trends: the overestimation of migration scale, and the underestimation of migrant assimilation. The first trend seems to vindicate the traditional perspectives of intergroup conflicts, notably those assuming a direct correlation between migrant hostility and the size of migrant communities. Yet, although economic concerns matter, empirical data on both sides on the Atlantic suggest that the magnitude of immigration-related fears results mostly from the exaggeration of the distinctiveness of some immigrants. As Jack Citrin and John Sides argue in their cross-national study of anti-migrant sentiment, "attitudes toward immigrants have become increasingly divorced from context as the issue has become politicized."[19]

Second, there is no empirical evidence to suggest that immigrants are more likely to engage in violent activity than "natives." On the other hand, evidence is plentiful that the level of criminal victimization is greater for immigrants than for the majority population. In Europe, for example, this is notably the case for Somali refugees in Finland, and Roma in Hungary, both of whom display a level of assault or threat victimization that is four times the rate of the majority population. Other minority groups with high rates of victimization (at least twice the rate of the majority population) are North Africans in France, Italy, and Spain.[20] Furthermore, the assumption that immigration poses a threat to national security has been disconfirmed by the fact that an increasing number of terrorists are not immigrants, while the vast majority of immigrants targeted by security measures are not terrorists.

Another shortcoming of the immigration-insecurity nexus is that the framing of immigration as a security issue started by the late 1980s and early 1990s. Even if we were to accept that restrictive immigration controls can prevent terrorism, while counterterrorist policies can manage immigration flows, the securitization process generated a long series of negative outcomes before 9/11, such as an increasing illegal immigration, despite enhanced border policing; the development of the people-smuggling industry; the implementation of a piecemeal counterterrorism legislation; and a growing tension between enforcing immigration controls and preventing terrorism. To the extent that all the measures that were intended to fight illegal immigration and to prevent terrorist attacks have failed, one can wonder why the post-9/11 approach looked a lot like the pre-9/11 one.

One common answer relates to the alleged decline of state sovereignty. In the aftermath of 9/11, U.S. and European restrictionists contended that the reassertion of state sovereignty in the field of immigration was long overdue. Arguing that border controls were too lax prior to 9/11, they advocated tougher measures aimed at counteracting the dark forces of globalization. Yet, upon close inspection, it appears that this stance has effectively been challenged in many ways by the record of the securitization process before 9/11 in many ways. The evolution of immigration and asylum policies in Europe and the United States illustrates that states are extraordinarily inventive in circumventing international norms, including human rights regimes. The multiplication of nonstate actors does not imply the decline of state sovereignty, especially in the field of the "governance of security."[21] Rather than a diffusion of authority to nonstate actors, this represents "a shuffling of cards within the state."[22] Consistent with scholars who are "bringing back the state,"[23] I argue that immigration policy remains one of the last bastions of the traditional Westphalian state. I therefore contend that the inability of Western states to manage the social dynamics of the migratory process before 9/11 should not be interpreted as an indicator of their limited capacity to rule.

CHAPTER 1

Newcomers, Old Threats, and Current Concerns

There are at least two ways in which immigration is perceived as challenging the societal integrity of receiving countries. The first one relates to the dramatic increase in the number of people who have immigrated (legally or illegally) into Europe and the United States. Both areas have previously experienced high levels of immigration, but the current sharp rise in the flows of new immigrants is nonetheless noteworthy. In Europe, excluding the former USSR, the number of immigrants rose from 14 million in 1960 to 33 million in 2000. The EU-15 member states hosted between 18.7 million and 20.1 million legal foreign residents in 2002.[1] In 2008 the estimated number of foreigners reached 30.8 million in the EU 27. The foreign-born population of the United States increased from 9.6 million in 1970 to 33.5 million in 2003.[2] According to the American Community Survey, the estimated number of foreign-born residents reached 38.5 million in 2009.[3] The rhetoric of "invasion" is always intrinsically linked to the issue of illegal immigration. The Pew Hispanic Center estimated that 10.3 million illegal immigrants resided in the United States by 2004–5, representing 29 percent of foreign-born persons.[4] In Europe, according to International Labor Office estimates, there were 2.6 million illegal immigrants in 1991, including asylum seekers whose applications were turned down but did not leave.[5] In 2005 the European Commission put the number in the vicinity of 3 million, with between 400,000 to 500,000 illegal immigrants arriving annually.

Second, much of the debate over the threats posed by immigration focuses on the qualitative characteristics of the newcomers. It is commonly argued that the vast majority of immigrants now consist of non-Europeans who are too "different" to assimilate and therefore pose a threat to national identity.[6] Samuel Huntington, for example, claimed that Asians and Hispanics challenge the substance of the American creed: "America's third major wave of immigration that began in the 1960s brought to America people primarily from Latin America and Asia rather than Europe as previous waves did. The culture and values of their countries of origin often differ substantially from those prevalent in America. . . . Cultural America is under siege."[7]

Although most Americans celebrate their heritage as a nation of immigrants, immigration raises fears about the preservation of national identity. Such a nativist stance has gained popularity since the 1990s, as illustrated by the widespread success of Peter Brimelow's book *Alien Nation: Common Sense about America's Immigration Disaster*. According to Brimelow, "there is no 'demographic destiny' compelling Americans to abolish their traditional identity and culture. . . . Whether America is shaped by immigrants or by Americans will be simply a consequence of public policy."[8] Brimelow believed that the first option would lead to "America's assisted suicide,"[9] echoing the diagnostic ("national suicide") made by the American Immigration Control Foundation.[10] Pat Buchanan claimed in 2002 that America was becoming "Mexamerica" and that an "immigration tsunami will make whites a minority in the US."[11] In 2006 he reiterated his anti-immigration position, denouncing a "Third World invasion" of America.[12] Similar concerns are raised in Europe by those who claim that immigration is likely to transform the cultures and national identities of Western countries. Opponents of immigration today raise the specter of the "Islamization" of Europe in a comparable way to how the fear of "Mexicanization" is exploited in the United States by some scholars and politicians. The Italian journalist Oriana Fallaci predicted that "Europe becomes more and more a province of Islam," although Muslims represent only 5 percent of the EU's total population. Like Oswald Spengler, the German philosopher and prophet of decline, she was convinced that European civilization was doomed: "Europe is no longer Europe, it is 'Eurabia,' a colony of Islam, where the Islamic invasion does not proceed only in a physical sense, but also in a mental and cultural sense. Servility to the invaders has poisoned democracy."[13] Populists like Pim Fortuyn, the Dutch politician, argued that most Muslims refuse to assimilate and indeed attack the values of their host countries. As Fortuyn put it, "We have a lot of guests who want to run the house, and the owners don't like that."[14]

He criticized Islam as a "backward culture," a view he expounded upon at length in his book *Against the Islamization of Our Culture.*

Those who fear that their country is already "swamped" by immigrants are indeed even more militant when they envisage the future. There are concerns, on both sides of the Atlantic, that low fertility rates combined with high immigration streams will eventually lead to a significant increase in the culturally distinct population and therefore change the host country's composition. In contrast to the past, Europe provides a smaller proportion of immigrants to the United States. In 1960, 75 percent of the foreign-born in the United States were from countries in Europe. By 2009, over 80 percent of the foreign-born were from countries in Latin America and Asia.[15] The U.S. Census Bureau estimates that by 2050, Asians will represent 8 percent of the total population, compared with 3.8 percent in 2000. Hispanics (of any race) will increase from 12.6 percent to 24.4 percent. Caucasians in America will still largely outnumber all other groups (72.1 percent, compared with 81 percent in 2000).[16] Nevertheless, they fear losing their identity. Europeans express similar concerns about their "ethnic future." In 2007 the EU-27 population reached 497 million. About 80 percent of this growth was due to immigration.[17] The EU-27 population is projected to increase from 495 million in 2008 to 521 million in 2035 and thereafter gradually decline to 506 million in 2060. From 2015 onward, deaths should outnumber births, and hence population growth due to natural increase would cease. From this point onward, positive net migration will be the only population growth factor. These estimated trends reinforce the argument developed by restrictionist experts in various European countries. David Coleman, co-founder of Migration Watch UK, provided scenarios of the changing ethnic and racial composition for seven European countries (covering half the population of Western Europe) and the United States by 2050. He envisaged widespread ethnic shifts, which he characterized as a "third demographic transition." In the Netherlands and Germany, 30 percent and 24 percent of the respective populations are expected to be of foreign origin by 2050 if the composition of European populations continues to change as he projected. The corresponding figure for Great Britain would be 36 percent. Coleman argued that these compositional shifts would mark the "cessation of a specific heritage" by changing the social and cultural fabric of receiving societies.[18]

Concerns about both the quantity and quality of immigrants have inspired restrictive immigration policies on both sides of the Atlantic. These policies in turn have institutionalized the perceived linkage between immigration and insecurity—thus increasing the politicization of immigration issues and the salience of immigration-related fears. To understand the dynamics of the securitization process, it is therefore crucial to examine the main assumptions that ground the "rhetoric of invasion." In doing so, I argue, first, that a characteristic vagueness in the evaluation of immigrant stocks and flows continues to fuel heated debates about the impact of immigration in receiving countries. Pressure from anti-migrant groups often results in the circulation of mythical numbers, in addition to a large degree of terminological confusion in the media devised to depict new major waves of immigrants as a threat to national cohesion and national identity. Second, the argument that newcomers pose a threat to national identity is based on the claim that descendants of earlier European immigrations could easily assimilate because their European origins made them culturally similar to core ethnic groups. Yet there is strong evidence that prior European immigrants suffered from discrimination. In the United States, the quality of immigrants from the Old World was indeed a constant issue of concern. In Europe, Italian, Spanish, Belgium, Irish, or Polish immigrants suffered from discrimination despite their European origin. Just as in the United States, they were perceived as irredeemably different, unable to assimilate and threatening to both societal cohesion and national identity. Third, natives on both sides of the Atlantic not only tend to overestimate the size of migrant communities, but they also underestimate the desire by immigrants to integrate. Recent studies reveal, for example, that Muslims and Hispanics are more eager to integrate into their host societies than believed by a large section of U.S. and European public opinion. I contend that there is no "clash of civilizations." Yet there is an increasing "clash of misperceptions" that aggravates ethnic tensions, and a sense of victimization and frustration.

Migration Scale and Hostility against Immigrants

It would be easy to dismiss the nativist concerns expressed in both the United States and European countries by recalling that immigration data reveal that the relative incidence of immigration in the total population is actually limited and remains well below the levels suggested by anti-migrant groups. Europe and the United States host today a comparable number of immigrants (all categories included): foreign-born individuals represent about 10 to 12 percent of the total population in the United States, and 8 to 10 percent in Europe. In the United States, while the number of immigrants and the growth rate of the immigrant population are higher than historical trends, the foreign-born percentage of the population is lower today than in previous decades.[19] There is no current "invasion" of Europe by immigrants either. The rate of migration in relation to total population is now lower than it has been historically. The total number of nonnationals living in the European Union was around 25 million in 2004, just below 5.5 percent of the total population. The Eurostat data for the period 2000–2004 indicates that the nonnational population ranged from less than 1 percent of the total population in Slovakia to 39 percent in Luxembourg, but this figure was between 2 and 8 percent in the majority of countries.[20] Contrary to the fears generated by EU enlargement, foreign citizens represented only 6 percent of the EU-27 population in 2008. The proportion of foreign citizens varied from 0.1 percent in Romania to 43 percent in Luxembourg, more than a third of whom were nationals from other EU member states.[21]

Yet the resilience of concerns about the potential negative impact of immigration suggests that the relationship between actual migration scale and the magnitude of perceived threats is not straightforward. We can identify at least three trends illustrating how the size of migrant communities is distorted—involving respectively U.S. and European public opinion, the media, and policymakers. First, it is worth noting that the U.S. and European public always overestimate the size of the foreign-born population.[22] Two-thirds of Americans give inaccurate responses to questions about the proportion of the population of foreign born, and about how racial and ethnic groups are distributed in the national population.[23] When asked in 2006 what proportion of the U.S. population was born outside the United States, most people tended to choose a figure much higher than the Census Bureau figure of 12 percent. Only 34 percent selected the correct answer ("closer to 10 percent"); 25 percent said the number was "closer to 25 percent"; and 28 percent believed it exceeded 25 percent of the total population.[24] Using the 2000 General Social Survey, Cara Wong found that respondents of all races underestimated the percentages of whites and overestimated the percentages of racial/ethnic minority groups and multiracial Americans in the United States. Overall, almost three out of four Americans underestimate the percentage of whites in the U.S. population, and a majority overestimates the percentages of all racial minority groups in the United States. All the subgroups tend to overestimate the percentages of racial minorities, and blacks and Hispanics seem to have an even more distorted perception of the composition of the U.S. population than do whites.[25]

A similar tendency is noticeable in Europe. When asked, in February 2007, what proportion of British residents were immigrants, respondents to an Ipsos MORI survey said it was about 26 percent, although the actual level was 6 percent. At the EU level, findings from the 2002–3 European Social Survey revealed that respondents to the survey in every country overestimated the percentage of immigrants in their country, up to 20 percent in the

Netherlands, Portugal, and the United Kingdom. Misperceptions of minority groups and innumeracy about immigration flows also play a key role in the construction of asylum seekers as a major threat. The proportion of asylum seekers and refugees entering the European Union and the United States is systematically overestimated. The estimated number of refugees stood at 13.5 million in 2005 (up from 4.5 million in 1970), accounting for 7 percent of the world's total migrant stock. Contrary to the idea that refugees are invading Europe and the United States, the overwhelming majority of these vulnerable populations are located in the third world, close to their country of origin. Nevertheless, the public dismisses empirical evidence and believes, for example, that the United Kingdom takes 24 percent of the world's refugees, when in fact the whole of Western Europe takes only 14 percent.[26]

A second distortion of migration scale relates to media coverage. There is evidence that the media play a role in public opinion formation, notably through the categorization of the "others," the exploitation of fears related to immigration, and the subsequent construction of immigrants as "enemies."[27] Facts do not really matter in the process. For example, the admission of ten new EU members in May 2004 was marked by a scare-mongering campaign in the United Kingdom. Some mainstream media engaged in a provocative game of guessing the numbers of immigrants who would invade the country. The *Sun* newspaper bet on "tens of thousands" of new arrivals, while the *Daily Express* estimated (with a heading of "The Great Invasion 2004") that 1.6 million people—mainly Roma—would be headed for Britain.[28] What actually happened? According to the Accession Monitoring Report of 2007, a cumulative total of 743,000 immigrants applied to register between May 2004 and September 2007 (of which 715,000 applications were approved).[29] Not only was Great Britain not invaded by immigrants from Central and Eastern Europe, but a majority of such immigrants (57 percent) intended to stay in the United Kingdom for less than three months (compared with 8 percent who wanted to stay more than two years). The media have a most powerful effect when they use preexisting negative opinions, in a way that both reinforces these opinions and transforms them into a securitarian "policy" discourse. Roma, for example, are perceived by Italian public opinion as posing a threat; they are depicted as "delinquents" and "criminal clandestine" by the mass media, and they are treated as "enemies" by public authorities— although their estimated number in Italy is 150,000 (0.3 percent of the total population, among the lowest percentages in Europe)—half of them being Italian citizens.[30]

The third distortion stems from the fact that data on immigration are provided by a wide range of authorities having different agendas and using different definitions. This large degree of terminological confusion and statistical uncertainty fuels, and is fueled by, the politicization of the debate over immigration issues. Puzzlingly, although immigration is perceived as a major issue by policymakers and public opinion on both sides on the Atlantic, little work has been done to clarify the definition and classification of immigrants. According to the current conventional wisdom, the phenomenon of international migration (both emigration and immigration) is defined as the movement of persons across national borders for purposes other than travel or short-term residence. An immigrant is therefore a foreigner or a nonnational who moved from his or her country of origin to another country for the purpose of settlement. This definition has been adopted—and promoted— by international organizations such as the United Nations and the Organization for Economic Cooperation and Development (OECD).[31] Yet this definition leaves unaddressed a series of important questions. If immigrants are basically defined as persons who are foreign born and who, at some stage, have immigrated into the country of residence, how should people born in their country of residence and nonetheless considered "foreigners" because they don't have access to citizenship rights in the country of residence be defined, even though they are not immigrants? Or what of those defined by some countries as "nationals" despite the fact that they are born and live in another country, yet with a privileged access to citizenship by virtue of their "bloodline"? What about foreigners who reside outside their country of origin but are not considered immigrants by the host country? Or, finally, nationals who are perceived as immigrants on the basis of their foreign origin but who are citizens? To complicate matters further, categories have varied over time and still vary from one country to another. The recent European citizenship provides a significant illustration of this issue. "Foreigners," in this context, are either EU nationals or third-country nationals (TCNs). Nationals from EU member states are allowed to live and work in another EU country without asking for a residency permit. They are not considered as "foreigners," *strictu sensu*, and the reliability of statistics concerning these persons is thus lower than that for non-EU citizens.[32]

Moreover, most countries have little information on "illegal," "irregular," or "undocumented" immigrants, despite this being obviously one of the most sensitive areas in current immigration trends. Technical reasons for this statistical uncertainty can be found in the use of contrasting sources of data, in the inability of administrative systems to collect information, or (perhaps more pointedly) in the lack of comparability due to different national views about who constitutes an immigrant. While the American Community Survey and the census questionnaires collect information about both legal and illegal immigrants, the majority of European sources of stock data do not provide reliable data on illegal immigrants. The Center for Information, Discussion and Exchange on the Crossing of Frontiers and Immigration (CIREFI) was set up in 1994 as the main EU body responsible for the collection of data on illegal immigration. But the CIREFI categories ("refused aliens," "illegal presence," "facilitators," "facilitated aliens," "removed aliens," and "regularizations") are not based on a common understanding by member states of what data are to be inserted in the EU database.[33] Whereas the U.S. legal categories are more precisely defined than their European counterparts, terms like "unauthorized immigrant" and "undocumented immigrant" are sometimes used interchangeably in the United States. But a large number of undocumented migrants have documents that are no longer legal. Visa overstayers, for instance, represented 25 percent to 40 percent of unauthorized immigrants in 2005. Other "quasi-legal" aliens include asylum applicants waiting for their cases to be adjudicated; persons with Temporary Protected Status (TPS) and Extended Voluntary Departure (EVD); immediate relatives waiting for their final papers; or green-card applicants. According to Jeffrey Passel, between 1 million and 1.5 million persons can be considered as having a "not yet fully legal" status.[34]

Data unreliability also stems from policy decisions. The evaluation of immigrant stocks and flows is clearly deeply political, and political interests often take precedence over the need for reliable comparable statistics. Disagreements among experts who endorse either pro- or anti-restrictionist arguments echo the political debate about the implementation of border controls. This was illustrated, for instance, by the "protracted numbers game" played by the Clinton and the George W. Bush administrations.[35] The Clinton administration's INS estimated there were 5.5 million unauthorized residents in 2000, compared with 3.8 million in 1990. Indeed, the INS reduced its estimate of the average net increment of illegal immigrants—"from 275,000 a year to 135,000 on the grounds that previous estimates of return migration were unduly low." Findings provided by the Clinton administration demonstrated that U.S. immigration laws have provided the government with broad powers to deny admission to any person suspected of attempting to violate U.S. laws or endanger public safety. In January 2003 the George W. Bush administration's INS released its own estimates, bringing the total of unauthorized residents as of 2000 to 7.1 million.[36] The report highlighted that the INS failed to bring illegal immigration under control during the Clinton years. The Bush INS raised the net entries from Mexico by about 1.2 million and took into consideration other categories (such as "quasi-legal migrants") that were assumed to have been undercounted by the previous administration.

Each of these trends—overestimation of migration scale, data inaccuracy, and biased use of statistics serving political purposes—is definitively part of the immigration landscape. Yet they do not explain the relationship between migration scale and hostility toward migrants, which is actually rather volatile and sometimes counterintuitive. One of the predominant traditional perspectives of intergroup conflict, for example, assumes that hostility toward migrants is a linear function of the size of migrant groups.[37] It is therefore commonly expected that ethnic exclusionism will be stronger in countries with a relatively high number of immigrants.[38] If that were true, we could anticipate that hostility toward migrants would be stronger in countries where there is a relatively high proportion of resident immigrants. Yet empirical studies have demonstrated that the relationship between the country level of prejudice and the size of the foreign-born population contradicts this hypothesis.[39] In his study of anti-immigrant and racial prejudice in Europe, Lincoln Quillian found that levels of anti-migrant sentiment in 1993 were about the same in France, Germany, and Denmark—although the proportion of non-EU nationals differed dramatically in these countries.[40] Conversely, levels of anti-immigrant prejudice were higher in Belgium than in the Netherlands, despite the fact that the percentage of non-EU nationals was about equal in these two countries. Both the 2002–3 Eurobarometer and European Social surveys confirmed that attitudes toward immigration at the country level were not related to the size of the foreign-born population. Recent influxes of migrants and asylum seekers have not always resulted in support for ethnic exclusionism in the main receiving countries. Countries where large minority groups were already settled, such as Belgium, polled below the EU average in support for exclusionism, as illustrated by table 1. Equally puzzling was the prominence of ethnic exclusionism where there was not a large presence of nonnationals. In Hungary, for example, where nonnationals represented 1.3 percent of the total population, more than 86 percent of the respondents expressed negative feelings toward immigrants.

Alternative measures that capture the distinctiveness of immigrant populations, such as the proportion of non-Europeans and the number of asylum seekers, confirmed a weak correlation between migration scale and ethnic exclusionism.[41] Using the Eurobarometer and European Social Survey data, Marcel Coenders et al. found "rather weak, non-significant yet positive effects of the presence of non-western nonnationals on most dimensions of ethnic exclusionism."[42]

In the United States, the correlation between negative public perceptions of immigrants and actual number of immigrants is also inconsistent. The 2004 American National Election Study revealed that Americans living in

Table 1.   Concentrations of non-nationals and negative feelings toward immigrants in selected EU countries

Country	Percent of non-nationals (a)	Resistance to immigrants (EU–25 average: 50%) (b) (%)	Immigrants perceived as a collective ethnic threat (EU average: 58%) (b) (%)
Luxembourg	38.6	52.74	39.58
Austria	9.4	64.37	52.03
Germany	8.9		
East Germany		47.54	65.99
West Germany		57.4	57.8
Belgium	8.3	44.16	62.88
Greece	8.1	87.48	84.73
Ireland	7.1	35.27	54.36
Spain	6.6	50.24	51.96
Denmark	5.0	50.45	49.97
UK	4.7	51.04	61.19
Netherlands	4.3	42.95	55.08
Italy	3.4	36.5	53.94
Slovenia	2.3	43.2	63.36
Portugal	2.3	62.47	61.54
Poland	1.8	43.77	57.48
Hungary	1.3	86.53	74.65

Sources: Adapted from (a) Eurostat, "Non-National Populations in the EU Members States," *Population and Social Conditions* 8 (2006); (b) ESS Round 1: European Social Survey Round 1 Data (2002). Data file edition 6.2. Norwegian Social Science Data Services.

states with large Hispanic populations tend to develop more favorable views toward Hispanics—a trend consistent with the contact theory.[43] Other studies have yielded disconfirming results about the relationship between the actual ethno-racial balance in a neighborhood and attitudes toward immigration and/or voting behavior.[44] Kenneth Scheve and Matthew Slaughter, for example, found no evidence that the relationship between work skills and immigration opinions is stronger in high-immigration communities: "Overall, people living in high-immigration areas do not have a stronger correlation between skills and immigration-policy preferences than do people living elsewhere."[45] Statistical and opinion survey data compiled in 2006 by the Pew Research Center showed (table 2) that the idea that immigrants take jobs from natives is indeed more widespread in areas with lower concentrations of immigrants.

The relationship between exposure to immigrants and opinions about them is consistent with these findings. As illustrated by table 3, people who live in areas that have high concentrations of immigrants are less likely to see them as a burden to society and a threat to traditional U.S. values. In contrast, people who live in areas with few immigrants are more likely to perceive immigrants as a threat.

Regina Branton et al. find that proximity to the U.S. border is an important component in explaining individual-level xenophobia, as illustrated by the California votes for Proposition 187 (in 1994) and Proposition 227 (in 1998). However, neither the size of the Hispanic community nor the distance to the border can fully explain the Californian voting behavior.[46]

Table 2. U.S. perception of immigrants according to region's level of immigrant concentration

Level of concentration of immigrants	Belief that immigrants take jobs from natives (%)
High	18
Medium	27
Low	33
National total	24

Source: Adapted from Pew Research Center, *America's Immigration Quandary: No Consensus on Immigration Problem or Proposed Fixes*, March 2006, p. 17.

Table 3. Perception of immigrants by U.S. public opinion in 2006 according to region's level of immigrant concentration

The growing number of new comers to the U.S.:	High concentration of foreign born in area	Medium concentration of foreign born in area	Low concentration of foreign born in area
Threaten traditional American customs and values	47	46	60
Strengthen American society	48	48	33
Mixed/don't know	5	6	7
Total	100	100	100

Source: Adapted from Pew Research Center, *America's Immigration Quandary: No Consensus on Immigration Problem or Proposed Fixes*, March 2006, p. 5.

To the extent that hostility toward migrants is not a linear function of migration scale, both at the national and local levels, we need to explore alternative explanations to the current migration phobia. As mentioned, much of the debate about immigration focuses on the qualitative characteristics of immigrants. The actual or perceived numbers of the "others," apparently, matters less than their presumed otherness. How do the newcomers actually differ from the previous immigrants? What are the peculiarities of current migration phobia compared with previous waves of anti-immigrant sentiment?

Historical Amnesia

Aristide Zolberg and Long Witt Woon persuasively argue that Islamic populations in Europe and Hispanics in the United States are both actually "metonyms for the dangers that those most opposed to immigration perceive as looming ahead: loss of cultural identity, accompanied by disintegrative separatism or communal conflict. . . . Seen in that perspective, Spanish bears a family resemblance to Islam in Europe. . . . It feeds fantasies of a malignant growth that threatens national unity."[47] Europe's Muslim population is extremely diverse—including different nationalities, ethnic groups, and different versions of Islam. "Yet in the eyes of the hosts, these disparate groups share an essentialized negative identity as dangerous strangers." Hispanics in the United States are equally diverse, and "yet here also, this highly disparate population has acquired an essentialized unified unity."[48]

Muslims and Hispanics are currently the most commonly targeted populations, but anti-immigrant feelings have consistently been overtly expressed in Europe and the United States. No historical period of immigration to Europe or the United States was characterized by a "happy welcome." The current wave of hostility to immigrants has been echoed throughout history. In Enoch Powell's "Rivers of Blood" speech in 1968, he predicted that Great Britain was "heaping up its own funeral pyre." Comparably, in the United States, as the sociologist Charles Hirschman notes, "each new wave of immigration has met with some degree of hostility and popular fears that immigrants will harm American society or will not conform to the prevailing 'American way of life.'"[49]

One of the many ironies of the history of immigration is that prior periods of mass immigration are now filtered through a collective historical amnesia that has given rise to enduring myths such as the inevitability of assimilation into the U.S. "melting pot," the French "cauldron" (*creuset français*), and Britain's multiethnic society. Newcomers are contrasted with previous immigrants in order to celebrate the successful assimilation of the "old" immigrants and to justify the exclusion of the current ones. Yet, as Richard Alba and Victor Nee note, "the view that the pathway of assimilation was smoothed for the descendants of European immigrants by their racial identification is an anachronism, inappropriately imposing contemporary racial perceptions on the past."[50] The assimilation of previous immigrants was, indeed, the result of a long, difficult, and often painful process. John Higham's classic book *Strangers in the Land* illustrated that sometimes it was the religion of the newcomers, sometimes their political ideas, and sometimes their race that provoked defensive reactions. Despite their European origin, for example, non-English immigrants to British North America were not perceived as similar to core "native" groups. In 1751, Benjamin Franklin complained about the "Palatine Boors" who were trying to Germanize the province of Pennsylvania. In order to preserve the English Protestant stock, he also argued that "white" excluded not only black and "tawny" immigrants but also Europeans of "what we called a swarthy complexion," such as Spaniards, Italians, Russians, and Germans—"the Saxons only excepted."[51]

Throughout the nineteenth century, Irish and other Catholic immigrants were not considered as fully American by "old line" U.S. citizens. They were viewed as minions of the pope and enemies of the Protestant character of the country. In his tract entitled *Imminent Dangers to the Free Institutions of the United States through Foreign Immigration*, published in 1835, Samuel F. B. Morse alleged that Roman Catholics were part of a Jesuit conspiracy to destroy American democracy. During the 1840s and 1850s, the Protestant crusade against Catholic immigration culminated in the burning of churches and the emergence of the native American movement. A secret organization, the Order of the Star-Spangled Banner, whose motto was "America for Americans," appeared in 1850. This anti-Catholicism formed the foundation for the Know-Nothing movement whose strength reached a peak in 1855 when it had six governors elected and sent a sizable delegation to Congress. Anti-Catholicism remained a powerful ingredient of nativism until at least the election of John F. Kennedy in 1960.[52]

Hostility to foreigners accelerated in the late nineteenth and early twentieth century as a racial ideological component, and anti-Semitism became part of the Anglo-American ethno-nationalism. Jews were not permitted to vote in some states until the late nineteenth century. They were discriminated against in employment and housing and excluded from membership in many clubs and organizations. Anti-Semitism found its way into the Populist Party, especially during the 1896 campaign, as a result of the J. P. Morgan bonds scandal. Democratic presidential candidate William Jennings Bryan suggested that this scandal, involving President Cleveland and the House of Rothschild, was an illustration of a Jewish conspiracy. Anti-Jewish sentiment flourished in political writings and novels, as illustrated by Henry Adams's letters of the 1890s and by W. "Coin" Harvey's book *A Tale of Two Nations* (1894). Anti-Semitism reached its peak during the period between the world wars, as illustrated by the rise of the second Ku Klux Klan, the pronouncements of Henry Ford, and the radio speeches of Father Charles Coughlin.

Nativism was increasingly tainted by eugenics, a pseudo-science of heredity and selective breeding aimed at improving human genetic qualities. Immigrants were perceived as a threat not only to the "national spirit" but also to the integrity of the "social body." They were blamed for all the perceived dysfunctions of American society, such as political corruption, urban expansion and related issues (noise, traffic, crime, and pollution), delinquency, alcoholism, and diseases (notably during the cholera scare of 1893). The belief in the social backwardness and racial inferiority of immigrants had an impact on immigration policy, with the adoption of a series of discriminatory measures against European and non-European immigrants alike. Restrictions led to the banning of prostitutes—a provision aimed at barring Chinese women from entry—and convicts (1875), and of "lunatics" and those "likely to become public charges" (1882). The Chinese Act of 1882 suspended the immigration of the Chinese into the United States for ten years and was renewed for an additional ten-year period in 1892. An 1891 act provided for deporting aliens already in the United States, stipulating that any alien who was a public charge could be expelled within a year after arrival.

In addition to establishing a literacy test, the Immigration Act of 1917 created an Asiatic barred zone. No person could be admitted legally who came from India, Indochina, Afghanistan, Arabia, the East Indies, or any smaller Asian countries. According to Madison Grant, one of the leaders of the Eugenics Record Office and founder of the New York Zoological Society, American society needed to be protected against the biological and ideological contamination spread by immigrants. In his book *The Passing of the Great Race* (1916), he provided a racial description of the "enemy inside": "The danger is from within and not from without. Neither the black nor the brown nor the yellow nor the red will conquer the white in battle. But if the valuable elements in the Nordic Race mix with inferior strains or die out through race suicide, then the citadel of civilization will fall for mere lack of defenders."[53] Ellsworth Huntington, a Yale professor, developed similar ideas in his 1924 book *The Character of Races as Influenced by Physical Environment, Natural Selection and Historical Development*. The same year, the Immigration Act accentuated the racial dimension of the national quota system introduced in 1921, and prohibited all immigration from Japan. It also enhanced legal provisions for the deportation of "unwanted" immigrants.

European immigrants to the United States were a familiar target for discrimination. In Europe many had suffered the same fate despite their European background, such as Poles in Germany, and Irish in England. Catholic immigrants from Italy, Belgium, and Poland suffered from discrimination in France in the late nineteenth century. Racial riots took place in Marseille in 1881 between French workers and Italian immigrants. Belgian immigrants were forced to leave the northern locality of Drocourt in 1892. Such xenophobic violence culminated in France in 1893 with the killing of a dozen Italian immigrants in Aigues-Mortes. The idea of "making Frenchmen from foreigners"[54] during the decades of the Third Republic (1870–1940) was illustrated by the reform of the educational system and the 1905 law on *laïcité* (secularism). However, the so-called French model of integration was undermined by nationalistic considerations supported by rightist and leftist groups. Specific minorities, such as Jews—either French or foreign—were accused of being unassimilable. Anti-Semitism peaked in France during the Dreyfus affair (1894–1905) and then again in the 1930s. Between 1940 and 1944 the Vichy regime persecuted those who were perceived as members of the "anti-France" lobby: specifically immigrants, Protestants, and Jews.

Racial nativism and the proponents of eugenics were as popular in Europe as they were in the United States. Various eugenics and racial hygiene movements developed throughout Europe, such as the German Race Hygiene Society (1905), the Eugenics Education Society in England (1907), and the French Eugenics Society (1912). Ernst Haeckel, a German zoologist, succeeded in popularizing social Darwinism with his first book, *The History of Creation*. He advocated a more "adequate use of the death penalty" as a way to prevent the transmission of criminality to the offspring of "degenerate outcasts." Robert Knox, a Scottish physician and anatomist, argued in his treatise *The Races of Man* (1850) that interracial breeding led to the corruption and decline of civilizations. Frenchman Arthur de Gobineau believed in the natural aristocracy of the white man. In his *Essay on the Inequality of the Human Races* (1853), he introduced the notion of "miscegenation" to describe the effect of blood mixing with inferior races. This theme was developed by Houston Stewart Chamberlain, a British-born but dedicated Germanophile, whose two-volume *Foundations of the Nineteenth Century* (1899) described the "Aryan" as the most superior human being. He portrayed the history of the West as a permanent conflict between the culture-creating Aryans and the materialist Jews. Racial essentialism was even more pronounced in the writings of Georges Vacher de Lapouge. He argued that the degenerative impact of cross-breeding, combined with the emigration of the best Aryan stock to America, had led to the unavoidable degeneracy of European civilization. The themes of eugenics were extended in the contributions of Karl Pearson and Julian Huxley in Great Britain, Eugen Fischer in Germany, and Alexis Carrel in France.

The specter of cultural degeneracy—popularized by Max Nordau's book *Entartung* (1892)—gained currency in other European countries within the context of a deep cultural pessimism, coupled with the appearance of xenophobic nationalism. The depression of the 1890s created ideal conditions for many political parties and organizations to ferment the appeal of racism and anti-Semitism. The most isolated areas, such as Ukraine and Russia, were also affected. Anti-Semitic pogroms took place at the turn of the century in the Black Sea areas. The notorious forgery *The Protocols of the Elders of Zion* first appeared in the 1890s, usually credited to the czarist secret police. From London to Odessa, Jews were both hated for trying to assimilate into gentile society as well as for remaining apart. Cultural xenophobia reached a peak in Germany when the notion of "degenerate art" was adopted by the Nazi regime to describe what was "un-German" or "Jewish Bolshevist," as opposed to the spiritual German *Volk*.

While it is difficult to predict the future sociocultural impact of immigration, it is clear that popular fears about immigrants expressed in the nineteenth and early twentieth centuries were completely mistaken. None of the pessimistic views about cultural or racial disintegration were justified. Current fears should be assuaged by noting that prior nativist concerns proved illusory. Sociologist Charles Hirschman notes that "looking backward, we can see that the impacts of the Age of Mass Migration from 1880 to 1924 were almost entirely opposite to those anticipated by contemporary observers. Based on standard measures of socioeconomic achievement, residential location, and intermarriage, the children and grandchildren of the 'new immigrants' of the early 20th century have almost completely assimilated into American society."[55] Immigrants adapted to American society, and American society gradually evolved as the result of this immigrant assimilation. The U.S. historian Oscar Handlin suggested, in 1951, that "the epic story of the Great Migrations . . . made the American people. . . . Immigrants were American history."[56]

Numerous studies provided evidence that assimilation was indeed the major trend among the descendants of the immigrants of the previous era of mass immigration. Assimilation diminished cultural differences, while immigrants and their descendants played a decisive role in the development of popular American culture.[57] Immigrants also played an important role in the transition to an industrial economy, and assimilation led to a massive population shift during the post–World War II era, with the development of ethnically integrated suburbs. As a result of high rates of ethnic intermarriage and ethnically mixed ancestry, ethnicity became symbolic.[58] Immigrants and their children increasingly participated in national politics, notably during the New Deal coalition in the 1930s and culminating with the election to the presidency of John F. Kennedy.

European immigrants similarly integrated in many European countries. Hostility toward Italians and Poles declined in France after 1945. By the 1980s, scholars and policymakers asserted the importance of immigration for French history.[59] They commonly depicted France as a country of immigration, with a strong emphasis on the effectiveness of the republican model of integration. The traditional republican mantra dismissed the tough realities of past integration by depicting a fictitious rosy picture of previous immigration. It claimed that anyone could become French, as long as there was a strong commitment to the ideals of republicanism, and that all individuals in the republic had equal rights as citizens, whatever their race, religion, class, or gender. As the U.S. historian Nancy Green notes, "a French model has emerged that distances itself from what is perceived as rampant American 'communitarianism,' the entrenchment of separate communities. Constructed in contradistinction to the American one, the French model ultimately has claimed to do better what many Americanizers have set out to do: create a melting pot."[60]

While using another national model, Great Britain has been described as a paradigmatic "integration nation" in Europe. Britain claimed—at least until the late 1990s—that it had achieved a multicultural society, constructed in contradistinction to French *assimilation*.[61] For at least three decades, it was assumed that the British model was both more efficient than the German one (because of the prevalence of the civic definition of the nation over ethnic criteria) and the French one (because of the British aversion toward "a series of carbon copies of someone's misplaced vision of the stereotypical Englishman," as secretary of state for the Home Department, Roy Jenkins, put it in 1966).[62] The implementation of an exceptionally elaborate system of harmonizing "race relations" was supposed to address the needs and aspirations of immigrant minorities in Great Britain. The final stage of this competition over which nation and which national model do better has reached its zenith within the European Union. The European project is built on universalist principles comparable to those found in the American creed. The U.S. motto *E pluribus unum* has inspired the European one: "United in Diversity."

While there are many instructive parallels between the end of the nineteenth century and the current situation, what worked yesterday may not work today, or tomorrow. The most common assumption of the supporters of a restrictionist agenda is that there is a "crisis of integration" resulting from the inability and/or unwillingness of new immigrants to integrate into their host society. On the basis of empirical studies, I suggest another reading of this "crisis of integration": although the socioeconomic context makes integration more difficult to achieve in most Western countries, immigrants are eager to become full members of their host society; and the most powerful barriers to their integration are those erected by discriminatory practices and the expanding perception of "symbolic threats."

The Clash of Misperceptions

Socioeconomic opportunities for immigrants are admittedly decreasing in both the United States and Europe. Western societies have become increasingly unequal over the last three decades, making it more difficult for immigrants and their children to integrate. The attainment of parity with the ethnic majority remains a distant goal, even for second- or third-generation immigrants. In the United States, for example, income does increase across generations of Hispanics: "Those who are the grandchildren of Mexican immigrants (the third generation) show an average income nearly 25 percent higher than those who are the children of Mexican immigrants (the second generation) and more than double that of the first generation."[63] However, the mean personal income of the third generation is 93 percent of the level of comparable non-Hispanic whites. Hispanics are more likely than non-Hispanic whites to work in low-skilled sectors (such as farming and construction), and third-generation persons of Mexican origin are only 80 percent as likely as whites to hold white-collar jobs. This economic disadvantage is reflected in a resilient income gap. In 2004 the median income of Hispanics was $35,929, compared with $48,784 for non-Hispanic whites. About 22 percent of Hispanics were living below the poverty rate, compared with 8.8 percent of non-Hispanic whites. This income gap mirrors the education gap, despite intergenerational progress in years of schooling. In 2004, 88.6 percent of non-Hispanic whites were high school graduates, compared with 59.9 percent of Hispanics; meanwhile, 29.7 percent of non-Hispanic whites had a bachelor's degree (or more), compared with 12.7 percent of Hispanics.[64] Furthermore, the recession that began at the end of 2007 had a severe impact on employment prospects for immigrants. The unemployment rate, for example, increased from 5.1 percent in 2007 to 8 percent in 2008 for foreign-born Hispanics, and from 6.7 percent to 9.5 percent for native-born Hispanics (compared with 3.7 and 5.5 percent respectively for non-Hispanic whites).[65] In June 2010, 12.4 percent of Hispanics were unemployed, compared with 8.6 percent of non-Hispanic whites.[66]

Similar differences between the immigrants and indigenous populations exist in many European countries where immigrants display, ceteris paribus, less favorable labor-market outcomes than natives. When compared to natives, immigrants generally experience a significant earnings gap, and immigrant unemployment rates are more than twice as high as those for natives in several countries, such as France, Belgium, Norway, and Sweden. Furthermore, second-generation immigrants' integration appears to remain problematic. In France, for example, second-generation immigrants with African ethnic background are found to be disproportionately vulnerable to unemployment and economic precariousness.[67] The recent PISA report "Where Immigrant Students Succeed" shows considerable performance gaps between second-generation immigrants and native students.[68] Many factors explain these gaps. Some of them relate to the characteristics of immigrants and members of minority groups, such as their national origin, socioeconomic status, and social capital, as well as family resources. Others include contextual factors, including the impact of discriminatory practices and other forms of exclusion such as racial stereotyping, residential disadvantages, and religiously drawn boundaries. Exclusion from the societal mainstream makes immigrant integration more difficult, which in turn fuels the belief that immigrants are unlikely to integrate. As Esses et al. argue in their study of public attitudes toward immigrants after 9/11, "threats can have a number of fundamental effects, and, in concert, they support the expression of existing forms of prejudice and discrimination, increase the likelihood that latent forms will be manifested, encourage the development of new biases, and orient intergroup relations in ways that promote escalating distrust, competition, and antagonism."[69]

Despite these constraints and limitations to socioeconomic integration, it is misleading to conclude that immigrants are reluctant to assimilate. Paradoxically, those who argue in the United States that Hispanics, mostly Mexicans, pose a threat to U.S. ethno-cultural homogeneity tend to underestimate the strength of the assimilation process they seek to preserve. The 2004 American Community Survey estimated the number of Hispanics to be 40.5 million (14.2 percent of the U.S. household population).[70] At that time, three-quarters of Hispanics were U.S. citizens, either by birth (61 percent) or by naturalization (11 percent). Only 28 percent had not become U.S. citizens. Most Hispanics (60 percent) were high school graduates, and about

13 percent had at least a bachelor's degree or more education. With regard to their command of English, about 23 percent spoke "only English" at home, and 38.5 percent spoke "English very well."[71] According to the 2005 U.S. Census Report, even in the 10 percent of households that were "Spanish speaking," 85 percent of the children spoke English "well or very well."[72] A survey conducted by the Pew Hispanic Center confirmed that the stereotype that Hispanics were resistant to learning English has thus proven false: most second-generation Latinos were either bilingual (47 percent) or "English-dominant" (46 percent). Only 7 percent remained "Spanish dominant." By the third generation, that figure fell to zero, while 78 percent were "English-dominant."[73]

In terms of racial identity, one question asked by the 2006 Latino National Survey was how Latinos identify themselves: as Americans, as Latinos, or as members of particular national groups? When forced to choose only one identity, the number of those who answered "American" was low. Yet when Latinos were allowed to report multiple identities, two-thirds of the respondents identified themselves with the United States, with a large majority emphasizing the importance of speaking English as being part of being American.[74] That same year, another survey conducted by the Pew Hispanic Center showed that most Latino immigrants (up to 63 percent) showed moderate attachment to their home country, both in terms of their attitudes and in the extent of their transnational activities (such as sending remittances, making phone calls at least once a week, and traveling back to their country of origin in the previous two years). Only 9 percent were engaged in regular transnational activities. Foreign-born Hispanics who have been in the United States for decades or those who arrived as children were less connected than those who arrived recently. Among those in this country for fewer than ten years, 63 percent sent remittances, and 62 percent phoned at least on a weekly basis. Among those here for thirty years or more, 36 percent only sent remittances, and 19 percent called at least weekly.[75]

Supporters of nativist arguments lump together all Hispanics, those who recently arrived and those whose families have been in the country for generations. Such aggregation is misleading because, as noted by Frank Bean and Susan Brown, "the characteristics of new immigrants are not static. Rather, immigrants change, both across time and across generations. Hence, reaching adequate conclusions about Mexican integration requires comparisons across generations."[76] While the number of Hispanic children has nearly tripled since 1980, their demographic profile has changed. Hispanics now make up 22 percent of all children under the age of eighteen in the United States (compared to 9 percent in 1980). A majority (52 percent) of the nation's

16 million Hispanic children are "second generation," and 37 percent are "third generation or higher."[77] In their intergenerational study of Mexican integration, Bean and Brown demonstrate that the Mexican-origin population is following a path of significant integration. In assessing sociocultural assimilation, they include various factors such as "speaking English, watching and listening to Spanish-language television and radio or English media, downgrading the importance of ethnic sub-group, having fewer children and being likely to live in extended family arrangements."[78] They find, for instance, that "virtually no one in the first generation prefers to speak English at home, but 39 percent of the 1.5 generation does, 63.3 percent of the second generation, and virtually all of the third generation." They also find that ethnic identity wanes between the second and third generation. By the third generation, the percentage reporting that ethnic identity was "very important" drops to "43.2 percent from 55.2 in the second generation. At the same time, more than half of the third generation has a spouse or partner of a different race or ethnicity." Furthermore, Mexicans are increasingly converging with whites in terms of having smaller families and attending religious services infrequently.

A similar misperception of migrant acculturation preferences and processes is noticeable in Europe. Concerns about the future "Europeaness" of Europe are stimulated by the growing presence of a Muslim population. At a very rough estimate, between 13 million and 15 million Muslims live in Western Europe today. Relatively large communities of indigenous Muslims live in Eastern Europe, especially in Albania, Bosnia, and Bulgaria. Smaller groups can be found in Greece, Romania, the Czech Republic, Slovakia, Hungary, and Poland. Three-quarters of the total Muslim population, however, is concentrated in Western Europe—predominantly composed of first- and second-generation immigrants. Muslims there are outnumbered by Christians (of various denominations) and by atheists: only 2 to 3 percent of the total population, on average, is Muslim. They are nonetheless perceived as a threat—to European identity and values, to national cohesion, and to security. Surveys demonstrate that Western publics, for instance, believe today that Muslims in their countries want to remain distinct from society rather than adopt their nation's customs and way of life. This perception, as illustrated by table 4, fuels the idea that Muslims have a growing sense of Islamic identity and therefore raises concerns about Islamic extremism.

Recent studies reveal, however, that immigrants and other ethnic minorities are more willing to be integrated than is commonly believed. In France, evidence suggests that Muslims are comparatively more open to French values and traditions than natives are. According to Sylvain Brouard and

Table 4.   Perceptions of Muslims in selected Western countries

	Muslims want to remain distinct (%)	Increasing sense of Islamic identity (%)	(Very) concerned about Islamic extremism in your country (%)
Germany	88	66	35
Spain	68	47	43
Netherlands	65	60	32
Great Britain	61	63	34
France	59	70	32
United States	49	50	31

Source: Adapted from the 17-Nation Pew Global Attitudes Survey, *Support for Terror Wanes among Muslim Publics* (July 2005).

Vincent Tiberj, 41 percent of Muslims believed that "immigrants can eas-ily integrate into French society" (compared with 33 percent of the native respondents). About 43 percent of Muslims contend that it is crucial to "value cultural differences," but 55 percent preferred to highlight "what the French people have in common." Finally, 88 percent believed that secularism is "a positive" value (compared with 80 percent of the natives), and 84 per-cent wished to enroll their children in public secular schools. Only 66 per-cent of the natives expressed such a wish.[79] In Great Britain, findings support the claim that ethnic and religious identities coexist with a strong attachment to a broader British national community. Neither ethnic concentration of neighborhood nor low levels of socioeconomic and cultural integration had a significant impact on British identification. Ethnically and religiously based mobilization did not perpetuate segregated identities, but rather a mutually reinforcing ethnic and national identification. Survey data from the 2003 Home Office Citizenship Study revealed that Muslims and South Asians were almost as likely as whites to identify as British. To the question "How strongly do you belong to Britain?" Muslims and South Asians were equal to whites in terms of a positive identification with British nationality: 86.70 percent of whites declared themselves "fairly strongly" or "very strongly" attached to Britain, compared with 85.97 percent of Muslims, 85.95 percent of Indians, 86.38 percent of Pakistanis, and 86.85 percent of Bangladeshis. By contrast, 2.91 percent of white respondents said they were "not at all strongly" attached to Britain, but only 1.77 percent of Indians and 1.89 per-cent of Pakistanis expressed such a lack of belonging.[80]

The Commission for Racial Equality published, in the aftermath of the London bombings, a survey entitled "Citizenship and Belonging: What Is

Britishness?" Members of Muslim and South Asian communities declared that while religion and ethnicity play an important role in their identity, there was no antagonism between these "markers" and being part of the mainstream British community. The final report argued that

> while some British Muslims may give priority to being Muslim over being British and see these identities in a hierarchical way, no one saw Islam and Britishness as fundamentally incompatible. Moreover, many Muslim participants deplored the fact that they, as they saw it, were implicitly or explicitly being asked to "choose" between these two identities, both by the British public and by the British government. They felt strongly that this test of their "loyalty" was both misguided and unfair, since nationality and religion are not mutually exclusive.[81]

A Pew survey in 2005 found that, given a choice of identifying as first Muslim or Christian or as first a citizen of their country, the majority of British, French, and German Muslims chose faith, while the majority of British, French, and German Christians chose country. Some have taken these results as substantiating the danger of overaccommodating religious differences. A Gallup poll conducted in 2006–7 by Zolt Nyiri, however, found that Muslims in Paris and Berlin tend to identify themselves as strongly with France and Germany (46 percent and 35 percent respectively) as members of the general public in those countries (46 percent do so nationwide in France, 36 percent in Germany). Muslims in London are even more likely to have a strong British identity (57 percent) than the British at large (48 percent). Only 35 percent of Germans, 41 percent of the French, and 45 percent of the British think that Muslims are loyal to the European countries in which they live. This is in sharp contrast to what European Muslims themselves believe: 74 percent of the Muslims in London, 73 percent in Paris, and 72 percent in Berlin think that Muslims are indeed loyal to the Western countries in which they live.[82]

The Peculiarities of Current Nativism

Expectations by natives that immigrants adopt their host culture are currently undermined in the United States and Europe by the mistaken belief that immigrants do not want to integrate—which in turn has negative consequences for intergroup relations.[83] Not only are cultural differences unappreciated, even in countries with a "multiculturalist tradition," but natives tend to also underestimate the elements of integration that already exist. As a result of this confusion, immigrants are asked to prove their loyalty in an increasingly hostile environment, obscuring the structural sources of inequalities and discrimination. From the immigrant viewpoint, such inequalities and discrimination produce a sense of victimization and frustration. The nativist overestimation of migrant ethnic identification therefore tends to strengthen immigrant alienation and separatist propensities. The tendency to characterize immigrants as a devalued "out group" increases prejudice toward them, and immigrants may therefore retreat from society and stay within ethnic enclaves. This mismatch between host and migrant perceptions increases ethnic tensions in host societies and consequently creates a greater sense of insecurity. The vicious circle is complete.

As mentioned, neither the actual or perceived migration scale provides a satisfactory explanation of the current anti-immigrant attitudes. A seemingly more powerful approach is provided by the realistic conflict theory, which commonly assumes that the level of anti-immigrant hostility is causally linked to the socioeconomic conditions in receiving countries. It emphasizes the perception of immigrants as the threat they pose to natives' material well-being when unemployment increases.[84] Nativism has indeed been stronger and more influential during periods of economic recession and unemployment, such as the Great Depression. In the aftermath of the oil crisis of the 1970s, anti-immigration hostility rose again. At the personal level, the self-interest theory postulates that individuals—especially those directly in competition with immigrants—develop negative sentiment toward immigrants when they fear they will lose their economic advantages. The main predictors relate to personal and socio-tropic concerns (such as people's perception of the economic well-being of society), although personal and collective interest–based explanations are often interactive.[85] It is assumed that poor or employed natives or people with only limited education are more negative toward immigration than those living in urban areas, from an immigrant background, or with a tertiary education. As summarized by Lauren McLaren and Mark Johnson,

> Immigrants pose the greatest threat to those of lower status—defined in terms of education, skill level, and income—because those of lower status fear competition for jobs, housing, schools and social services. . . . Thus, based upon general self-interest arguments and research specifically on attitudes to minorities and immigrants, it is expected that individuals at the lowest levels of skill, income and education would indeed be the most worried about immigration and thus the most hostile to it.[86]

The current migration phobia, however, confounds these traditional approaches of intergroup conflict and ethnic competition theory. There is evidence, on both sides of the Atlantic, that the impact of "realistic threats" is more complex than commonly expected. In Europe, Jason Kehrberg examined in 2007 the influence of the national economy on attitudes toward immigrants by using data from the Eurobarometer survey conducted in 1997.[87] He found that the coefficient for GDP per capita had a negative correlation with public attitudes: in countries with a high level of economic development, such as Sweden and Denmark, a large majority of natives still perceived immigrants as a threat. The correlation between the unemployment rate and anti-immigrant hostility was also less consistent than expected. In countries with low levels of unemployment, negative public opinion was widespread, while a decrease in unemployment resulted in only a 1.6 percent increase in the probability of positive attitudes toward immigrants.

Actually, variations across countries tend to challenge the anticipated correlation between ethnic exclusionism and economic factors. A closer examination of the 2003 European Social Survey data, combined with the results of the 2000 and 2003 Eurobarometer surveys, confirms that economic contextual factors often play a small role in explaining attitudes toward immigrants. Generally speaking, ethnic exclusionism prevails to a greater extent in less-prosperous countries, such as Greece. However, the "ethnic competition" theory is challenged by puzzling variations. As illustrated by table 5, the correlation was quite weak in 2003 between GDP per capita and anti-immigrant hostility levels. It did not work for many different dimensions of ethnic exclusionism, nor did it explain variations across countries. Portugal and Greece, for example, had a similar GDP per capita, yet ethnic exclusionism was higher in Greece (which ranked first on all the different components of ethnic exclusionism) than in Portugal (where resistance to multiculturalism was nevertheless lower than in more prosperous countries such as Ireland and West Germany). In terms of "resistance to immigrants," high scores in Austria and Finland were inconsistent with their economic wealth (with GDP per capita reaching 26.9 and 24.8 respectively). With a similar level of GDP per capita (24.5), Sweden was far more tolerant toward immigrants than Finland (14.6 percent in Sweden versus 59.2 percent in Finland). In Luxembourg, the country with the highest GDP per capita, both "resistance to immigrants" and "resistance to multicultural society" reached a higher score than in Italy (where GDP per capita was only 24.55).

In terms of the effects of unemployment, the common hypothesis is that ethnic exclusionism is stronger in countries with a larger proportion of unemployed natives. Yet table 6 shows that high levels of unemployment are often unmatched by high levels of support for ethnic exclusionism. In Belgium, for example, the unemployment rate reached 7.3 percent in 2003,

Table 5. GDP per capita and level of ethnic exclusionism in selected European countries

	GDP per capita (PPP)	Resistance to multicultural society (EB 2003) (%)	Limits to multicultural society (EB 2003) (%)	Resistance to immigrants (ESS 2003) (%)	Resistance to diversity (ESS 2003) (%)	Immigrants perceived as a collective threat (ESS 2003) (%)
Finland	24.79	23.5	21.6	59.24	44.96	41.83
Sweden	24.50	12.5	40.7	14.64	39.9	32.81
Denmark	27.80	22.3	55.4	50.45	43.76	49.97
Great Britain	24.77	20.3	68.1	51.04	34.75	61.19
Ireland	30.12	16.9	72.1	35.27	28.92	54.36
Netherlands	27.05	21.6	67.5	42.95	30.8	55.08
Belgium	25.97	37.3	69.2	44.16	41.98	62.88
Luxembourg	45.46	16.2	63.0	52.74	33.03	39.58
West Germany	26.50	32.6	71.5	37.8	39.56	57.4
East Germany	16.45	36.2	74.6	47.54	42.1	65.99
Austria	26.90	27.0	61.3	64.37	43.01	52.03
France	24.65	22.2	64.1			
Spain	20.23	14.6	49.3	50.24	47.87	51.96
Portugal	16.49	18.2	59.2	62.47	68.29	61.54
Italy	24.55	23.9	45.5	36.5	48.14	53.94
Greece	15.82	59.0	80.6	87.48	77.23	84.73

Sources: Adapted from Eurostat, *Basic Figures on the EU* (2003); Eurobarometer and European Social Survey in *Majorities' Attitudes towards Minorities: Key Findings from the Eurobarometer and the European Social Survey* (Vienna, EUMC, March 2005).

Table 6. Unemployment rate and level of ethnic exclusionism in selected European countries

	Unemployment rate (2003) (%)	Resistance to multicultural society (EB 2003) (%)	Limits to multicultural society (EB 2003) (%)	Resistance to immigrants (ESS 2003) (%)	Resistance to diversity (ESS 2003) (%)	Immigrants perceived as a collective threat (ESS 2003) (%)
Finland	9.1	23.5	21.6	59.24	44.96	41.83
Sweden	4.9	12.5	40.7	14.64	39.9	32.81
Denmark	4.5	22.3	55.4	50.45	43.76	49.97
Great Britain	5.1	20.3	68.1	51.04	34.75	61.19
Ireland	4.4	16.9	72.1	35.27	28.92	54.36
Netherlands	2.7	21.6	67.5	42.95	30.8	55.08
Belgium	7.3	37.3	69.2	44.16	41.98	62.88
Luxembourg	3.8	16.2	63.0	52.74	33.03	39.58
West Germany	6.5	32.6	71.5	37.8	39.56	57.4
East Germany	15.2	36.2	74.6	47.54	42.1	65.99
Austria	4.3	27.0	61.3	64.37	43.01	52.03
France	8.8	22.2	64.1			
Spain	11.3	14.6	49.3	50.24	47.87	51.96
Portugal	5.1	18.2	59.2	62.47	68.29	61.54
Italy	9.0	23.9	45.5	36.5	48.14	53.94
Greece	10.0	59.0	80.6	87.48	77.23	84.73

Sources: Adapted from Eurostat, *Basic Figures on the EU* (2003); Eurobarometer and European Social Surveyy in *Majorities' Attitudes towards Minorities: Key Findings from the Eurobarometer and the European Social Survey* (Vienna, EUMC, March 2005).

while only 44 percent of the population expressed resistance to immigrants. In Denmark, about 50 percent of the population perceived immigration as a major threat, while the unemployment rate was 4.5 percent. A similar effect was observable in Central and Eastern Europe, where countries with relatively lower unemployment expressed a stronger rejection of foreigners than those with a proportionately higher percentage of unemployment.[88]

Jack Citrin and John Sides reached a similar conclusion in 2007, pointing out that collective economic factors are becoming less significant than during prior decades. They argued that the current predictors of opposition to immigration were mostly unrelated to contextual factors, such as the size of migrant communities and the overall state of the economy.[89] In the United States, a report by the American National Election Studies (for 1992 and 1996) found a weak correlation between assessments of personal and national well-being and opposition to immigration.[90] Interestingly, approximately 50 to 70 percent of Americans continued to express negative views on immigration in the second half of the 1990s despite the rapid growth of the U.S. economy and a low level of unemployment.[91]

These puzzling variations suggest a need to analyze the influence of other factors, such as individual economic conditions. The analysis of the direct effect of contextual factors reveals that opposition to immigration is grounded more in individuals' attitudes and perceptions than in objective national economic conditions. Six main personal characteristics have been identified that commonly affect an individual's perception of immigrants: education, occupation, income, age, political affiliation, and residence. Of these, it appears that people who have prolonged their education tend to be less xenophobic. Conversely, support for "ethnic exclusionism" is more prevalent among people with lower education levels. People with professional careers show weak support for "ethnic exclusionism." Conversely, xenophobia is supported by people performing manual labor or among the self-employed. People with low income tend to be more xenophobic than those with higher income. In general, young people exhibit less support for ethnic exclusionism than older people. People on the right wing of the political spectrum show more support for all aspects of ethnic exclusionism than those on the left. Finally, populations living in urban areas tend to show less support for ethnic exclusionism than those living in rural areas. These results are consistent with studies on the impact of education, age, gender, and income.[92]

Yet the correlation between personal self-interest and ethnic exclusionism is often less consistent than expected.[93] In Great Britain, for example, none of the predictable individual factors (such as age, gender, left–right ideological position, job skill, income, and education) achieves statistical significance. According to Lauren McLaren and Mark Johnson, "Those with better incomes, better education and higher-status occupations are just as hostile to immigration as their low-status counterparts. Moreover, being unemployed or a recipient of government benefits also appears to make little difference in one's attitudes to immigration."[94] In their study of the individual factors shaping attitudes toward immigrants in the United States, Thomas Espenshade and Katherine Hempstead noted that the "effects of education are generally in the hypothesized direction, although not all are significant." They identified an "anomalous group" whose members failed to complete high school but whose views toward the desired level of immigration "are more positive than those of college graduates, when controlling for all other covariates."[95] They also found no consistent pattern with respect to respondents' age, while the effect of political affiliation was insignificant.

How can we explain these variations? Consistent with scholars who refer to symbolic politics theory, I argue that the current migration phobia confirms the impact of "symbolic threats," with an unprecedented focus on security-driven concerns.[96] There is plentiful evidence that concerns about racial, religious, and cultural identities—both at the group and individual levels—in host countries matter more than material circumstances.[97] Migrant phobia has less to do with ascertainable facts about immigration than with unarticulated fears that immigrants are threatening national integrity and societal security. Regarding economic conditions, what really matters is not the actual GDP per capita or the level of unemployment, but rather the perceptions of economic changes. People who believe that the economy is getting worse have more negative feelings about immigrants than those who feel that the economy is improving. Empirical data has confirmed this trend on both sides of the Atlantic, casting doubts on the economic deprivation model of out-group hostility. At the individual level, the effects of personal economic and financial concerns outweigh the actual socioeconomic status. Those who express economic anxiety about their situation tend to be more opposed to immigration. In the United States, for example, a Pew Research Survey found in 2006 that 30 percent of respondents who say their personal finances are only fair or poor believed that immigrants take jobs from Americans—compared with 18 percent of those who have a positive view of their personal finances.[98] Finally, concerns about cultural unity are more strongly associated with anti-migrant feelings than any other predictors, both at the group and individual levels.[99] This leads to a rather circular situation: immigrants are perceived as a security threat on the basis of fears fueled by speculative concerns about values and identity.

The central question has been, for many years, if and how actual ethnic competition affects perceived ethnic threats. The characteristics of nativism today suggest asking a slightly different question: how perceived ethnic threats have been consolidated to the extent that they are largely indifferent to realities. Addressing this question has major implications for the understanding of the current framing of immigration as a security issue by policymakers on both sides of the Atlantic. First, when speculative concerns inform restrictive immigration policies, they become more credible and thus reinforce the spiral of suspicions and fears. As noted by Mikhail A. Alexseev, "the more migration is feared as a security threat, the more of a security threat it becomes."[100] Second, and subsequently, persistent anti-immigrant hostility on both sides of the Atlantic is fueled—and to some extent legitimized and reinforced—by security-oriented public policies. Professor Will Jennings, in his study of "risk regulation" applied to immigration and asylum, stresses that "if the formulation of immigration policy is informed by responsiveness to public opinion that overestimates the existing level of immigration and is prejudiced on the national origin of immigrants on a racial dimension . . . aims of opinion-responsiveness may distort regulatory outcomes if public opinion is mainly determined by unrelated factors."[101] We may also wonder if the politics and policies that have consolidated the immigration-security nexus before 9/11 were actually determined by the most relevant factors. This I do in the next chapter.

CHAPTER 2

Securitization before 9/11

President George W. Bush, speaking before Congress on September 20, 2001, declared that "we are a nation at war." Terrorism was no longer a *crime*. It was an unprecedented form of *warfare*. Thus, counterterrorism was no longer a fight against criminals but rather a war against "those nations, organizations or persons [who] planned, authorized, committed, or aided the terrorist attacks that occurred on September 11, 2001, or harbored such organizations or persons."[1] Tony Blair's statement in March 2004 reflected the feelings that many Europeans shared at that time:

> If the 20th century scripted our conventional way of thinking, the 21st century is unconventional in almost every respect. This is true also of our security. The threat we face is not conventional. It is a challenge of a different nature from anything the world has faced before. . . . From September 11th on, I could see the threat plainly. There were terrorists prepared to bring about Armageddon.[2]

The policy known as the "war on terror" became the top priority of the U.S. authorities and their allies. On both sides of the Atlantic, the horrific events of 9/11 were described and analyzed as "exceptional" and "unprecedented." This popular narrative hinged on the notions of "global insecurity" and a "third type" of terrorism, which, by signaling the emergence of new threats, called for equally exceptional policy responses. Furthermore, the nineteen hijackers who committed the terrorist attacks epitomized the worst fears related to immigration. The consequence was tougher immigration enforcement policies, both designed and legitimized as effective antiterrorist measures.

However, 9/11 did not constitute a dramatic departure from either the U.S. or the EU pre-9/11 stances on the immigration-terrorism nexus. I argue in this chapter that the current securitization of immigration issues uses traditional rhetorical arguments—formulated increasingly and more openly by politicians, officials, and the media—which again take up the classic pattern of the social construction of internal enemies already observed in the late nineteenth century and during the cold war. This process has commonly encompassed two interrelated dimensions: suspicion toward foreign-born people who are perceived as potential members of a "fifth column," and the classification of those crossing a border as criminals.

Significant policy changes were introduced in the aftermath of the terrorist attacks, and my point is not to minimize them. Yet with regard to the emphasis on immigration as a key component of the terrorist threat, 9/11 marked a turning point in intensity but not in the nature of policy. According to Deborah Meyers, former policy analyst at the U.S. Commission on Immigration Reform, "even as the September 11 attacks provided the high-level political support necessary to advance a broader understanding of border enforcement, it has also been characterized by a reflexive tendency to do *more of the same*."[3] Both the United States and the EU member states enacted a series of measures that were designed to do "more of the same." The terrorist attacks of September 2001 therefore created a paradoxical situation. On the one hand, the exceptional character of 9/11 led to exceptional forms of counterterrorism, blurring the limits between the conventional and the exceptional. On the other hand, both the United States and Europe responded to these attacks by either the accelerated adoption of measures that were on the table for years or by strengthening existing regulations.

Addressing this paradoxical situation requires analyzing how and why this linkage between terrorism, other criminal activities, and immigration had been constructed in the United States and Europe before 9/11. This securitization of immigration shared strong similarities with previous "unprecedented" states of exception. For example, fears of religious, political, and racial subversion have played a key role in periodic anti-immigrant backlashes throughout both American and European history. Concerns about the impact of immigrants on criminality during the mid-1990s echoed the late nineteenth-century nativist discourse about the "criminal traditions" of migrant groups. However, there are two major differences, each having crucial implications in terms of the capacity for law enforcement. First, many of the previous restrictive measures targeting immigrants or members of minority groups were adopted during wartime, while the current securitization began at the end of the cold war—when the specter of a military confrontation with the traditional enemy (the Soviet empire) was replaced by metaphoric wars and existential threats. Second, most of these measures were temporary, invalidated when contextual changes took place. By contrast, the gradual securitization of immigration has no time horizon, reflecting a "permanent" state of exception,[4] and justifying a "no wartime warfare." This process has in turn informed U.S. and European policies, which were designed as durable, as well as allegedly efficient.

Previous "Unprecedented" States of Exception

There is abundant evidence that immigrants were regarded with suspicion as early as the late eighteenth century. Antiradical American nativism emerged in response to the French Revolution, leading to the notorious Alien and Sedition Acts (1798–1801), which provided for the expulsion of aliens on political grounds. The fear of foreign radicals resurfaced during the late nineteenth and early twentieth centuries. World War I generated an intense patriotism, a "One Hundred Percent Americanism" mobilization based on the assumption that immigrants could be the bearers of perverted and subversive ideologies. In such a climate of fear and suspicion, the proponents of "Americanism" demanded action to be taken against persons of German and Austro-Hungarian origin, as well as "hyphenated Americans." Wartime security concerns also fostered restrictive border controls, such as the Immigration Act of 1917, which added new excludable categories and extended the period of deportability to five years. In the aftermath of World War I, the campaign against radicals was further fueled by the fear of Bolshevik contagion. Congress passed the Espionage Act in 1917 and the Sedition Act in 1918. The Sedition Act made it a crime to criticize the U.S. government. It was designed to target anarchists and Communists, preventing departure from and entry into the United States "contrary to the public safety." Decades before the McCarthy era, U.S. attorney general A. Mitchell Palmer predicted that the country would experience a "Red Revolution." He ordered the arrest of thousands of "alien radicals" and deported five hundred "seditious men and women," many to Russia. Congress passed a law in 1921 that punished aliens for possessing subversive literature and showing sympathy for radical organizations.

In Europe the fear of the spread of subversive ideologies was related to the increasing influence of "foreign propaganda." In France, for example, foreigners suspected of espionage were listed by police authorities (in the *Carnet B*). Detention camps that had been set up during World War I in order to address the alleged subversive threat posed by immigrants coming from belligerent countries were reconstituted in 1938 to detain Spanish Republicans who had fled the dictatorship established by Franco. Meanwhile, the fear of Bolshevik contagion coupled with the specter of a Fascist fifth column increased suspicions about immigrants and foreign-born citizens. Discrimination against immigrants and other foreigners perceived as a threat culminated during World War II. Various categories of "suspects" were sent by the French Vichy regime to concentration camps (including anti-Fascist refugees from Italy and Spain, Communists, and Freemasons). Jewish refugees from Germany and Austria were categorized in Great Britain as "enemy aliens" and sent to internment camps in Canada and Australia.

In the United States the Alien Registration Act (the Smith Act) was enacted in 1940 and continued to fuel prosecution of alleged subversives well into the 1960s. The vast majority of unnaturalized Germans and Italians were left at liberty, but they were required to register annually. By contrast, the belief that the Japanese "race" was "an enemy race" led to the internment of residents of the West Coast of Japanese origin, including not only forty thousand foreign born (who remained alien by virtue of the prohibition of their naturalization) but also seventy thousand U.S.-born citizens of Japanese extraction. The cold war reactivated national security considerations. In the United States, for example, the McCarran-Walter Immigration Act of 1952 excluded any aliens who might "engage in activities which would be prejudicial to the public interest, or endanger the welfare, safety or security of the United States." Other laws dealing with the "red scare" were enacted, such as the Internal Security Act of 1950 and the Communist Control Act of 1956.

In addition to the specter of a potential fifth column, the criminalization of immigration was consolidated by the classification as illegal aliens of those crossing borders without authorization. The emphasis on border controls generated new restrictions, thus creating a new category of persons—illegal aliens—within the nation. As the U.S. historian Mae Ngai argues, "The processes of defining and policing the border both encoded and generated racial ideas and practices that, in turn, produced different racialized spaces internal to the nation."[5] Illegal aliens from Europe and Canada were treated differently from Mexicans and Chinese. Border controls had been mainly designed to restrict Chinese immigrants, the first illegal aliens racially constructed as "unwanted." Canadians were allowed to move freely into the United States until the 1920s; and Mexican immigration was perceived not as a threat but rather as a source of cheap labor regulated by the labor market demands in the southwestern states. It was not until 1919 that Mexicans were required to apply for admission at lawfully designated ports of entry.

The quota laws of 1921 and 1924 marked a turning point in immigration policy by imposing new numerical restrictions and creating enforcement mechanisms, such as the United States Border Patrol. The Border Patrol increasingly focused on the U.S.-Mexico border, where illegal crossings increased considerably throughout the 1940s and 1950s. In the summer of 1954, the Eisenhower administration launched "Operation Wetback," which resulted in the deportation of hundreds of thousands of Mexicans. The emergence of Mexicans as iconic illegal aliens and criminals was consolidated by the "War on Drugs," initiated by President Nixon and escalated by President Reagan. The antidrug offensive had a dramatic impact upon both the number of incarcerated immigrants and the number of deported criminal aliens. According to Judith Warner, professor of sociology and criminal justice, "increasingly, the use of zero tolerance policing, three strikes and you're out, preventative detention, and post-detention surveillance has created a prison industry geared to containment for citizens and incarceration followed by deportation for non-citizens, rather than rehabilitation for the purpose of re-integration into the social fabric."[6]

Meanwhile, the structural dependence of Western European economics on foreign labor in the aftermath of World War II led to the active recruitment of migrant workers by private employers and governments. Immigrants were not perceived as a societal threat as long as they addressed the need for manpower. Until the middle to late 1970s, the major Western immigration-receiving countries (such as France, West Germany, and the United Kingdom) welcomed the mass movement of workers from the less-developed European countries (notably Mediterranean countries, Poland, East Germany, and Yugoslavia) and selected third world countries (mainly former colonies in North and West Africa, East and South Asia). This immigration wave was expected to have a negligible effect on the host societies because the common assumption was that these "guest workers" would return home once the demand for their labor slackened. Concerns started to emerge when it appeared that European immigrants were outnumbered by non-European immigrants. In France, for example, Italians were the major source of labor during the 1950s. By 1970 the Italian proportion of the immigrant population had fallen to 18 percent, while North Africans (mainly Algerians) represented 28 percent of the total. Furthermore, the "internal migration" from North Africa "became a 'foreign migration' as decolonization progressed."[7] The United Kingdom faced similar challenges, with a total of 1.5 million persons of "New Commonwealth" ethnic origin in 1971. In the face of economic recession and mass unemployment precipitated by the oil shock of the early 1970s, immigration policies evolved dramatically in the major Western European receiving countries. Governments enacted a series of restrictive measures designed to freeze the recruitment of new workers, in addition to voluntary repatriation schemes. When it became evident that the "guest workers" intended to stay permanently, immigration morphed into a security issue.[8]

However, in terms of policy enforcement, immigration and terrorism were nonetheless regarded as two different issues in Europe and the United States until the mid-1980s. According to Derek Lutterbeck, former expert at the Geneva Center for Security Policy, "these two domains were considered separate: while challenges to a state's internal security were understood in terms of criminal or otherwise disturbing activities within the boundaries of the state, threats to external security were seen as arising first and foremost from the aggressive behaviour of other states."[9]

Gradual Convergence of Immigration and Counterterrorist Policies before 9/11

In the United States the process started when the Clinton administration reinforced the strategy of "border escalation" initiated by President Reagan,[10] announcing new initiatives against illegal immigration in July 1993. This policy shift was reflected by the Border Patrol's 1994 strategic plan, which became the basis of the "new security agenda" based on "prevention through deterrence." The linkage between immigration and terrorism was confirmed by the adoption in 1996 of the Antiterrorism and Effective Death Penalty Act (AEDPA) and the Illegal Immigration Reform and Individual Responsibility Act (IIRIRA). AEDPA expanded the aggravated felonies classification (by adding gambling, prostitution, commercial bribery, vehicle trafficking, and passport fraud) and made non-U.S. citizens retroactively subject to mandatory detention and deportation without consideration for extenuating circumstances. It also introduced the elimination of judicial review of certain kinds of deportation cases, and a new type of radically streamlined removal proceeding (including the possibility of using secret evidence) for immigrants suspected of terrorist activities. Finally, it increased the number of immigrants who could be detained and deported for non terroristic-related reasons and made it harder for aliens to secure employment and to qualify for the benefit of citizenship. IIRIRA included many provisions dealing with border enforcement, such as the increase of Border Patrol agents by a minimum of one thousand for each year of the succeeding five years; the construction of physical barriers (including second and third fences); and the acquisition of military technology and equipment for the "detection, interdiction, and reduction of illegal immigration."[11] New regulations stiffened civil and criminal penalties for illegal entry and limited the ability of aliens to challenge INS decisions and deportation rulings in federal courts. In this setting, the linkage between immigration and terrorism was reinforced by a security rhetoric. As the U.S. Commission on Immigration Reform explained, "immigration can be, under certain circumstances, a threat to traditional ideas of national security even if one concludes it has not yet posed such a threat to the United States."[12] In 1999 the Supreme Court upheld the administration policy of targeting immigrants for deportation on the basis of their rhetorical support for terrorist groups. The Court's decision stated that

> the Executive should not have to disclose its "real" reasons for deeming nationals of a particular country a special threat—or indeed for simply wishing to antagonize a particular foreign country by focusing on that country's nationals, and even if it did disclose them a court would be ill equipped to determine their authenticity and utterly unable to assess their adequacy. . . . When an alien's continuing presence in this country is in violation of the immigration laws, the Government does not offend the Constitution by deporting him for the additional reason that it believes him to be a member of an organization that supports terrorist activity.[13]

In Europe, the securitization of immigration issues was initiated by the Trevi group (Terrorisme, Radicalisme, Extrémisme, Violence Internationale)— a multilateral forum initially designed for improving the cooperation of European governments in the field of counterterrorism. Its 1989 "Palma Document" prestructured the Program of Action adopted in Dublin in June 1990. This program was defined as a "synthesis of the arrangements between police and security services . . . in relation to terrorism, drug trafficking or any form of crime including organized illegal immigration." The interface between policing, terrorism, drug trafficking, and immigration controls also informed the work of the Schengen group and led to the adoption of the 1990 convention implementing the Schengen Agreements. The main objective was to "assure the protection of the entire territory" of the signatory states "against illegal immigrants and activities which could jeopardize security."[14] In 1992 the Maastricht Treaty introduced a Third Pillar on Justice and Home Affairs (JHA), which institutionalized the securitization of immigration and asylum policies.[15] This trend was confirmed by the 1997 Treaty of Amsterdam, which transferred the sections related to immigration and asylum from the Third to the First Pillar and incorporated the Schengen framework into the *acquis communautaire*.[16] These institutional developments were complemented by a closer collaboration between law enforcement agencies on internal security issues within the Third Pillar. The securitization of the field of JHA included cooperation between the customs administrations, the police forces, and the justice administrations of the member states. Europol, the European police office, became fully operational in 1999. Along with this communitarization of immigration policies, the EU official focus shifted from border controls to "threat management." As in the United States, this shift was justified by a security rhetoric. According to the Reflection Group in charge of setting the EU agenda for the Amsterdam Intergovernmental Conference, "we all agree that the Conference should strengthen the Union's capacity to protect its citizens against terrorism, drug trafficking, money laundering, exploitation of illegal immigration and other forms of internationally organized crime."[17] As in the United States also, the assumed necessity to combine antiterrorist and immigration policies resulted in the amalgamation of immigrants and terrorists.

The gradual securitization of immigration policies that took place during the mid-1980s and early 1990s can be analyzed as a result of the blurring of this distinction between internal and external security. Criminal threats, including terrorism and illegal immigration, were constructed as security issues with both internal and external dimensions. One of the major effects of this reconceptualization of security was the reclassification of a wide range of activities as security problems, such as drug trafficking, organized crime, illegal immigration, and "bogus" asylum seekers. Three interrelated trends played a key role in this process: the resilience of terrorist threats; the enduring immigration pressures fueled by illegal immigration and asylum issues; and, in this problematic context, the need to balance the downgrading of internal frontiers initiated by the North American Free Trade Agreement and the Single European Act. None of these trends in itself explains the emergence of the immigration-terrorism nexus. It is, in fact, the dynamic interplay of their combined impact that lies at the heart of the securitization process. They all derived from concerns about a potential "security deficit." They all fueled a sense of vulnerability that in turn informed security-driven measures.

External Threats, Internal Security

In this period the United States faced, indeed, domestic terrorist attacks orchestrated by either foreign nationals (as illustrated by the February 1993 bombing of the World Trade Center, carried out by a group of foreign terrorists from Egypt, Iraq, and the Palestinian Authority) or by U.S. citizens (as illustrated by the destruction of a federal building in Oklahoma City in April 1995).[18] However, terrorism derived mainly from overseas. The United States became the most popular single target of international terrorism during the 1980s. U.S. citizens, officials, diplomats, and military officers were victimized by both state-sponsored terrorism (originating from Libya, Syria, and Iran) and international groups (Islamic fundamentalists such as Hezbollah, or Palestinian groups such as the Popular Front for the Liberation of Palestine–General Command, or Abu Nidal).[19] Following the Persian Gulf War (Operation Desert Storm) in 1991 and the emergence of al-Qaeda, numerous attacks were directed against U.S. interests abroad in the 1990s. One hundred and seventy attacks were recorded against the Gulf War coalition members, but most were against Americans. In October 1993, terrorists ambushed U.S. military personnel in Mogadishu, Somalia. This event was followed by a truck-bomb attack at Khobar Towers in Dhahran, Saudi Arabia, which destroyed a U.S. Air Force housing complex and killed nineteen soldiers (June 1996); truck bombings outside the U.S. embassies in Nairobi, Kenya, and Dar es Salaam, Tanzania (August 1998); and the suicide bombing of the destroyer USS *Cole* in Aden Harbor in Yemen (October 2000).

As the number of terrorist attacks increased abroad, the counterterrorist strategy focused on the "enemy" outside the U.S. borders. According to Laura Donohue, professor of law and expert on national security at Georgetown University, "domestic terrorist incidents were seen as related to law enforcement, with terrorism reserved for attacks levied by foreign nationals abroad."[20] This approach informed most of the counterterrorist measures introduced in this period. These included the adoption of bilateral and international treaties relating to aviation security, hostages, diplomatic security, hijacking, maritime safety, and terrorist financing. The United States also resorted to more-coercive measures, including designating "state sponsors of terrorism," conducting military strikes (such as in Iraq in 1993 and Afghanistan and Sudan in 1998), and initiating extraterritorial searches. Overseas security activities included the deployment of regional security officers in 131 countries, overt and covert intelligence operations, and the strengthening of "incident management" structures.

Despite this focus on the international nature of terrorism, there was evidence that concerns about external threats started to fuel fears about internal security. In the aftermath of the 1993 World Trade Center and 1995 Oklahoma City bombings, when it became evident that terrorism could happen on U.S. soil, U.S. authorities started to develop domestic preparedness programs aimed at reducing vulnerability to terrorist attacks against "sensitive" infrastructures (such as airports, public transportation, and nuclear plants). These programs also addressed the potential terrorist use of chemical, biological, or nuclear weapons and involved all the federal agencies (such as the FBI, CIA, and FEMA) and departments of the government (notably the Departments of Defense, Justice, Energy, and Health and Human Services). Under the Defense against Weapons of Mass Destruction Act of 1996, the Nunn-Lugar-Domenici Preparedness Program trained first-responders (such as fire, police, and emergency medical staff) in 120 of the largest U.S. counties. Additionally, the United States enacted domestic measures designed to address the transnational character of terrorism. The federal government made use of the powers included in the 1978 Foreign Intelligence Surveillance Act to monitor citizens and noncitizens located within the United States suspected of having ties with terrorist organizations. Other initiatives, under Executive Order 12947 of 1995, included the freezing of suspected groups' U.S.-based assets and the criminalization of providing resources or material support to terrorists.

Despite all these legislative initiatives, the multiplication of terrorist attacks targeting U.S. citizens at home and abroad generated a greater sense of vulnerability. Led by Vice President Al Gore, a White House commission report highlighted in February 1997 the risks of terrorist attacks in the United States. Calling for increased aviation security, the report noted that

> the threat of terrorism is changing in two important ways. First, it is no longer just an overseas threat from foreign terrorists. People and places in the United States have joined the list of targets, and Americans have joined the ranks of terrorists. The bombings of the World Trade Center in New York and the Federal Building in Oklahoma City are clear examples of the shift, as is the conviction of Ramzi Yousef for attempting to bomb twelve American airliners out of the sky over the Pacific Ocean. The second change is that in addition to well-known, established terrorist groups, it is becoming more common to find terrorists working alone or in ad-hoc groups, some of whom are not afraid to die in carrying out their designs.[21]

The Bremer Report, published by the National Commission on Terrorism in 1999, concluded that terrorism was posing an increasingly dangerous threat to America. That same year, the FBI suspended all public tours of its headquarters in Washington, D.C., and the State Department closed diplomatic posts in "high-risk areas."[22]

In Europe various countries were also involved in combating internal and international terrorism. The most active domestic terror groups were the left-wing Red Army Brigade in Italy, the French "libertarian communist" Action Directe, the Basque ETA group, and the Irish Republican Army (IRA). Furthermore, pro-Palestine groups were very active in Europe, as illustrated by the kidnapping and slaying of Israeli athletes at the 1972 Olympic Games in Munich. Internal and international terrorist groups often made common cause. West Germany's Red Army Faction and Italy's Red Brigades used PLO training camps and cooperated on operations like the seizure of an OPEC summit meeting in Vienna in 1975. European governments enacted counterterrorist measures at the national level (such as the United Kingdom's Terrorism Act of 1974) and created multilateral consultative forums, such as the Police Working Group on Terrorism in 1979. EU member states also signed in 1977 the European Convention on the Suppression of Terrorism, which listed terrorist acts by using the classification defined by the 1973 UN convention on terrorism. Intergovernmental cooperation covered a broad range of issues: terrorism, public order, football hooliganism, drug trafficking, safety and security at nuclear installations, civilian air travel security procedures, and contingency measures to deal with emergencies (disasters, fire prevention, and firefighting). All these measures proved insufficient. Terrorist threats reemerged as a high priority in the 1980s. France, for example, faced a fast escalation of terrorist attacks during the early 1980s committed by either domestic groups (such as Action Directe and the National Front for the Liberation of Corsica) or international movements (such as Abu Nidal and the Secret Armenian Army for the Liberation of Armenia). Germany was also the target of Abu Nidal terrorist activities, in addition to several national groups (such as the Red Army Faction, the Military Sports Group Hoffmann, and the German Action Group). France and Germany, as well as Italy and the United Kingdom, therefore enacted new counterterrorist measures while pushing EU initiatives addressing terrorism and other serious forms of international crimes. These initiatives included the ratification of the Europol Convention and the creation of a new Directorate General for Justice and Home Affairs (DG-JHA).[23]

Yet, in the 1990s, European countries faced the rise of radical Islamist terrorism, as illustrated by the Algerian Armed Islamic Group, which hijacked an Air France flight in 1994 and conducted a series of bombings in France in 1995 and 1996. This form of radicalism challenged the traditional distinction between domestic and international terrorism because terrorist groups directed their recruitment efforts not only at foreign-born young people (such as Frenchman Kaled Kelkal, born in Algeria, and the members of the

"Hamburg cell" who planned 9/11) but also at native residents. Furthermore, European governments became aware of the development of transnational networks, as exemplified by the case of the "Frankfurt cell" composed of five Algerians living in Germany who, together with co-nationals in France, planned to bomb targets in Strasbourg in 2000. Three months after the members of this cell were arrested, the Italian authorities revealed the existence of the "Milan cell" connected to other cells in France, Great Britain, Spain, Belgium, and Switzerland. According to French authorities, it was time to "terrorize terrorists."[24] However, as in the United States, the main result of the multiplication of terrorist incidents was an increasing sense of vulnerability. Terrorism was depicted as a "threat to democracy, to the free exercise of human rights and to economic and social development."[25] The European Council, in its conclusions of the Tampere meeting (October 1999) and the Santa Maria da Feira meeting (June 2000), asked the EU member states to strengthen their cooperation in order to prevent further terrorist attacks and improve all aspects of military and nonmilitary crisis management. In July 2001 the European Parliament published a report on the role of the EU in combating terrorism. This report expressed concerns about the growing "security deficit" in Europe and stressed the "inadequacy of traditional forms of judicial and police cooperation in combating" the new "transnational terrorism."[26]

Single Market, Multiple Threats

Against this background, concerns about transnational threats were reinforced by fears that national borders were becoming more porous, mainly as a result of the implementation of the 1985 Single European Act (SEA) and the 1992 North American Free Trade Agreement (NAFTA). SEA highlighted new security challenges by creating the internal market, an "area without internal frontiers in which the free movement of goods, persons, services and capital is ensured in accordance with the provisions of this Treaty" (SEA, art. 13). According to Jef Huysmans, professor at the United Kingdom's Open University,

> The reasoning can be summarized as follows: if we diminish internal border controls then we must harmonize and strengthen the control at the external borders of the European Community to guarantee a sufficient level of control of who and what can legitimately enter the space of free movement. . . . To make the issues of border control a security issue, the internal market had to be connected to an internal security *problematique*.[27]

This led to the adoption of the Schengen Agreements, which created a territory without internal borders (the Schengen area or "Schengenland") by abolishing checks at the internal borders of the signatory states. It created, subsequently, a single external border. The main objective became to balance the downgrading of internal border controls with a strengthening of external border controls. Several "compensatory measures"—designed to balance the potential risks of a "security deficit" created by free movement—were enacted, based on the assumption that control of illegal flows happens primarily at the border. Common rules regarding visas, right of asylum, and checks at external borders were adopted, as well as new initiatives aimed at improving cooperation and coordination between the police and the judicial authorities in order to safeguard internal security. The alleged causal relation between the abolishment of internal borders and an increase in insecurity was consolidated by the Dublin Convention, which entered into force in 1997. Designed to prevent refugees from making multiple asylum applications, the convention determined which of the signatory states was responsible for handling an asylum seeker's claim. The most effective innovative measure was the notion of a "safe country," designed to permit states to return asylum seekers without strictly violating international refugee law. Nationals of a state judged to be a "safe country of origin" were thus regarded as having an unfounded claim to asylum and could be deported. The notion of "safe country" was complemented by the concept of "safe third country," which denoted the last "safe" state through which asylum seekers had transited and to which they could be returned. More to the point, the convention explicitly connected immigrants and asylum seekers to issues of crime and security. It stated, for example, that "aliens" should be denied the right to entry when they posed "a threat to public order or national security and safety." Security should be considered at stake not only in the case of "aliens that have been previously convicted for a criminal offense" but also in the case of "aliens who have the intention to commit" a serious offense (art. 96).

Although much debate about NAFTA had centered on its economic dimensions, the new liberalized trade regime had a significant impact on the border security environment.[28] Designed to stimulate transborder economic linkages by eliminating barriers to trade in goods and services (art. 102), NAFTA was suspected of facilitating human movement as well, especially illegal flows. As in Europe, the challenge was therefore to combine a "borderless economy" with a "barricaded border." The United States began building its "Great Wall" shortly after NAFTA was implemented. The most significant illustration of the emergence of a new security continuum on the U.S. agenda was provided by a 1993 initiative named "Operation Blockade," later renamed "Operation Hold the Line," which sought to close the border at El Paso, Texas, to undocumented workers attempting to enter the United States. It involved the deployment of 450 Border Patrol agents and the erection of a 1.5-mile steel fence along the border. This constituted the "the vanguard border securitization initiative, becoming the model for U.S. policy as a whole in the 1990s."[29] In 1994 a more comprehensive border enforcement plan was unveiled by U.S. authorities, involving a 40 percent increase in the number of Border Patrol agents (up to five thousand), additional fences along crossing points in California, Texas, and Arizona, and the use of advanced electronic surveillance equipment. "Operation Gatekeeper" was launched in October 1994 in the vicinity of San Diego. This was followed by "Operation Safeguard" in Arizona and, finally, "Operation Rio Grande" in 1997, intended to secure the south Rio Grande Valley of Texas.[30] As a result, drug trafficking and undocumented immigration were increasingly framed as a "national security threat," along with terrorism and other criminal activities.

This trend was consolidated by the reform of the deportation system and tougher measures dealing with asylum. According to the Commission on Immigration Reform, chaired by former Texas representative Barbara Jordan, it was urgent to improve the management of criminal and noncriminal aliens: "Both criminal and noncriminal aliens must be removed to protect public safety (in the case of criminals) and to send a deterrent message (to *all* who have no permission to be here)."[31] Hence, IIRIRA introduced the expedited removal process: an immigration officer could determine that an arriving alien was inadmissible and could order him or her removed without further hearing unless the alien claimed a fear of persecution and intention to apply for asylum.[32] This legislation also retroactively expanded criminal grounds for deportation and permitted the use of secret evidence for noncitizens accused of terrorist activities. In addition, the asylum process was modified in 1995 in order to deter "abusive claims." Affirmative applicants who were turned down would immediately be put into deportation proceedings, much as would defensive applicants.[33]

Enduring Immigration Pressures

The sense of "invasion" and the subsequent rise of insecurity feelings were actually confirmed by the negative outcomes of restrictive immigration measures adopted on both sides of the Atlantic. The actual outcomes of the 1990 Immigration Act and IIRIRA did not address the main concerns—both qualitative and quantitative—expressed by restrictionists. The implementation of tougher border controls was followed by a dramatic increase in the numbers of illegal immigrants. According to the Office of Immigration Statistics, about 1.9 million undocumented immigrants entered the United States between 1990 and 1994, and 3.2 million between 1995 and 1999.[34] Regarding legal immigration, family reunion remained the largest category (up to 86.6 percent of admissions in 2000). Legal immigration also remained heavily Hispanic, with Mexico retaining the top position it achieved in the 1960s—a trend fiercely criticized by those agitating against the specter of the "Mexicanization of America." The most dramatic change related to asylum seekers and refugees: while they represented 19.8 percent of admissions in 1991, they accounted for only 7.8 percent in 2000. The 1995 reform of the asylum system was apparently effective, and the number of applications decreased during the late 1990s. Objections from human rights advocates, who denounced the overuse of some provisions, such as expedited removals, received little public attention.

In Europe, EU initiatives were strengthened by new regulations adopted at the national level. In addition to tougher border controls designed to deter illegal immigration, these regulations focused on asylum seekers—increasingly depicted as frauds and abusers of the EU "hospitality." The United Kingdom, for example, adopted the 1988 Immigration Act (or Carrier's Liability Act) and the 1993 Asylum Act (revised in 1996). In Germany the status of *Aussiedler* (emigrants of German descent) was reformed by a series of measures limiting their right to emigrate. The Asylum Law Reform of 1993 modified article 16 of the Basic Law by introducing important restrictions to asylum policy. However, restrictive measures produced mixed results, both at the EU and national levels. Between 1993 and 1998, the annual number of asylum seekers in Europe fell below a quarter of a million. However, more-stringent rules on asylum in some member states led to an increase in the number of asylum seekers in other member states. For example, the strict policy applied in Germany after 1992 contributed to the increase in the number of asylum seekers in the Netherlands, which rose to fifty-three thousand in 1994.[35] Furthermore, the number of asylum seekers reached new peaks in 1999–2000 when the war in Kosovo in 1999 reignited the European asylum crisis. Several traditional emigration countries in Southern Europe, such as Italy, Spain, Greece, and Portugal, developed into countries of immigration, due both to return migration and to an increase in immigration flows from North Africa and Asia. Former sending countries in Eastern and Central Europe, such as Bulgaria, Romania, and Poland, became receiving countries because of their peripheral location to "Fortress Europe." Facing unexpected flows of "unwanted" immigrants, these countries reacted to what was described as a state of emergency by introducing further immigration controls. Meanwhile, the estimated number of illegal immigrants rose from about two million in 1991 to more than three million in the early 2000s. This increase was partly the result of restrictive asylum measures. According to Gil Loescher, senior expert at the International Institute for Strategic Studies, "the restrictive asylum practices introduced by EU states have converted what was a visible flow of asylum seekers into a covert movement of irregular migrants that is even more difficult for states to count and control."[36]

These policy outcomes raised serious concerns about the ability of Western governments to manage illegal immigration. It was during this period that anti-immigrant groups and extreme-right-wing parties became more influential. Critics of immigration policy flourished. Public opinion expressed reservations about the capacity of political leaders to elaborate and implement effective measures. As a result both U.S. and European authorities tried to compensate for the ineffectiveness of border controls by amplifying their commitment to border controls. More resources were allocated to achieve this goal, not *despite* the fact that border controls were less efficient than expected, but *because* they were. This paradoxical strategy led to the multiplication of new "war style" practices and the emergence of new security actors. It also generated discriminatory measures against refugees and asylum seekers.

The Security Continuum Before 9/11

As the distinction between internal and external security blurred, the emergence of a new security continuum connecting border controls and counterterrorism was characterized by two interrelated trends: the increasing militarization of border control, and a close linkage between law enforcement and foreign intelligence.[37] A "new security agenda" led to a "new management style": the focus on counterterrorism efforts enhanced collaboration between law enforcement and foreign intelligence agencies and strengthened the investigative power of police forces.

The U.S. Border Patrol strategic plan, for example, included expanding the use of infrared scopes, upgrading sensors, and erecting secondary fences. Many of these technologies originated with the military, which played a major role in the construction and maintenance of security systems. Based on the U.S. Navy's Identification and Tracking System, a new fingerprint system was introduced in 1994 intended to identify criminal aliens and repeat crossers. It actually served as the underlying architecture of the US-VISIT tracking system introduced in the aftermath of 9/11.[38] IIRIRA continued this trend of adapting military technologies for the strengthening of border controls. This legislation authorized historically unprecedented increases in the size of security agencies and their operational budgets. From 1993 to 2000, for example, the overall annual INS budget increased from $1.5 billion to over $5 billion.[39]

European states, especially at the eastern and southern frontiers, developed regimes and sets of practices that formerly would have been possible only in wartime but were in fact considered as "normal"—even prior to 9/11. In Germany and Austria, police forces resorted to using a growing amount of military-style technology and instruments (such as night-vision goggles, spy planes, radars, and cameras similar to the ones used at the U.S.-Mexico border). In Spain, the Guardia Civil—a paramilitary force—became the lead agency in dealing with illegal immigration and trafficking by sea. Naval forces of various European countries (such as Italy, France, Spain, Portugal, and the United Kingdom) engaged in anti-immigration operations. Furthermore, there was a general trend toward the adoption of more preemptive measures, especially at the European Union's maritime borders, where border patrols try to catch immigrants before they come ashore. In addition to this "naval blockade," an EU-wide information technology system for the comparison of the fingerprints of asylum seekers—commonly known as Eurodac—was adopted in December 2000. People who violated the Eurodac process were either deported or detained in one of the detention centers that multiplied within Europe.

The militarization of border controls was coupled with the "policisation of intelligence and intelligence-isation of policing."[40] The German Foreign Intelligence Service, the British MI6, and the French Direction Générale de la Sécurité Extérieure, for example, shifted their main focus to areas such as drug trafficking, money laundering, and transnational terrorism. Conversely, police forces started to use surveillance technology that was originally conceived for foreign intelligence activities. Furthermore, the military forces started to play a key role in counterterrorism. In France, for example, military forces were deployed internally during the Gulf War of 1991 in order to prevent potential retaliatory actions by Islamic extremists (the *Vigipirate* plan). In Italy, military forces took part in ten antiterrorism missions between 1990 and 2000, carrying out search-and-seizure operations and protecting sensitive public buildings. Analyzing this militarization of the fight against terrorism, Derek Lutterbeck persuasively notes that

it could be argued that the growing involvement of military forces and foreign intelligence services in domestic security issues is not just simply an adaptation of such institutions to a changing security environment, but is to a large extent also driven by the desire of such agencies to secure their continued existence despite the disappearance of their traditional adversaries and the absence of direct military threats.[41]

These "war style" practices were indeed promoted by a growing number of security actors. In the United States the expansive field of "national security" became overcrowded. It encompassed the intelligence community (the CIA and FBI, the Bureau of Intelligence and Research at the State Department, the Defense Intelligence Agency, the National Security Agency, and intelligence units of the armed services), the agencies in charge of "domestic preparedness" (such as FEMA, the Department of Defense, the Department of Energy, the National Institutes of Health, and the Drug Enforcement Agency), FAA's experts on aviation security, the INS—in addition to a multitude of legislative committees and special bodies (such as the House Task Force on Terrorism). In 1993 the Clinton administration established the Office of the National Coordinator for Security, Infrastructure Protection and Counter-Terrorism. As explained by Richard Clarke, national coordinator from 1998 to 2001, the task of improving "coordination between dozens of government departments, agencies and offices" was hard to achieve, many being "uninterested in a unified strategy."[42] Yet all these actors played a role in the process described by Laura Donohue: "fear of possible attack, the introduction of measures, the allocation of greater resources, increased publicity, and increased fear."[43]

In Europe a new security network was established, including national governments, transnational police agencies, and security professionals. At the national level it involved the different actors playing a role in controlling borders (police, customs, borders guards), counterterrorist agencies, intelligence services, and the military, as well as new security agencies that mushroomed in various countries. This security network played a key role in the transformation of immigration into a security issue through struggles over power, resources, and claims of expertise.[44] A similar competition took place at the EU level between the security experts who were involved in the different intergovernmental forums (Trevi, Ad Hoc Working Group on Immigration), the various working groups included in the JHA Pillar, the Horizontal Information Group, the DGs/Departments within the European Commission, other EU institutions (as well as their specialized bodies dealing with security issues), and the Strategic Committee for Immigration, Frontiers and Asylum. As a result, these actors formed a network of "securitarian significance," using their expertise by focusing on the "new migratory threats."[45]

The last element in the emergence of a new security continuum connecting border control, terrorism, and immigration was based on the assumption that immigrants (both legal and illegal) and asylum seekers were social enemies. Refugees and asylum seekers were no longer perceived as victims of insecurity but described—and managed—as sources of insecurity in Europe. As a result, French expert Didier Bigo explains, "the issue was no longer, on the one hand, terrorism, drugs, crime, and on the other, rights of asylum and clandestine immigration, but they came to be treated together in the attempt to gain an overall view of the interrelation between these problems and the free movement of persons within Europe."[46]

Liza Schuster (former researcher at the Center on Migration at Oxford University) reaches a similar conclusion, arguing that "asylum seekers are a group of people that the state has singled out as legitimate targets for hostility." She contends that such discriminatory assumptions and practices can be characterized as "racist":

> Asylum seekers have been constructed, not solely as a legal category—those awaiting a decision on their entirely lawful application for recognition as a refugee—but as something more. "Asylum seeker" is now a term that is used unambiguously, and immediately conjures up cheat, liar, criminal, sponger—someone deserving of hostility by virtue not of any misdemeanour, but simply because he or she is an asylum seeker.[47]

Actually, one tangible result of the securitization process before 9/11 was the increasing criminalization of immigrants. Although both U.S. and European experts have concluded that immigrants commit proportionately no more—and possibly even fewer—crimes than native-born citizens, Western governments used national origin as a proxy for evidence of dangerousness, thus increasing suspicion and stigmatization of immigrants and resident ethnic minorities.[48] In the United States this was illustrated by the passage of laws aimed at controlling illegal immigration and related crime, such as the 1994 Violent Crime Control and Law Enforcement Act, as well as the sections of AEDPA and IIRIRA that expanded the range of criminal convictions. The hallmark of this increasing criminalization was the blurring of the distinction between the crime of crossing the border without authorization and serious offenses such as burglary, drug trafficking, and homicide. As a result, noncitizens accounted for two-thirds of the growth in the federal prisons' population from 1985 to 2000—a trend that strengthened further criminal stereotyping of immigrants.[49] A similar association of immigration with crime took place in Europe, where the overrepresentation of foreigners in prisons was mainly the result of the reclassification of immigration offenses and the detention of a growing number of immigrants awaiting deportation. Yet the securitarian thesis of the "criminal alien" was spread by the media, adopted by policymakers, and finally institutionalized by public policies. In Italy, for example, the stereotype of the criminal Albanian migrant was fueled by a media campaign that culminated in 1997 and resulted in the restrictive Turco-Napolitano Act adopted in 1998.

Critical Evaluation of the Securitization Process Before 9/11

Given that the U.S. and European governments began to mix antiterrorist measures (to fight illegal immigration) and anti-immigration measures (to combat terrorism) during the 1990s, a key question concerns whether the securitization of immigration policies helped achieve the official goals of limiting unwanted flows of immigrants and apprehending terrorists. In fact, border escalation produced new channels for illegal immigrants and more-efficient people smugglers and therefore aggravated the problems it was supposed to solve. The other outcome was the failure of both U.S. and European intelligence agencies to prevent the 9/11 attacks.

Border Controls and "Unwanted" Immigration

As the "hold the line" strategy was replicated along the Mexican-U.S. border, apprehensions of illegal crossers rose by 68 percent from 1994 to 2000. According to the Clinton administration, this increase reflected the efficiency of the enforcement buildup itself. As former commissioner of the INS Doris Meissner stated, "We have achieved more in the past five years than has been done in decades."[50] This, in turn, legitimized increased resources for the Border Patrol and other INS divisions. After more than doubling in size since 1993 (up to a total of more than nine thousand agents in 2000), the Border Patrol received additional funding (up to $1 billion in 2000, compared with less than $600 million for inspections and $200 million for consular activities). In some sectors, such as San Diego, the number of apprehensions declined. This trend was attributed by Patrol Border officials to the deterrent effect of concentrated border enforcement. Nevertheless, questions remained about the effectiveness of this strategy, as well as its consequences. The INS overstated the apprehension statistics by including data on repeat entry attempts (recidivism) instead of counting the actual number of persons trying to enter the United States. Furthermore, the alleged deterrent effect of border controls was mitigated by a geographical shift in attempted crossings. After triple fencing was constructed in San Diego, apprehensions of undocumented immigrants fell from 450,152 in 1994 to 100,000 in 2002, but apprehensions in the Tucson sector increased by 342 percent during the same period.[51] This variation was attributed mainly to immigrants' having shifted their routes eastward, looking for easier places to cross.

In addition to rerouting illegal entry attempts, border enforcement operations stimulated illegal immigration in two ways. First, immigrant smuggling became a growth industry. The share of undocumented immigrants apprehended along the southern border who reportedly were smuggled into the United States rose from 5.5 percent in 1992 to 22.2 percent in 2004.[52] In all probability, the increasing use of "professionals" reduced the likelihood of apprehension. Second, fees charged by people smugglers tripled or even quadrupled in some sectors. In Arizona, for instance, the average fee increased from $150 in 1999 to more than $800 in 2000.[53] Such inflation generated a higher rate of permanent settlement among illegal immigrants. As Wayne Cornelius, director of the Center for Comparative Immigration Studies at the University of California, San Diego, argues, "By making it more costly and difficult to gain entry illegally, the U.S. government has strengthened the incentives for permanent settlement in the United States. Thus, it is entirely possible that the current strategy of border enforcement is keeping more unauthorized migrants *in* the United States than it is keeping out."[54]

A similar border escalation took place in Europe, with similar negative outcomes. Around Ceuta and Melilla, two Spanish enclaves on the North African coast, the Spanish army erected a double fence equipped with intrusion detectors and barbed wire. A new surveillance system, SIVE (Integrated External Vigilance System), was installed, as well as radar systems in patrol boats and helicopters. Some EU countries, like Austria, deployed military forces along the eastern border (up to two thousand soldiers in 1990 in order to prevent illegal immigration from Hungary and Slovakia). In Italy the Guardia di Finanza, a semi-military police force, was equipped with military-style technologies such as thermal cameras and infrared night-vision equipment The Italian army was involved in immigration control operations in support of the traditional police forces such as the Polizia dello Stato and the Carabinieri. Under the legal decree of May 1995, the army was sent to the coastline of Salento (in southern Apulia) in order "to obtain a more pervasive control of public order and guarantee citizens' security"—leading to about three thousand arrests of clandestine crossers. During the Albanian crisis of 1997, fifteen hundred soldiers were transferred to the southern Adriatic coast to deter illegal immigrants from entering the country.

As in the United States, the border escalation resulted in a spatial redistribution of illegal immigration. For example, while Italian authorities imposed a naval blockade in the Strait of Otranto, new routes developed along the borders between Treviso and Trieste (the preferred path for East European immigrants); through Germany, Austria, and Switzerland (used by South Americans and Filipinos); and along the southern Sicilian coast, notably the island of Lampedusa (where North Africans landed).[55] Border enforcement had also fostered the sophistication of the migrant smugglers. While there was no strong evidence that the restrictive measures implemented by the Italian authorities were efficient, the "Albanian mafia" became increasingly well organized, extending its activities to other smuggling operations such as trafficking in drugs, arms, and illegal cigarettes. Costs of transit varied from $800 for clandestines coming from Albania to over $10,000 for those coming from Asia. Like Albania, Morocco was not just a country of origin for an increasing number of individuals who tried to cross the Strait of Gibraltar, but also a transit country for immigrants coming from farther south. Spanish authorities, in their efforts to secure this gateway, had to deal with the growing professionalism of smuggling networks that operated from both sides of the strait.

Border Controls and Counterterrorism

In the aftermath of 9/11, the claim for harsher immigration measures was based on the assumption that more-efficient border controls could have prevented terrorist attacks. In the United States, various studies consolidated the belief that the immigration system was dysfunctional, allowing terrorists to enter the country. According to the restrictionist Center for Immigration Studies, of the ninety-four foreign-born terrorists known to have operated in the United States between 1993 and 2004, fifty-nine committed immigration fraud prior to or in conjunction with taking part in terrorist activities. Once in the United States, twenty became naturalized U.S. citizens.[56] However, these finding have to be kept in context. As Bill Ong Hing of the University of San Francisco School of Law notes, "More than 500 million individuals (citizens and non-citizens) cross U.S. borders at over 200 designated crossing points every year; about 330 million of them are non-citizens, and some of that group may remain in the country longer than their visas permit. . . . We also know from experience that the overwhelming numbers of individuals arriving on our shores are not entering to engage in terrorism."[57] This means that, according to the U.S. historian Aristide Zolberg,

> border inspectors would have to make 1.3 billion correct decisions every year to keep terrorists and their weapons out of the country,

including in that count the inspection of ships and cargo containers, of passengers arriving by air, and of persons crossing the borders by land. . . . Approximately 1 of every 500,000 visas issued in the two-year period preceding 9/11 went to a hijacker or one of their suspected associates. . . . Some 120,000 visas were issued to Saudi nationals, of which 15 went to future hijackers—approximately 1 per 8,000 or .0001 percent.[58]

From a security standpoint, border controls are a needle-in-a-haystack approach to intercepting foreign terrorists. Terrorist organizations—notably al-Qaeda—choose their members carefully to avoid detection. The Migration Policy Institute, an independent and nonpartisan think tank, concluded a report on U.S. domestic security by noting that "immigration measures are an important tool in the domestic war against terrorism, but they are not effective by themselves in identifying terrorists of this new type . . . *clean operatives* who have not been identified by intelligence methods for special scrutiny."[59] Even under the tightest immigration controls, most of them would still have been admitted to the United States. According to Walter Ewing, senior researcher at the American Immigration Council, "attempting to locate terrorists by sifting through every foreign-born person who enters the country is not a promising means of unraveling a terrorist plot."[60] This strategy is ineffective in guarding against terrorist attacks launched by native-born perpetrators. Profiling would not have identified Atlanta Olympics bomber Eric James Rudolph, American Taliban fighter John Walker Lindh, or al-Qaeda recruit José Padilla.[61] On the European side, immigration controls would have been ineffective to spot the natives who participated in the 2004 Madrid and the 2005 London bombings.

Paradoxically, evidence suggests that the efficiency of the U.S. immigration system was also undermined by the securitization of immigration controls. The reforms adopted in 1996 by the U.S. government, for example, were supposed to enhance national security. In reality, they caused the INS to focus on the deportation of illegal immigrants for reasons unrelated to terrorism. The U.S. system became so complicated that INS agents did not apply it as intended. Law enforcement agencies spent more time and resources capturing illegal Mexicans who posed no threat to national security than they did effectively tracking potential terrorists. Similarly, while the EU member states were obsessed with protecting the internal market from potential external threats, they underestimated the threat posed by potential homegrown radicals. European border forces targeted instead illegal Albanians, refugees and asylum seekers from sub-Saharan Africa, and Roma from

Eastern Europe. By contrast, little attention was paid to the new terrorist networks that set up bases in Europe.

Intelligence and Security

Finally, there is strong evidence that failure to stop the 9/11 attacks was more the result of intelligence lapses than of immigration-enforcement failures. In addition to signing the Antiterrorism and Effective Death Penalty Act of 1996, President Clinton had, the previous year, issued Executive Order 12947, which named twelve foreign terrorist organizations and froze their properties in the United States.[62] The name of Osama bin Laden was added to the list following the 1998 attacks in Sudan and Afghanistan, and Clinton signed Executive Order 13099 imposing sanctions against al-Qaeda. Yet a 2002 joint inquiry, conducted by the Senate Select Committee on Intelligence and the House Permanent Select Committee on Intelligence, revealed serious management and resource deficiencies in intelligence collection and information sharing. The joint inquiry noted that the intelligence community "had considerable evidence before September 11 that international terrorists were capable of, and had planned, major terrorist strikes within the United States" and that "Osama bin Laden's role in international terrorism had also been well known for some time before September 11."[63] The National Security Agency, for example, reported at least thirty-three communications indicating a possible imminent attack in 2001. In June 2001 a CIA report on Khalid Sheikh Mohammed (KSM)—who would subsequently be identified as the alleged mastermind of the 9/11 attacks—emphasized his ties to bin Laden and expressed concern about his continuing travel to the United States in order to recruit future terrorists. Yet KSM obtained a U.S. visa in late June, under an alias of a Saudi citizen. In July 2001 an FBI agent in Phoenix sent a report to the Radical Fundamentalist Unit and the Osama bin Laden Unit at FBI headquarters. The agent expressed his concerns that a coordinated effort was under way by bin Laden to send students to the United States for civil aviation–related training. This claim generated no interest. In August 2001 a closely held intelligence report for senior government officials mentioned that members of al-Qaeda, including some U.S. citizens, had resided in or traveled to the United States for years and that the group maintained a support structure in the country. The INS arrested Zacarias Moussaoui in August because his visa to stay in the United States had expired. But no one at the FBI connected the Moussaoui case with the heightened threat environment in the summer of 2001.

Among the major intelligence deficiencies it identified, the joint inquiry found that a lack of coordination and exchange of information between the FBI, CIA, INS, FAA, and other agencies resulted in missed opportunities to identify and arrest some of the hijackers. The CIA, for example, failed to update the TIPOFF system, a watch list for suspected terrorists used by INS to screen visa applicants. Nor did the FBI keep the NSA or the CIA adequately informed. In addition, the quality of counterterrorism analysis was inconsistent. Many analysts were inexperienced, undertrained, and lacked access to critical information. At the FBI, for example, a 2002 internal study found that 66 percent of the strategic analysts were unqualified. The staff and resources dedicated to counterterrorism could not keep pace with the amount of incoming intelligence reporting. Before 9/11, 35 percent of Arabic language materials derived from the Foreign Intelligence Surveillance Act were neither reviewed nor translated.

U.S. intelligence agencies were not alone in their failures. The pilots who flew the September 11 planes lived in Hamburg and met in Spain to make their final preparations. None of them were spotted by European intelligence agencies. With regard to the Madrid bombings, for example, German authorities noticed Rabei Osman Sayed Ahmed ("Mohammed the Egyptian") as a vocal lay preacher. Although he was investigated, German authorities concluded he was not dangerous. By the time that intelligence officers decided to investigate him further in the aftermath of the attacks in the United States, Osman Sayed Ahmed had already left Germany for Spain, where he participated in the preparation of the terrorist attacks. European governments were so obsessed by the external enemy than they underestimated the threats posed by the emergence of homegrown terrorists. Three members of the so-called 7 July Group—Mohammad Sidique Khan, Shehzad Tanweer, and Hasib Hussain—were actually second-generation British citizens whose parents were of Pakistani origin. They grew up in Beeston (near Leeds), apparently well integrated into British society. Tanweer, the son of a prominent businessman, excelled at school and played for a local cricket team. Hussain went on to college in an advanced business program. Khan worked for the Benefits Agency and then joined the staff of a local primary school, taking part in a school trip to the Houses of Parliament in 2004. Intelligence agents and investigators in the United Kingdom apparently had no idea that an attack was imminent, and shortly before the London bombings, the Joint Terrorism Analysis Center suggested the terrorism alert level be lowered from "severe general" to "substantial." According to the *Report of the Official Account of the Bombings* published by the House of Commons, the social life of the terrorists did not reveal any obvious sign of extremism prior to the attacks. Their behavior was not unusual enough to cause concern—although the report added that "camping, canoeing, white-water rafting and other outward bound type activities are of particular interest because they appear common factors for the 7 July bombers and other cells disrupted previously and since."[64]

The United States and European countries were already drawn into a security/insecurity spiral prior to 9/11. The hierarchical classification of the threat level was based on the assumption that illegal immigration was a security threat because it was not possible to regulate it; and because it was a security threat, illegal immigration was to be managed by enacting regulations similar to counterterrorist measures. Western countries reached this conclusion by conflating the notions of illegal immigrant (or "bogus" asylum seeker) and social enemy. The impact of this confusion was detrimental to both immigration policy and counterterrorist strategy. Neither the United States nor the European countries achieved their stated goals. Rather, stricter enforcement efforts produced a counterproductive dynamic whereby negative policy outcomes gave legitimacy to attempts of further securitization, border militarization, and surveillance. This process generated two trends with long-term effects.

The first one was a growing infringement of human rights and civil liberties. In 1993 the Electronic Communication Privacy Act entitled the FBI to obtain certain telephone subscriber information without a court order or subpoena for use in counterintelligence investigations. Other measures enacted before 9/11 included special courts, "secret evidence" in making deportation decisions, classified deportation procedures, and extraordinary renditions.[65] It is also worth noting that many provisions of the controversial USA Patriot Act, rushed into law in October 2001, had been put forward in early drafts of the AEDPA, such as a widening of the definition of "terrorist" to include foreigners with tangential connections to groups identified as terrorist by the president, indefinite detention of noncitizens, and modifications in the implementation of the Foreign Intelligence Surveillance Act standards in cases of alien deportation. These provisions were pulled out of the 1996 legislation but would find their way into federal law after 9/11. In the United Kingdom, the Anti-Terrorism Act of 2000 was adopted in order to bring existing laws into compliance with the European Convention on Human Rights. Yet this 2000 act broadened the definition and scope of the crime of terrorism (through, for example, the notion of accomplice liability in the United Kingdom or abroad) and created new substantive criminal offenses (such as failing to disclose information about a potential terrorist attack). It also shifted the burden of proof from the government to the defendant, thereby rejecting the "presumption of innocence" principle. Other provisions empowered police forces to arrest suspects without a warrant, allowed the detention of terrorism suspects for forty-eight hours without contact with counsel and family members, and extended the detention without charge in certain cases for up to an extra five days.

Furthermore, both the U.S. and European governments proved extremely creative in finding a way to circumvent the most basic international human rights, notably the non-refoulement principle as defined by the Geneva Convention relating to the status of refugees.[66] In Europe, one solution was provided by the Dublin Convention, notably with the notions of "safe country of origin" and "third safe country," which allowed European governments to deny asylum status or apply a fast-track deportation procedure. Another solution was the multiplication of interceptions at high sea. This "dissuasion and control strategy" legitimized the naval blockades imposed by southern countries and increased the number of shipwrecks.[67] As in Europe, the practice of extraterritorializing asylum flows became part of the new deterrence strategy. The Clinton administration resumed the George H. W. Bush administration practice of intercepting refugees on the high seas, sending them back without an interview. In its 1993 *Sale v. Haitian Centers Council* ruling, the Supreme Court argued that "exclusion protection under the Refugee Act and non-refoulement obligations existed only within U.S. territory."[68]

The second trend related to the abuse of "emergency policy" in the absence of actual war—as opposed to "wars" through military metaphors ("war on crime," "war on drugs," "invasion," "border under siege") that flourished before the declaration of the "war on terror." Historically, the most extreme security measures targeting immigrants or members of minority groups suspected of posing a threat were invalidated when "emergency times" ended. With regard to wartime mistreatment of the Japanese, for example, the Presidential Commission on the Wartime Relocation and Internment of Civilians concluded in 1983 that it "was not justified by military necessity, and the decisions which followed from it—detention, ending detention and ending exclusion—were not driven by analysis of military conditions. The broad historical causes which shaped these decisions were race prejudice, war hysteria and a failure of political leadership."[69] Both AEDPA and IIRIRA were criticized by legal experts and advocacy groups notably for their retroactivity effect.[70] Yet they endured and informed the post-9/11 legislation. The normalization of extraordinary measures was also noticeable in Europe, either through the reform of criminal codes (as in Germany) or as a result of counterterrorist legislation (as in France and Great Britain). Initially designed to deal with the "Basque problem," article 55 of the Spanish Constitution allowed the declaration of "state emergency or siege" and the subsequent suspension of all civil liberties (such as freedom of movement, and right of assembly). Under this article, Spanish authorities could adopt "emergency measures" suspending or restricting individual rights in cases "involving certain persons with respect to investigations having to do with the activities of armed bands or terrorist elements."[71] Although article 55 warned the government against an "abusive utilization" of these powers, the very notion of "emergency" remained vague. Similarly, the notions of "public order" and "national security" remained indeterminate legal concepts in the legislation passed by other European countries.

The stage was set for the strengthening of the securitization of immigration issues that took place in the aftermath of 9/11. As the next chapter illuminates, policy choices were to be deeply influenced by the legacy of the immigration and security measures adopted in the pre-9/11 era. Both the U.S. and European governments subsequently followed the same circular path: the introduction of restrictive measures with mixed actual outcomes; the subsequent allocation of additional resources; and, finally, an increased feeling of being unable to secure the borders, which in turn increased existential anxieties and actual threats.

CHAPTER 3

Securitization after 9/11

          The terrorism-immigration nexus was solidly consolidated by the events of 9/11 in two ways. First, the belief that foreigners were more liable than citizens to commit terrorist attacks was sufficient to justify a zero-tolerance approach to immigration offenses, tougher controls on borders, and even extraterritorial controls beyond borders. The conflation of the notions of "immigrant" (broadly defined) and "terrorist" (equally broadly defined) relied on inflated risk assessments: terrorists might infiltrate the United States and the EU by legally seeking admission or by attempting illegal entry, and therefore all immigrants should be perceived as would-be terrorists. This reliance on worst-case scenarios fueled suspicion and legitimized extrajudicial powers and practices. Second, the notion of the "war on terror" suggested that the scope of U.S. counterterrorism policy should be broadened in order to respond to the global nature of the threat. In Europe, where military metaphors have remained less popular, many countries nonetheless also passed legislative measures similar to those adopted in the United States to strengthen their ability to prevent, investigate, and respond to terrorist threats. They expanded the legal definition of terrorism to cover all kinds of terrorist organizations and to include new offenses. They also expanded the powers of the police, law enforcement, and intelligence services. In the aftermath of the London and Madrid terrorist attacks, European governments took further steps toward the completion of their counterterrorist arsenal, both at the national and EU levels.

In July 2002 the George W. Bush administration issued its first National Strategy for Homeland Security (NSS). This document listed the key strategic objectives, such as preventing terrorist attacks within the United States, reducing America's vulnerability to terrorism, and minimizing the damage from attacks that could occur.[1] These objectives—"prevent, protect against, respond to, and recover from terrorist attacks"—were reaffirmed by the National Security Strategy of March 2006, the National Strategy for Combating Terrorism of September 2006, and the National Strategy for Homeland Security of October 2007. European countries rallied around similar goals, as illustrated by the European Security Strategy (ESS) adopted in December 2003 and written in direct reference to the 2002 NSS.[2] Both the NSS and ESS also focused on dangers posed by failed/rogue states and weapons of mass destruction (WMD) proliferation—although the Europeans praised the virtue of multilateralism, while the NSS only referred to "American internationalism."

Regarding the terrorism-immigration nexus, three dimensions of the war on terror deserve particular attention: first, security measures designed to protect homeland safety; second, extraterritorial actions such as the military interventions in Iraq and Afghanistan; third, measures targeting immigrants, especially some specific nationalities and/or categories (illegal immigrants and asylum seekers). All these trends have defied the traditional distinction between domestic and international security, as well as between military and nonmilitary (such as illegal immigration) challenges.

The U.S. War on Terror

In October 2001 the USA Patriot Act (Uniting and Strengthening America by Providing Appropriate Tools Required to Intercept and Obstruct Terrorism) was signed into law by President Bush. The act expanded the definition of "terrorism" and introduced new criteria and processes for designating "terrorist organizations." It amended a variety of regulations dealing with law enforcement tactics and tools in gathering intelligence during the course of an investigation, with new broad powers to conduct searches, employ electronic surveillance, and detain suspected terrorists. The Patriot Act invested the Department of Justice with the authority to investigate all offenses relating to terrorism. It also enlarged the federal government's power to conduct criminal investigations. Section 213 gave law enforcement authorities the power to conduct "sneak and peak" searches (which involve a delay in delivering notice of the execution of a search warrant). This section granted federal law enforcement the authority to secretly enter a premise without notifying the occupant until some "reasonable" time after the search. Section 216 granted law enforcement authorities the ability to intercept e-mail and Internet activity. Section 218 authorized the monitoring of phone conversations without a warrant. Additionally, the act gave the U.S. attorney general the authority to retrieve and store DNA samples from any defendant convicted of any federal crime of violence or terrorism. The act amended immigration law to strengthen the powers of federal law enforcement to deport certain individuals. It also granted the attorney general the authority to certify aliens as suspects and detain them if there existed "reasonable grounds to believe" they were involved in unlawful terrorist activities. Once suspected aliens were in custody, section 412 of the act allowed the government to detain them for up to seven days without a hearing—after which the person had to be released, charged, or deported. If the attorney general believed an individual's release would threaten national security, he could request that the detention be extended indefinitely, with six-month renewable periods of detention.

In his Homeland Security Presidential Directive 2 on "combating terrorism through immigration policies," President Bush stated that "it is the policy of the United States to work aggressively to prevent aliens who engage in or support terrorist activity from entering the United States and to detain, prosecute, or deport any such aliens who are within the United States."[3] He announced the creation of a Foreign Terrorist Tracking Task Force designed to accomplish the following objectives: first, to deny entry into the United States of aliens associated with, suspected of being engaged in, or supporting terrorist activities; and second, to locate, detain, prosecute, or deport any such aliens already present in the United States. In the pursuit of enhanced INS and customs enforcement capabilities, Bush asked for the development and implementation of multiyear plans increasing the number of customs and INS special agents assigned to joint terrorism task forces. The directive also delineated measures dealing with the abuse of student visas, the use of advanced technologies for data sharing and enforcement efforts, and initiated new negotiations with Canada and Mexico designed to ensure the maximum possible compatibility of immigration, customs, and visa policies.

In November 2001 John Ashcroft, then attorney general, called for the voluntary interviewing of up to five thousand aliens from countries suspected of harboring terrorists. The State Department also slowed the process of granting visas for men ages sixteen to forty-five from certain Arab and Muslim countries. On November 13 President Bush issued an executive order authorizing the creation of military tribunals to try noncitizens on charges of terrorism. The trials could be held in secret; classified information could be used against a defendant; conventional rules of evidence would not apply; there would be no jury nor appeal to civil courts; and the penalty could include execution. In March 2002 the Department of Justice announced it was conducting interviews with more than three thousand more Arabs and Muslims living in the United States as visitors or students. The following September Ashcroft ordered the INS to launch a "prompt review" of political asylum cases in order to identify any potential members of terrorist organizations. In November the INS expanded the National Security Entry-Exit Registration System (NSEERS) and required male nationals ("special registrants") of Iran, Iraq, Libya, Sudan, and Syria admitted prior to 9/11 to register with the INS.[4] This first phase was intended to enable the U.S. government to keep track of the arrival and departure of these special registrants. They were required to be fingerprinted, photographed, and interviewed under oath at U.S. ports of entry. The second phase required special registrants who had already been admitted to the United States to register at designated INS (later U.S. Citizenship and Immigration Services) offices. Those who did not abide by these procedures ran the risk of being considered out of status and deportable. Additionally, the Enhanced Border Security and Visa Entry Reform Act of 2002 sought to improve the visa issuance process abroad as well as immigration inspection at the border.

The INS was subsumed into the Department of Homeland Security (DHS) in March 2003. It included two new divisions: the U.S. Citizenship and Immigration Services (USCIS), which handles immigrant visas, naturalization, and refugee and asylum application; and the Directorate of Border and Transportation Security. Three departments were charged with playing a key role in administering the new laws and policies on the admission of aliens: the Department of State, the Department of Homeland Security, and the Department of Justice. With the implementation of the new immigration infrastructure, the State Department curtailed certain immigration programs, such as the visa revalidation program and the exemption for Commonwealth citizens from visa requirements. In March 2003 the Bush administration launched Operation Liberty Shield, designed to "increase security and readiness in the United States." As part of this initiative, DHS implemented a temporary policy of detaining asylum seekers from thirty-three countries where al-Qaeda was known to have operated. The attorney general announced an order (issued in December 2002) allowing FBI agents and U.S. marshals to detain noncitizens for "alleged immigration violations" in cases where there was insufficient evidence to hold them on criminal charges. Subsequent to the NSEERS, the USCIS implemented in January 2004 the U.S. Visitor and Immigrant Status Indicator Technology (US-VISIT), which required nonimmigrants to provide fingerprints, photographs, and other biometric identifiers when arriving in, or departing from, the United States.

The REAL ID Act of 2005 (HR 418) further expanded the applicable definition of the term "engage in terrorist activity." Under the new law, an alien who solicited on behalf of or provided material support for a designated terrorist organization would be inadmissible "unless he demonstrated by clear and convincing evidence that he did not and should not have reasonably known that he was soliciting on behalf of or providing material support for a group that met the definition of 'terrorist organization' found in INA §212(a)(3)(B)(vi)(III)." The act contained a number of immigration- and identification-related provisions intended to improve homeland security. Among these were provisions that made changes to the Immigration and Nationality Act (INA), expanded the terrorism-related grounds for alien inadmissibility and deportation, and set standards for state-issued driver's licenses and personal identification cards. The REAL ID Act expressly limited the process of federal habeas reviews and certain other nondirect judicial review for certain matters relating to the removal of aliens under INA §242, while permitting appellate court review of constitutional claims and questions of law. It also allowed the secretary of homeland security to waive the application of any legal requirements when it was believed such a waiver was necessary to ensure the "expeditious construction" of certain barriers along U.S. land borders. In April 2008 Michael Chertoff, then secretary of homeland security, actually issued waivers suspending more than thirty laws that he said could interfere with the construction of new fences in Arizona, California, New Mexico, and Texas. The list included laws protecting the environment, endangered species, antiquities, farms, deserts, forests, Native American graves, and religious freedom.

Finally, the Protect America Act of 2007 (S 1927) authorized the collection of international communications on a massive scale, without court order, including not only calls between two foreign countries but also when one party was in the United States. It gave the administration the power to choose how to collect, store, and use the private communications of Americans. The attorney general was required to report to Congress twice a year but was not obliged to give any details about "secret procedures," including the number of U.S. citizens targeted. This act left the executive unchecked and also stated that "judicial proceedings shall be concluded as expeditiously as possible."[5]

War on Terror in Europe

The events of September 11, 2001, were a catalyst for changing laws in Europe. Not only were Europeans—including sixty-seven British citizens—

among those who died at the hands of the 9/11 terrorists, but Spain and the United Kingdom had their own versions of 9/11 (3/11 in Madrid, and 7/7 in London). Europeans demonstrated beyond doubt their solidarity with the Americans after 9/11. The NATO alliance invoked its article 5 self-defense clause for the first time in its fifty-two-year history, and the Europeans stood together to support their Western friend and ally. "We are all Americans" proclaimed Jean-Marie Colombani, then editor of *Le Monde*.[6] Tony Blair, Jacques Chirac, Gerhard Schröder, and other European leaders rallied around this idea. Memorial services were organized in London, Paris, and other European capitals. Spontaneous demonstrations of sympathy took place in many cities. Millions of Europeans held candle vigils, rallies, and prayer services. The Western alliance suddenly entailed an emotional sense of community, a widespread feeling of common destiny.

International and regional organizations, such as the United Nations and the European Union, implemented new provisions. On September 28, 2001, the UN Security Council passed Resolution 1373, which consolidated key provisions from a variety of treaties dealing with terrorism. The resolution mandated that countries change their domestic laws to prevent the financing of terrorism and to designate terrorist acts as serious criminal offenses, and that they take appropriate measures before granting refugee status, to ensure that asylum seekers were not planning terrorist attacks.

The EU reaction was equally swift. By September 14 the EU issued a declaration affirming the intention of the member states to develop a common foreign and security policy, to facilitate the implementation of the European security and defense policy, and to promote international action to create a sustainable counterterrorism network. On September 20 the JHA Council decided on a package of thirty-eight antiterrorist measures dealing with judicial and police cooperation, some of which had been debated for years. This package was endorsed by a special European Council on September 21. Political agreement was reached among EU member states in November on both the terms of a European arrest warrant and the common definition of terrorist acts and sanctions. In addition, the EU made significant progress on a number of sensitive issues, such as the amendment of the Money Laundering Directive, the setting up of a permanent Eurojust cross-border prosecution unit, and the creation of joint investigative teams. The European Commission suggested a series of urgent measures in October, which included establishing a mechanism for the short-term joint assessment of threats, updating regularly the list of terrorist organizations compiled by national police forces, and agreeing on a framework decision for penalties on terrorist activities. The EU adopted a Common Position in December 2001 on the application of specific measures to combat terrorism. It listed individuals and groups whose funds and financial assets must be frozen, including the IRA, ETA, Palestinian Islamic Jihad, as well as Osama bin Laden and individuals or groups linked to al-Qaeda.[7]

In June 2002 the EU adopted a Framework Decision on combating terrorism, which defined a "terrorist offense" and laid down the penalties that member states had to incorporate in their national legislation.[8] The Framework Decision on the European Arrest Warrant of June 2002 provided for the arrest of wanted persons by the police and judicial authorities of one member state on demand by the authorities of another member state. Other measures strengthened cross-border operational cooperation, such as the Council Decision on the Implementation of Specific Measures for Police and Judicial Cooperation to Combat Terrorism (December 2002), and the Council Decision on the Exchange of Information and Cooperation Concerning Terrorist Offenses (September 2005). In the fight against financing terrorism, the EU adopted several instruments, such as the Council Framework Decision on the Execution of Orders Freezing Property or Evidence (July 2002), and the Directive on the Prevention of the Use of the Financial System for the Purpose of Money Laundering and Terrorist Financing (October 2005). The EU Council added new functions for the Schengen Information System (SIS) to combat terrorism more effectively, and gave access to the data stored in the SIS to Europol, member states of Eurojust, and national judicial authorities responsible for investigating and prosecuting crime.[9] Access to the Visa Information System was also given to Europol and national authorities responsible for internal security in order to prevent and detect terrorist offenses and other serious criminal offenses.[10]

The Hague Program, adopted in November 2004, included various antiterrorist measures among its ten priorities. The European Commission emphasized the need for terrorist prevention and listed a series of objectives, such as improved exchanges of information, a better understanding of the radicalization and recruitment of terrorists, and the prevention of misuse of charitable organizations for the financing of terrorist organizations.[11] The EU Counter-Terrorism Strategy was adopted by the European Council in November 2005, partly as a response to the London bombings. It listed the main measures under the four headings of Prevent (radicalization), Protect (EU citizens, values, and infrastructures), Pursue (terrorists), and Respond (to terrorist attacks). It was followed in December 2005 by the EU Strategy for Combating Radicalization and Recruitment to Terrorism, which focused on al-Qaeda as the main terrorist threat to the European Union. Harmonization of law enforcement was enhanced by the Council Decision on the Exchange of Information Extracted from Criminal Records (November 2005) and the Directive on Retention of Telecommunication Data (March 2006). Finally, in 2007, the EU established a specific program aimed at supporting projects in the prevention of, preparedness for, and consequence management of terrorism.[12]

As in the United States, counterterrorism activities led to institutional innovations, such as the creation of a twenty-four-hour alert unit within Europol and joint investigation teams comprising terrorism experts from the police and the judiciary, representatives of Eurojust, and Europol officers. The Office of the Coordinator for Counterterrorism was established in the aftermath of the Madrid bombings, and the EU Police Chiefs Operational Task Force was charged with organizing high-level meetings of the heads of EU counterterrorism units. The Situation Center was created in June 2005, intended to stimulate cooperation between security and intelligence services. Other EU structures dealing with terrorist threats included the Terrorist Working Group (under the supervision of the JHA Council), the Working Party on Terrorism (within the General Affairs and External Relations Council), and the Monitoring and Information Center (set up at the European Commission).

Many European countries additionally passed legislation in response to terrorist threats. Belgium passed the Terrorist Offense Act in 2003, which amended the criminal code by introducing definitions relating to terrorism and spelling out punishment for belonging to or supporting terrorist organizations. In 2004 Belgium became the first country to introduce biometric-based electronic passports, and adopted a law addressing the issue of financing of terrorism. In 2007 a royal decree entered into force making it easier for financial authorities to freeze the assets of individuals involved in terrorist offenses. In Greece, Law 3241/2004 was introduced in July 2004 and amended the first anti-terrorist law, Law 2928/2001. It listed twenty-two types of offenses considered as terrorist acts and introduced a number of provisions enabling the authorities (subject to special judicial scrutiny) to infiltrate a terrorist group, record terrorist activities by all technical means, and to use DNA testing. In Norway the penal code was amended in 2002 with a view to establishing effective legislative measures against acts of terrorism, and in 2005, new laws on police methods to prevent terrorist attacks came into force. They included provisions for police surveillance of individuals suspected of being members of terrorist groups, and the detention of suspects for a maximum of forty-eight hours. If the authorities had reasonable grounds to believe that investigation required a further period of detention, they were allowed to extend it up to several weeks. The Swedish counterterrorist legislation was amended by the 2002 Act on Criminal Responsibility for the Financing of

Particularly Serious Crimes and the 2003 Act on Criminal Responsibility for Terrorist Offenses. The Danish parliament adopted an updated antiterrorism package in June 2006, and a new provision of the Administration of Justice Act entered into force in 2007, allowing for the storage of Internet and tele-communications data for a one-year period.

In October 2001 Italy issued a new law decree (374/2001) amending antiterrorist legislation to introduce the new criminal category of "asso-ciation with the aim of international terrorism." It applied the provisions of Italy's anti-Mafia laws to crimes committed for the purpose of inter-national terrorism. This amendment and other measures approved by the Italian government made it possible to prosecute and punish anyone pro-moting, assisting, organizing, or financing a terrorist organization. The same decree law increased the powers of the judicial police, extending pre-emptive and court-authorized wiretapping and interception of communi-cations. In 2005, urgent measures to counter international terrorism (such as law no. 144) were passed, providing that individuals could be kept in custody for up to twenty-four hours (compared with twelve hours prior to the enactment of the law) without charge and without a lawyer present. The new legislation also allowed law enforcement authorities to take hair or saliva samples without consent in order to trace the suspect's DNA; to have access to Internet and cell phone records; and introduced the incen-tive to reward immigrants with residence permits if they cooperated with police investigations. Additionally, it reinforced the rules concerning crimi-nal offenses such as "public provocation to commit terrorist offenses" or "recruitment for terrorism." The definition of terrorism in article 270 *bis* of the Italian Penal Code was widened by Law 155/2005, which came into force in August 2005. The new definition included promoting, organizing, managing, and financing terrorist organizations, or assisting any individual who participated in such organizations. It also included enrolling or train-ing individuals to carry out violent activities. This law gave the police and other investigating authorities increased powers to pursue terrorists—such as the right to use false identities and to intercept communications. In 2007, new measures to prevent and combat financing of terrorism, as well as concerning expulsion in case of terrorism, were introduced through EU Directive 2005/60/CE.

In France a law on "everyday security and combating terrorism" was passed in November 2001. This law added the financing of terrorist activity to the list of terrorist offenses and lightened the procedural requirements for car, body, and luggage searches. It also increased surveillance of areas consid-ered dangerous and allowed prosecution services to decipher messages (such as e-mails and other digital information). The national database of genetic information was extended beyond sex offenses to other crimes (including theft). Under Law 2004-204 passed in March 2004, a ninety-six-hour special custody regime was extended to a wider range of offenses. Persons suspected of terrorism or drug trafficking could be held incommunicado for the first forty-eight hours without access to a lawyer. Under Law Perben II of October 2004, new types of covert investigative methods in the investigation of organized crime and terrorism were permitted. The French parliament then adopted another antiterrorism bill in December 2005, in response to the London bombings. It amended the French legislation concerning incrimination of terrorist acts as well as rules governing criminal proceedings for terrorists.

A few days after 9/11, the German federal government adopted the first "security package" (September 19), followed three months later by a second one (December 20). The first one led to the abolishment of the "religious privilege" by allowing the banning of religious organizations if their purpose or activities ran counter to the provisions of criminal law. It also amended the penal code by criminalizing the support of, or membership in, terrorist organizations based not only in Germany, but also in other countries. The second package strengthened the rights and capabilities of the security authorities. Federal police institutions, intelligence services, and law enforcement agencies were granted the power to obtain information from various public and private services and to access private information (such as mail, bank accounts, and employment or university records). In June 2004 the parliament adopted the Act for the New Regulation of Air Security Tasks, which provided the legal basis for the use of military force in cases of hijacked or suspicious civilian planes inside German airspace.

In December 2001 the United Kingdom adopted the Anti-Terrorism Crime and Security Act (ATCSA), which reinforced the most stringent and repressive components of the 2000 act. The ATCSA allowed for much more invasive documentation taken from a suspect during detention (DNA samples included) and extended police powers. It also contained several provisions relating to the combating of terrorism through financial provisions. This act allowed the home secretary to detain foreign nationals pending deportation, even if removal was not currently possible, if the secretary of state reasonably believed that the person's presence in the United Kingdom was a risk to national security and reasonably suspected that the person was involved with international terrorism linked with al-Qaeda.[13] Six months before the London bombings, the British government adopted the Prevention of Terrorism Act of 2005. It further strengthened the tools at the disposal of law enforcement, notably by creating "control orders"—"against an individual that imposed obligations on him for purposes connected with protecting members of the public from a risk of terrorism." This act allowed the secretary of state to make a control order against an individual if reasonable grounds existed for suspecting the individual was or had been involved in terrorism-related activity and the secretary of state considered it necessary to do so for purposes connected with protecting members of the public from a risk of terrorism.

The London terrorist attacks of July 7 and the attempted bombings of July 21 prompted another round of legislation, with the adoption of the UK Terrorism Act of 2005–6. It created new criminal-law offenses relating to terrorism and further enhanced the tools of law enforcement to prevent terrorist acts. For example, it made it a crime to engage in the glorification of terrorism, either in the United Kingdom or abroad. It also became a criminal offense to frequent the same locations where terrorist training took place. The 2005–6 act tried to extend the period for detention without levying charges from fourteen to ninety days, but the House of Commons opposed the measure. The detention period was therefore limited to twenty-eight days, compared with six days in France and thirteen days in Spain. The antiterrorism arsenal was completed in February 2006 by the adoption of a long-term plan to collect biometric information about UK citizens, and the extensive use of closed circuit television for purposes of national security and criminal investigations. The Terrorism Act of March 2006 created a number of new offenses, including preparatory acts, training, encouragement to terrorism, and dissemination of terrorist publications. In 2007, new proposals were put forward to extend the precharge detention for terrorist suspects beyond the previous limit of twenty-eight days and enable the full use of DNA in terrorist cases. Finally, the Counter-Terrorism Act of 2008 created new powers to gather and share information for counterterrorism; to make further provision for the detention and questioning of terrorist suspects and the prosecution and punishment of terrorist offenses; to impose notification requirements on persons convicted of such offenses; and to act against terrorist financing.

In Spain many of the antiterrorist provisions were passed before 9/11, mainly to deal with the domestic terrorist threat posed by ETA. However, in the aftermath of 9/11, Spain expanded the scope of criminal offenses relating to terrorism to include direct or indirect forms of support for terrorist organizations. Article 573 of the criminal code created a new offense involving the storing or possessing of weapons or explosives for potential use by a terrorist organization. The search powers of police were expanded, as well as the use of intercepted evidence. The law authorized the surveillance and interception of communications during the course of an investigation. It also gave law enforcement the power to detain suspected terrorists for an extra forty-eight hours beyond the initial period of three days, to keep them incommunicado, and to deprive them of legal counsel by court order. In October 2007 Spain passed Law 25/2007 on Electronic Communications, in accordance with EU Directive 2006/24/EC. The new legislation required the providers of public electronic communications services to retain the data for a year and make it available to the authorities in charge of terrorist investigations.

Both the U.S. and European governments have devoted increased funds to intelligence and law enforcement programs. In Great Britain, for example, MI5 continued to expand substantially, from 1,800 staff in 2001 to approximately 3,500 in 2008, and tracked more than 1,600 known active militants (up from 250 in 2001). Belgium spent almost 2 percent of its GDP on public order and safety functions in 2005, as well as funding a new intelligence and policing agency, the OCAM/CODA, designed to perform threat analysis. In 2003 the French government allocated €52 million to additional counterterrorist activities for the next five years and spent approximately 1 percent of its GDP on public security and safety. The importance of external border management within the EU's overall activities was demonstrated by the financial resources made available for this purpose. With a commitment of over €282 million in the 2008 budget, the policy area covering external borders formed the most important expenditure of the Area of Freedom, Security and Justice (AFSJ). Commitments under this heading amounted to 39.6 percent of the total commitments for the AFSJ, with those for the external borders fund amounting to 23.8 percent of the total, 9.5 percent for Frontex, and 3.7 percent for the Schengen Information System. In 2009 the EU increased by 18 percent its funding of AFSJ commitments in the areas of terrorism and immigration (up to €866 million).[14] In 2010 the part of the EU budget to receive the biggest boost in spending included projects to fight crime, terrorism, and manage migration flows, increasing by 16.2 percent to a little more than €1 billion.[15] Meanwhile, the U.S. administration and Congress authorized a 145 percent increase in funding for border security, 118 percent for immigration enforcement, and 61 percent for Department of Defense operations between 2001 and 2007. By 2008 approximately $426.8 billion had been appropriated for Defense Department operations in the "Global War on Terror," and $2.5 billion had been spent in investments in "critical crime fighting" operations. The 2008 budget provided $3.8 billion for the FBI's counterterrorism and intelligence programs and $3.5 billion for the Border Patrol.[16]

Extraterritorial Actions Designed to Enhance Homeland Security

President Bush made it clear immediately after 9/11 that the strategy of the United States to combat terrorism included foreign intervention. He subsequently reaffirmed the necessity to "prevent attacks by terrorist networks, deny weapons of mass destruction (WMD) to rogue states and terrorists who seek to use them, deny terrorists the support and sanctuary of rogue states, and deny terrorists control of any nation they would use as a base and launching pad for terror."[17] Accordingly, the United States sent troops into Afghanistan to fight the Taliban regime and disrupt al-Qaeda operations. On September 13, 2001, President Bush issued Military Order Number One dealing with the detention, treatment, and trial of certain noncitizens in the war against terrorism.[18] It specified that individuals tried for international terrorism could be tried by military courts, rather than civilian courts. It also allowed treating a suspected terrorist as an "enemy combatant," subject to indefinite military detention. This provision was confirmed by the Military Commission Act of 2006, which gave the president the absolute power to designate enemy combatants.

President Bush announced his "strategic doctrine of preemption" at the Military Academy at West Point in 2002. According to this doctrine, which extended the notion of self-defense very broadly, the United States would "intervene against oppressive regimes that produce, hide, and prepare to use weapons of mass destruction." The United States accordingly invaded Iraq, invoking the right of self-defense, as defined by article 51 of the United Nations charter. Although, as it turned out, Saddam Hussein's regime lacked weapons of mass destruction, the Bush administration continued to justify the military intervention in Iraq as part of the war on terror. Engagements in Iraq and Afghanistan enabled the United States to capture, detain, and interrogate suspected terrorists abroad. To accommodate detainees and prisoners, the United States set up a variety of detention centers, such as "salt mine" detention facilities in Afghanistan, Guantanamo Bay in Cuba, and the Abu Ghraib prison in Iraq.

U.S. military intervention in Afghanistan was supported by European countries as part of the war on terror, but the EU made it clear that intervention had to be planned in the context of a UN mandate. This was reflected in an explicit reference to UN Security Council Resolution 1368 in the European Council's conclusions of September 21, 2001. Forces from France, Germany, Italy, the Netherlands, Poland, and the United Kingdom joined the International Security Assistance Force (ISAF) under the command of

NATO. European involvement also included Eurocorps, with troops drawn from Belgium, France, Germany, Luxembourg, and Spain—although 40 percent of them were based outside Afghanistan. Engagement in Iraq was more problematic, but the United States found a few European allies, such as Great Britain, Italy, Poland, Spain, Bulgaria, Ukraine, and Hungary. The EU counterterrorism strategy, however, emphasized the need for international cooperation and consensus, through and in conjunction with the United Nations and other international or regional organizations. This strategy focused on countering radicalization and recruitment to terrorist groups such as al-Qaeda, notably by "working to resolve conflicts and promote good governance and democracy . . . as part of the dialogue and alliance between cultures, faiths and civilizations."[19]

The connection drawn by President Bush between the war on terror and the concept of preventive war, as defined by the National Security Strategy of September 2002, worried the U.S. allies. The "Bush doctrine," with its credo of "military dominance in perpetuity" was critically regarded as an imperialist doctrine and accelerated the divergence in opinion.[20] For Gilles Andreani, then a French Foreign Ministry official, the "war on terror" was a "good cause" but a "wrong concept." His analysis captured the dominant perceptions on the European side:

> Calling the fight against terrorism a "war" entails some major draw-backs. . . . The United States bent both its internal judicial rules and international law to accommodate the concept of the war on terror. . . . The connection drawn by the Americans between the war on terrorism and the concept of preventive war has undermined the anti-terrorist coalition. . . . The linkage with the war against Iraq has aggravated the problem, while heightening anti-Western and anti-American feeling in the Middle East and the Islamic world. Finally, the "war on terror" has detracted from the consideration of some urgent political problems that fuel Middle East terrorism.[21]

For European public opinion, the war in Iraq remained a major bone of contention. When it became evident that the promised weapons of mass destruction were not to be found, the sharp drop in America's global popularity—prompted initially by the start of the military intervention—further accelerated in most European countries. More than two-thirds of the public in Spain (69 percent) and Poland (67 percent) thought by 2005 that their countries were wrong to support military action in Iraq. In Great Britain the support of military intervention declined from 61 percent in 2003 to 39 percent in 2005. Furthermore, 92 percent of the French public and 87 percent of the German public reaffirmed their support for nonintervention.

Another controversial issue was the treatment of prisoners held at Guantanamo Bay (a "no law zone"). Under the 2006 Military Commission Act, captives could be convicted (and eventually face the death penalty) based on secret evidence or detained indefinitely without being charged with a crime. On the European side, the refusal to treat the Taliban and al-Qaeda prisoners as prisoners of war raised fears that the United States was simply making its own rules in defiance of international law. Apart from humanitarian concerns, Europeans were inflamed by the U.S. decision to consider the detainees as "unlawful combatants." Europeans claimed that no such category exists in international law, insisting that the captives were either entitled to the rights of POWs or those of common criminals. The Guantanamo controversy was closely linked to the issue of U.S. opposition to the International Court of Justice. In 2002, in an unprecedented move, Bush withdrew the United States as a signatory to the International Criminal Court's statute (which had been ratified by all other Western democracies), demanding immunity from ICC prosecution for American nationals as a condition of recognition. For Europeans, the refusal to adhere to international law seriously undermined both U.S. legitimacy and U.S. democracy. On the issues of human rights and civil liberties, Europeans underlined the view that the new U.S. regulations (such as the Homeland Security Act and the USA Patriot Act) violated the main ingredients of the American creed, such as a faith in liberty, constitutionalism, and democracy.

EU member states particularly criticized the United States for nondemocratic practices, such as the so-called extraordinary renditions, whereby people are transferred involuntarily across borders without due process—for example, transportation of suspected terrorists to camps such as in Guantanamo Bay and other "black" sites. There were, however, many cases of irregular rendition, extradition, and abduction carried out by EU member states, or by the U.S. authorities with the support of European countries. The Swedish government, for example, in 2005 deported Muhammad Muhammad Suleiman Ibrahim El-Zari and Ahmed Hussein Mustafa Kamil Agiza with the assistance of U.S. security services, flying them to Egypt. The two men were deprived of the opportunity to contest their expulsion. The Swedish government recognized that the men had a well-founded fear of persecution in Egypt, but refused them protection on the basis of secret evidence. The same year, the Dutch immigration authorities deported to Syria Abd al-Raham al-Musa, a Syrian who had previously been deported from the United States to the Netherlands. Upon arrival in Syria, al-Musa was transferred to an unknown location.[22]

Furthermore, several European countries played an active role in the U.S. High Value Detainees program. This program was set up by the CIA with the cooperation of European partners and kept secret for many years, thanks to strict observance of the rules of confidentiality laid out in the NATO framework. It involved illegal transfers of detainees by the CIA, and their detention in secret sites in Europe, notably in Poland and Romania. The Council of Europe reported in 2006 that detainees were subject to inhumane and degrading treatment, including torture. It also deplored the fact that "the concepts of state secrecy or national security are invoked by many governments (the United States, Poland, Romania, the former Republic of Macedonia, Italy, and Germany, as well as the Russian Federation) to obstruct judicial and/or parliamentary proceedings aimed at ascertaining the responsibilities of the executive in relation to grave allegations of human rights violations."[23]

The transatlantic partnership was also strengthened soon after 9/11 as part of the global antiterrorist arsenal. In November 2001 Eurojust representatives traveled to Washington in order to improve collaboration between U.S. authorities and the EU agencies in the field of justice and home affairs. A Eurojust magistrate was appointed by the United States, implying a more direct operational contact with the U.S. liaison officer at the U.S. Embassy in Paris. In December 2001 an agreement was signed between Europol and U.S. authorities concerning the exchange of liaison officers and information in the fight against terrorism. The United States and the European Union also agreed to systematically share information on security measures relating to border control and investigation techniques, and signed an agreement in June 2003 on Extradition and Mutual Legal Assistance. Among the key features of this agreement was the requirement that each side identify bank accounts of suspected terrorists in each other's territory. The agreement permitted the establishment of joint task forces under the direction of the United States or an EU member state consisting of personnel drawn from different countries. It also allowed for the taking of evidence in each other's territory by means of videoconferencing (in order to reduce the time required to obtain evidence). After extended and difficult negotiations, the United States reached an agreement with the EU on the transfer of Passenger Name Record data and on the use of biometrics in travel documents. According to Monica den Boer, academic dean of the Police Academy of the Netherlands, "It is clear that the transatlantic axis against terrorism has opened the EU-door to the USA far more widely than before, and that there is a spill-over from terrorism to other security or mobility-related issues. Border controls, criminal justice cooperation, immigration and asylum policy have thus become elements inserted in a wider transatlantic security policy continuum."[24]

U.S. Security-Driven Immigration Policy

The Immigration and Nationality Act (INA) was broadened after 9/11 to deny entry to representatives of groups that endorsed terrorism, prominent individuals who endorsed terrorism, and spouses and children of aliens who were removable on terrorism grounds. The INA listed a series of criteria that constituted grounds for inadmissibility and deportation, including grounds for inadmissibility based on foreign policy concerns. In addition, it stated that even if an alien did not fall under terror-related categories or was inadmissible or deportable, he might still be denied entry or removed from the United States on separate, security-related grounds. A catchall provision also allowed that "any alien who either the Secretary of State or Attorney General, after consultation with others, determines has been associated with a terrorist organization and intends while in the United States to engage . . . in activities that could endanger the welfare, safety, or security of the United States is inadmissible."[25]

As criminal justice expert Michael Welch notes, recent changes in U.S. immigration policies have been "driven primarily by a criminal justice agenda."[26] Both legal and illegal immigrants have been affected by the government's war on terrorism and left without remedy for governmental acts that would be unconstitutional if directed at U.S. citizens. The Supreme Court has confirmed that all noncitizens, irrespective of their legal status, have less constitutional protection despite the First, Fourth, Fifth, and Fourteenth Amendments.[27] The 2001 Patriot Act admittedly restricted the civil rights of noncitizens. Illegal immigrants, like prisoners, were denied access to increasing numbers of social rights and benefits. They were detained for longer periods, in facilities that were designed for criminals rather than immigrants. Individuals who were accused of civil violations were denied many of the constitutional protections (such as the right to a public defender) usually accorded to criminal defendants.[28] Before the advent of the Patriot Act, aliens were deportable for engaging in or supporting terrorist activity. The new law made them deportable for virtually any associational activity with a terrorist organization, irrespective of whether the alien's support had any effective connection to terrorism or any other act of violence. For many human rights NGOs, this resulted in an expansive notion of "guilt by association" because aliens were considered culpable not only for their own acts, but for the acts of those with whom their conduct was allegedly associated.

Furthermore, the U.S. government authorized unprecedented secret proceedings (closed to the public, the press, and family members) as well as the use of secret evidence to detain and deport immigrants. The Department of

Justice refused to disclose the most basic information about the number of detainees and the average period of detention. Under the new regulation, the immigration services could keep an alien locked up (even if the immigration judge ruled that he should be released) simply by filing an appeal of the release order. In some cases, detained aliens did not have the opportunity to respond to the charges against them. Some might be preventively—and indefinitely—detained if they were suspected of terrorist activity, and without any hearing. Finally, the Patriot Act enhanced the government's authority to deport or deny admission to alien terrorists. Any person or organization could be declared inadmissible if the secretary of state determined that person or organization to be a political or social group who endorsed terrorist acts that undermined the efforts of the United States to thwart or eliminate terrorism. In the same vein, the REAL ID Act of 2005 modified the eligibility for asylum and withholding of removal, limited judicial review of certain immigration decisions, and expanded the scope of terror-related activity making an alien inadmissible or deportable.

The 2005–6 immigration debate focused heavily on security concerns. President Bush proposed a temporary guest-worker program that would allow workers who lived in the United States a reprieve from deportation if employers agreed to give them jobs for three years and were unable to find American citizens willing to do the job. Illegal workers would pay a fee to apply immediately for a green card for permanent U.S. residency. The applicant would still have to compete for the visa, but would not be deported for three years while the application was under consideration. Bush also called for tougher work site enforcement, as well as more personnel and equipment at the U.S.-Mexican border. In May 2006 the White House reiterated its support for comprehensive immigration reform and announced the stationing of six thousand National Guard troops at the U.S.-Mexican border. President Bush declared that "first, the United States must secure its borders. This is a basic responsibility of a sovereign nation. It is also an urgent requirement of our national security. Our objective is straightforward: The border should be open to trade and lawful immigration and shut to illegal immigrants, as well as criminals, drug dealers and terrorists."[29] The other components of Bush's plan were a temporary worker program that "would create a legal path for foreign workers to enter our country in an orderly way, for a limited period of time," "a better system for verifying documents and work eligibility," and the opportunity for illegal immigrants to become legal workers and to apply for citizenship under specific requirements—as a result of "a rational middle ground between granting an automatic path to citizenship for every illegal immigrant, and a program of mass deportation."

Yet the House of Representatives restricted its attention to border controls, without addressing the other issues. The Border Protection, Antiterrorism, and Illegal Immigration Act of 2005 (HR 4437) was introduced by Representative James Sensenbrenner and passed the House by a vote of 239–182. It called for an estimated $2.2 billion worth of fences to be erected along part of the southern border and the installation of additional cameras and sensors in various locations. It also required the federal government to take custody of undocumented aliens detained by local authorities and mandated employers to verify workers' legal status. It called for the elimination of the Diversity Immigrant Visa (the Green Card Lottery) and an increase in penalties for aggravated felonies (including marriage fraud). It would have allowed deportation of any undocumented aliens convicted of driving under the influence and prohibited the acceptance of immigrants from any country that refused to accept its nationals who were deported from the United States. In addition, it would have made it a crime to assist an illegal immigrant attempting to remain in the United States. Furthermore, the prison term applicable to a removed alien would also be applicable to anyone who assisted that alien in reentering the United States. The act was strongly opposed by a broad range of organizations, such as the U.S. Chamber of Commerce, the American Farm Bureau, the National Association of Homebuilders, the United Auto Workers, and religious and humanitarian NGOs. A "day without immigrants," where illegal immigrants and their supporters went on strike, was organized in May 2006. Huge protests took place in Los Angeles, New York, Chicago, and other, smaller cities—with at least a million marchers nationwide.

Although it did not pass the Senate, the Sensenbrenner Act was followed by the Secure Fence Act (HR 6061), which did pass Congress and was signed by President Bush in October 2006. It doubled funding for border security, deployed thousands of National Guard members to assist the Border Patrol, and added thousands of new beds in detention facilities. In addition, the U.S. government unified its air and marine assets and personnel under the Customs and Border Protection (CBP) Office of Air and Marine, the largest civilian law enforcement arm in the world with almost 600 pilots, more than 250 aircraft, and 200 marine vessels. This civilian structure intended to use military technology to achieve war-style objectives, such as "to deter and combat the threat of illegal activity." It also implemented a collaborative CBP / Coast Guard operations program focused on "joint targeting, vessel boardings, and training."[30]

Meanwhile, various bills were filed in the Senate in 2005–6. The McCain-Kennedy proposal (S 1033), for example, included a path to citizenship for guest workers and increased the number of visas available for low-skilled workers while expanding family-based flows. Undocumented immigrants present in the United States on the date of the legislation's introduction to Congress—May 12, 2005—would be eligible for an "H-5B" temporary visa. The temporary visa would be granted contingent upon payment of a thousand-dollar fine and other fees, and proof of work history and of no criminal record. Spouses and children would also be eligible. Immediate relatives of U.S. citizens would not be counted toward the existing 480,000 annual ceiling applied to family-sponsored green cards. This provision would have expanded the number of visas in all other categories of family-sponsored immigration, thereby reducing the backlog for available visas. The Cornyn-Kyl bill (S 1438), in contrast, was more restrictive. It created a new "W" nonimmigrant visa for a guest worker program, which would allow employers to temporarily hire foreign citizens to fill jobs that could not be filled by Americans. Workers would be required to undergo background checks and biometric documentation. The bill also provided for "mandatory departure," permitting an alien who illegally entered the United States within the past year to apply for a guest worker visa, leave, and then reenter through legal means. The proposal also boosted interior enforcement of immigration laws with tougher penalties against employers who illegally hire undocumented workers. On the border security and enforcement side, the Cornyn-Kyl bill increased criminal penalties for immigrant smuggling, document fraud, and drug trafficking. It also authorized ten thousand more Border Patrol agents; ten thousand additional detention beds to house illegal immigrants; ten thousand new homeland security officers to patrol work sites and businesses for illegals; five hundred new federal attorneys to prosecute illegals, smugglers, and scofflaw employers; and $5 billion in new technology over five years to monitor the border.

After the adoption of the Sensenbrenner Act by the House, the Senate Judiciary Committee devoted more energy to drafting a new bill. Committee Chairman Arlen Specter of Pennsylvania (at that time a Republican) tried to synthesize various competing proposals while numerous meetings took place—including senators John Cornyn, Jon Kyl, Edward Kennedy, John McCain, Chuck Hagel, Mel Martinez, and others involved in the debate. Months of negotiations, procedural strategizing, delay tactics, and political maneuvers finally resulted in the Comprehensive Immigration Reform Act (S 2611 and S 2612), known as the "Hagel-Martinez compromise." The bill advocated the creation of a temporary worker program (H-2C visa program), with a potential path to legal permanent residence for individuals currently outside the United States, subject to two main conditions. First, employers seeking to hire foreign workers through this program would initially have to undergo recruitment efforts to find an available U.S. worker, including advertising the job at the prevailing wage. Second, a worker would have to pay a five-hundred-dollar fee (plus application costs), and undergo background, security, and medical checks. The bill also provided work authorization and a path to legal permanent residence for long-term undocumented immigrants who had resided in the United States for at least five years prior to April 5, 2006, and had worked a minimum of three years during the five-year period (and continued to work at least six years after its enactment). Undocumented immigrants would have to pass national security and criminal background checks, pay all federal and state income taxes owed, register for military selective service, and meet English and U.S. civics learning requirements.

Security concerns were illustrated by Title I (border enforcement) and Title II (law enforcement). The bill called for increased border and other personnel enforcement, required the detention of certain undocumented immigrants located at or between ports of entry, and created new grounds of inadmissibility for withholders of biometric information, and new criminal penalties for evading inspection. More to the point, the bill expanded the definition of "criminal alien smuggling," as well as the types of offenses that can be classified as an "aggravated felony"—a label for criminal conduct that leads to mandatory detention, deportation, and ineligibility for most immigration relief. The bill also restated the obligation of any alien ordered deported to cooperate with the attempts of the Department of Homeland Security to deport him, and undercut two Supreme Court decisions by also allowing DHS to indefinitely detain foreign nationals. As a result, the bill made every person identified in the newly expanded category of passport, visa, and document-related offenses inadmissible and/or deportable. This could be applied to individuals who omitted any piece of information on an immigration application, even if the information was minor.

The return of immigration reform to the Senate floor following the Hagel-Martinez compromise was damaged by other delaying tactics and procedural mechanisms that either froze or multiplied competing amendments. Differences between the House and the Senate bills could not be resolved. When Congress reconvened in early September 2006, midterm election concerns took precedence over the reform of the immigration system. In March 2007 President Bush initiated a new round of bipartisan negotiations leading to the proposed Comprehensive Immigration Reform Act of 2007 (S 1348)—also known as the Secure Borders, Economic Opportunity, and Immigration Reform Act of 2007. The bill was portrayed as a compromise, providing a path to citizenship for illegal immigrants while increasing border enforcement: it included funding for three hundred miles (480 km) of vehicle barriers, more than one hundred camera and radar towers, and twenty thousand more Border Patrol agents, while simultaneously restructuring visa criteria around high-skilled workers. The legalization provisions for undocumented immigrants included "enforcement triggers," ensuring that the earned legalization and temporary worker program would not go into effect until border security and work site enforcement benchmarks were met. The bill was introduced in the Senate on May 9, 2007, but was never voted on, though a series of votes on amendments and cloture took place. The last vote on cloture (on June 7, 2007) failed by a vote of 34–61, effectively ending the bill's chances of passage. After months of debate and multiple revisions of the bill, the reform process ultimately failed.

The failure to reform the U.S. immigration system had many causes, including the intricacies of the policymaking process and several sets of electoral considerations. Like prior proposals, S 1348 was heavily criticized by both sides of the immigration debate. The "grand bargain" was supposed to appeal to restrictionists and moderates in both parties, with provisions on stringent new standards on workplace enforcement and border security, in addition to a point system for future immigration based not only on family ties but also education, work skills, and English-language proficiency. The legislation also required tougher penalties for a range of immigration-related crimes. The compromise was designed to be attractive to free-marketers by offering illegal immigrants the option to reenter the country legally if they paid a fine and any back taxes they owed, and legitimized their status within six years if they broke no additional laws and continuously held a job. Opposition to the bill, however, came from both ends of the political spectrum. Half a dozen Democrats joined conservative opposition from a dozen Republicans, allied with think tanks (such as the Heritage Foundation and the Center for Immigration Studies) and other restrictionists who described the bill as an "amnesty for lawbreaking foreigners." Free-marketers called the proposed temporary guest-worker program unrealistic. Business groups also protested against a provision that would have forced employers to verify the legal status of every worker, and expressed concerns about the lack of flexibility of the point system for green cards. Labor unions contended that the guest worker program would depress U.S. wages and create an underclass of abused foreign workers. Immigration advocates, such as the National Council of La Raza and the National Immigration Law Center, tried to introduce a proposal that would require employers to pay a fair wage to illegal workers; and civil rights groups (including the National Urban League) were divided over the issue of legalizing undocumented immigrants. For the New York

Immigration Coalition, the proposal was "unacceptable." For the Mexican American Legal Defense and Educational Fund, it was "immoral, unworkable and unacceptable." John Trasvina, the group's president, said the push against allowing new U.S. citizens to sponsor family members for green cards was an "anti-immigrant drive to end cultural diversity."[31]

Immigration reform was also undermined by the impact of security concerns. Bush reiterated his support for comprehensive reform while compromising this goal by sending a series of mixed messages. In January 2004 he said that "we must make our immigration law more rational and more humane, and I believe we can do so without jeopardizing the livelihood of American citizens." He added, "Illegal entry across our borders makes more difficult the urgent task of securing the homeland."[32] In 2006, while still asking Congress to act on issues related to immigration, the White House endorsed the restrictive enforcement bill adopted by the House (HR 4437), yet remained reluctant to support the comprehensive compromise reached in the Senate. In June 2007 Bush again campaigned for the adoption of a comprehensive reform. In a speech peppered with Spanish phrases, he thanked Latino religious leaders "for making comprehensive immigration reform your top priority," adding, "I share that priority."[33] Meanwhile, supporters of the Secure Borders, Economic Opportunity, and Immigration Reform Act (S 1348) complained about Bush's ineffective support.

The result of this inconsistent behavior was the withdrawal of all significant immigration reform proposals in a context characterized by weakening poll numbers, controversies about policy in Iraq, and the increasing erosion of Republican support for the president's policies. "There is not a lot of credibility right now with the administration on securing the border and enforcing the law," Representative Ric Keller of Florida told the *Washington Post* in June 2007.[34] One of the last attempts by the White House to restore its image was a new plan designed to enlist state and local law enforcement authorities in cracking down on illegal immigrants, which previously had largely been a federal function. In August 2007 the administration unveiled a series of tough border-control and employer-enforcement measures designed to compensate for security provisions that failed when Congress rejected a broad set of revisions to the nation's immigration laws in June. Ignoring the issues of the temporary worker program and legalization of undocumented immigrants, the plan focused only on restrictive measures. It called for the Bush administration to "train growing numbers of state and local law enforcement officers to identify and detain immigration offenders whom they encounter in the course of daily law enforcement." As part of the package, "the Departments of State and Homeland Security will expand the list of international gangs whose members are automatically denied admission to the U.S." Furthermore, "the Department of Homeland Security will raise the civil fines imposed on employers who knowingly hire illegal immigrants by approximately 25 percent."[35]

By the time President Bush left the White House, there was a widespread belief in Washington, D.C., that border controls and integration of immigrants were two interrelated but separate issues. Even Senator McCain, one of the main backers of comprehensive immigration reform, endorsed this approach when he addressed a GOP convention in Utah. "The present system is broke. It's a failed federal policy," he told the GOP delegates. "We need a comprehensive approach, but first we have to fix our borders."[36] On the other hand, proponents of a comprehensive reform argued that focusing on border controls was not the best way to enhance the nation's security. According to Daniel T. Griswold, associate director of the Center for Trade Policy Studies at the Cato Institute, "the problem is not that we are letting too many people in but that the government is not effectively keeping the wrong people out. . . . Instead of expanding scarce resources to hunt down construction workers and raid restaurants, our border control efforts should focus on tracking potential terrorists and smashing their cells before they can blow up more buildings and kill more Americans."[37]

Europe's Security-Driven Immigration Policy

As in the United States, the European Union's response to 9/11 reinforced the security logic of immigration. The conclusions adopted by the Council of the European Union on September 20, 2001, reflected this security-driven approach by advocating the "immediate strengthening of surveillance measures under article 2.3 of the Schengen Convention," "utmost vigilance" in the issuing of residence permits, and "more systematic checking of identity papers."[38] In the same vein, the Common Position on Combating Terrorism adopted in December 2001 provided that "appropriate measures" be taken ("before granting refugee status") to ensure that an asylum seeker had not planned, facilitated, or participated in terrorist activities.[39] In June 2002 the Seville European Council adopted a plan to form a joint border police force designed to patrol shores, ports, and crossing points against illegal immigrants and refugees.[40]

To secure its external borders, the EU created in 2005 the European Agency for the Management of Operational Cooperation at the External Borders (Frontex), paid by a new external borders fund of €1.82 billion for 2008–13.[41] Frontex was designed to plan and coordinate a number of operations at the EU's expanded land, air, and sea borders. Its priorities included strengthening surveillance of the southern maritime borders, enhancing cooperation with bordering Mediterranean countries, and establishing procedures for emergency situations. Frontex developed a permanent Coastal Patrol Network, in addition to the deployment of the Rapid Borders Intervention Teams.[42] Specific prefrontier measures included visa requirements, imposing sanctions on transport carriers, the posting of immigration/airport liaison officers, biometrics requirements, and the use of information databases for immigration. European states shared a common list of 128 countries whose nationals were subject to a visa obligation (including refugee-producing countries such as Afghanistan, Somalia, Sudan, and Iraq). The EU's Common Consular Instruction was intended to target some particular "risk groups" such as "unemployed people, those with no regular income, etc."[43] Immigration/airport liaison officers were deployed by twenty-five of the twenty-seven EU member states to prevent irregular immigration and to deal with potential refuges and asylum seekers. Meanwhile, sanctions against air carriers were enhanced by the 2004 council directive on the obligations of carriers to communicate passenger data in advance to the relevant authorities. The directive also imposed financial penalties, as well as the obligation to return unwanted third-country nationals in transit to their country of origin. A number of EU information systems were developed, such as Eurodac in the field of asylum; the Schengen Information System in the field of immigration, police, and judicial cooperation; and the Europol Information System in the field of criminal law. Additionally, in 2004 the EU established the Visa Information System (VIS), which contains data on visa applications. As in the United States, operational capacity for interception at sea has been expanded. Conducted by EU member states, and sometimes supported by Frontex, interception at sea involves the diversion of a vessel "actually using any level of force to constrain a migrant vessel to alter a course or return to its port of departure."[44]

The strengthening of a security continuum was evident in the Prüm Convention, concluded on May 27, 2005, by seven EU member states—the Benelux countries, Germany, Austria, France, and Spain.[45] Also referred to as Schengen III, this convention explicitly linked terrorism, cross-border crime, and illegal migration. A security logic, rather than a free-market rationale, formed the driving force behind the EU's preoccupation with the external borders and cooperation in justice and home affairs. The Lisbon Treaty (Treaty on the Functioning of the EU, or TFEU) of December 2008 reflected the European conception of a "permanent" state of "exceptional" emergency. Article 67(3) of the treaty stated that the EU should strive for "a high level of security" through the "coordination and cooperation between police and judicial authorities and other competent authorities." Article 64(2) allowed the European Council to take emergency measures in situations characterized by the "sudden inflow of nationals of third countries."

The wording of all the major EU documents consistently reflected the linkage between terrorists, immigrants, asylum seekers, and refugees. The Laeken European Council Declaration stated, for example, that better management of the external borders would help fight not only terrorism, but also illegal immigration networks and the trafficking of human beings.[46] In the Declaration on Combating Terrorism of March 25, 2004, issued shortly after the Madrid bombings, the European Council emphasized that "improved border controls and document security play an important role in combating terrorism."[47] The 2005 European Union Counter-Terrorism Strategy further stated that the EU had to "enhance protection of [its] external borders to make it harder for known or suspected terrorists to enter or operate within the EU."[48] In 2008 the European Commission declared that "while Member States remain responsible for controlling their own borders, the Union's common policy in support of Member States' efforts should be continuously developed and strengthened in response to new threats, shifts in migratory pressure and any shortcomings identified."[49] The commission also stated, in its Communication on the Development of a European External Border Surveillance System (Eurosur), that "border surveillance has not only the purpose to prevent unauthorised border crossings, but also to counter cross-border crime such as the prevention of terrorism, trafficking in human beings, drug smuggling, illicit arms trafficking, etc."[50]

EU member states introduced new regulations to reinforce the security-immigration nexus. National initiatives were allowed, if not encouraged, by the lack of effective supranationalism in the areas of immigration, asylum, and security. In the United Kingdom, the 9/11 attacks gave added momentum to efforts to tighten immigration and asylum procedures. The main objective was to prevent terrorists and other criminals from abusing the UK's asylum system—despite the fact that none of the terrorists arrested by British police forces was a refugee or an asylum seeker. The intersection of immigration laws and antiterrorism measures went to extremes with the adoption of the 2001 Anti-Terrorism, Crime and Security Act. Although many of the immigration/detention provisions were repealed by the House of Lords, the most restrictive rules were reintroduced by the 2005–6 Terrorism Act. Under this legislation, the secretary of state is allowed to certify a person as a suspected terrorist if the secretary "a) believes that the person's presence in the United Kingdom is a risk to national security and b) suspects that this person is a terrorist." Authorities can detain the person indefinitely pending deportation. These rules have been challenged as being in violation of the European Convention on Human Rights; yet detention and deportation procedures have been maintained on condition of a more-exacting judicial scrutiny by British courts. Security concerns also had an impact on the Nationality, Immigration and Asylum Act of 2002, which led to new measures aimed at the repatriation of refused asylum seekers. Part of the act (section 55) was ruled in fundamental conflict with human rights laws in 2004. Yet the Asylum and Immigration Act of 2004 has continued to fuel anti-asylum rhetoric and policies. Following the 2005 London bombings, the government announced a series of measures designed to make it easier to deport foreign individuals who advocate violence and incite hatred, and to refuse asylum to anyone with possible terrorist connections.

In Germany, the amended Asylum Procedure Act stipulated that those seeking asylum had to provide a voice recording, in addition to requiring other increased data on foreigners (face recognition, fingerprints, and other biometric data). Correspondingly, the new sections of the Alien Act stipulated that persons who "constitute a threat to democracy and freedom or to the security of the Federal Republic or who engage in acts of violence in the pursuit of political goals, who incite the use of force in public, or who are proven members or supporters of a terrorist organization" should not be granted entry visas or resident permits. In addition, the new immigration law, which entered into force in January 2005, included provisions related to the fight against terrorism. Before naturalization, applicants must be investigated and certified by the Federal Bureau of the Protection of the Constitution. The automatic right of relatives of applicants to remain in Germany has also been revoked. The major goal of this law was to hasten deportation procedures by creating the possibility of issuing a deportation order without having to prove the involvement of asylum seekers and other immigrants in any planned or committed crime. A deportation order could be issued on the basis of an "evidence-based threat prognostic," which meant that suspicion sufficed to justify deportation.

In Denmark the Liberal-Conservative government elected in November 2001 presented a legislative package that included the Aliens Act, the Integration Act, and the creation of a Ministry for Refugees, Immigrants and Integration. The objective of this legislation was to reduce the attractiveness of Denmark for potential asylum seekers, as well as to restrict the number of immigrants, to introduce tougher requirements on access to permanent residence, and to ensure the loyalty of newcomers. France's new immigration and integration law, adopted in July 2006, introduced further restrictions to family reunification. It also limited access to residence and citizenship and simplified the procedure whereby the government could deport illegal immigrants—especially those disturbing "public order." In Italy a similar tendency to ease the terms whereby aliens could be removed was illustrated by the adoption of Law no. 144 on Urgent Measures to Counter International Terrorism. Under this legislation, the Ministry of the Interior was allowed to expel an alien if there was any reason to believe that this alien might pose a security threat. Expulsion of non-Italian nationals was expanded to encompass terrorism-related concerns. Legislative Decree 286/1998 was amended by Law 189/2002, Law 271/2004, and Law 155/2005—specifying how expulsions could be carried out (including administrative expulsions). The new legislation required immigrants to have a job before entering Italy, made family reunification more difficult, and mandated fingerprinting for all immigrants requesting (or renewing) a residence permit.

As in the United States, security concerns damaged the prospect for the adoption of a comprehensive immigration policy at the EU level. In 1999 the Tampere program listed a series of ambitious measures designed for the adoption of a comprehensive immigration and asylum policy:

> The European Union needs a comprehensive approach to migration addressing political, human rights and development issues in countries and regions of origin and transit. This requires combating poverty, improving living conditions and job opportunities, preventing conflicts and consolidating democratic states and ensuring respect for human rights, in particular rights of minorities, women and children. To that end, the Union as well as Member States are invited to contribute, within their respective competences under the Treaties, to a greater coherence of internal and external policies of the Union.[51]

The new area of Freedom, Security and Justice (AFSJ) was supposed to include partnerships with immigrants' countries of origin; a common European asylum system (based on a full application of the Geneva Convention); a fair treatment of third-country nationals, combined with a "vigorous integration policy" granting them rights and obligations comparable to those of EU citizens; and a more-efficient management of migration flows. The Tampere program focused on the mutual recognition of judicial decisions and judgments in both civil and criminal matters within the EU to encourage a comparable, if not universal, system of justice. The European Council also called for the "integration of crime prevention aspects into actions against crime, as well as for the further development of national crime prevention programs."[52] These objectives were reinforced by the 2004

Hague Program—the EU's blueprint for realizing its vision in the areas of access to justice, international protection, migration and border control, terrorism and organized crime, and police and judicial cooperation and mutual recognition.[53] The Hague Program listed ten priorities: strengthening fundamental rights and citizenship; enhancing anti-terrorist measures; defining a balanced approach to migration; developing integrated management of the EU's external borders; setting up a common asylum procedure; maximizing the positive impact of immigration; striking the right balance between privacy and security while sharing information; developing a strategic concept on tackling organized crime; creating a genuine European area of justice; and sharing responsibility and solidarity. Achieving these priorities required a mixture of both "inclusive" and "exclusive" measures. Inclusion referred to the strengthening of freedoms and other initiatives, thereby ensuring fair treatment for immigrants. By contrast, exclusive measures related to the securitization of both border controls and integration policies.

A brief assessment of the most significant EU initiatives, summarized in table 7, reveals that the EU member states have been unable to establish a common European immigration and asylum system. Over a decade after the Tampere program, EU member states mostly agree on common principles and minimum standards—as illustrated by the various proposals, plans, green papers, and pacts (all without binding force). The Lisbon Treaty, which entered into force in December 2009, brought about an important change in that it broadened the scope of the articles dealing with migration and asylum, providing for a common immigration and asylum policy rather than minimum standards, to be decided on under the "ordinary legislative procedure"—that is, co-decision.[54] Still, the Lisbon Treaty, in a new provision, explicitly confirmed that the member states are ultimately responsible for the number of immigrants they allow to enter their territory.[55]

EU member states invoked security-related concerns in order to delay the actual harmonization of most aspects of EU immigration policy, either by blocking supranational initiatives[56] or making sure that the harmonization that did occur was weighted in favor of their law-and-order and security objectives. EU member states were therefore more likely to support the most restrictive elements of the AFSJ while ignoring the inclusive measures listed by the Hague Program. In the field of asylum, for example, progress has been limited to the harmonization of minimum standards (the Reception Conditions Directive, 2003/9/EC) and the introduction of a mechanism for determining responsibility for asylum claims (Dublin Regulation). As the European Commission noted in its 2007 report, important inconsistencies remain in terms of both national definitions and procedures for identifying

Table 7. EU's AFSJ legislation

Protection of fundamental rights	Basic freedoms	Common asylum system	Migration and integration	Border management
• Creation of the Fundamental Rights Agency (2007 • Data Protection Directive (Directive 95/46/EC, Council Framework Decision 2008/977/JHA)	• Directive concerning the status of TCNs who are long-term residents (Council Directive 2003/109/EC) • Directive on the right to family reunification (Council Directive 2003/86/EC) • Directive on the right of citizens of the EU to move and reside freely within the member states (Directive 2004/38/EC)	• Dublin II regulation establishing the criteria and mechanisms for determining the member-state responsible for examining an asylum application lodged in one member state by a TCN (Council Regulation EC no. 343/2003) • Minimum standards for reception conditions in the member states (Council Directive 2003/9/EC) • Green Paper on the future European asylum system (COM(2007) 301 final)	• Green Paper on an EU approach to managing economic migration (COM (2004) 811 final) • Policy Plan on legal migration (COM (2005) 669 final) • EU blue card (COM (2007) 637 final and COM (2009) 50/EC) • Proposal for a Directive providing sanctions against employers of illegally staying TCNs (COM (2007) 249 final) • Common Agenda for integration of TCNs in the EU (COM (2005) 389 final) • European Funds for integration (Council Decision 2007/435/EC) • Common Immigration Policy for Europe: principles, actions and tools (COM (2008) 359 final) • European Pact on Immigration and Asylum (Council Document 13440/08)	• Schengen Border Codes (Regulation EC no. 562/2006) • Rapid Border Intervention Teams (Regulation EC no. 863/2007) • Schengen Information System / SIS I and SIS II (Council Regulation EC no. 1104/2008 and Council Decision 2008/839/JHA) • Frontex (Council Regulation EC No. 2007/2004) • Eurosur (COM (2008) 68 final) • Exit-Entry System (COM (2008) 69 final) • Directive on common standards and procedures for returning illegally staying TCNs (Directive 2008/115/EC)

the most vulnerable asylum seekers.[57] Furthermore, the Reception Conditions Directive allowed national authorities to "reduce or withdraw reception conditions" if the applicant "presents a threat to national security."

The 2003 directives on third-country nationals included a similar restrictive clause.[58] The right to family reunification, for example, is subject to
mandatory respect for public order and public security. Applicants for long-
term resident status "must not constitute a threat to public security or public
policy." Member states who had generous legislation on family reunification before the adoption of the EU law (such as France and Belgium) were
therefore given the opportunity to weaken their own domestic legislation
by introducing new restrictive measures. Others used the security-driven
clauses to restrict immigration. In Italy, for example, three legislative decrees
were prepared by the government in 2009 with a view of modifying existing
legislation that had implemented the EU directives on EU citizens' freedom
of movement and residence and on family reunification. EU citizens wish-
ing to reside in Italy for more than three months have to prove that they
have sufficient means to sustain themselves and their family. They may be
expelled from the territory on grounds of "public security," which include,
for example, not registering with the competent authorities within ten days
after the three-month residence period, or being classified as a serious threat
to public morals.

Freedom of movement has been far from being adequately enforced. An
important development was the adoption in 2004 of the directive on the
rights of citizens of the EU and their family members to move and reside
freely within the territory of the member states.[59] This directive reaffirmed
the right to equal treatment on the grounds of nationality and reinforced
the rights of family members by extending family reunification rights for
registered partners. It created an unconditional permanent right of residence
after five years of continuous legal residence in the host member state. This
directive, however, allowed two exceptions to the principle of equal treatment. First, during the first three months of residence, member states are
not obliged to grant to EU citizens entitlement to social assistance, other
than those who are workers, self-employed persons, or their family members. Second, member states are not obliged to grant educational aid prior
to the acquisition of a permanent right of residence. These limitations may
appear as rather insignificant. Yet they become problematic when combined
with other difficulties, such as lengthy administrative procedures in obtaining
residence documents and unresolved issues regarding the enforcement of the
rights of family members at the national level. The European Commission
published its fifth report on the Citizenship of the Union in 2008. Reviewing

compliance with the 2004 directive, the commission found that "many national laws transposing the EU law were deeply flawed. Not one country has managed to transpose the EU law fully, effectively, and accurately."[60] Most of the violations of the directive concern third-country family members who, through marriage to Europeans, have the right to live and move freely in the EU. According to the commission, some member states require them to present documents or undergo procedures not allowed by the directive, such as requiring non-EU spouses to have resident rights in another EU state before they can get a permit in the new one. Some states also require EU citizens to submit additional documents when they apply for residence. Finally, a growing number of complaints concern obstacles to free movement encountered by EU citizens traveling to another state, due to the documents arbitrarily demanded by border authorities and air carriers.

Security concerns also have an impact on the naturalization process at the national level—and thus access to EU citizenship. National authorities can reject an application on many grounds, including "serious crimes" or "other offenses." In the Netherlands, for example, an applicant can be rejected not only on the basis of a serious crime but also the "serious suspicion" that an immigrant will be a threat to public safety. In Portugal there is no right of naturalization per se, even if all the conditions for naturalization required by the law are fulfilled. All these examples raise concerns about the effective implementation of the rights granted to third-country nationals, despite the efforts made by EU institutions to introduce some degree of coherence and fairness.

All the measures dealing with the humanitarian aspects have been therefore delayed or watered down, while border enforcement has been strengthened at both the EU and national levels. The communitarization of immigration and asylum policies remains thus rather limited, framed by the securing of the very few options granted to immigrants. In contrast, EU members aggressively pursue the strengthening of border controls and the policing of "risky populations." This approach includes a strict implementation of the Schengen *acquis*, a greater involvement of Frontex in border controls, and the removal of illegal third-country nationals under the terms of the 2008 directive. According to the European Commission in its evaluation of the implementation of the Hague Program, "This uneven progress can be to a large extent explained by the unique challenges faced by the AFSJ: a relatively young *acquis*, an insufficient role of the European Parliament in certain policy areas, a limited jurisdiction of the European Court of Justice and a limited competence of Commission to bring infringement, and the requirement for unanimity for decision-making in several areas. Therefore the ambition of measures was often scaled down in certain areas such as legal migration."[61] Although these factors partially explain the inability of the EU to achieve a truly harmonized and comprehensive immigration policy, the focus on security is the key reason why the ambitious goals listed by the Tampere and Hague programs are unlikely to be achieved in the near future. As Adam Luedtke argues, "Not only did 9/11's aftermath shift the nature of the immigration laws that did pass, but it also warped the entire EU immigration policy agenda by shifting resources and attention away from the topic and towards terrorism and policy matters."[62]

The European Pact on Immigration and Asylum adopted in September 2008 clearly illustrates this shift.[63] Compared with the global framework developed in 1999, this pact (a document only specifying political intent and therefore a non–legally binding act) contains only five basic commitments: (1) to organize legal immigration to take account of the priorities, needs, and reception capacities determined by each member state, and to encourage integration; (2) to control illegal immigration by ensuring that illegal immigrants return to their countries of origin or to a country of transit; (3) to make border controls more effective; (4) to construct a Europe of asylum; and (5) to create a comprehensive partnership with the countries of origin and of transit in order to encourage synergy between migration and development. Stating that the "EU does not have the resources to decently receive all the migrants hoping to find a better life here," the pact lists a series of measures designed to ensure the management of migration flows, such as the conclusion of readmission agreements with sending countries (to ensure that illegal immigrants are expelled), policies of cooperation with the countries of origin and of transit in order to deter or prevent illegal immigration, the deployment of additional technological tools at the external borders, and the allocation of more powers and resources to Frontex. It is worth noting that the pact does not mention the directive on the right to family reunification for third-country nationals. Its wording also avoids endorsing a respect for human rights and the respect of the rule of law as key principles, or "basic commitments" of any future common policy on migration, borders, and asylum.[64] Finally, the pact is driven by a predominantly intergovernmental logic, prioritizing the competences of the member states over those of the EU. By doing so, it fosters the predominance of the national level over the policy domains of immigration, asylum, and borders, and prevents the consolidation of any "common" policy in the years to come.

PART II

The Dynamics of Policy Failure

Similar policies often produce convergent results. Hence it is not surprising that the border control strategy implemented in the aftermath of 9/11 as a continuation of the measures adopted during the 1990s has generated comparably negative outcomes: a geographical redistribution of illegal entries; a growing number of illegal immigrants; and the development of the people-smuggling industry. Furthermore, whether the strengthening of immigration control yields benefits to the fight against terrorism remains to be seen. In addressing these issues, I analyze in the following chapters three interlocking processes that fuel what can be described as the dynamics of policy failure: the spillover effect of "border escalation" by which tougher border controls produce more "unwanted" immigrants; the security/insecurity escalation by which security policies have led to both less-tangible and perceived security; and the emergence of a new "enemy within." A growing body of evidence indicates that the securitization of immigration has not only proven ineffective in achieving its prescribed goals but in fact aggravates the problems it is supposed to solve.

Border controls create the illusion of effectiveness without regard to the actual costs and results. Despite the rising investment in border enforcement, both in terms of spending and staffing, repressive border enforcement policies do not effectively manage migration flows (as illustrated by the recent increase of illegal immigrants); instead, they boost the development of smuggling networks and the immigration security business. A continuation of illegal immigration, in turn, fuels political distrust—one of the major sources of anti-immigrant feelings. As senior policy analyst Marc Rosenblum notes, current outcomes "suggest that the marginal costs of 'more of the same' enforcement techniques exceed their marginal benefits."[1]

Furthermore, restrictive security-related immigration policies actually undermine the fight against terrorism in many ways: by increasing the number of illegal immigrants who avoid security controls; by diverting scarce resources from more-pressing security priorities; by targeting and alienating minorities whose cooperation is essential to counter terror efforts; and by providing new incentives for terrorist radicalization and recruitment. Consequently, not only have all these actions been largely ineffective in terms of their stated goal of preventing foreign terrorists to plot attacks, but they have also contributed to the proliferation of "homegrown" terrorists. Being born and/ or raised in the United States or Europe no longer prevents radicalization— as illustrated by Adam Gadahn (known as "Azzam the American"), who converted to Islam at the age of seventeen and became the first American in more than fifty years to be charged with treason. The case of twenty Somali American students from the University of Minnesota is equally disturbing. They had integrated into American society, embracing basketball, the prom, and the mall. Yet they became affiliated with the Shabaah, a militant group aligned with al-Qaeda in Somalia. One of them, Shirwa Ahmed, blew himself up in Somalia in October 2008—becoming the first known U.S. suicide bomber. As the director of the FBI pointed out, "Ahmed was radicalized in his hometown of Minnesota."[2] In the aftermath of the Madrid bombings, Fidel Sendagorta, then head of policy planning at the Spanish Ministry of Foreign Affairs, asked a crucial question: "What drives a young Moroccan, with a job and a good command of Spanish, a fan of Real Madrid and resident of a welcoming and cosmopolitan district such as Lavapiés—in short, someone reasonably well integrated in our society—to take part in the murder of 192 people in the city in which he lives?"[3] There is no easy answer to this question. The threat posed by homegrown terrorists seems to support the assumption that immigrants and their progeny have trouble integrating into Western societies. From this perspective, more integration, coupled with enhanced social control, should provide more security. Yet the profile of some homegrown terrorists—those well educated and apparently well integrated—challenges this common perception. In the case of natives and converts, the process of radicalization seriously undermines the belief that a better control of immigration would provide more security.

CHAPTER 4

Border Escalation as a Policy Failure

Depicting immigration as the ultimate challenge to state sovereignty is a convenient way to explain the gap between stated objectives and actual outcomes. That is, the more that states do to strengthen border controls, the less effective they appear to be. Policymakers are usually inclined to selectively support this explanation when they are blamed by public opinion for their failure. Yet it is crucial to bear in mind the distinction between state sovereignty, state capacity, and governmental efficiency. The "gap hypothesis" does not reflect the decline of state sovereignty but rather identifiable policy failures. In the field of immigration policy, both the European and U.S. governments have been able to effectively expand their domain of action despite the emergence of new international and domestic pressures. They have reacted to the rising numbers of asylum seekers and illegal immigrants by introducing successive reforms in order to deter them. Doing so has encouraged policymakers to adopt policies that further mismanage immigration. It is therefore the inability of both U.S. and European governments to address the issues they have partially created that needs to be explained.

States also tend to compensate for the ineffectiveness of border controls by amplifying their commitment to border controls. The "state is back" as a result of a discursive strategy that, at least symbolically, reaffirms the traditional boundaries of an "imagined community." In his analysis of the escalation of immigration control at the U.S.-Mexico border, Peter Andreas, for example, concludes that "the unprecedented expansion of border policing has ultimately been less about achieving the stated instrumental goal of deterring illegal border crossers and more about politically recrafting the image of the border and symbolically reaffirming the state's territorial authority."[1] The "art of impression management" is indeed a widespread practice in Europe as well as in the United States. Andrew Geddes, an expert on EU policies, notes that the notion of "Fortress Europe" has become "associated more with a politics of symbols—of national and cultural identities and 'ways of life' that are supposedly threatened by immigration and are to be 'protected'—and less with state capacity to control immigration (or match the rhetoric of control with the reality of restriction)."[2] On both sides of the Atlantic, the border has become a "theater," and Western states use "symbolic rituals" to reaffirm their sovereignty despite the evident decline of their efficacy.[3]

This situation raises major concerns. The false impression that borders are under control—at least symbolically—cannot hide the negative impact of the ineffectiveness of border escalation on public opinion. Citizens expect concrete results beyond the self-confidence often expressed by policymakers about their ability to manage the border. Policy failure, therefore, fuels political distrust and increases anti-immigrant feelings, which in turn encourage policymakers to do "more of the same." Furthermore, the main effect of political distrust is that natives tend to underestimate the government's capacity to act, while anti-immigrant feelings characteristically lead to the public's overestimation of the number of immigrants (both legal and illegal) actually living in the United States and Europe. As a new influx of "others" may be ascribed to policy failure, natives are likely to develop a suspicion that their government is becoming weaker, even though the opposite may be the case.[4] Subsequently, one of the most problematic aspects of contemporary immigration policy is the large and systematic gap between public opinion, state capacity, and public policy in Western democracies.[5]

The Spillover Effect of Border Escalation

In addition to the USA Patriot Act, the US-VISIT program, and the NSEERS program, the Bush administration adopted a series of measures purportedly designed to improve border controls. The Enhanced Border Security and Visa Entry Reform Act, for example, in 2002 allocated an increase of 150 consular officers per year from 2006 to 2009. The United States signed the Smart Border Accord with Canada in December 2001 and with Mexico in March 2002. The 2005 Strategy for Protecting America stated that the priority mission of U.S. Customs and Border Protection (CBP) was to prevent terrorists and terrorist weapons from entering the country, and also extended the zone of security beyond the physical borders themselves. These activities enhanced the militarization of border controls at ports of entry (strategic goal number 1) and between ports of entry (strategic goal number 2) as part of the America's Shield Initiative.[6] This strategy also relied on expanded intelligence-driven operations. In order to support tactical and strategic operations, it was decided in 2005 that the Border Patrol "will enhance its intelligence program by coordinating with the CBP Office of Intelligence," especially regarding the Arizona Border Control Initiative.

By 2007, CBP increased the number of Border Patrol agents by 21 percent (from 12,349 in 2006 to 14,923), the largest yearly increase in the history of the Border Patrol. It completed 154 miles of primary fencing along the southern border and announced an additional 215 miles would be constructed by the end of 2008. This strategy was consolidated in 2008: the entire CBP workforce increased by 11 percent (up to 51,553 staff, including 17,499 Border Patrol agents); more than ninety-three miles of new fencing was completed; the total budget reached $8.8 billion (including $6.6 billion for border security); marine and air operations were expanded; and visa regulations were modified with the introduction of the Electronic System for Travel Authorization. New Mexico governor Bill Richardson questioned the utility of this strategy, saying "I believe that if you build a 12-foot wall, pretty soon they'll start making 13-foot ladders."[7]

What were the actual outcomes of all these measures? As illustrated by figure 1, the apprehension of illegal immigrants declined after 2001. Fiscal year 2001 brought a decline of 25 percent in apprehensions along the southwest border. With the exception of a slight increase in 2005–6, the trend was toward reduced arrests. Apprehensions by Department of Homeland Security authorities dropped by 17 percent in 2008 (to 791,568, from 960,756 in 2007). About 97 percent of all apprehensions took place along the southwest border, where apprehensions declined by 18 percent. The El Paso sector, for instance, saw a reduction of 60 percent, a trend attributed to the highly successful concentrated border strategy, and more precisely to Operation Streamline and other "prevention-though-deterrence" measures.

Proponents might claim the decline in apprehensions was a success, attributable to reduced traffic caused by the introduction of a new deterrence strategy. Yet other explanations are equally plausible. First, the decrease in the apprehensions is partly due to a change in reporting practices and data collection introduced in 2006. As explained by Department of Homeland Security officials,

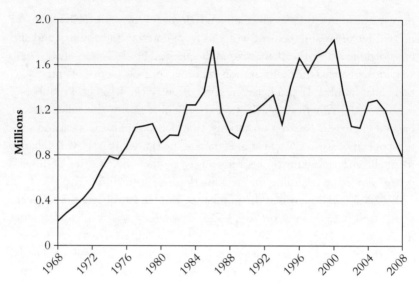

FIGURE 1. Apprehensions at the U.S. borders, fiscal years 1968–2008.
Source: DHS, Office of Immigration Statistics, *Annual Report*, July 2009, p. 3.

Recent changes in data systems, definitions, and reporting requirements have affected the annual removal and apprehension data series. . . . A change in [Immigration and Customs Enforcement] administrative arrests between 2006 and 2007 was largely attributable to the internal transfer of the Criminal Alien Program (CAP) from Investigations to Detention and Removal Operations (DRO). What would have been previously recorded as a "CAP administrative arrest" is now recorded as "Charging Documents Issued" and not included in this report.[8]

Second, there is some evidence that immigrants and people smugglers have adapted their tactics for entering the country. As the land border with Mexico tightens with the construction of new fencing, U.S. authorities are facing a sharp increase in the number of people (and drugs) being smuggled into the country by sea off the San Diego coast. In 2008, for example, Coast Guard and CBP agents arrested 136 illegal immigrants sneaking in by sea, double the number of 66 arrests made in 2007. In 2009 more than one hundred illegal immigrants were apprehended between January and June, while attempts at smuggling accelerated to unprecedented levels. According to the Coast Guard in San Diego, "it is like spillover from a dam."[9]

In addition to this rechanneling effect, there is an upsurge in attempted entry by persons using false documents. This trend is partly illustrated by the increasing number of "expedited removals." Expedited removal procedures allow DHS to quickly remove certain inadmissible aliens from the United States. Until recently this procedure had been mainly used as a way to limit the number of asylum applications. In 2008 DHS started to apply these procedures to aliens arriving at ports of entry who illegally attempted to gain admission by fraud or misrepresentation, or to those with no entry documents, or those using counterfeit, altered, or otherwise fraudulent or improper documents. Aliens from Mexico accounted for nearly 68 percent of expedited removals in 2008. Of the total number of 246,851 Mexicans who were removed, only 71,650 were deported for "criminal activities" (such as drug activities and immigration violations). Among the 175,201 other Mexicans removed, a large number of them carried false documents.

More to the point, figure 2 illustrates that the restrictive measures applied by U.S. authorities after 9/11 did not significantly reduce the flows of illegal immigrants. The Department of Homeland Security did not produce any reliable data on illegal immigration between 2001 and 2004. Yet after several adjustments and reclassifications, DHS estimated that the unauthorized immigrant population increased by 37 percent between 2000 and 2008.

Nearly 4.3 million (37 percent) of unauthorized immigrants in 2008 had entered the United States between 2000 and 2007 (see table 8). An estimated 3.3 million (28 percent) came between 2000 to 2004, and 1.1 million (9 percent) came to the United States between 2005 and 2007.

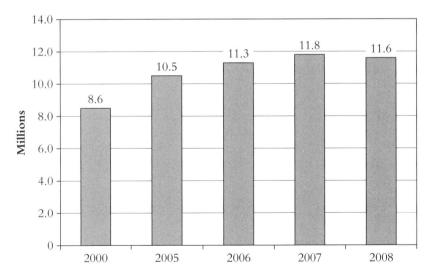

FIGURE 2. Unauthorized immigrant population in the United States, 2000–2008. DHS estimates not produced for 2001–2004.
Source: Office of Immigration Statistics, Estimates of the Unauthorized Immigrant Population Residing in the United States, *Population Estimates*, February 2009, p. 2.

These estimates suggest that restrictive border controls may have slightly slowed the increase of illegal flows. Yet the amplitude of this trend remains difficult to evaluate because DHS estimates rest on the assumption that the number of immigrants has declined from 11.8 million in 2007 to 11.6 million in 2008. This decrease may be due to a sampling error in the evaluation of the foreign-born population in the 2007 American Community Survey, especially in the estimates of the foreign-born population, as well as emigration of legally resident immigrants.

Fears that terrorists might attempt to infiltrate the United States as refugees or asylum seekers led to enhanced screening measures applied in the aftermath of 9/11, dramatically reducing the opportunities for eligibility under these categories. The total number of refugees admitted decreased by 23 percent, from 53,739 in 2005 to 41,150 in 2006 (compared with 68,925 in 2001). The total number of asylum seekers also declined, from 38,625 in 2001 to 26,113 in 2006, due to changes in security procedures and admission requirements introduced by the USA Patriot and REAL ID acts. However, the total ceiling for refugee admissions increased from 70,000 in 2007 to 80,000 in 2008, due to the expected resettlement of Iraqi, Bhutanese, and Iranian refugees. The 2008 ceiling was 65 percent lower than in 1980 (231,700). Yet more than 60,000 refugees were admitted in 2008 through the resettlement program. The proportion of Iraqi refugees increased from 0.5 percent of the total in 2006 to 23 percent in 2008. The State Department anticipated admitting at least 17,000 refugees from Iraq in 2009 (compared with 13,823 in 2008). Meanwhile, nearly 23,000 individuals were granted asylum in 2008. This represented an 8.7 percent decrease compared with the corresponding number in 2007 (25,124) and a 12.5 percent decline

Table 8.   Period of entry into the U.S. of the unauthorized immigration population, 1980–2007

Period of entry	Estimated population, January 2008	
	Number	Percent
All years	11,600,000	100
2005–2007	1,070,000	9
2000–2004	3,250,000	28
1995–1999	3,260,000	28
1990–1994	1,800,000	16
1985–1989	1,310,000	11
1980–1984	900,000	8

Source: DHS, Office of Immigration Statistics, Estimates of the Unauthorized Immigrant Population Residing in the United States, *Population Estimates*, February 2009, p. 3.

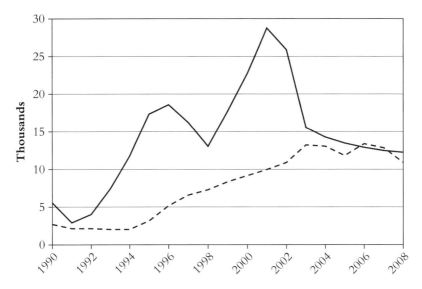

FIGURE 3. Annual flow of affirmative and defensive asylees in the United States, 1990–2008.
Source: DHS, Office of Immigration Statistics, *Annual Flow Report, Refugees and Asylees: 2008*, p. 6.

compared with 2006 (26,203). As illustrated by figure 3, restrictive measures had an impact on both affirmative and defensive asylum seekers.[10] Approximately 53 percent were granted asylum affirmatively, and 47 percent were granted asylum defensively in 2008. Citizens from China (23.8 percent), Colombia (7.2 percent), and Haiti (5.4 percent) accounted for more than a third of all asylum seekers admitted.

As in the United States, a dramatic escalation in the number of border controls took place in Europe in the aftermath of 9/11, both at the EU and national levels. In January 2003 the navies of France, the United Kingdom, Spain, Portugal, and Italy launched Operation Ulysses, intended to prevent illegal immigration across the Strait of Gibraltar and from the Western Sahara toward the Canary Islands. In November the EU adopted a program design to combat illegal immigration across the EU's maritime borders. It authorized the expansion of paramilitary border police forces, leading to a growing number of maritime interception operations by Frontex and individual EU member states. In Italy, the Bossi–Fini immigration law of 2002 was supplemented by the "anti-landings decrees" of June 2003. These decrees granted special powers to the police to send back boats before they entered Italian waters "if the vessels seem seaworthy and if the passengers on board are not genuine asylum seekers."[11] Meanwhile, attempts to address the Lampedusa crisis failed. This small Sicilian island became a major gateway to Europe for

Africa's immigrants soon after the intensification of controls in the Adriatic during the late 1990s. The Channel of Sicily thus replaced the Strait of Otranto: the number of illegal immigrants intercepted in Sicily jumped from 848 to some 14,000 between 1998 and 2004 (or from 0.02 percent to more than 98 percent of all apprehensions along Italy's southern borders).[12] About 180 boats arrived in Lampedusa between January and July of 2006, with more than 10,000 people on board (twice the island's population). Unable to manage the situation, the Italian government finally requested EU assistance. Officials from Frontex arrived in August 2006 to organize joint EU naval patrols in the area and stem the influx of immigrants. An Italian coast guard expressed some reservations: "It's our job not just to stop these people but to save them from drowning. . . . But to prevent them from coming? We can't do that."[13] Approximately 31,700 immigrants landed in Lampedusa in 2008, a 75 percent increase from the previous year. Half of all the immigrants who traveled from Africa by boat to Europe in 2009 arrived first in Italy, and 33,000 of the 36,000 who did so made their first landfall on Lampedusa.[14]

The continuous upgrading and militarization of border controls had no significant impact on the overall inflow of illegal immigrants, asylum seekers, or refugees. This increase in border controls diverted the flows of immigrants toward other routes along the EU southern borders and the Mediterranean (mainly from the Strait of Otranto to the Channel of Sicily, and from the Strait of Gibraltar to the Canary Islands), as well as Eastern European borders. Immigrants tried to reach Greece via the Aegean or Ionian seas, Italy from Tunisia and Libya, and the Spanish Canary Islands from the Saharan coast. Others tried to enter Slovakia from Ukraine, Poland and Lithuania from Chechnya, or Cyprus and Malta from Iraq. The rechanneling effect was clearly illustrated by the issue of the Red Cross camp located at Sangatte, about 1.2 miles from the Eurotunnel and 2 miles from the French town of Calais, from where thousands of illegal immigrants tried to sneak into Great Britain. Following an agreement between the British and the French governments, the Sangatte camp was closed in December 2002 in a bid to stem the flow of illegal entries. Official figures showed that the number of illegal immigrants detected entering Kent from Calais decreased by 80 percent in the aftermath of the closure, from more than 10,000 in 2002 to 1,500 in 2006. The British Border and Immigration Agency thwarted 18,000 illegal entries in 2008 and additionally spent millions of pounds on scanning equipment. Yet immigrants and smugglers responded to the closure by simply moving three miles away and taking advantage of poor fencing at Calais to initiate attempts at illegal entry into the UK. Thus, up to 1,500 illegal immigrants a year have successfully crossed the Channel since 2003.

The reality at the EU's external borders shows that although visa require-ments and sanctions on carriers may constrict official air routes and ferry connections, this has not stopped people from attempting to reach Europe using irregular means. A 2007 report on illegal migration in Central and Eastern Europe found that, since 2004, there had been an increase in the use of official road border posts for illegal crossings, although in many countries the most common way of crossing the border irregularly remained on foot, outside designated crossing points. According to a 2004 report of the Inter-national Center for Migration Policy Development, an estimated 100,000 to 120,000 undocumented migrants try to cross the Mediterranean each year.[15]

More-stringent border controls, therefore, did not curtail the number of illegal immigrants in Europe. With few legal migration routes into the EU from third countries, immigrants are forced to resort to irregular means of travel. The greater reliance upon smugglers, in turn, supports a call for new and more sophisticated security responses. Potential asylum seekers increas-ingly decide to circumvent the new restrictive regulations by crossing the bor-der illegally. For those who successfully overcome detention or deportation, other problems arise. Many European states have reduced the rights conferred upon asylum seekers whose applications are accepted, such as the right to work and access to welfare benefits. During the admission process, asylum seekers and refugees are regarded as "potentially guilty" until they prove themselves innocent. The 2003 Directive on Reception Conditions includes limitations to the right to have access to social benefits, residence permits, or travel documents. The directive only requires EU member states to issue residence permits "as soon as possible" after the status has been granted. Sub-sequently, an increasing number of refugees find themselves undocumented in the country of asylum and prevented from enjoying the rights attached to their legal status. Many of them therefore prefer to become illegal, as the status of illegal immigrant tends to appear, paradoxically, more appealing than an asylum status.

The number of applications for asylum has decreased in recent years, totaling 240,000 in 2008 (compared with 369,550 in 2002).[16] This trend results from an expansive use of the notions of "safe country" and "safe third country," as well as a sharp increase in the number of deportations and rejected applications. In 2008 there were 141,730 rejections (73 percent of the cases examined) and only 51,960 positive decisions—of which 24,425 applicants (13 percent) were granted refugee status, 18,560 (10 percent) were granted subsidiary protection, and 8,970 (5 percent) were granted authoriza-tion to stay for humanitarian reasons.[17] The proportion of positive decisions considerably varied among EU member states. In some countries, like Italy and Sweden, about 50 percent of requests got a positive response; but in others (such as Greece, Slovakia, and Slovenia) the proportion was only 3 percent. According to EU officials and European governments, the decreasing number of asylum seekers illustrates the highly successful asylum strategy adopted since 2001. However, the EU continues to face a constant pressure, which in turn legitimates the most controversial aspects of its asylum policy in terms of human rights.

EU member states also face a "boomerang effect" with regard to the redistribution of applications. The major receiving country in the EU throughout the 1990s was Germany. This changed in 2000, when the number of asylum applications in the United Kingdom reached 98,900, outnumbering applications to Germany by about 20,000. The decrease in asylum applications in the EU 15 was offset by an increase in those countries acceding to the EU in May 2004. In these ten countries (Estonia, Latvia, Lithuania, Poland, Slovakia, Slovenia, the Czech Republic, Hungary, Malta, and Cyprus), 37,300 people lodged asylum applications in 2003, compared with 32,100 the preceding year, a rise of 16 percent. The 2006 figures revealed that while the number of applications was decreasing in Slovenia (by 70 percent) and France (by 40 percent), it was increasing in Lithuania (by 44 percent), Sweden (by 38 percent), and Greece (by 35 percent). This "boomerang effect" increased the number of illegal immigrants as well. For example, when the Netherlands decided in 2005 to remove thousands of rejected asylum seekers, 3,085 of them (35 percent of the cases reexamined) "departed to an unknown destination"—a euphemism for illegally crossing the border into another EU member state in order to evade deportation.

Finally, the strengthening of "Fortress Europe" has not significantly reduced the flows of legal immigrants. Total immigration into the EU increased between 2002 and 2006. In 2006 the number of immigrants (3.5 million) was nearly 25 percent higher than in 2002. The annual average increase was more than one hundred thousand people during this period. As figure 4 shows, the increase in the total population of EU member states was mainly due to high net migration.[18] From 2003 to 2007, the population of EU member states increased on average by 1.7 million per year, solely because inflows outweighed outflows. As a result, net migration contributed up to 71 percent of the total population increase. The main reason for immigration remained family reunification, accounting for 70 percent of the entries from non–European Economic Area countries and 33 percent of the entries from EEA countries between 1992 and 2002.[19] Puzzlingly, there is no EU data on the comprehensive impact of family reunification. Yet recent estimates show that more than three-quarters of the EU's annual inflow is based on family reunification for labor immigrants and asylum seekers. Various national data confirm that this kind of "migration chain" plays a key role in the increase of immigration flows. In Greece, for example, the number of applications for family reunification increased from 28,902 in 2002 to 138,110 in 2006. Family reunification accounted for 67.8 percent of long-term migration inflows in Sweden in 2006, 64.3 percent in France, 63.5 percent in Austria, 61.7 percent in Italy, and 49.8 percent in the Netherlands.[20] As a consequence of the legal restrictions imposed by EU member states, family reunification is likely to remain a major immigration gateway into the EU 27 for third-country nationals. Clearly, any further restrictive border controls would not address this issue.

Furthermore, escalation of controls at the external borders does not address the issue of EU internal migration either. More than a third of foreign citizens (37 percent) in the EU 27 came from another member state in 2008. The largest groups of intra-EU migrants were from Romania (1.7 million or 15 percent of the total number of foreign citizens from another EU member state), Italy (1.3 million or 11 percent), and Poland (1.2 million or 11 percent).[21]

The economic crisis in the United States and Europe that began at the end of 2007 certainly has had an impact on immigration flows. Recent census data from the Mexican government, for example, indicate a slight decline in

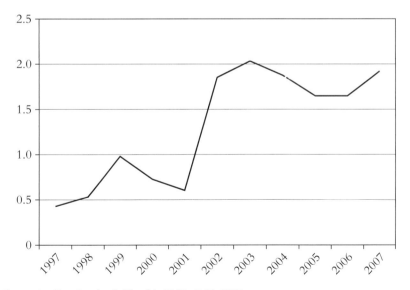

FIGURE 4.   Net migration (millions) in EU 27, 1997–2007.
Source: Eurostat, *Key Figures in Europe*, 2009, p. 54.

the number of Mexican immigrants going to the United States. This trend is substantiated by a decrease in arrests along the border as a result of Mexicans' deciding to delay illegal crossing because of the lack of jobs in the United States. Still, many of them are ready to pay smugglers' fees (reaching now $3,000 to $5,000) in the hope that the U.S. economy will improve soon. Conversely, there has been no large exodus: only 450,000 Mexicans returned to Mexico in 2008 (as in 2007), and at least 11 million illegal immigrants remain in the United States. According to Mónika Oropeza Rodríguez, executive director of the Albergue del Desertio, the explanation is quite simple: "Our people are not stupid. There may be a crisis in the United States, but they know that we have been in an economic crisis in Mexico for many years."[22] In Europe, increasing unemployment rates in some countries have an impact on intra-European migration. Between April 2008 and May 2009, about fifty thousand immigrant workers returned home from Ireland, mostly to Eastern Europe. Yet, as in the United States, there was no large-scale exodus. For the majority of immigrants (both legal and illegal) residing in EU member states, low wages and uncertain employment are still better than the conditions they would face in their country of origin. Several countries, such as the Czech Republic and Spain, offered financial incentives to leave. The Czech government offered to pay €500 and to provide a one-way plane ticket to each unemployed worker who wanted to go home. This measure met with little enthusiasm. In Spain, only three thousand immigrants (out of a total of 5.2 million foreigners) agreed to leave in 2009.

A Cost/Benefit Evaluation

Restrictive measures against illegal immigrants have failed to address the complex relationship between border controls and migration flows. The presence or absence of border controls plays a role in determining migration flows, but immigrants are also motivated by external factors (such as economic deprivation). Despite the supposed deterrent effect of tougher border controls, there is no evidence that large numbers of migrants are discouraged from trying.[23] Furthermore, anti-immigrant measures generate both direct and indirect costs. Among the direct costs is the increasing funding devoted to tougher border enforcement, including additional fences, surveillance technologies, weapons, and manpower labor costs. For example, in June 2004, Border Patrol units in Arizona began using two Hermes 450 unmanned aerial vehicles (drones) for surveillance. The purpose was to relay digital pictures of people and vehicle movements at the border. In the eight months the drones were used, they accounted for less than 0.5 percent of the sector's total apprehensions of illegal immigrants, for a total cost of $10 million. Furthermore, not a single terrorist was identified.[24] The Department of Homeland Security contract for the American Shield Initiative cost $2.5 million in 2004. It included funding for technology to patrol the borders, from drones to ground sensors—which a government audit in December 2005 found of little use. The General Services Administration also found that the government has paid up to 300 percent more than it should have for cameras and ground sensors by contracting with the International Microwave Corporation (for a total of $239 million) in 2004. Since then, several other contracts have been awarded, including one with Man Tech for $33.1 million and another with Cross Match Technologies for $33.1 million (as part of the US-VISIT program).

In 2004 DHS spent nearly $50 billion, including $9 billion in contracts awarded to private corporations for protection against terrorism and illegal immigration.[25] The immigration-industrial complex has continued to expand since then, with a growing number of departing high-level DHS officials joining corporations, such as former DHS secretary Tom Ridge, who in 2005 joined the board of directors of Savi Technologies, a multinational contractor that supplies equipment to forces in Iraq.[26] Other security-driven programs have received increasing funding over the last few years. The National Fugitive Operation Program, for instance, spent a total of $625 million between 2002 and 2007. Despite its controversial results, its budget rose from $218 million in 2008 to $350 million in 2009. Congress also asked Immigration and Customs Enforcement to redirect an additional $850 million to catch and deport criminal immigrants. Meanwhile, ICE supported local initiatives (such as neighborhood sweeps and traffic stops) through a $60 million-a-year training program. The Secure Communities Program, aimed at checking the legal status of immigrants booked into local jails, received a budget of $200 million in 2009.

The Obama administration has sought to expand this program to all inmates in federal and state facilities. Based on initial projections, ICE estimated that screening and removing all "level 1 offenders" would cost $1.1 billion over four years. Removing all criminal illegal immigrants would cost $3 billion. In May 2010 President Obama also announced his decision to deploy an additional 1,200 National Guard troops at the southern border and to request $500 million in extra money for border security. Yet the U.S. Government Accountability Office (GAO) published a report entitled "Secure Border Initiative: Technology Deployment Delays Persist and the Impact of Border Fencing Has Not Been Assessed." According to the GAO, Customs and Border Protection could not account for the impact of tactical infrastructure despite a $2.4 billion investment. The GAO also reported that CBP's effort to deploy Secure Border Initiative SBInet technology had fallen behind its planned schedule. For example, CBP had awarded thirteen orders to Boeing for a total of $1.1 billion in 2009, but Boeing was unable to provide a system with the capabilities required to control the border in Arizona. The GAO noted that fencing costs dramatically increased over the years. Fencing miles completed in October 2008 cost an average of $3.9 million per mile for pedestrian fencing and $1.0 million per mile for vehicle fencing. Once new contracts were awarded, however, the average per-mile costs had increased to $6.5 million for pedestrian and $1.8 million for vehicle fencing. Furthermore, total life-cycle costs for all infrastructure constructed to date were estimated at about $6.5 billion. The GAO report concluded that much of the United States' six thousand miles of international borders with Canada and Mexico remains vulnerable to illegal entry, although SBI's funding has amounted to over $3.7 billion since 2005.[27] Finally, in January 2011, DHS canceled the "virtual fence" program across the southwest border. According to Janet Napolitano, the homeland security secretary, border agents should instead use less-expensive technology, as well as surveillance equipment tailored to the rough terrain along much of the border.[28]

Chasing after immigrants in Europe is not cheap either. Although it is impossible to estimate total expenses at the national level, Frontex illustrates the increasing cost of both interception and deportation activities at the EU level. In the first year of its existence, the Frontex budget was €6.2 million. It was amended twice in 2006, with a final sum of €19.2 million. For 2007 Frontex was awarded a budget of €42 million, while the number of staff members was almost doubled in two years.[29] To this can be added the costs that European governments pay to carriers to transport deportees. When commercial airline pilots and cabin staff members refused to fly with deportees on board, European authorities had to use private companies. The cost of chartering a plane may be prohibitive. For example, it cost £75,000 to the British government in 2005 to hire a private jet to deport a single Algerian failed asylum seeker who was banned as a passenger by commercial airlines.[30] More generally, in 2006 the average cost of deporting one individual was estimated by the UK Home Office at £11,000.[31] The willingness of EU member states to cooperate in these fields is admittedly motivated financially, in the hope of reducing the marginal costs of their repressive policies. Yet it remains unclear whether the communitarization of anti-immigrant policies is achieving this goal. Furthermore, the EU's aim to externalize questions of immigration and asylum management not only involves the violation of the basic rights of immigrants but also absorbs an increasing portion of the

EU budget. Between 2004 and 2008, the EU spent about €120 million on migration and asylum initiatives through the Aeneas program. In July 2005 the European Commission allocated €2 million to the ARGO program to "support operational activities to address the emergencies caused by illegal immigration in the Mediterranean." In 2007 the EU launched the Thematic Program on Migration and Asylum aimed at supporting third countries in their efforts to "ensure better management of migration flows"—by focusing on the fight against illegal immigration and the readmission of illegal immigrants. This program was awarded a budget of €205 million for 2007–10, of which 34 percent was devoted to the southern migratory route (flows from sub-Saharan African countries and North Africa) and 24 percent to the eastern migratory route (flows from or transiting through the Russian Federation, Ukraine, Moldova, Belarus, the southern Caucasus, and Central Asia). Within this global framework, the EU developed bilateral relations with countries of origin and transit, as illustrated by a series of agreements with Libya. For example, despite the reservations expressed in April 2005 by a European Parliament delegation regarding the violation of human rights in Libya, the EU allocated additional support intended to develop a number of coordinated initiatives, including a partnership for infectious-disease control (known as the Benghazi Action Plan) designed to limit the propagation of HIV/AIDS. Under the EU's National Indicative Program for Libya, the EU allocated €60 million in aid for Tripoli for 2011–13.

Meanwhile, Italy bilaterally began the construction of a detention camp in northern Libya to facilitate deportations, and two additional camps in Kufra and Sebha were under discussion. Little information has filtered out regarding the funding of these facilities. The Italian government also provided Libya with training and equipment to assist in surveillance and management. In 2005 the Italian minister of the interior reportedly pledged to give Libya €15 million over a three-year period for border control equipment.[32] In a similar vein, France paid €2.6 million in 2006 to finance immigrants who agreed to return to Mali. Mali, in return, exchanged a letter of understanding with the French government on facilitating the deportation process. More broadly, France also made available €20 million for small grants to immigrants (both legal and illegal) from thirty-four countries if they agreed to return home. Fewer than two thousand accepted the deal, with half a million preferring to stay. In 2008 the French government budgeted €42 million for the deportation of twenty-six thousand illegal immigrants (based on an average cost of €2,186 for deporting one individual), and €5 million for the detention of thirty-five thousand people (held in the 42 detention centers and the 185 administrative facilities across the country). By fiscal year 2009, the total budget for the ministry in charge of immigration and asylum policy reached €513.8 million.[33]

Sociopolitical Effects of the Immigration Policy Failure

On both sides of the Atlantic, anti-migrant alarmism persists, despite the introduction of a large range of statutory and nonstatutory measures. In 2005 only 21 percent of Americans approved of the way President Bush was dealing with immigration. Three-quarters said that the government was not doing enough to keep illegal immigrants from crossing into the United States.[34] An opinion poll survey conducted by the Pew Research Center the following year confirmed that the American public lacked confidence in the capacity of its political leadership to deal with immigration: 62 percent then disapproved of the way the president was handling immigration policy.[35] By 2007, 81 percent believed that the government was not doing enough to keep illegal immigrants from coming to the United States.[36] A similar level of political distrust is noticeable in Europe, with ineffective border controls fueling suspicion about the possibility of an effective immigration policy at the national level. According to the MORI Social Research Institute, 44 percent of the British public and 42 percent of the Spanish expressed concern over the lack of effectiveness of immigration controls in 2006. Only 25 percent of respondents in the United Kingdom, and 32 percent in Italy, expressed confidence in the government when it comes to the issue of promoting the integration of foreigners.[37] In 2007, 56.8 percent of Italians wanted the armed forces to enforce border security.[38] The same year, 64 percent of Britons urged tougher immigration laws.[39] A large majority of the EU-25 population also wanted the control of external borders (72 percent), as well as asylum and migration policies (65 percent), adjudicated at the EU level.[40]

Addressing both public criticism and the threat posed by immigration to state sovereignty therefore requires further restrictive policies designed to curb the number—and control the quality—of immigrants. The absolute necessity of restoring state capacity also calls for "law and order" measures that would enhance internal safety. Yet the ineffectiveness of these measures fuels migration phobia, which in turn increases the level of political distrust, contributing to uncertainty and concern about security. Governments then face an immigration policy dilemma: "The appearance of being soft on immigration is likely to undermine domestic support for the government. But pursuing a tough restrictionist policy may . . . criminalize immigration—exacerbating exactly the problems that need to be resolved."[41]

While economic factors do not seem to provide a sufficient explanation for the persistent migration phobia, as argued in chapter 2, the relationship between political distrust and distrust of immigrants provides useful insights. In Eastern Europe, prejudice against immigrants and anti-Gypsy attitudes are closely linked to opposing the political system, distrust, and general malaise, as illustrated by the findings of the Political Capital Institute's Demand for Right-Wing Extremism (DEREX) index.[42] In Hungary, for example, anti-establishment attitudes dramatically increased from 12 percent to 46 percent of the population between 2003 and 2009, due to striking dissatisfaction with political institutions and democracy itself. Meanwhile, antiforeigner sentiment increased from 37 percent of respondents in 2003 to 55 percent in 2007. The number of Ukrainians who expressed antagonism toward the political establishment doubled, from 25 percent to 52 percent, during the two years following the 2005 Orange Revolution—a time when many Ukrainians felt their new leaders had let them down. In 2007, 48 percent expressed a high level of prejudice against immigrants.

According to the DEREX findings, two sets of factors demonstrate the relationship between political distrust and migrant phobia. The first one, the "public morale" index, measures people's relationship with the national political and social institutions, the perception of their leaders and their fellow citizens, as well as their views on politics and the economy.[43] The second one corresponds to the "value judgments" index, which probes people's attitudes toward outsiders and minority groups (homosexuals and immigrants), conformity to social norms, religiosity, and obedience to authority. The highest levels of prejudice are found in countries where people express a low level of public morale and negative value judgments. These two series of factors also influence the demand for far-right extremism, as illustrated by a comparison of Poland and Hungary. These two countries started at about the same base in 2003: 10 percent of Hungarians and 9 percent of Poles were potential supporters of the extreme right. By 2009 Poland's DEREX score had dropped by nearly a third, and Hungary's had doubled. The biggest difference was the improvement in public morale in Poland. After 2005, public opinion was "consolidated" where the anti-elite trend began to reverse itself and people began to feel more positive about the economy. Meanwhile, support for immigration crumbled in Hungary. Poland, the country with the most restrictive attitude in the European Social Survey round 1, became more liberal, with a significant decrease in anti-immigrant feelings between 2002 and 2007.[44]

In Western Europe, levels of prejudice and xenophobia are more significant than antiestablishment attitudes. However, political distrust impacts anti-immigrant feelings to a significant degree. The European Social Survey included five questions in 2003 examining factors affecting individual attitudes. These questions focused on left-right placement, perceived insecurity, social distrust, political distrust, and perceived ethnic threat. As illustrated by table 9, respondents' answers suggested that these factors were consistently influential: the more people perceived that their personal safety was reduced, and the more they distrusted political leaders, the more they considered themselves to be politically right wing, and the more they perceived ethnic minorities to pose a collective threat. They were therefore increasingly likely to favor different aspects of ethnic exclusionism as a consequence of their fear and alienation.

Political distrust is by no means the only source of anti-immigrant feelings, as illustrated by the case of Austria, where there is a low level of economic and political distrust but a strong resistance to immigrants. However, linking the levels of economic pessimism and political distrust to the dimensions of ethnic exclusionism provides insights as to what is happening, explaining a substantial part of long-term evolution in migrant phobia, as well as variations among countries. With the exception of Italy, all the countries where political distrust is higher than the EU average also expressed high levels of support for ethnic exclusionism.

Political distrust affects not only those who express concern about the effectiveness of national government. It also has an impact on state actors—those who are supposed to address the problems that need to be solved. At the EU level, political distrust among member states related to border management has been a key ingredient of the logic of border escalation since the foundation of the Trevi group. The multiplication of "compensatory measures" to free movement within the EU was motivated by the fear that some member states—namely the Mediterranean countries that joined the EU in the 1980s, without an immigration policy and without strong border controls—would become a gateway for irregular entry to the EU as a whole. These concerns were exacerbated by the dominant perspective on the EU enlargement: the old EU-15 states did not trust the ability of the ten new member states to carry out their sovereign roles of controlling their borders and managing immigration and asylum systems in a way that met established EU norms and standards. This mistrust still prevails, despite the fact that the ten new member states had to accept all existing EU decisions on immigration, asylum, and border control policies, including the Schengen protocol, prior to accession. In addition to transitional agreements by which EU-15 states have limited the right to free movement for citizens from the EU 10, this mistrust fuels the border escalation along the new external EU borders,

Table 9. Economic pessimism, political distrust, and xenophobia in the EU

	Employment pessimism (UE 15 = 47%)	Economic pessimism (UE 15 = 46%)	Dissatisfaction with national democracy (EU 15 = 43%)	Distrust for national government (EU 15 = 60%)	Insecurity feelings (crime as a major issue) (EU 15 = 28%)	Limits to multicultural society (EU 15 = 60%)/ EB 2003	Resistance to immigrants (EU average = 50%)/ESS 2003	Perceived collective ethnic threat (EU average = 58%)/ESS 2003
Belgium	59	51	38	54	29	69	44.1	62.8
Denmark	44	23	10	39	34	55.4	50.4	49.9
Germany	62	57	45	65	18	73	42.6	61.7
Greece	55	56	46	50	27	80.6	87.4	84.7
Spain	26	24	27	50	11	49.3	50.1	51.9
France	53	52	42	64	30	64.1		
Ireland	41	40	25	59	41	72.1	35.2	54.3
Italy	44	50	65	62	28	45.5	36.5	53.9
Luxembourg	55	46	23	31	15	63	52.7	39.5
Netherlands	64	62	39	57	52	67.5	42.9	55
Austria	44	32	30	51	20	61.3	64.3	52
Portugal	58	52	64	55	23	59.2	62.4	61.5
Finland	43	25	26	64	24	21.6	59.2	41.8
Sweden	41	35	26	49	32	40.7	14.6	32.8
UK	28	34	37	68	48	68.1	51	61.1

Sources: Adapted from Eurobarometer 60 (2003), Public Opinion in the EU (February 2004), and Majorities' Attitudes towards Minorities: Key Findings from the Eurobarometer and the European Social Survey (Vienna, EUMC, March 2005).

while the United Kingdom still refuses to be fully part of Schengenland. Yet the EU has already invested heavily in new technology and institutional assistance to help manage its new eastern border. In 2003 the EU's PHARE program, in cooperation with the Hungarian government, spent over €3.6 million developing the National Operational Control System of the Hungarian Border Guard. In Poland the PHARE Small Infrastructure Project Fund is focusing on increasing cooperation between Polish border institutions and their counterparts in neighboring countries.

Furthermore, the issue of distrust has an impact on EU relationships with third countries. The EU Schengen Catalogue establishes, for example, that "as regards cooperation with adjacent states, it is considered necessary that transit states lend their active assistance by ensuring that their borders are thoroughly secured and by taking measures away from the border, i.e. consistent repatriation practice."[45] The European Neighborhood Policy (ENP) adopted in 2003 perfectly illustrates the ambiguous relationship between political distrust, security concerns, and border escalation. The ENP framework was proposed to sixteen of EU's closest neighbors.[46] It sets out in concrete terms how the EU proposes to work more closely with these countries with the goal of "strengthening the prosperity, stability and security of all." It is designed, according to the European Commission, "to prevent the emergence of new dividing lines between the enlarged EU and its neighbours and to offer them the chance to participate in various EU activities, through greater political, security, economic and cultural co-operation."[47] The ENP includes enhanced preferential trade relations and increased financial and technical assistance, as well as cooperation in the fields of energy, transport, social policy, and the environment. In exchange, the ENP requires the EU's neighbors to reinforce controls and security to avert threats before they reach EU territory: "Action Plan priorities could furthermore include co-operation on migration, asylum, visa policies, measures to combat terrorism, organised crime, trafficking in drugs and arms, money laundering and financial and economic crime. Action Plans will identify concrete steps to strengthen the judiciary and to increase police and judicial co-operation, including in the area of family law as well as co-operation with European Union bodies" such as Europol and Eurojust.[48] The EU therefore suggests to its partners an "intensified cooperation to prevent and combat common security threats" as a way to keep out of the EU those third-country nationals whom the member states consider personae non gratae.

This EU strategy has had two results. First, ENP partners have actually strengthened their border management capacities to combat cross-border and organized crime. They also converged toward border and law-enforcement standards of those of the EU. According to the European Commission, "a greater capacity to ensure effective border controls and surveillance led, in certain cases, to improved detection of smuggling, illegal migration and customs fraud. Efforts to professionalize and civilianise border management services need to be consistently pursued. Improvements to risk assessment techniques and analysis remain critical in this regard. Closer cooperation and communication between national authorities at regional level remains necessary for ENP partner countries whose borders still need to be demarcated and delimited."[49] Technical cooperation arrangements with Frontex are in force with Georgia, Moldova, and Ukraine, while arrangements remain under discussion with Egypt and Morocco. Readmission agreements were implemented with Moldova and Ukraine in 2009 and with Georgia in 2010. Yet there is no evidence that all these measures actually curb the number of immigrants originating from these countries. Second, this strategy illustrates what Ruben Zaiotto calls a "gated community syndrome" fueled by the "Schengen culture of internal security." The message to neighbors is: "we appreciate your support, but we do not trust you; we want your cooperation and friendship, but we build protective fences; we share interests, but we define what these interests are; and we believe in promoting collective security, but our own security comes first."[50]

Mexico and the United States have been engaged in a similar love-hate relationship for many years. Suspicion and distrust work both ways. On the Mexican side there are concerns about U.S. "imperialistic" motives. Mexico also insists that the trafficking of drugs would not exist without the enormous and growing market in the United States, thus placing responsibility on its northern neighbor. Furthermore, 90 percent of the firearms recovered from crime scenes in Mexico originated in the United States. According to the U.S. Bureau of Alcohol, Tobacco, Firearms and Explosives, the greatest proportion of firearms trafficked to Mexico originate from U.S. states in the Southwest—especially Texas, Arizona, and California. With regard to Mexican illegal immigrants (accounting for almost 59 percent of the total estimated illegal alien population in the United States), Mexico takes the view that the migrants are "undocumented workers," making the point that since the U.S. market attracts and provides employment for the migrants, it bears some responsibility. Mexico regularly voices concern about alleged abuses suffered by Mexican workers there and for the loss of life and hardships suffered by Mexican migrants as they risk increasingly dangerous routes and methods to circumvent tighter border controls. After President Bush approved the Secure Fence Act of 2006, Mexico denounced the proposed border fence at the Organization of American States, with the support of twenty-seven other nations.[51] President Felipe Calderón, during his first official visit to the United States in May 2010, criticized the authorization of seven hundred miles of fencing along the U.S.-Mexico border, noting that it complicated the two nations' relations. He asserted that job creation and increased investment in Mexico would be more effective than constructing a new border fence.

Even at times when U.S.-Mexican relations have been at their best, successive U.S. administrations have viewed Mexico's government as corrupt and unable to address the issues of drug-trafficking and illegal border crossing. On the U.S. side there is suspicion that the Mexican government is not doing enough to limit the number of workers who try to enter the United States illegally, because Mexico benefits from illegal migration in at least two ways. First, it is a "safety valve" that dissipates the political discontent that could arise from higher unemployment in Mexico; and, second, it is a source of remittances by workers in the United States to families in Mexico. Furthermore, even when the Mexican government strongly reaffirms its commitment to fighting illegal immigration and drug trafficking, as illustrated by counternarcotics efforts during the Vicente Fox administration (2000–2006), the U.S. government often expresses reservations about the efficacy of these initiatives. The growth and dramatic character of the violence related to drug cartels in Mexico have also led some U.S. officials and observers to question the strength of the Mexican state.[52] In order to compensate for Mexican weakness, the U.S. government has increased its assistance to Mexico in the fields of drug trafficking, human smuggling, trade, migration, human rights, and security. One major program is the Mérida Initiative, a multiyear, $1.4 billion effort, which started in 2007 and is intended to combat drug trafficking, gangs, and organized crime. In total, U.S. assistance to Mexico rose from $65 million in 2007 to $403 million in 2008. In 2009 the U.S. Congress appropriated an estimated $369 million for Mexico. The Obama administration also requested $66 million in a fiscal 2009 supplemental request.[53] However, some have questioned whether such measures are enough to address Mexico's security troubles and shore up its weak institutions. The Department of Justice National Drug Threat Assessment report stated in 2008 that "Mexican drug trafficking organizations represent the greatest organized crime threat to the United States."[54]

In 2010 the U.S. and Mexican governments unveiled a revised strategy for continued bilateral security cooperation, framed by the notion of "co-responsibility" and based on four pillars: disrupting the ability of organized crime to operate, strengthening institutions to sustain the rule of law and human rights, building a twenty-first-century border, and fostering strong and resilient communities. However, the adoption of a restrictive immigration law by the Arizona legislature in April 2010 reignited frustration and distrust on both sides of the border. President Calderón described this law as "anti-Mexican,"[55] while Arizona's two Republican senators—John McCain and Jon Kyl—justified the law by arguing that Mexico is responsible for an "unacceptable" situation. "The violence has crossed the border and escalated to a point where many Arizonans do not feel safe within their own homes or on their own property," stated McCain and Kyl in a joint press release. "It would be irresponsible not to do everything we can to stop the escalating violence along the border with Mexico."[56] It is worth noting that the law does not tackle the issue of violence at the border—which is mainly related to drug trafficking—but gives local police broad authority to stop and demand documents from anyone they suspect is an illegal immigrant. It also calls for aggressive prosecution of illegal immigrants, and officers can be sued if they do not enforce the law.

Proponents also defend the Arizona law by blaming Washington for its failure to move on immigration reform. "We in Arizona have been more than patient waiting for Washington to act," Governor Jan Brewer said. "But decades of federal inaction and misguided policy have created a dangerous situation."[57] From this perspective, the debate around the Arizona law is the most recent example of how political distrust generates a "higher political bid" tendency, influencing the relationship between the federal and state governments. President Obama's response to the Arizona law in May 2010 was the deployment of twelve hundred additional National Guard Troops and $500 million in extra funding for border security. This decision was obviously intended to deflect conservative criticism following the passage of Arizona's harsh immigration law and to appease congressional Republicans, who have refused to support an immigration overhaul unless the White House boosted border security first. Yet Republicans remained dismissive of Obama's promise to enhance border security, while immigration reformers feared that he could end up following Bush's failed path on immigration reform—by being unable to make a persuasive case for reform and letting the conservatives take over the debate.

● ● ● Chapter 5

The Security/Insecurity Spiral

The main assumptions that justified the war on terror can be summarized as follows: terrorism constitutes the major threat to security; immigration poses a major terrorist threat; and Islamist terrorism currently represents the major threat to national security. These assumptions have been admittedly strengthened by the horrific events of 9/11, the Madrid and London bombings, as well as failed or foiled terrorist attacks since 2001. In response to a changing insecurity environment, both the United States and Europe have adopted new security frameworks—such as the European Security Strategy, the U.S. National Security Strategy, and comprehensive antiterrorist strategies with similar objectives. In the United States the National Strategy for Combating Terrorism listed four key concepts (the four *D*s): *defeat* terrorists and their organizations; *deny* sponsorship, support, and sanctuary to terrorists; *diminish* the underlying conditions that terrorists seek to exploit; and *defend* U.S. citizens and interests at home and abroad. The European Union Counter-Terrorism Strategy aimed at covering four comparable strands (the four *P*s): *protect* citizens and infrastructure and reduce Europe's vulnerability to attacks, including through improved security of borders, transport, and critical infrastructure; *prevent* people from turning to terrorism by tackling the factors or root causes that can lead to radicalization and recruitment, in Europe and internationally; *pursue* and investigate terrorists across EU internal borders and globally (by impeding planning, travel, and communications, disrupting support networks, cutting off funding and access to attack materials, and bringing terrorists to justice); and *prepare* member states, in the spirit of solidarity, to manage and minimize the consequences of a terrorist attack, by improving capabilities to deal with the aftermath, the coordination of the *response*, and the needs of victims.[1]

Both the U.S. government and EU member states have often been eager to trumpet their satisfaction in terms of effective policy outcomes. According to the European Commission, "The EU's experience and success in issues such as border management and fighting organized crime are a useful point of reference for other countries facing similar challenges."[2] In October 2007 President Bush argued that "despite grave challenges, we have also seen great accomplishments. Working with our partners and allies, we have broken up terrorist cells, disrupted attacks, and saved American lives."[3] Such self-confident claims are indeed justified by some tangible results. In the United States, only four of the homegrown plots since 9/11 progressed to an actual attack (notably the 2009 shooting at Fort Hood by Major Nidal Malik Hasan, who killed thirteen). Law enforcement had some success against jihadist terrorists, especially in 2009 and 2010, with a total of seventy-six arrests (almost half the total since 9/11). According to a report published by the New America Foundation and Syracuse University's Maxwell School of Public Policy, this increase was driven by arrests in FBI sting operations, as well as the thirty-one people who were charged with fund-raising, recruiting, or traveling abroad for the Somali terrorist group Al-Shabaab.[4]

British authorities did not prevent the 2005 London bombings. Yet other groups plotting to carry out bombings in Britain have been successfully arrested and prosecuted. "Operation Crevice," the biggest antiterrorist operation, led to the arrest of seven plotters in March 2004, including Omar Khyam, who was in contact with Mohammad Khan and Shehzad Tanweer while the two men were organizing the 7/7 attacks. Dhiren Barot, a Hindu convert to Islam who planned several attacks, was also arrested in 2004 and received a forty-year prison sentence in 2007. That same year, Khyam and four other suspects were sentenced to life imprisonment. Meanwhile, more than one hundred suspects awaited trial on terrorism charges. The Home Office has recorded statistics on terrorism in Great Britain for the period of September 11, 2001, to March 31, 2009. During that time there were 1,661 terrorism arrests (of which 598 resulted in a charge). The main offenses for which suspects were charged under terrorism legislation were possession of an article for terrorist purposes, membership in a banned organization, and fund-raising—all offenses under the Terrorism Act of 2000. On March 31, 2009, 121 persons were in prison for terrorist-related offenses, and

22 persons were classified as domestic extremists/separatists. The majority (62 percent) of the 121 persons imprisoned were UK nationals.[5]

In Greece the effectiveness of counterterrorist legislation was illustrated by the investigation and subsequent trial of nineteen alleged November 17 terrorists arrested in 2002. Of the nineteen, fifteen were subsequently convicted of a number of crimes, including creating and participating in a terrorist organization. In Germany three men suspected of planning several coordinated bomb attacks were arrested in September 2007. In the so-called Glasvej case, the Danish police arrested eight people in September 2007 on suspicion of planning a massive attack.

At the EU level, Europol registered a total of 1,044 individuals who were arrested for terrorism-related offenses in 2007, an increase of 48 percent over the previous year. France, Spain, and the United Kingdom reported the largest number of arrests. That same year 418 individuals were tried on terrorism charges in the EU member states, in a total of 143 proceedings.[6] After this peak, the number of attacks decreased in 2009 by 33 percent compared with 2008, and was almost half the number of attacks carried out in 2007. The majority of court decisions pronounced in 2009 were related to separatist terrorism (involving 268 individuals tried, out of a total of 408), in contrast with 2008, when the majority related to Islamist terrorism. The highest number of individuals tried for terrorism charges in 2009 was reported by Spain (including twenty-five tried for Islamist terrorist activity, out of a total number of eighty-nine tried on similar charges in other European countries).[7]

My point is not to deny these accomplishments. Yet reservations remain about the effectiveness of the war on terror, as well as the relevance of anti-migrant measures to enhancing homeland security. To assess the effective outcomes of policies in relation to the war on terror requires evaluating their impact on national security. In doing so, I believe that it is important to address two interrelated questions: Do the policies address the previous intelligence deficiencies? And do they improve the fight against terrorism by identifying the right targets and by providing reliable information on terrorist cells?

Answering these questions is a difficult task, because the assessment of terrorist threats is associated with a high degree of uncertainty for at least three reasons. First, terrorists adapt their strategy to changes in the security environment in which they operate. Since little is known about how they will respond (because the number of available strategies is very large), it is not clear how security policies or other relevant changes affect the probabilities of new attacks. As a result, "actions by governments to guard one venue cause the terrorists to shift to another venue."[8] Furthermore, the profile of terrorists is also changing. In Europe, for example, almost 40 percent of the arrested suspects are younger than thirty. Yet suspects arrested for Islamist terrorism are older than those arrested for separatist terrorism. The vast majority are men. Yet in 2009, 15 percent of the arrested suspects (mostly for separatist terrorism) were women—compared with 10 percent in 2007.[9] There is no typical terrorist profile in the United States, either, because the pool of radical individuals is growing more and more diverse—from Adam Gadahn (raised Jewish in California) to Colleen LaRose (a white woman from Pennsylvania). Furthermore, suicide bombers in Muslim countries have little in common with anarchist terrorists in Europe or domestic right-wing terrorists and white supremacists in the United States.

Second, intelligence services gather and interpret information on terrorist activity, so they are particularly well placed to form opinions on the likelihood and nature of future attacks. It is, however, less obvious that this information can be used in overall policy design, because of secrecy restrictions. As argued by experts in a recent report published by the Organization for Economic Cooperation and Development, "secrecy requirements pose a principal-agent problem: the principal wants security, and needs to monitor agents' operations to attain that objective, but monitoring is difficult because of the secrecy requirement. More broadly, strict secrecy policies create a problem of accountability and potentially of legitimacy. Authorities could argue that policies are justified by the information available to them but which cannot be made public."[10] Cost-benefit analysis has difficulty dealing with security issues, mainly because the benefits are uncertain or, at least, extremely hard to quantify.

Third, there is a counterfactual problem, because there is no true way to know what terrorism would have been had certain policies not been taken. On the other hand, it appears that the war on terror has not only decreased the number of incidents, but also on average resulted in incidents with more casualties. This changing pattern over time has been combined with a geographical relocation of terrorist attacks—from the Western Hemisphere to the Middle East and Eurasia.[11] According to U.S. figures, terrorist attacks worldwide increased by 300 percent between 2003 and 2004.[12] In 2005 there were 360 suicide bombings, resulting in three thousand deaths, compared with 472 such attacks spread over the five preceding years.[13]

Bearing in mind these difficulties, it is crucial nonetheless to evaluate whether counterterrorist policies have attained their objectives on both sides of the Atlantic. I focus on the security/insecurity spiral, by which I mean that a real or perceived sense of insecurity leads to the implementation of further security measures. I demonstrate that the overgeneralized character-ization of terrorism undermines governmental legitimacy because a continu-ing sense of insecurity is interpreted as a sign of incapacity, and thus fuels an increasing feeling of insecurity in an endless circle.

When Counterterrorism and Restrictive Immigration Policy Collide

Whether the strengthening of immigration controls yields benefits in the fight against terrorism remains to be seen. What evidence there is so far indicates that border controls create a misleading appearance of effectiveness without regard to the tangible results. Border fences and similar security measures are a continuation of the ineffective border control strategy imple-mented more than a decade ago. Despite the rising investment in border enforcement, in spending on technology, materials, and staffing, estimated undocumented flows have increased, while immigration enforcement has proven to be of nominal effectiveness as a counterterrorist measure.

Such a counterproductive approach has been illustrated in the United States by the raids on homes and in neighborhoods conducted by Immigra-tion and Customs Enforcement (ICE) agents as part of the National Fugitive Operation Program and "Operation Return to Sender." These raids were billed as carefully planned hunts for dangerous immigrant fugitives and ter-rorists. Spending on these programs grew from $9 million in 2003 to $219 million by 2008, as the number of seven-member teams multiplied from 8 to 104. However, internal directives gradually revised immigration policy enforcement and thus its results. In January 2004 an ICE memo stated that "no less than 75 percent of all fugitive operation targets will be those clas-sified as 'criminal aliens'—noncitizens with a criminal record as well as an order of deportation." It added that "collateral apprehensions" (illegal immi-grants encountered by chance during an operation) would not be counted in calculating that percentage. In January 2006 ICE raised arrest quotas for each team from 125 to 1,000. A new directive, however, removed the require-ment that at least 75 percent of those sought out for arrest be criminals but maintained that "collateral apprehensions will not count." Yet this standard was subsequently dropped in September 2006, and ICE teams were allowed to count nonfugitives toward their 1,000 arrest quota. As a result, 73 percent of the 96,000 illegal immigrants arrested between 2003 and 2008 had no criminal conviction. In 2007, 51 percent of those arrested had a deportation order but no criminal record, and 40 percent were termed "ordinary status violators" who did not fit any of the program's priority categories. Fugitives with criminal records dropped to 9 percent of those arrested (compared with 39 percent in 2004). By 2008 the number of fugitives with criminal background accounted for only 16 percent of total arrests. In order to appear tough on immigration enforcement and counterterrorism, the Bush administration created incentives for ICE teams to target "window washers" rather than criminals, drug smugglers, and potential terrorists. According to Peter L. Markowitz, a Cardozo law professor who reviewed ICE activities, "it looks like what happened here is that the law enforcement strategy was hijacked by the political agenda of the administration."[14]

Another result of racial profiling, illegal searches, random raids, and false arrests was the dramatic increase in the number of immigrants imprisoned in federal or state jails. Congress gave additional funding to ICE but required that all fugitives be identified, arrested, and removed. Yet the shift from trying to capture the most dangerous criminal immigrants to boosting total arrests undermined deportation proceedings. Furthermore, it became more difficult to remove illegal immigrants convicted of crimes after their sentences were served, despite new initiatives designed to check the immigration status of immigrant inmates (such as the Secure Communities Program). In 2007, for example, the number of immigrants evading deportation orders rose to 634,000.

Various antiterrorist measures produced similar counterproductive outcomes. The REAL ID Act suggested improving security by denying driver's licenses to illegal immigrants. As a result, this measure has driven the undocumented further beyond the government's reach. Racial profiling programs, such as the NSEERS, have failed to detect terrorists. They also have discouraged immigrants from complying and registering because immigrants understandably fear detention and deportation. Security concerns have also perverted the debate on the reform of the U.S. immigration system. In September 2003 Tom Ridge, former secretary of homeland security, suggested that some sort of legalization program was necessary "to come to grips with the presence of 8 to 12 million illegals."[15] Opponents of "earned legalization" (upon payment of fees) and guest worker programs argued that punitive law enforcement measures and stricter border controls were the only options in fighting against illegal immigration. They opposed any form of legalization that appeared to them to be rewarding those who have broken the law. The other side of the coin was that an increasing number of illegal immigrants remained "below the radar." Meanwhile, legal residents were turned into unlawful suspects because of the backlash effects of the tightening of the naturalization process. In 2007 the government denied 89,863 applications for naturalization, about 12 percent of those presented. Though precise figures are not publicly available, an increasing number of these denials involved immigrants who believed they were in good legal standing and would have continued to live in the United States legally—had they not sought to become citizens. In April 2008 the *New York Times* reported a series of cases, including Brad Darnell, an electrical engineer from Canada who came legally to the United States in 1991. When he applied for naturalization in 2007, he discovered that a ten-year-old conviction for domestic violence—although reduced to a misdemeanor and erased from his public record—made him ineligible to become a U.S. citizen or to stay in the country. In Florida, aspiring citizens believed that their green cards entitled them to vote. When they reported their election activities on their applications, their naturalization was rejected, and U.S. authorities ordered them deported.[16] Other cases have been reported by NGOs and advocacy groups, and many of these long-term legal immigrants had no other option than to become illegal in order to stay in the country.

Last but not least, the bureaucratic restructuring of immigration into homeland security has actually created more problems than it has solved. According to Margaret Stock, immigration attorney and lieutenant colonel in the U.S. Army Reserve, assigned to West Point, "policies and practices that fail to properly distinguish between terrorists and legitimate travelers are ineffective security tools that waste limited resources, damage the U.S. economy, alienate those groups whose cooperation the U.S. government needs to prevent terrorism, and foster a false sense of security by promoting the illusion that we are reducing the threat of terrorism."[17] Critics of "Fortress America" highlighted the negative effects on the U.S. economy, education, and research. Overseas travel to the United States declined 17 percent from 2000 through 2006. Certain security processes imposed extraordinary delays on many legitimate travelers such as businessmen, international students, and researchers. In a report published by DHS, experts admitted that "traveling to the United States is becoming viewed as at least an uncertain, potentially unpleasant experience and at worst a major hassle."[18] In 2006 the Rice-Chertoff Initiative initiated the "Secure Borders and Open Doors" policy in order to address the issues raised by excessive security measures. However, crucial dysfunctions still undermine the U.S. system. Individuals are sometimes falsely identified, with unpleasant results ranging from secondary questioning to arrest. Security measures increase the amount of time CBP officers spend on average with each passenger, leading to congestion in Federal Inspection Services facilities and "exacerbating the underlying and historically inadequate staffing" at U.S. ports of entry."[19] Finally, a decade after 9/11, the United States still has no reliable system for verifying that foreign visitors have actually left the country. In 2009, for example, DHS officials admitted that they did not know if more than two hundred thousand visitors had left or overstayed their visas. One of them was Hosam Maher Husein Smadi, a nineteen-year-old Jordanian who had overstayed his tourist visa and was accused in court of plotting to blow up a Dallas skyscraper.[20]

The Intelligence Reform and Terrorist Prevention Act of 2004 has required an in-person consular interview of most applicants for nonimmigrant visas between the ages of fourteen and seventy-nine. Visa applications are now automated in the Consular Consolidated Database, and the system is linked with other databases to flag problems that might affect the issuance of a visa. Consular officers are also required to send suspected names, especially for applicants from Muslim countries, to the FBI for a name check program called Visa Condor, which is part of the broader Security Advisory Opinion system. Since the United States has suspended its longtime practice of reissuing or revalidating visas, visa holders must now often travel abroad to a consular post to refile their application. As a result backlogs have swelled in some posts in Canada, as the number of visa overstays has increased. In addition, DHS experts express strong reservations about the NSEERS process, which is "intrusive and time consuming, not only for travelers but also for CBP officers."[21]

The processing of citizenship applications is marked by similar lengthy delays and backlogs. In a context characterized by counterterrorist measures targeting immigrants and heated debates over immigration reform, an increased number of permanent residents want to guarantee their status by becoming U.S. citizens. This trend has been encouraged by citizenship campaigns organized since 2005 by immigrant advocacy groups, such as the Illinois Coalition for Immigrant and Refugee Rights. Furthermore, uncharacteristically large numbers of permanent residents sought naturalization in 2006 and 2007 in order to vote in the November 2008 presidential election. While being overwhelmed by this surge in applications, the U.S. Citizenship and Immigration Services decided in January 2007 to increase the cost for filing naturalization applications by 80 percent. As a result it received 460,000 applications in July 2007 and was unprepared to deal with this "350 percent increase in one month."[22] During fiscal year 2007 nearly 1.4 million applications were filed, and the processing time rose to eighteen months, from formerly seven. By the end of that year, USCIS had approximately one million cases on file pending adjudication.

Moreover, courts have been overwhelmed by cases challenging immigration administrative decisions. The implementation of the most restrictive measures led to increasingly lengthy periods of detention and a failure to conduct custody reviews during the mandated time frame. In 2001 the U.S. Supreme Court ruled that an alien with a final order of removal should not be detained for longer than six months. Yet Immigration and Customs Enforcement remains unable to properly oversee the growing detention caseload generated by DHS's planned enhancements to secure the borders. The DHS Office of Inspector General has recently admitted that, among the Post-Order Custody Review (POCR) files reviewed by ICE, "custody decisions were not made in over 6% of cases, and were not timely in over 19% of cases."[23] The POCR program is, according to the Office of Inspector General, an "outdated, difficult to use, inefficient case management system." Therefore,

> some aliens have been suspended from the review process without adequately documented evidence that the alien is failing to comply with efforts to secure removal. In addition, cases are not prioritized to ensure that aliens who are dangerous or whose departure is in the national interest are removed, or that their release within the United States is adequately supervised. Finally, ICE has not provided sufficient guidance on applying the Supreme Court's "reasonably foreseeable future" standard, and does not systematically track removal rates—information that is necessary for negotiating returns and for determining whether detention space is used effectively.[24]

It is unlikely that this process effectively enhances national security. In 2007 the Office of Inspector General examined the situation of forty-five persons who were detained for more than six months. Only three of them were considered to be a threat to national security, and eight were violent criminals—compared with fifteen who had no criminal record, eight who were accused of sexual assault or domestic violence, and seven who suffered from mental problems. Additionally, for those POCR cases whose deportation should have been prioritized, it appeared that ICE did not always advise the Travel Document Unit that these cases required expedited processing.

Counterterrorist Strategies and Insecurity

The current expansive use of the notion of national security entails an equally expansive perception of what defines terrorism. The rules governing the war on terror highly depend on what terrorism entails. Conversely, such a definition affects criminal laws and mechanisms of enforcement. The attempt to define and contain terrorism goes back at least to the Roman occupation of Palestine (around 67–73 CE) when the *Sicarii* were regarded as a terrorist movement. Since then, the question of how to define terrorism has remained a sensitive one, which could not be detached from the question of who is the defining agency—especially when one man's terrorist is another man's freedom fighter.[25] Almost all the proposed formulations prior to 9/11 have condemned terrorism without clearly defining it. These formulations were also affected by particular political motivations. The Arab Convention for the Suppression of Terrorism adopted by the League of Arab States, for example, explicitly prevented the Palestinian fight against Israel from being defined as terrorism. With regard to the European Convention on the Suppression of Terrorism, the main concern of EU member states was to avoid militant groups, such as the Basque ETA, claiming that countermeasures used against them constituted terrorism.

In the post-9/11 era, terrorism has been interpreted very broadly, creating a new normative balance between civil liberties and the requisites of national security. The USA Patriot Act, for example, defines "terrorist activity" to include virtually any use or threat to use a weapon against a person or property. In an effort to counter terrorism, the law also targets individuals who support a group. Thus, as professor of law at Georgetown University David Cole notes, "an immigrant who offered his services in peace negotiating to the IRA in the hope of furthering the peace process in Great Britain could be deported as a terrorist."[26] The Border Protection, Antiterrorism, and Illegal Immigration Control Act of 2005 has raised similar concerns. According to many legal and humanitarian NGOs, it would not only harm refugees and asylum seekers by treating them as criminals, but would also criminalize social workers, church volunteers, and others who are simply doing their jobs assisting asylum seekers, unaccompanied children, or trafficking victims in need. In addition, Title II of the Patriot Act, entitled Enhanced Surveillance Procedures, expanded the government's powers to intercept wire, oral, and electronic communications; to gain access to certain medical and library records; to block notification of the search to the person whose records have been searched; and to permit information sharing between law enforcement and intelligence agencies. In 2008 the Department of Homeland Security disclosed the existence of a database collecting information on all travelers—American citizens included—entering the country by land. Exempted from Privacy Act protections, this data would be stored for fifteen years and could be used in criminal investigations or shared with foreign agencies when relevant to their hiring or contracting decisions.

In the EU the 2002 Council Framework Decision on Combating Terrorism provided a very broad definition of terrorist activities, including acts "causing extensive destruction to a government or public facility, including an information system, a fixed platform located on a continental shelf, a public space or private property likely to endanger human life or result in major economic loss."[27] The Framework Decision identifies terrorism, in its article 1, as "one of the most serious violations of the universal values and principles" on which the EU is founded, as well as a "threat to democracy, and economic and social development." Thus terrorism is perceived not only as a threat to citizens' lives but also as a global threat to the very foundations of the EU in terms of both its political and economic structures, and its fundamental principles (such as dignity, solidarity, rule of law, and democracy). However, according to Jörg Monar, expert on security governance at the College of Europe,

> If one wants to assess this definition of a common threat, one has to say that it is most vague on what is actually threatened besides citizens' lives. By repeating all the time that the values of the EU are threatened it is not made any clearer how post-9/11terrorism actually threatens certain EU declared values. . . . The argument about threats posed to the economic and social development of the EU is not developed in any clearer terms either.[28]

As the fight against terrorism still resides with the EU member states, the Framework Decision sets only minimum standards. Member states are free to go further, by establishing their own list of terrorist groups and by listing additional terrorist offenses. There is no judicial scrutiny related to the establishment of these lists. The EU's broad and vague definition of terrorism thus allows European governments to extend the list of criminal offenses, which may serve agendas distinct from fighting terrorism. Yet the connection between the fight against terrorism and some of these "antiterrorist" measures is sometimes less than evident. In France, for example, the Day-to-Day Security Law of October 2001 requires all motorbikes to be registered, makes speeding of forty kilometers per hour or more above the limit subject to a revocation of the driver's license, and makes the organization of music festivals subject to approval of local councils. It allows the seizure of any amplifying sound equipment during a private party if the "public peace is deemed to be violated" (article 53). It also imposes tighter regulations on owners of domestic animals and allows for the killing of the pets if they represent a danger to the public (article 45).[29] In Germany, official security experts exhibit a wide understanding of insecurity as they assess the present threats deriving from different sources, such as attacks against critical infrastructures, but also macroeconomic instability, man-made environmental threats, migratory pressure, ethnic conflicts, and cyber attacks.[30] In other

European countries the fight against terrorism has been similarly extended to various issues, such as football hooliganism and child pornography.

As in the United States, the growth in the scope of privacy encroachment has been fueled by the escalation of antiterrorism policymaking. In many European countries, notably France, Great Britain, and Germany, bank accounts, postal data, and Internet and phone records can be accessed by the police or security forces—without the knowledge or consent of the person under surveillance. In countries where ID cards have been part of daily life for many years, the obligation of citizens to carry identification documents has now been coupled with the extension of biometric data involving the scanning of fingerprints, retinas, or facial structures. In France, new antiterrorist legislation extended the national database of genetic information beyond sex offenses and advocated the introduction of lesser crimes, such as theft. In 2007 the government suggested introducing DNA tests for asylum seekers and refugees. In 2008 the French government suggested creation of a database aimed at collecting information on all kinds of activists involved in politics, unions, NGOs, and religious groups since the age of thirteen— without any limitations in the range of information collected nor any time limit in retaining the data.

Security measures at border checkpoints have generated an upward spiral of controls for a broad range of law enforcement and intelligence purposes. In the United States the Aviation and Transportation Security Act of 2001 was followed by the Enhanced Border Security and Visa Reform Act of 2002 and the Intelligence Reform and Terrorism Prevention Act of 2004. In Europe the Visa Information System was created with the intent of supporting the coordination of data between EU consular officials, immigration, asylum, and border authorities for the 134 countries that require EU entry visas. Reportedly, the system would store the personal and biometric data of approximately 20 million Schengen visa applicants. EU databases additionally include the Schengen Information System, Eurodac (for asylum applicants and illegal immigrants), and the proposed entry-exit system that would facilitate nonborder identity checks based on biometric data, performed by law enforcement authorities.[31] In addition to these databases, the Prüm Treaty, signed in May 2005 by seven EU countries, has allowed the exchange of data from DNA and fingerprints. The European data protection supervisor, Peter Hustinx, has expressed concerns that "all travelers are put under surveillance and are considered a priori as potential law breakers." Furthermore, the use of sensitive data with little oversight or accountability "significantly weakens protections of personal data of European citizens."[32]

The lack of a cohesive counterterrorist framework is coupled with institutional and technical deficiencies. Both the United States and European countries have reorganized their domestic and border protection institutions to enhance homeland security and prevent terrorism. In addition to other new initiatives, the British government created the Joint Intelligence Analysis Center, drawing together about one hundred officials from eleven intelligence agencies, including MI5, MI6, the police, and the defense and transport ministries. In Germany, federal and state ministers of the interior implemented new measures in 2004 to improve coordination between intelligence and law enforcement agencies. As a result, a Joint Coordination Center was established in Berlin, consisting of state- and local-level agencies. Furthermore, the twelve new EU member states have joined the oldest fifteen members in their efforts to harmonize their instruments to combat terrorism and reinforce operational capacity according to the EU's Counter-Terrorism Strategy. This strategy set out four objectives: to prevent new recruits of terrorism; better protect potential targets; pursue and investigate members of existing networks; and improve EU's capacity to respond to and manage the consequences of terrorist attacks. In its introduction to the revised 2004 EU Plan of Action on Combating Terrorism, the European Council emphasized the importance of various EU agencies (such as Europol and Eurojust), and the Office of the Coordinator for Counterterrorism, as well as the crucial role of the European Arrest Warrant and other law enforcement measures.

Nevertheless, sparring over control and resource issues continues among the various entities subsumed within DHS or the EU framework. In the United States, problems persist in interagency coordination, as illustrated by the issue of a terror database. In 2003 President Bush ordered the intelligence community to centralize data on terrorism suspects. This led to the creation of TIDE, the Terrorist Identities Datamart Environment, which is a storehouse for data about individuals who the intelligence community believes might harm the United States. Information collected by TIDE (from field reports, captured documents, and sometimes rumors) feeds other databases used by the Transportation Security Administration, the Consular Lookout and Support System at the State Department, the Interagency Border and Inspection System at DHS, the Justice Department's National Crime Information Center, and the Terrorist Screening Center at the FBI. Once someone is on the list, it is virtually impossible for them to get off it—even for U.S. citizens, who represent 5 to 10 percent of the listings. In addressing one problem, TIDE has spawned others. First, TIDE has more than quadrupled in four years, from fewer than 100,000 files in 2003 to about 435,000 in 2007. Russ Travers, in charge of TIDE at the National Counterterrorism Center, admitted that the growing database threatens to overwhelm the people who manage it, and expressed his concerns about the long-term quality control.[33] Actually, the Government Accountability Office reported in 2004 and 2005 that misidentifications accounted for about half of the ten thousands of times a traveler's name triggered a watch-list "hit." Second, the Transportation Security Administration, the Terrorist Screening Center, and other agencies decide to use TIDE information according to different criteria, which are classified. As a result, nine federal agencies operate twelve different watch lists, and the Office of Inspector General has recently criticized DHS for failing to consolidate a single database of terrorist suspects. As a result, these intelligence failures let a would-be bomber fly to Detroit from Amsterdam in December 2009, despite the fact that his own father had reported him to the U.S. authorities.

The process can lead to errors at any stage because of mixed-up names and unconfirmed information. For example, in 2006 Senator Ted Stevens, an Alaska Republican, complained that his wife, Catherine, was repeatedly delayed by the TSA because she was listed as "Cat Stevens"—the name of the British pop star who converted to Islam. That same year, CBS's *60 Minutes* revealed that fourteen of the nineteen terrorists who committed the 9/11 attacks were still listed—five years after their deaths. As the homeland security expert and president of the Center for National Policy Stephen Flynn argues, the U.S. system is now a combination of "security-at-any-cost" with a "cure-is-worse-than-the-disease" approach. Although the Department of Homeland Security was supposed to minimize homeland vulnerability, inadequate funding and bureaucratic intricacy have limited its preventive capacity. Tellingly, more than a dozen intelligence professionals declined the position of DHS intelligence chief; and all the federal departments (such as the Defense, Homeland Security, Justice, and State) whose missions include national security received dismal grades in 2006 and 2007 (with an average of D-plus), according to the assessment of federal agencies' compliance with the Federal Information Security Management Act.

As in the United States, European countries suffer from a dysfunctional institutional architecture in combating terrorism. In most of these countries, responsibility for different aspects of homeland security remains scattered across several ministries and intelligence and law enforcement agencies.[34] In Germany, for example, the most important domestic and intelligence authorities (the Federal Bureau of Criminal Investigation and the Federal Bureau for the Protection of the Constitution) are still divided among one federal and sixteen state bureaus. In Italy coordination between different ministries and intergovernmental agencies remains limited despite the creation of various structures designed to break down institutional barriers, such as the Committee for Strategic Anti-Terrorism Analysis. Furthermore, Italy still does not have a central database for terrorist suspects, and there is no national prosecuting office for terrorism offenses. Antiterrorist investigations instead are led by twenty-six different regional prosecutors, who rarely share their findings with the intelligence services. The reluctance of European countries to share information and intelligence raises concerns about their capacity in fighting terrorism. After the Madrid bombings, for example, Spanish police officials refused to share information with the French authorities on the types of explosives that had been used in the attacks. "The reason for this attitude," Davide Casale argues in his study of EU counterterrorism, "can ultimately be identified as mistrust" between national intelligence agencies.[35] As in the United States, many efforts have been undertaken and important steps forward made by the European countries. Yet more coordination is utterly necessary.

At the EU level, measures to combat terrorism have been hastily adopted on a piecemeal basis. Existing structures and instruments have been extended, while new ones have been created and implemented. For example, Europol was asked to establish a Task Force for the Fight against Terrorism, as well as an operational center known as the Counter Terrorist Task Force. In addition, Europol launched new programs, such as the Counter Terrorism Program, the Counter Proliferation Program, the Preparedness Program, and the Networking Program. A data protection officer has been appointed to Eurojust, which was asked to work in close cooperation with Europol. Alongside Europol and Eurojust, joint investigation teams were created, in addition to the EU Police Chiefs Operational Task Force and the network of Counterterrorist Liaison Officers, which belongs to the Police Working Group on Terrorism. The Second Pillar Counterterrorism Working Party and the Justice and Home Affairs Terrorism Working Group were also expanded. Many experts have expressed strong reservations about this hectic and haphazard process. According to Monica den Boer, "the involvement of all these agencies, groups, and individuals means that the EU's counterterrorism venue may well be characterized as a crowded policy area, which is mainly caused by a gradual and incremental form of policy-making."[36] The consequential question is whether these agencies and instruments are sufficiently coherent and robust to make an impact on terrorism. To date, this multidimensional and multiagency approach has created problems, including bureaucratic obstacles that are difficult to overcome. Furthermore, according to Doron Zimmermann, an expert on international security at the National Defense University in Washington D.C., "it is not to be taken for granted that the Union is the right vehicle in Europe for the multilateral fight against terrorism." He suggests that

> the lack of the EU's executive powers with respect to regulating the behavior of member states relative to a common threat such as terrorism raises the fundamental question of whether the Union itself, as opposed to its constituent members, is an appropriate body for initiating, driving, coordinating, and to some extent even assuming the role of political leadership in counterterrorism in Europe. . . . The implications for robust European counterterrorism, finally, are grave. They must be sought on the structural level of this institutionalist cooperative framework, where the undue importance conceded to processes, and the bureaucratic infrastructure they require, in many different fields of Union activity up to and including counterterrorism is neither intended nor unintended, but *inherent*.[37]

The twenty-seven EU member states remain fully sovereign when it comes to implementing the EU counterterrorist initiatives. Although they agree in principle that cooperation at the EU level is needed because of the cross-border nature of terrorist activities, they remain reluctant to give the EU the powers that could interfere with their own security legislation, limiting their national sovereignty. As a result, the EU lacks a harmonized framework, and its operational capabilities suffer from major limitations. This leads to the proliferation of agencies and expert groups, while the majority of EU antiterrorist measures are either only partially implemented or not implemented at all.

Admittedly, some argue that more terrorist attacks would have happened in the United States and Europe without the introduction of these counterterrorism measures. As I mentioned in the opening of this chapter, there is no way to address this counterfactual problem when it comes to evaluating the efficiency of the war on terror. There are also many asymmetries between terrorists and their targeted governments that work to the terrorists' advantage. First, unlike many challenges, Todd Sandler and Daniel Arce argue in their study of counterterrorist strategies, "there is no solution to transnational terrorism because it is a cost-effective tactic of the weak against a more formidable opponent. . . . Even effective antiterrorism campaigns will only temporarily work until the terrorists either find new leaders or sources of resources. Even if a terrorist group is annihilated, a new group may surface for some other cause. Thus, terrorism can be put into remission but it cannot be eliminated."[38] Second, "liberal democracies present terrorists with target-rich environments. In contrast, terrorists take a low profile and hide among the general population, thus they offer a target-poor environment to the government. Governments have to protect everywhere, while terrorists can focus on vulnerable targets. Terrorists have a second-mover advantage, while the governments have a first-mover disadvantage, because terrorists can observe how governments harden potential targets and then attack accordingly."[39] Yet the fact that the war on terror has not properly addressed the pre-9/11 intelligence deficiencies raises legitimate concerns about security in Western countries.

Furthermore, the introduction of restrictions on individual freedom of assembly, religion, speech, and the right to privacy have often been unrelated to effective efforts to fight terrorism. In February 2008, for example, the French government announced that the number of closed-circuit television (CCTV) cameras would triple by 2009 and that spy drones would be deployed across French skies in order to tackle the problem of urban violence in poor suburbs. The Italians are today among the most spied-upon people in the world, with seventy-six intercepts per one hundred thousand inhabitants each year.[40] Wiretapping and electronic eavesdropping are widely used by the secret services, the police, and the judiciary, even though the Italian constitution guarantees privacy of information. Do these practices enhance the fight against terrorism? The answer is unclear, although we do know that they have fueled several recent political scandals because conversations of high-profile politicians are routinely taped and then leaked to journalists. The probability is that these practices will over time come to be used increasingly against not only suspected terrorists but anyone involved in various forms of civil protests or suspected of antisocial behavior. In 2008 the London police threatened protestors with arrest under antiterror laws during the protests over Tibet that greeted the arrival of the Olympic flame in the city. In Spain a group of musicians were accused of the terrorist offense of "glorification" (*enaltecimiento*) for a song whose lyrics talked about ETA and the Guardia Civil. Any kind of designated deviant group may become the target of security measures if it is perceived as a source of potential security threats. As noted by Professor Ronald Crelinsten of the Center for Global Studies at the University of Victoria, "this includes not only immigrant and refugee communities, but also different ethnic communities, gay and lesbian communities, religious and cultural minorities, or deviant subcultures."[41]

The Issue of Target Hardening

As mentioned, the war on terror has been based on the assumption that the people who are perceived as the highest threat to homeland security are immigrants, Muslim foreigners, and Muslim nationals. In the United States, Sunni and Shiite Muslims (both U.S. citizens and nonnationals) were the fastest-growing categories listed by TIDE and other watch lists. In Europe, the idea that Islamist terrorism constitutes the major threat has been strengthened by the Madrid and London bombings, as well as by failed or foiled terrorist attacks involving members of Islamist networks on both sides of the Atlantic. The 2005 Strategy for Combating Radicalization and Recruitment to Terrorism did refer to "other types of terrorism" that continue to pose a serious threat to EU citizens, but it focused on "violent religious extremism." However, this strategy is somewhat misleading, because it blurs the distinction between actual and existential threats, limiting the efficacy of antiterrorist measures.

In the United States many of the initiatives taken in the aftermath of 9/11, such as roundups of individuals based on their national origin and religion, were poorly planned and have undermined their own objectives in terms of security. They have helped, however, to extend the scope of the counterterrorist fight and to consolidate the practice of scapegoating. In August 2002, for example, the INS announced the deportation of about one hundred Pakistanis. They were held for months and deported at the urging of top Pakistani officials. The majority of the deportees were arrested for violation of the new immigration regulations. None had ties to terrorist organizations. No terrorist has been found, either, among Mexicans arrested at the southern border, and the DHS has recently indicated that no chemical materials, explosives, or terrorists have been seized at the U.S.-Mexico border since 9/11. With regard to those classified as Other Than Mexicans, their share of apprehensions along the U.S.-Mexico border rose from 1.1 percent in 1997 to 5.8 percent in 2004. The majority of these were from Honduras, El Salvador, Brazil, and Guatemala—none of which countries was a likely source of terrorists intent on attacking the United States. There is also no evidence that the extremely small number of Arabs and Muslims apprehended at the border constituted a threat to national security. From 1999 to 2004 the number of Special Interest Aliens (SIAs)[42] apprehended reached 1,615 (0.02 percent of all apprehensions along the southern border). The threat to national security cannot be quantified only through the number of SIAs apprehended by the Border Patrol, yet not one of the SIAs apprehended had been involved in terrorist attacks.

Indeed, concerns about terrorist infiltration increased in the aftermath of 9/11, based on the false assumption that illegal immigrants from Mexico were potential terrorists. A senior fellow at the Foreign Policy Research Institute argued, for example, that "the greatest threat to homeland security comes from illegals who enter the country through its porous borders in order to attack. . . . As Mexicans have known for years, the border is wide open, and anyone who wants to can easily enter the United States covertly." He suggested that the United States should "put more people on the border, either using volunteers like the Minutemen, or using the U.S. Army Reserve and the border states' National Guards."[43] This rhetoric was echoed by high-level officials (such as retired admiral James Loy, DHS acting deputy direc-tor) and congressmen. Representative Solomon Ortiz, a Texas Democrat, stated in 2005 that "the southern border is literally under siege, and there is a real possibility that terrorists, particularly al-Qaeda forces, could exploit this series of holes in our law enforcement system."[44] Again, despite widespread alarms raised over terrorist infiltration, not a single known terrorist entered the United States from Mexico, before or after 9/11. Robert Leiken, director of the Immigration and National Security Program at the Nixon Center, came to this conclusion in a study of the biographical data of 373 terror-ists in Western Europe and North America.[45] Yet he continued to raise the specter of terrorists coming through the southern border, because, he argued, "Moroccan affiliates of al-Qaeda who have learned Spanish may well come in on the Mexican border."[46]

Another urgent task, according to U.S. authorities, is to screen "high risk" populations residing in the United States by implementing racial profiling measures. To date, however, these measures have been mostly ineffective. The NSEERS program, which required male noncitizens from twenty-five mostly Arab and Muslim countries to register with the INS between November 2002 and April 2003, proved quite unsuccessful. Of the eighty-three thousand who came forward, nearly thirteen thousand were placed in deportation proceedings in return for their cooperation. It seems that many were actually deported (the INS never revealed the total number), but no one was charged with crimes related to terrorism. James Ziglar, INS com-missioner before the creation of DHS, admitted that "the people who could be identified as terrorists weren't going to show up. This project was a huge exercise and cost us resources in the field that could have been much better deployed. As expected, we got nothing out of it."[47] Other profiling measures have also failed. The interviewing of Arab and Muslim men launched in March 2002 did not identify a single terrorist. The Department of Jus-tice interviewed about two thousand subjects, and twenty were taken into custody, most of whom were charged with immigration violations. None was linked with terrorism.[48] In July 2002 the Justice Department required immigrants to report changes of address within ten days. The INS was over-whelmed and unable to process the majority of the notices. Furthermore, since this program operates on an honor system, terrorists can simply provide false information.

The U.S. government's actions in the aftermath of 9/11 have directly impacted more than sixty thousand individuals, through religiously based interrogations, the singling out of Arabs and Muslims at airports because of their distinct names or appearance, or the termination or denial of employment because of religious discrimination, detentions, raids, and the closures of charities. According to *Statewatch*, more than seventy-one thousand stop-and-searches were conducted in Great Britain in 2002–3 as part of the war on terror. Arrests were made in only 1.18 percent of cases, mainly for reasons not connected to terrorism.[49] During 2007–8 the police stopped and searched 1,035,438 persons and 10,485 vehicles, totaling 1,045,923 stop-and-searches. This was 9 percent more than the 2006–7 total of 962,897 under section 1 of the Police and Criminal Evidence Act of 1984, as well as other legislation. Meanwhile, 444 stop-and-searches were made under section 44 of the Terrorism Act of 2000, of which 0.6 percent resulted in arrests.[50] In the Netherlands the leader of the Christian Democrat group in Parliament declared, shortly after the assassination of Theo van Gogh: "If it is about preventing an attack it is better to have temporarily ten innocent people in jail than one terrorist with a bomb on the street."[51] Unfortunately, the detention of ten innocent people does not always provide more safety; it may instead facilitate further radicalization.

According to Peter Clarke, the head of the counterterrorism branch of London's Metropolitan Police, "most terrorism-related investigations begin with intelligence gathered from foreign governments, intelligence agencies or electronic eavesdropping." He added that, because of the increasing suspicion of Muslims, many of them are "reluctant to report co-religionists to the police, even if they disagree with their militant view."[52] In Spain in 2003, after a series of anti-Muslim raids throughout Catalonia, several Muslim organizations issued a joint statement complaining of "unnecessary violence" that "wiped out years of collaborative work with the local authorities."[53] For the Central Council of Muslims in Baden-Württemberg, the arbitrary nature of police raids conducted in December 2002 had broken down trust and all possibilities of future collaboration with German law enforcement authorities. As in many European countries, Liz Fekete argues, "the police and intelligence services, by alienating potential allies in enhancing the security of all, exacerbated and made more opaque any potential genuine threat."[54]

Some U.S. experts and NGOs have reached a similar conclusion. The broadened powers and increased activity of security agents and immigration authorities have greatly concerned some Arab Americans and American

Muslims. This has damaged the ability to obtain information from members of the Muslim community about possible terrorist-related suspects. The Arab American Institute noted, for example, that an effort by the FBI to recruit Arabic-speaking agents in New Jersey was met with suspicion by Muslim community members upset by the detention of relatives, friends, and acquaintances by federal authorities.[55] According to the Migration Policy Institute, "the government conducted roundups of individuals based on their national origin and religion. These roundups failed to locate terrorists, and damaged one of our great potential assets in the war on terrorism: the communities of Arab- and Muslim-Americans."[56]

Counterterrorism and the Sense of Insecurity

By linking terrorism and immigration, current counterterrorism policies foster the mistaken belief that measures such as limiting the number of immigrants will reduce the threat. Yet the actual increase of illegal immigration raises both the fears (of being attacked) and expectations (to be protected) of U.S. and European citizens who are drawn into supporting the spiraling effects of counterterrorism: more security measures generate more fears, which in turn increase the demand for further security measures. In the long term, this approach may damage the credibility of the authorities involved in the war on terror, undermining governmental legitimacy because a continuation of insecurity may be interpreted as a sign of incapacity and fuel new feelings of insecurity.

Effective antiterrorist campaigns can also, paradoxically, reinforce a sense of insecurity, as illustrated by the announcement in June 2002 that José Padilla, a U.S. citizen and alleged al-Qaeda associate, had been arrested while plotting to explode a "dirty bomb" in an American city. The public's view of terrorism as a major problem for the country increased from 22 percent in May to 33 percent in June.[57] By multiplying counterterrorist measures, policymakers generate high expectations. But the continuation of insecurity is interpreted as a sign of governmental incapacity and thus fuels an increasing feeling of insecurity. Meanwhile, by planting fear in the public (through, for example, the color-coded alarm), policymakers fuel a growing political distrust—as illustrated in May 2010 by the reaction of U.S. public opinion in the aftermath on the arrest of the failed Times Square bomber. Only 46 percent of American respondents believed at that time that the federal government was doing everything it could to prevent terrorist attacks in the United States. More to the point, only 33 percent believed that the government was effective in preventing the bombing, while 49 percent considered that the government had been simply lucky.[58] According to a Rasmussen Reports survey, 52 percent said the country is less safe today, up from 42 percent and the highest level measured over the prior three years.[59] More important, 60 percent believed that terrorists would always find a way to commit further attacks.[60]

In assessing the evolution of public opinion in both the United States and Europe, this section outlines a series of basic findings that are often troublesome. First, it appears that the multiplication of antiterrorist measures and tactical operations increases the public's concerns about the efficacy of the war on terror. In September 2007 the Center for American Progress Terrorism Index revealed that 84 percent of U.S. citizens did not believe that the United States was winning the war on terror, and more than 80 percent expected a terrorist attack on the scale of 9/11 within a decade. Fully 91 percent said the world has become more dangerous for Americans and the United States, while only 2 percent believed the world was safer.[61] A survey for the BBC found in December 2006 that 53 percent of the respondents believed the UK government was losing the war on terror, and 56 percent thought it was being lost by other Western governments. Four out of ten people questioned said they felt less safe now than when the war on terror began, while only 11 percent felt safer.[62] A large proportion of Americans and Europeans surveyed also believed that the war on terror had failed to weaken its prime target, al-Qaeda. An opinion poll survey conducted in twenty-three countries in September 2008 for the BBC World Service revealed that only 22 percent of the respondents believed that al-Qaeda had been weakened, while 29 percent believed that the U.S.-led war on terror had no major effect, and 30 percent feared that it had made al-Qaeda stronger. As illustrated by table 10, France had the largest number saying that al-Qaeda had been strengthened (48 percent), while only 7 percent believed that al-Qaeda had been weakened. Even in the United States, only 34 percent said that al-Qaeda had been weakened.

Second, concerns about the efficacy of the war on terror increase political distrust. During the George W. Bush administration there were brief spikes in approval ratings of the president in general and of his handling of terrorism. Yet the general pattern was one of a gradual decrease in both these ratings. The proportion of Americans who approved of the way Bush was handling terrorism dropped from 90 percent in September 2001 to 28 percent by June 2008.[63] In 2003, 71 percent believed that the government was effectively protecting the country from terrorism.[64] In 2007, only 50 percent

Table 10.   Public perception of the war on terror in selected countries (in % of respondents)

	Al-Qaeda has been weakened	Al-Qaeda is stronger	The war on terror has no effect on al-Qaeda
United States	34	33	26
France	7	48	33
Germany	34	31	24
UK	13	40	36
Italy	13	43	36

Source: Adapted from "US 'War on Terror' Has Not Weakened al Qaeda, Says Global Poll," World Public Opinion.Org (September 28, 2008). See http://www.worldpublicopinion.org/pipa/pdf/sep08/BBCAlQaeda_Sep08_rpt.pdf.

expressed such a belief.[65] A series of opinion poll surveys conducted by ABC News and the *Washington Post* confirmed the weak impact of securing the homeland in terms of public perception, as illustrated by table 11. Recent findings have confirmed this trend. The election of President Obama was followed by higher ratings of confidence and an increasing sense of security. In May 2009, 55 percent approved of the way Obama was handling terrorism.[66] Yet confidence in America's efforts in the war on terror dropped again in 2010. Shortly after the Christmas Day attempted bombing on a Detroit-bound plane, 44 percent of American respondents said the president was doing a good or excellent job on national security issues. However, in January 2010, only 21 percent believed that the government has made a "great deal of progress" in protecting Americans from acts of terrorism.[67]

As in the United States, European leaders faced a growing political distrust. When Gordon Brown, then prime minister, announced new antiterrorist measures in August 2007—including a new unified border force, and allowing police to detain terror suspects for longer than the current maximum of twenty-eight days—73 percent of the British population agreed that the government should give police whatever powers they need, putting combating terrorism ahead of concerns for civil liberties. Yet this claim for further counterterrorist actions was balanced by a high level of political distrust. Approximately 60 percent said that Brown's proposed new counterterrorism measures were more about looking tough on terrorism than actually making Britain safer, and 51 percent believed that new laws would make no difference to the level of terrorist threat facing Britain.[68] At the European level, only the Spanish expressed their satisfaction with the way their government handled terrorist threats after the Madrid bombings (up to 53 percent approval in 2007).[69]

Table 11. Evaluation of threat: Do you think the country is safer from terrorism? (in % of respondents)

	Much safer	Somewhat safer	Less safe	No difference
September 2003	24	42	27	4
September 2004	26	38	28	5
September 2006	19	36	37	6
September 2007	24	36	29	11

Source: *AEI Studies in Public Opinion*, July 24, 2008. See http://www.aei.org/publicopinion3.

Third, security concerns fueled demands for tougher measures despite resilient doubts about the efficacy of counterterrorism. In the United States 60 percent of the respondents to an ABC News / *Washington Post* poll survey claimed in 2006 that the government should do more to try to prevent further terrorist attacks (compared with 27 percent in 2001).[70] In 2007, 52 percent believed that the United States was inadequately prepared to deal with another terrorist attack (compared with 29 percent in 2003), demanding further security measures.[71]

Finally, when it comes to identifying both the nature of terrorism and the identity of the terrorists, there are variations among countries that deserve further inquiry. In Europe, for example, some states treat terrorism as a national issue (such as France, Spain, and the Netherlands). Others deem it to be a transnational issue (including Italy, Portugal, and Poland).[72] In both cases, the general public tends to believe that radical Islam poses the major threat, although the data collected by Europol show that this assumption is wrong. In 2007, for example, nine EU member states reported a total of 583 failed, foiled, or successfully executed attacks. This represented a 24 percent increase from what was reported in 2006 despite the implementation of tougher counterterrorism measures. Of the 583 attacks, only 4 were attributed to Islamist terrorism (2 failed and 2 attempted attacks), while 517 were claimed or attributed to separatist groups, mainly in Spain and France.[73] This trend raises the question of why Europeans tend to overestimate the threat of radical Islam. In contrast, Americans seem to underestimate the domestic origin of terrorism despite the multiplication of attacks committed by homegrown terrorists (either native-born or naturalized). In April 2010, to the question "Which do you think is the more serious threat to Americans?" 46 percent of the respondents mentioned international terrorism (committed by citizens from other countries), while 38 percent indicated a concern about domestic terrorism (committed by U.S. citizens).[74] In the aftermath of the failed Times Square attack, 46 percent believed that radical foreign Muslims pose a greater risk to the United States, and 24 percent mentioned homegrown radicals (like Oklahoma City bomber Timothy McVeigh). Yet although Faisal Shahzad, who confessed to the Times Square bombing attempt, was not native born, he was a U.S. citizen.

Actual and Existential Threats

It is commonly expected that the overall volume of threat messages and actual terrorist attacks affects how the public ranks terrorism as a major problem. Yet there is evidence that while both Americans and Europeans are to one degree or another worried about terrorism, they are less concerned by this threat than by other issues, such as unemployment, health care costs, and even global warming. This trend suggests a disjuncture between the evolution of public opinion and policy developments based on a "culture of hysteria."[75]

When Americans and Europeans are asked to evaluate the risk posed by terrorism to their countries, they express a high level of concern. The same proportion of Americans, for example, were worried in 2006 as were five years previously—and a strong majority (67 percent) were still very or somewhat worried, as illustrated by table 12.

Five years of intensively fighting against terrorism did little to reassure the American people. Furthermore, concerns about terrorism fuel an increasing personal sense of insecurity. In 2003 a poll survey conducted by Gallup/CNN/*USA Today* revealed that 60 percent of respondents had a stockpile of food and water at home in order to prepare for a terrorist attack.[76] In 2006 only 12 percent of American respondents felt personally safer (compared

Table 12.   Evaluation of threat: How worried are you that there will soon be another terrorist attack in the United States? (in % of respondents)

	Very worried	**Somewhat worried**	**Not too worried**	**Not at all worried**
October 10–14, 2001	27	40	19	12
October 2–6, 2002	20	46	22	11
August 5, 2003	13	45	29	12
October 15–19, 2004	17	43	27	12
July 13–17, 2005	25	44	19	11
August 9–13, 2006	23	44	21	10

Source: AEI Studies in Public Opinion, July 24, 2008. See http://www.aei.org/publicopinion3.

Table 13.   Evaluation of threat: How worried are you that you or someone in your family will become a victim of a terrorist attack? (in % of respondents)

	Very worried	**Somewhat worried**	**Not too worried**	**Not worried at all**
November 7, 2001	13	27	29	19
October 10–11, 2002	16	27	35	21
August 21–22, 2003	18	26	26	28
October 27–29, 2004	13	28	32	26
August 2–4, 2005	14	26	32	27
August 9–13, 2006	16	28	35	20

Source: AEI Studies in Public Opinion, July 24, 2008. See http://www.aei.org/publicopinion3.

with 31 percent in 2003).[77] Although a majority (55 percent) did not worry about being a victim of a terrorist attack in 2006, as illustrated by table 13, 44 percent expressed concerns (compared with 40 percent in November 2001).

In Europe 66 percent of respondents in Great Britain, 72 percent in Germany, and 85 percent in Spain said in 2004 that they worried about the threat of terrorism in their respective countries.[78] In France 66 percent declared that global terrorism was a major threat to their country.[79] In late June and early July 2007, two attempted car bombings were reported in London, and a car filled with gas cylinders and fuel crashed into the doors of Scotland's Glasgow Airport in another attack. Following these events, 52 percent of respondents in Great Britain expected a major attack to take place in the next twelve months.[80]

These trends, however, have to be put in perspective. In Europe the French and Italians worried more about global warming than terrorism in 2006. Terrorism was ranked first by the British (up to 43 percent of the respondents, compared with 26 percent in France and 29 percent in Spain).[81]

In 2009, 51 percent of European citizens considered unemployment to be the most important issue that their country faces—compared with 4 percent who mentioned terrorism. As illustrated by table 14, respondents in Spain expressed one of the highest levels of concern (up to 12 percent)—which can be explained by the fact that this country faces both ethno-nationalist terrorism (from the ETA) and Islamic terrorism (such as the Madrid bombings). In Great Britain, however, only 6 percent of respondents believed that terrorism was one of the two major issues facing the country—despite the London bombings.

Americans worry about terrorism as much as they worry about federal government debt—as illustrated by responses in May 2010 to the question

Table 14. List of the main concerns expressed by European citizens, in response to the following question: What do you think are the two most important issues facing (our country) at the moment (maximum two answers)? (in % of respondents)

	Unemployment	Economic situation	Crime	Rising prices/ inflation	Healthcare system	Immigration	Pensions	Taxation	Educational system	Housing	Terrorism	Environment	Energy	Defense/ foreign affairs
EU 27	51	40	19	19	14	9	8	7	7	5	4	4	3	2
BE	42	35	15	24	3	18	18	11	4	6	2	5	8	1
BG	48	51	33	25	14	1	9	3	4	1	1	1	3	1
CZ	50	53	17	22	13	4	14	5	5	7	1	2	2	1
DK	36	29	39	4	24	15	2	2	14	1	9	16	4	3
DE	58	46	13	16	21	4	7	7	14	0	3	4	2	1
EE	68	53	19	10	22	0	6	7	3	1	0	1	3	1
IE	61	50	23	14	24	2	3	8	5	3	1	2	1	0
EL	46	60	22	23	7	8	4	8	6	0	5	3	0	2
ES	66	55	11	10	2	6	2	6	3	7	12	2	0	2
FR	59	31	16	22	11	6	14	6	8	10	2	1	1	1
IT	45	41	18	31	6	10	4	15	3	3	4	3	2	1
CY	31	43	36	26	6	14	4	3	5	6	1	1	2	4
LV	64	50	17	6	20	4	8	11	8	1	0	0	1	0
LT	64	49	19	19	7	3	7	16	3	1	1	1	7	0
LU	52	29	12	24	6	8	8	4	14	21	3	4	3	2
HU	58	51	12	30	16	1	9	5	3	3	1	1	3	0
MT	21	32	5	41	10	34	4	8	2	2	0	8	24	0

NL	32	50	21	7	26	8	19	4	11	2	3	7	3	1
AT	**43**	36	18	28	11	17	9	7	13	2	2	5	2	2
PL	**48**	25	10	27	34	2	15	7	4	4	1	1	4	3
PT	**57**	36	18	29	11	1	11	10	4	2	1	1	0	2
RO	36	**53**	23	39	13	1	9	8	4	4	1	2	1	0
SI	**56**	52	16	19	12	1	10	10	2	4	0	2	1	7
SK	**64**	45	20	18	13	2	10	4	4	6	1	2	3	1
FI	**58**	27	10	9	35	11	12	10	5	2	1	7	7	2
SE	**63**	30	14	2	26	9	6	3	16	3	1	20	6	1
UK	**38**	28	36	8	10	29	6	5	6	8	6	2	6	5

Source: European Commission, EB 72, December 2009, p. 12. In bold, the highest results per country. Boxed figures show the highest results per value.

"How serious a threat to the future well-being of the United States do you consider each of the following issues?" Some 79 percent of the respondents believed that terrorism was an extremely or very serious threat, the same percentage expressed concerns about the future of the federal budget, and 83 percent cited unemployment as the major threat.[82] On a personal basis, the main concerns of Americans were being hurt in a car accident (54 percent) and not being able to pay bills (51 percent).[83] There is at least a consistent relationship between this ranking of concerns and actual risk threat. As Jessica Wolfendale notes, "Even after 9/11, there is a significantly greater likelihood of being killed by lightning strikes, bee stings, or do it yourself (DIY) accidents than being killed in a terrorist attack. The number of annual deaths from sport utility vehicles (SUVs) is reported to be greater than the total number of deaths caused by all terrorist acts combined."[84] The point is not to deny that terrorism is not a threat. Yet it is not the major threat, as argued by Richard Jackson, who notes that "the estimated 1,000–7,000 yearly deaths from terrorism pales into significance next to the 40,000 people who die every *day* from hunger . . . and the millions who die annually from diseases like influenza (3.9 million annual deaths), HIV-AIDS (2.9 million annual deaths), diarrhoeal (2.1 million annual deaths) and tuberculosis (1.7 million annual deaths)."[85] The European think tank Copenhagen Consensus points out, in a similar way, the gap between perceptions and realities:

> The number of lives lost or ruined by transnational terrorism is rather minor compared with other challenges. . . . On average only 420 people are killed and another 1249 are injured each year from transnational terrorist attacks. Nevertheless, the public in rich countries views transnational terrorism as one of the greatest threats. This is rather ironic since over 30,000 people die on US highways annually, yet highway safety is not as much of a public concern.[86]

These developments suggest that the principal challenge is how to develop new security mentalities and policing forms able to properly address the actual fears of U.S. and European citizens. They also suggest focusing on what constitutes the major threat to security posed by the emergence of homegrown terrorists. It is to this exploration that I turn my attention in the next chapter.

CHAPTER 6

Radicalization in the West

September 11 did not create anti-Muslim suspicion. The post-9/11 period, however, amplified previous prejudice and initiated a climate of harassment. Muslims have come under intense scrutiny on the chance they might be terrorists. At first the objective was to catch foreign radicals, as illustrated in the United States by mass arrests shortly after the attacks. Some twelve hundred Arab or Muslim males (presumably noncitizens) were arrested and detained under high-security conditions. In an effort to screen people coming from twenty-six Arab and Muslim-majority countries, the State Department imposed in October 2001 a mandatory twenty-day hold on all nonimmigrant visa applications submitted by men ages eighteen to forty-five. These measures were followed by FBI interviews, the "Absconders Initiative" designed to deport noncitizen males (usually for overstaying their visas), and the Special Registration Program. This massive roundup of male Arab and Muslim foreigners produced no terrorists.

Then a series of events on both sides of the Atlantic reflected the so-called "terrorist next door" phenomenon. In the United States, it started as soon as 2002, with the "Lackawanna Six" and the "Portland Seven." In these two cases, the majority of the terrorists were U.S. citizens (both first and second generation). Mohammed Reza Taheri-azar, who tried to kill people with his SUV on the campus of the University of North Carolina at Chapel Hill in 2006, was an Iranian-born U.S. citizen. Abdulhakim Mujahid Muhammad, who attacked a Little Rock, Arkansas, military recruiting office in 2009, was an American citizen (previously known as Carlos Bledsoe) who converted to Islam. Three of the suspects arrested in May 2009 on charges of plotting to bomb two synagogues in the Bronx and to shoot down planes at a military base in New Jersey were African American U.S. citizens. Of the 175 post-9/11 cases of Americans or U.S. residents convicted or charged of some form of Islamist terrorist activity directed against the United States, half involved U.S.-born citizens, and another third were naturalized citizens.[1] Evidence shows that the number of cases involving homegrown terrorists has risen sharply since 2008. Professor Bruce Hoffman of Georgetown University has identified fifteen plots to attack the United States in 2009, the majority from citizens or naturalized immigrants. That year, according to a report published by the Bipartisan Policy Center, at least forty-three American citizens or legal residents aligned with militant groups were charged or convicted in terrorism cases in the United States and elsewhere.[2] In 2010 the number of homegrown terrorists convicted or charged of terrorist offenses declined to thirty-three, but the number of victims reached fourteen (out of a total of seventeen since 9/11).

Likewise, in Europe, the Madrid terrorists were primarily composed of first-generation North African Muslim men but included nine Spaniards. The Hofstad group, tied to the van Gogh assassination, was a cluster of young Dutch Muslims as well as a small group of converts.[3] Three of the four London bombers were second-generation British citizens of Pakistani descent. Even more troubling was the multiplication of cases involving converts like the Walters brothers in the Netherlands, Germaine Lindsay in Great Britain, and Muriel Degauque, who lived in Belgium. The most crucial finding of the 2007 Europol report was that the vast majority of terrorist suspects were EU citizens (91 percent). This trend was due not only to the fact that the majority of attacks were plotted or committed by national separatist groups but also reflected an increase in the number of homegrown Islamist terrorists. In the United Kingdom, where two car bombs failed to explode in central London and one failed at Glasgow International Airport in July 2007, officials reported an increasing number of arrests of Islamist British nationals. Jacqui Smith, then home secretary, declared that the Security Service estimated the number of people in the UK believed to be operating terrorists increased from sixteen hundred in 2006 to two thousand in 2007. While some of this increase reflected the improved intelligence work done by police and counterterrorist agents, some was undoubtedly due to more-intensive recruitment by local terrorist groups.[4] In other EU countries, such as France, Austria, Bulgaria, Belgium, and Germany, the majority of Islamist terrorists arrested were also nationals. Dutch authorities reported in 2007 an increasing number of Dutch nationals and residents willing to participate in jihad inside and outside Europe.

In 2009, although the number of Islamist terrorist attacks had decreased in Europe, 110 suspected terrorists were arrested in relation to Islamist terrorism in eight countries (mainly in Spain, France, and Italy). Individuals born in North African countries represented 42 percent of all arrested persons. Nearly one-third of all suspects (30 percent) were EU citizens. The proportion of homegrown terrorists remained unchanged compared with 2008, at around one-fifth of all arrested suspects. According to Europol, "of particular concern are radicalized EU nationals who travel to conflict areas with the intent to take part in acts of illegal violence or join training camps. On their return, they may use their newly acquired skills and experience to act on their terrorist intentions, in actions that may be ordered by terrorist organizations from abroad. Furthermore, they can encourage others to follow their example."[5] In addition to these homegrown terrorists, Europol pointed out the issue of marginalized Somali youth as a target for radicalization and recruitment for terrorist activities.

Addressing the root causes of radicalization is therefore crucial, albeit complex and often controversial. The spectrum of perceived causes is extremely wide and includes both broad structural and individual motivational factors. Structural factors relate to long-term conditions of terrorism. These include recurrent political conflicts; extremist ideologies; inequality of power; rigid class structure; a sense of relative deprivation; the experience of social injustice; and the role of mass media. Motivational causes consist of the actual grievances that people experienced, motivating them to act, such as discrimination at work and racial profiling.[6] The relationship between securitization and radicalization is thus admittedly extremely complex and requires multidimensional theories of causation.[7] A real or perceived sense of alienation does not always lead to radicalization, and the radicalization process may take various forms, such as the desire to disengage from the host society, the rejection of the principles and institutions of liberal democracy, and the growing acquisition of violent attitudes. Terrorist recruitment represents the final stage of the radicalization process, which involves only a tiny minority of Muslims. Most of them are "unremarkable" people, suffering from a real or perceived sense of alienation, often self-radicalized and influenced by the jihadist narrative. According to Bruce Hoffman, these radicals pose a particular problem in the United States, as well as in Europe. They have less resources and abilities than al-Qaeda sleeper agents, but "because they are not part of actual terrorist groups, members of the network are much more difficult to identify and track. They have no terrorist record, no modus operandi, and no connections to known terrorists."[8] Europol reached a similar conclusion, noting that the threat is "increasingly likely to originate from self-radicalized individuals and a diversity of militant extremist groups, including those who are, or claim to be, affiliated with al-Qaeda."[9] In 2008 and 2009, for example, two-thirds of the individuals arrested on suspicion of involvement in Islamist terrorism could not be linked to specific terrorist organizations identified by EU authorities.

Furthermore, as Lydia Khalil, a former counterterrorism analyst for the New York Police Department, argues, "A law enforcement agency trying to ferret out a radical homegrown terrorist is looking for the proverbial needle in the haystack."[10] As demonstrated in this chapter, the homegrown terrorists do not fit any particular socioeconomic profile, neither in the United States nor in Europe. For example, of the cases for which ethnicity could be determined, only a quarter of the 175 U.S. citizens or residents convicted or charged of jihadist activity between 2001 and 2010 were of Arab descent— while 10 percent were African American, 13 percent Caucasian, 18 percent South Asian, 20 percent of Somali descent, and the rest either mixed race or of other ethnicities.[11]

The emergence of a new "enemy inside" raises two issues. The first relates to the efficiency of the counterterrorist measures implemented since 9/11. Did these measures target the real threat? Did both the U.S. and European security strategies pay enough attention to the homegrown radicalization process? If so, did these strategies address the key factors explaining the radicalization of young Americans and Europeans? There is evidence that both U.S. and European authorities did not do enough to prevent or limit the radicalization process. The Bush administration underestimated this threat on the assumption that radical jihad was unlikely to find fertile ground in the United States, where the Muslim population is among the most integrated, assimilated, and wealthy in the Western world. The 2006 National Security Strategy made only passing reference to this threat. In 2007 the Department of Homeland Security noted that "the United States is not immune to the emergence of homegrown radicalization and violent extremism within its borders."[12] The prevention of radicalization, however, was not prioritized on the security agenda. Europeans, by contrast, overestimated the threat posed by native Muslims—a trend fueled by high levels of Islamophobia before 9/11. Yet the EU waited until 2005 before developing a strategy designed to address the factors contributing to violent radicalization. The measures set out were a combination of soft measures (such as intercultural exchanges among young people) and hard ones (such as the prohibition of satellite broadcasts inciting terrorism). The European Commission also planned to deepen the dialogue with the Mediterranean countries on antiradicalization measures and to promote moderate Islam in third countries where Islam is the predominant religion.[13] I provide evidence that this strategy, however, did not address most of the factors contributing to the radicalization of young Muslims in Europe.

The second issue related to the counterproductive outcomes of the war on terror was the development of a culture of fear that justified racial profiling and discrimination. Both in the United States and Europe, there is evidence that the war on terror has increased the sense of alienation among Muslim communities. In response, a fragment of alienated minorities tends to radicalize—a trend beneficial to terrorist recruitment. As a result, policies designed to enhance security actually produce more insecurity. In the long term, both the United States and Europe may achieve a tragic self-fulfilling prophecy, as the current management of the Islamist threat encourages discourse and practices that actually increase the number of enemies within. The key paradox of the war on terror is therefore that it provides further opportunities to homegrown terrorists by imposing measures designed to address the issue of the "enemy inside."

Discrimination and Resentment

The European Monitoring Center on Racism and Xenophobia reported that Islamophobia dramatically increased in the EU member states in the aftermath of 9/11. It noted that "Muslims, especially Muslim women, asylum seekers and others, including those who 'look' Muslim or of Arab descent were at times targeted for aggression. Mosques and Islamic cultural centers were also widely targeted for damage and retaliatory acts."[14] Since then, Islamophobia has strengthened in Europe, prompted by a series of events such as the murder of Theo van Gogh in the Netherlands, the London and Madrid bombings, and the debate on the cartoons of the Prophet Muhammad published in a Danish newspaper in September 2005.[15] The monitoring center found that Islam is seen in many European countries as a monolithic bloc, engaged in a clash of civilizations, aggressive and supportive of terrorism. Conversely, anti-Muslim hostility was regarded as normal and often used to justify discriminatory practices. According to Baroness Warsi, cochair of Britain's Conservative Party and the first Muslim woman to serve in the Cabinet, prejudice against Muslims had "passed the dinner-table test."[16]

The highest proportion of respondents among Europeans who perceive that relations between Muslims and Western countries are generally bad is to be found in Germany. A 2003 survey found that 46 percent of respondents agreed that "Islam is a backward religion," 34 percent said that they were "distrustful of people of Islamic religion," and 27 percent believed that "immigration to Germany should be forbidden for Muslims." A subsequent survey, in 2004, reported that 93 percent of Germans associate "Islam" with "oppression of women" and 83 percent with "terrorism." In 2006 only 30 percent of Germans reported a "favorable opinion of Islam."[17] Several Muslim organizations have been accused of being a threat to internal security by both the media and the Verfassungsschutz (Federal Office for the Protection of the Constitution), especially groups connected to Millî Görüş. A similar tendency was noticeable in other European countries. In Italy a 2005 polling survey on intolerance among young people, conducted by UCEI (Unione delle Communità Ebraiche Italiane), found that more than 50 percent of the respondents stated that Muslims "support international terrorism" and have "cruel and barbaric laws."[18] In 2006, senior politicians in Italy's government launched a policy manifesto vowing to protect Western civilization from what they called "threats of Islamic fundamentalism" and a "moral vacuum." The manifesto, a document entitled "For the West, Force of Civilization" begins with the statement: "The West is in crisis. Attacked externally by fundamentalism and Islamic terrorism, it is not able to rise to the challenge. Undermined internally by a moral and spiritual crisis, it can't seem to find the courage to react." A 2004 opinion poll in the Netherlands revealed that 68 percent of respondents felt threatened by "immigrant or Muslim young people," 53 percent feared a terrorist attack by Muslims in the Netherlands, and 47 percent feared that eventually the Netherlands would be ruled by Islamic law.[19] In Spain the Real Instituto Elcano (a think tank that declares itself to be independent but has strong links with the Spanish Ministry of Foreign Affairs) published a survey in 2007 showing that 96 percent of those polled thought that Muslims were sexist, 90 percent thought that that they were authoritarian, and 68 percent that they were violent.[20]

Being part of the most affluent and integrated Muslim community in the Western world does not protect American Muslims against prejudice. A majority of Americans still have a negative perception of Muslims, despite the group's socioeconomic achievements and its overwhelming rejection of Islamic extremism. According to the Council of American-Islamic Relations (CAIR), 26 percent of Americans in 2006 expressed negative comments about Muslims (such as "terrorists," "towel-heads," and "rag-heads"), while only 6 percent had positive comments (such as "good people," and "faithful"). Nineteen percent agreed that the civil liberties of American Muslims should be restricted because of security needs.[21] Anti-Muslim fervor reached a new peak in 2009–10, as illustrated by a series of violent controversies including the planned "International Burn a Quran Day" (on the anniversary of the 9/11 attacks) sponsored by pastor Terry Jones in Florida, the proposed building of Islamic centers or mosques in California and Tennessee, as well as a similar project near Ground Zero, the site of the former World Trade Center towers in New York City.

On both sides of the Atlantic, Islamophobia fuels anti-Muslim violence and discriminatory practices. Europe-wide statistics on the extent of anti-Muslim attacks are unavailable because figures are hard to collect in many countries or, as in France, the authorities remain vague about the ethnic origin and religion of complainants. When data are reliable, they reveal an alarming level of intolerance toward Muslims. Germany recorded a 40 percent increase in racist crimes in 2004, while the London-based Islamic Human Rights Commission reported a thirteen-fold increase in backlash complaints about such activities in Britain since the 9/11 attacks. FAIR, the UK's leading NGO on Islamophobia, recorded over fifty cases of violence against Muslims property, including places of worship, and over one hundred cases of verbal threats and abusive behavior in 2004–5. In the aftermath of the London bombings, there was an upsurge in "faith hate" incidents. Furthermore, new antiterrorist legislation was used overwhelmingly against Muslim defendants. Few arrests have led to convictions related to terrorism, and they have been used to cover routine immigration violations. In the Netherlands, acts of aggression against Muslims increased in the aftermath of 9/11 and reached a peak after Theo van Gogh's assassination in 2004—including the burning of a Muslim school in Uden. Muslims responded by organizing nightly surveillance of mosques in many Dutch towns. At that time, one opinion poll showed that 68 percent of the respondents felt threatened by "migrant or Muslim youth" and 53 percent feared a terrorist attack by radical Muslims.[22]

As in Europe, racial profiling and anti-Islamic sentiments have increased in the United States since 9/11. The government's actions against Arabs and Muslims have fueled the belief that discrimination against them is legitimate, if necessary to prevent further terrorist attacks. Racial profiling can take place while Muslims are driving, walking, shopping, traveling through airports, and even while at home, since U.S. legislation allows speculative raids of public housing. As in Europe, rights groups have also recorded a dramatic increase in profiling complaints and backlash attacks carried out against American Muslims. According to CAIR, this post-9/11 anti-Muslim backlash increased the number of civil rights complaints by 64 percent in 2002. Since then, Islamophobia has continued to have an impact on the daily life of Muslims in several ways. In 2003 CAIR reported that there were 1,019 civil rights complaints, representing an increase of 15 percent over the previous year. CAIR processed a total of 1,522 cases in 2004, constituting an increase of 49 percent in the reported cases of harassment, violence, and discriminatory practices over the previous year. In 2006 the total number of cases rose to 2,467, compared with 1,972 in 2005—an increase of more than 25 percent. In addition, CAIR received about 141 reports of anti-Muslim hate crimes in 2004, a 52 percent increase from 2003. In 2006 CAIR reported 167 anti-Muslim hate crimes, a 9.2 percent increase compared with the 153 complaints received in 2005.[23] Although anti-Islamic hate crimes remained more limited than in Europe, they represented about 9.3 percent of the total hate crimes recorded by the FBI in 2009 (compared with 7.7 percent in 2008). In a bulletin entitled "Multiple Controversies Regarding Muslim Communities Raise the Potential for Violent Reactions," the FBI warned in September 2010 that anti-Muslim sentiment could "lead to more hate crimes against Muslims and encourage extremist rhetoric or actions against the United States." The bulletin added that "this can serve to isolate American Muslim youths and possibly drive them toward extremism."[24]

Substantial majorities of Muslims living in Western countries thus express concerns about anti-Muslim sentiment, being viewed as terrorists, ignorance of Islam, and negative stereotyping. A large portion of American Muslims declared that "a quiet but persistent bias, like an undercurrent in work and social interactions, is commonly felt."[25] A University of Michigan study of Arab Americans in the Detroit area (one of the largest such communities in the United States) found in 2004 that about "15 percent say that, since 9/11, they personally had a bad experience due to their ethnicity. These experiences included verbal insults, workplace discrimination, special targeting by law enforcement or airport security, vandalism, and in rare cases, vehicular and physical assault."[26] According to a survey conducted by the Pew Research Center in 2007, a majority of Muslim Americans (53 percent) said "it has become more difficult to be a Muslim" in the United States since 9/11. Beyond expressed discrimination itself (19 percent), their main concerns were being viewed as terrorists (15 percent) and stereotyping (12 percent).[27] A deeper problem is a growing sense of alienation among Muslims, who often do not feel part of the American "success story." This sense of alienation, in turn, fuels a tendency toward isolation. In the aftermath of 9/11, "people who had never recognized and seen themselves as Muslims had no choice but to see themselves as Muslims," argued Muzaffar Chishti, director of the Migration Policy Institute at the New York University School of Law.[28]

Surveys show that most Muslims in Western countries are strongly opposed to extremism. In Great Britain about 79 percent of British Muslims shared the view that the "use of suicide bombings against civilian targets to defend Islam is never justified." The same views were expressed by 83 percent of French Muslims, 89 percent of German Muslims, and 78 percent of Spanish Muslims.[29] Most Muslims in Great Britain (69 percent), France (59 percent), and Germany (53 percent) are also worried about extremism—almost as much as the general publics in Western countries. Consistent with these concerns, majorities or pluralities of Muslims in Great Britain (58 percent), France (56 percent), and Germany (49 percent) believed in 2006 that "there is a struggle in their country between moderates and Islamic fundamentalists." In European countries those who do see a struggle heavily side with the moderates.[30] Radicalization, therefore, involves only a tiny minority of Muslims. In Europe, where the total Muslim population is estimated to be fifteen million, fewer than ten thousand militants are considered even to be a threat by the security services. This equates to less than 0.07 percent of the Muslim community.[31]

There is, however, a residual support for extremism in several Western countries. A Pew Research Center survey found that in Great Britain a minority of Muslims (15 percent) believed in 2006 that "suicide bombings are often or sometimes justified." A similar trend was noticeable in France and Spain (with 16 percent in each country).[32] These findings, as well as other empirical studies, have emphasized the correlation between (real or perceived) discrimination and radicalization. Furthermore, the feeling that Muslims are under attack in Western countries facilitates the anti-Western propaganda spread by jihadist groups worldwide. Issues such as the *hijab* (head-scarf) controversy in France, the controversy over a ban on the burqa in public places in several countries, and the anti-Muslim cartoons in Denmark are exploited by international terrorist groups to construct further political and ideological grievances and to justify further acts of terrorism. In this context what is crucial is a better understanding of the radicalization process in order to evaluate the respective impact of different factors, including economic deprivation, political disaffection, the role of religion, and an identity crisis correlated to personal factors.

The Deprivation/Radicalization Conundrum

The development of socially deprived immigrant communities has raised major concerns in Europe, on the assumption that that socioeconomic deprivation plays a key role in the radicalization process. This correlation has been emphasized by numerous studies demonstrating that Muslims in many European countries suffer from socioeconomic exclusion. The European Monitoring Center on Racism and Xenophobia, for example, noted in 2006 that "differences in wages, type of employment or unemployment rates of migrants, of which a significant proportion belong to Muslim faith groups, indicate persistent exclusion, disadvantage and discrimination."[33] In Great Britain, Muslims had the highest male and female unemployment rate (13 and 18 percent respectively) in 2004. A report published by the Open Society Institute's EU Monitoring and Advocacy Program confirmed that Muslims were three times more likely to be unemployed than the Christian majority and had the highest level of economic inactivity (52 percent). Pakistani and Bangladeshi men suffered the greatest "ethnic penalty," with key nonethnic factors (such as age, education, timing of migration, and economic environment) explaining only 7 percent of the wage gap between them and non-Muslims.[34] In Germany in 2006, the largest Muslim group (Turks) had an unemployment rate of 21 percent, contrasted with only 8 percent for the general population. In the Netherlands, unemployment among Moroccan and Turkish communities was higher than the national average in 2006: a 9 percent unemployment rate for native Dutch, compared with 27 percent for Moroccans and 21 percent for Turks.[35] In Ireland 11 percent of Muslims were unemployed, compared with a national average of 4 percent. In Belgium the unemployment rate for Moroccan and Turkish nationals (38 percent) was five times higher than the unemployment rate for native Belgians (7 percent).

It would be misleading to attribute this socioeconomic exclusion only to religious factors. Other interrelated factors (such as educational and professional qualifications, as well as language skills) also have an impact on the situation of Muslims. Nevertheless, there is evidence, based on experiments in employers' recruitment practices, that discrimination based on religion does play a prominent role. In 2004 the French Monitoring Center on Discrimination, for example, found that a person from the Maghreb had a 20 percent chance of that of a native of getting a positive reply from a prospective employer.[36] Muslims achieve substantially poorer educational outcomes compared with non-Muslims in France, Spain, Germany, and the Netherlands—although such outcomes are comparable in Italy and the United Kingdom. In Germany only 5 percent of Muslims have advanced degrees, compared with 19 percent of the broader population. The EUMC report showed that housing is overall much poorer for immigrants, who often face discrimination and sometimes are violently excluded. The report stated that, in Germany, minorities clearly live in spatially segregated areas with poorer quality housing. In the United Kingdom, over two-thirds of Pakistanis and Bangladeshis live in low-income households. Nearly a quarter live in overcrowded houses, while only 2 percent of the white population does the same.[37]

Socioeconomic exclusion has explained the recruitment of some terrorists in Europe during the 1990s (such as Khaled Kelkal in France), but its importance is currently challenged by the profile of the new generation of homegrown terrorists: they are mainly well-educated young men, from middle-class families, with no criminal records, who seem well integrated. In Spain, for example, Javier Jordan et al. found that the so-called 11-M terrorists (those who committed the Madrid bombings) did not suffer from socioeconomic exclusion prior to their radicalization.[38] In contrast, other homegrown terrorists have suffered from such exclusion prior to their radicalization, like Hasib Hussain (one of the terrorists involved in the London bombings), who dropped out of school at age sixteen with no qualifications. The existence of homegrown terrorists therefore epitomizes a new integration conundrum: being born and raised in Europe does not prevent radicalization, either when young Muslims suffer from socioeconomic deprivation or when they seem perfectly well integrated.

It is commonly believed in the United States that the situation of Arabs and Muslims living there is better than that in Europe. Such a belief partly explains why the radicalization of young U.S. Muslims has for many years been perceived as less alarming than the situation in Europe, even after 9/11. While focusing on border controls to prevent foreign terrorists from entering the country and applying tight surveillance on Muslim foreign nationals, American policymakers tended to dismiss the very possibility of second- or third-generation immigrants joining the jihadist ranks. It is true that Arab Americans and American Muslims are highly assimilated and close to parity with other Americans in terms of income and educational attainment.[39] According to the Vera Institute of Justice, 15 percent of the U.S. population in 2006 had earned a bachelor's degree, mirroring exactly the national figure for Arab Americans (15 percent). Arab Americans (although predominately non-Muslim owing to waves of Christian Arab immigration to the United States during the early 1900s) also reported a higher median income than that of the general U.S. population ($47,459, compared with $41,994 respectively).[40] A 2007 Pew survey, "Muslim Americans: Middle Class and Mostly Mainstream," found that Muslim Americans had a generally positive view of U.S. society, in which they felt well integrated. Compared with the general population, fewer Muslims have finished high school, but just as many have earned college degrees and attended graduate school. About

22 percent are currently enrolled in college classes, with similar rates among both the foreign-born (22 percent) and native-born (20 percent) population. Similar to the U.S. general public, about 24 percent have a college degree. Economically, family income among American Muslims is comparable with that of the population as a whole. Among Americans in 2007, 44 percent reported household income of $50,000 or more annually, as did 41 percent of Muslim Americans. At the higher end of the income scale, 16 percent of Muslim Americans (compared with 17 percent of the general population) reported household incomes of $100,000 or more. At the lowest level, a similar proportion of Muslim Americans (35 percent) and adults nationwide (33 percent) reported household incomes of less than $30,000. In terms of employment, 41 percent of Muslim Americans said they work full time, compared with 49 percent of the general population. The survey reported that 43 percent of Muslim Americans believed that Muslims coming to the United States should adopt U.S. customs instead of trying to remain distinct from broader society. According to Amaney Jamal, an assistant professor at Princeton University who was a senior adviser on this poll, "what emerges is the great success of the Muslim population in its socio-economic assimilation."[41]

American Muslims have also achieved high levels of civic and political integration, as illustrated by the large percentage who are registered to vote, and the percentage of those registered who actually turn out to vote—79 percent and 85 percent, respectively.[42] In a similar fashion Arab Americans were registered to vote in 2000 at a rate of 88.5 percent, surpassing the national average that year of 70 percent.[43] In the 1980s and early 1990s, Arab Americans and new Muslim immigrants focused on U.S. foreign policy issues pertaining to the Islamic world, such as the Israeli–Palestinian conflict, U.S. sanctions against Iraq, and conflicts in Afghanistan and Chechnya. African American Muslims, by contrast, tended to focus on domestic issues, and they largely supported the Democratic Party. Formulating a united political platform between the two groups was not easy, as evidenced by the recurrent tensions between African American organizations and immigrant Muslim organizations, such as the Islamic Society of North America. Despite these tensions U.S. Muslims increased their political visibility, mainly as the result of the activism of the Muslim Public Affairs Council and the American Muslim Council. Former congressman Paul Findley estimated that 65 percent of the 3.2 million Muslims who turned out to vote in 2000 supported Bush, but just 15 percent of African American Muslims did.[44] According to a Zogby poll, Bush support among Arab Americans was 45 percent, whereas Gore secured 38 percent of their vote.[45] Furthermore, about seven hundred

Muslim Americans ran for various local, state, and federal offices in the 2000 elections. At least 152 of them were elected to local and state offices. Muslim turnout in the 2008 U.S. presidential election was even higher, reaching an unprecedented 95 percent, according to a poll conducted by the American Muslim Taskforce on Civil Rights and Elections.

These trends fuel the assumption that Arab Americans and American Muslims are highly integrated and therefore less inclined to radicalize. Indeed, a Pew Research Center survey conducted in 2007 showed that 78 percent of U.S. Muslims said that "the use of suicide bombings against civilian targets to defend Islam is never justified."[46] Since 9/11, U.S. Muslims have reaffirmed their commitment to America, its institutions, and its values. According to Karen Leonard, "the Muslim organizations have now rallied and declare themselves even more fervently to be American, democratic and supportive of civil liberties."[47] In 2006 the Council on American-Islamic Relations conducted a survey of American Muslim voters. Results showed that American Muslims were strongly politically and socially integrated in American society—89 percent said they vote regularly; 86 percent said they celebrate the Fourth of July; 64 percent said they fly the U.S. flag; and 42 percent said they volunteer for institutions serving the public (compared with 29 percent nationwide in 2005).[48] The terrorist attacks of 9/11 were followed by an unprecedented mobilization. The American Muslim Council, for example, urged Muslims to apply for law enforcement jobs to help with the investigation of terrorism. Other Muslim organizations collaborated with the FBI and developed partnerships with local and state authorities, as illustrated by the Muslim Public Affairs Council's "National Grassroots Campaign to Fight Terrorism" and Southern California's Muslim-American Homeland Security Congress. Muslim religious bodies publicly condemned terrorism, and the Fiqh Council of North America issued an opinion stating that it was religiously permissible for enlisted American Muslims to take part in the fight against terrorism.[49] U.S. Muslims also viewed al-Qaeda very unfavorably (up to 58 percent) or somewhat unfavorably (10 percent).

This rosy picture, however, is somewhat tempered by the situation of native-born African American Muslims, who are the most disillusioned segment of the U.S. Muslim population. When compared with other Muslims, they are less educated, and they earn less, although they match the full-time employment rate for all Muslims (45 percent and 41 percent respectively). They expressed a strong sense of alienation that leads them to question the American dream. They are less convinced that hard work brings success (only 56 percent compared with 75 percent of other native-born Muslims) and complain more about increased surveillance and monitoring related to antiterrorist policies than do other Muslims (72 percent and 54 percent respectively). African Americans who are Muslim appear to bear a double burden, as they say they face racial as well as religious intolerance. About 50 percent of them say they suffer from Islamophobia, compared with 28 percent of white Muslims and 23 percent of Asian Muslims. They are more than twice as likely as other Muslims to say they have been singled out by police, or physically threatened or attacked. Furthermore, native-born African American Muslims are considerably more likely than immigrant Muslims to express support for al-Qaeda. Nine percent of them expressed a favorable attitude toward bin Laden's terrorist organization, while 36 percent said that they held a very negative view. By contrast, 3 percent among foreign-born Muslims had a favorable view of al-Qaeda, while 63 percent had a "very unfavorable" view.[50]

Recent studies and surveys indeed show more acceptance of Islamic extremism in some segments of the U.S. Muslim public than others. One of the most striking findings of the 2007 Pew survey, for example, was that younger Muslims in the United States are much more likely than older Muslim Americans to say that suicide bombings can be at least sometimes justified (up to 26 percent). They are also more likely to primarily identify themselves as Muslims rather than Americans. Indeed, most Muslim Americans under the age of thirty defined themselves primarily as Muslims (60 percent, compared with 40 percent of people older than thirty), and about 50 percent said they attend mosque at least once a week. According to the Pew survey, 39 percent of Muslim Americans between eighteen and twenty-nine years old believe that newly arrived Muslims should remain distinct from society at large, compared with 17 percent of Muslims older than fifty-five.[51] Yet radicalization involves only a tiny minority of Muslims in the United States. In 2006, 5 percent of U.S. Muslims believed that the use of violence was justified "rarely," 7 percent said "sometimes," and 1 percent said "often." The most troubling finding was that "13 percent of those who think of themselves primarily as Muslims believe that suicide bombing to defend Islam from its enemies can be often or sometimes justified."[52]

A brief assessment of recent terrorist threats in the United States reveals that the relationship between economic marginalization and radicalization is more complex than commonly assumed. Like in Europe, some terrorists are well educated and well integrated, as illustrated by Ryan Anderson, a Muslim convert and member of the Washington National Guard, who was convicted in September 2004 of providing military intelligence to al-Qaeda. Neither his bachelor's degree from Washington State University nor his professional activities prevented him from becoming radicalized. The American-born Major Nidal Hasan, who killed thirteen people at Fort Hood in Texas, was an army psychiatrist. Since 9/11, of the ninety-four cases where education could be ascertained, two-thirds of the U.S. terrorists pursued at least some college courses, and one in ten had completed a master's degree, PhD, or doctoral equivalent.[53] Nevertheless, as in Europe, the profile of other terrorists is consistent with the presumed correlation between socioeconomic status and radicalization, as illustrated by Colleen Renee LaRose ("Jihad Jane"), Bryant Neal Vinas (who traveled to Pakistan to join al-Qaeda), the four members of the domestic cell who plotted to carry out terrorist attacks near New York City in May 2009, and the two New Jersey men who were arrested at John F. Kennedy International Airport while trying to fly to Somalia in order to join Al-Shabaab. Despite different family backgrounds, they all suffered from some form of socioeconomic exclusion.

We can deduce two conclusions from these contrasting examples. First, deprivation is not a sufficient motivational factor. What really matters is the sense of frustration and resentment expressed by young Muslims. Alienation may be either real or perceived; but in both cases it may lead to radicalization when dashed expectations regarding social status generate a sense of humiliation. Second, socioeconomic exclusion remains a fertile ground for terrorist recruitment. While this correlation has been recognized by European policymakers prior to 9/11, their American counterparts have continued to ignore this dimension of the radicalization process until recently. Yet the securitization of immigration and integration policies is today producing similar results on both sides of the Atlantic: discrimination against Muslims limits their opportunities to integrate, and thus aggravates their sense of alienation.

The Domestic Impact of the Global War on Terror

How has the fight against terrorism outside the United States and Europe had an impact on the situation of Muslims and created a permissive environment of terrorism in Europe? There is growing evidence that the war on terror abroad has provided many terrorist groups with the ammunition they need to promote their message, helping them to recruit new militants. External factors, such as conflicts in the Middle East and foreign military occupation, are commonly perceived as playing a key role. The war in Iraq, for instance, was depicted by the United States and its allies as a way to take the war on terror to the terrorists. Regrettably, however, the invasion and occupation of Iraq brought terrorism back to Western democracies— as illustrated by the London and Madrid bombings, as well as other foiled terrorist attacks on both sides of the Atlantic—and has fueled both national and international insecurity. A growing number of U.S. and European experts agree that the war in Iraq worsened insecurity in many ways. Both the CIA and the National Intelligence Council admitted that "the war in Iraq could provide an important training ground for terrorists, and the key factors behind terrorism show no signs of abating over the next 15 years."[54] The war in Iraq also helped al-Qaeda's terrorism network to be rebuilt in the Afghan and Pakistani tribal areas—where it has recovered much of its ability to attack from the region and broadcast its messages to militants across the world. Senior American and Pakistani officials today admit that the lawless badlands, where ethnic Pashtun tribes have resisted government control for centuries, have become a natural place for a dispirited terrorism network to find refuge. The war in Iraq consistently diverted resources and high-level attention from this problem. Yet in the spring of 2006, Taliban leaders based in Pakistan launched an offensive in southern Afghanistan, increasing suicide bombings by 60 percent and NATO and American casualty rates by 45 percent. According to Seth Jones, a Pentagon consultant and a terrorism expert at the RAND Corporation, "the United States faces a threat from al Qaeda that is comparable to what it faced on Sept. 11, 2001. The base of operations has moved only a short distance, roughly the difference from New York to Philadelphia."[55]

The United States is also facing the issue of U.S. citizens fighting for the Taliban abroad, such as John Walker Lindh (sentenced to twenty years in jail in 2002) and Bryant Neal Vinas, who moved from Long Island to Peshawar (where he was arrested in 2008). There is also the case of the estimated thirty Somali Americans who left their communities in California, Minnesota, and Ohio to fight with an Islamist militia in Somalia—where the main leader is Omar Hammami (known now as Abou Mansoor Al-Amriki), born in Alabama. "Even when individuals plan to support terrorist activity abroad, we remain concerned that once they reach their foreign destinations they may redirect against targets back home, as we've seen in the past," Raymond W. Kelly, the New York police commissioner, said in a news release shortly after the arrest at JFK Airport of Mohamed Mahmood Alessa and Carlos Eduardo Almonte (who were seeking to travel to Somalia).[56] The most troubling finding of the report published by the Bipartisan Policy Center in 2010 related to the increasing "Americanization" of the leadership of al-Qaeda and aligned groups:

> Anwar al-Awlaki, the Yemeni-American cleric who grew up in New Mexico, is today playing an important operational role in Al-Qaeda in

the Arabian Peninsula, while Adnan Shukrijumah, the Saudi-American who grew up in Brooklyn and Florida, is now effectively al-Qaeda's director of external operations. In 2009, Shukrijumah tasked Najibul-lah Zazi and two other Americans to attack targets in the United States. Omar Hammami, a Baptist convert to Islam from Alabama, is both a key propagandist and a military commander for al-Shabab, the Somali al-Qaeda affiliate, while Chicagoan David Headley played a role in scoping the targets for the Lashkar-e-Taiba attacks on Mumbai in late 2008 that killed more than 160 people.[57]

A similar trend involves Europeans. Europol reported an increasing num-ber of European nationals and residents who are being recruited for jihad in Iraq and Afghanistan. The French and Dutch authorities admit that Western military intervention in Afghanistan is a motivating factor for the jihadists to recruit in these two countries. In 2007, Iraq attracted the largest number of recruits from EU member states. The expansion of the "al-Qaeda fran-chise" in Iraq, Algeria, Egypt, and Somalia provides Islamist terrorism with access to new centers of support and new resources for the recruitment and training of EU nationals and residents. An increasing number of EU nation-als are trained in Pakistan, as illustrated by the arrests made in Germany and Denmark in 2007. The trial of the perpetrators of the failed attacks in London in July 2005 also revealed that they were trained both in Pakistan and the United Kingdom. European governments have expressed concerns about the situation outside the EU. In July 2007 eight Spanish nationals were killed in Yemen, and three German officers were killed in Kabul the follow-ing month. That same year French nationals were targeted in Saudi Arabia in February and in Mauritania in December (where four tourists were killed near Aleg). Al-Qaeda in the Islamic Maghreb (AQIM, formerly the Salafist Group for Preaching and Combat in Algeria) has strengthened its influence and carried out several suicide attacks that specifically targeted European citizens, as in Algiers in September and December 2007. Direct threats were made by both al-Qaeda and AQIM toward the Spanish cities of Ceuta and Melilla. Camps in Mali, according to French intelligence, are being used to initiate operations in Algeria and Mauritania. The merger of AQIM with al-Qaeda brings fresh risks and a reinvigorated zeal for Western targets. As Abdelmalek Droukdal, one of the top leaders of AQIM, argues, "If the U.S. administration sees that its war against the Muslims is legitimate, then what makes us believe that our war on its territories is not legitimate?"[58]

The war on terror has damaged America's global image in predominantly Muslim countries, as well as among close U.S. allies. A Pew survey in 2006 found that only 23 percent of the Spanish public expressed positive views of the United States, down from 50 percent in 2000 and 41 percent in 2005. In Great Britain, favorable opinion of the United States declined from 83 percent in 2000 to 56 percent in 2006. The belief that the war in Iraq has made the world a more dangerous place was supported by 60 percent of the respondents in Great Britain, 66 percent in Germany, and 68 percent in Spain. Large majorities in Muslim countries shared this belief, notably in Egypt (70 percent), Jordan (74 percent), and Turkey (70 percent).[59] The war on terror has been extremely unpopular among Muslim minorities: about 78 percent of French Muslims opposed it in 2006, as well as 77 percent of Muslim respondents in Great Britain, 62 percent in Germany, and 83 percent in Spain.[60]

The war in Iraq remains the major source of contention, but Muslims also refer to military actions and prisoner abuses in Afghanistan, the Israeli-Palestinian conflict, the crisis in Lebanon, and discrimination against Muslims in Western countries as sources of discontent. In 2007, publics in Muslim countries were inclined to see the United States as the greatest threat to their countries, a view expressed by 72 percent of respondents in Bangladesh (compared with 47 percent who cited India as a major threat), 64 percent in Turkey (compared with 13 percent who feared Iraq), 64 percent in Pakistan, and 63 percent in Indonesia. In addition, large majorities, in the range of 34 and 40 percent, cited U.S. policies as the most important cause of Islamic extremism.[61]

More to the point, numerous studies show that many Muslims have an aggrieved view of the West. Noting that many Muslims in the United States feel angry about U.S. foreign policy, Jerrold Post of George Washington University and Gabriel Sheffer of Hebrew University of Jerusalem contend that "the apparent resistance to radicalism among U.S. Muslims heretofore may well change." They observe, for example, that "the Palestinian-American community is increasingly active, organized, and angered by its perception of a one-sided U.S. policy towards Israel. . . . The U.S. Iraqi communities are similarly beginning to show their dissatisfaction with the U.S. presence and role in Iraq."[62] The so-called clash of civilizations, in fact, works both ways: a large portion of Westerners share a negative image of both Islam and Muslims; this trend provides ammunition to certain militant groups in promoting their message that there is a fundamental conflict between the West and Islam. This symmetrical construction of a West-Islam antagonism normalizes restrictive and punitive counterterrorist measures while simultaneously "creating a self-fulfilling prophecy in which imprisoned, tortured and harassed activists decide that the use of violence is their only recourse."[63]

Self-proclaimed crusaders therefore depict terrorism as a necessary means, justifying their criminal activities by listing *state and war crimes* committed by Western democracies. Radical preachers and jihadist activists make capital out of institutional discrimination (as illustrated by racial profiling, arbitrary detention, and deportation), as well as a range of international and domestic issues including the Guantanamo prison camp, the Abu Ghraib abuses and other examples of the use of torture, the practice of extraordinary rendition (also associated with torture), and the designation of "unlawful enemy combatant."[64]

These perceived injustices galvanize the notion of a "just cause," calls for revenge, and a culture of martyrdom. Islamist radicals actively promote a collective solidarity and ideological orientation fueled by a "de-territorialized altruism."[65] In his analysis of British-born terrorists, Brendan O'Duffy of the University of London notes that the perceived lack of a coherent British foreign policy, coupled with domestic political grievances, helps to radicalize young Muslims who feel ignored and undervalued in contemporary British society: "When perceptions of injustice at national and international levels mirror local and personal experience, or when local discrimination is consonant with perceptions of liberal imperialist foreign policies, a larger pool of recruits becomes available for potential indoctrination."[66] In this process, political disaffection is increased by a sense of political impotence, such as that witnessed in the wake of demonstrations in Europe that failed to stop the war in Iraq. Terrorist attacks are therefore committed in the name of a global jihad, as a response to Western occupation of the holy land in the Middle East, and the killing of Muslims in Bosnia, Iraq, and Afghanistan. For example, Nizar Trabesi, a Tunisian accused of plotting a bombing attack against U.S. forces in Belgium, explained that he decided to join al-Qaeda after seeing pictures of a Palestinian girl killed by Israeli forces in Gaza in 2001. The London bombers reportedly watched videos of Iraqi victims of U.S. forces. Both Mohammad Sidique Khan and Shehzad Tanweer described themselves in their martyrdom tapes as soldiers defending Islam and avenging their Muslim brothers and sisters.

This sense of collective identity, as expressed by "altruistic" empathy for fellow Muslims, fuels social networks with channels of communication and provides material support for terrorist attacks.[67] It is also related to the now common phenomenon of jihadist websites, forums, and blogs.[68] Terrorist organizations use these tools in order to promote their agenda, collect information on future targets, plot new attacks, and recruit members (with new sections in Western languages being developed in prominent websites advocating Islamist terrorism).

The expansion of the "al-Qaeda franchise" in Iraq, Algeria, Egypt, and Somalia provides Islamist terrorism with access to new centers of support, and new resources for the recruitment and training of EU and U.S. nationals or residents. Islamist terrorists use these transnational links for organizing—and justifying—terrorist attacks in Western countries or against Western interests abroad. While the number of terrorist incidents in Afghanistan more than doubled in 2009 compared with 2008, violence by several militant Islamist groups escalated in Yemen, Somalia, and North and West African countries (notably in Mauritania, Niger, and Mali). Most of the attacks in 2009 targeted nationals of Western countries, including tourists, diplomats, and members of NGOs.

Political Disaffection

Resentment against the West is coupled with a growing hostility toward Western societies among Muslims living in the United States and Europe. Domestic factors, such as political discontent and disaffection from mainstream politics and society, can lead to disillusion with democratic principles and nonviolent activism. Some young Muslims therefore turn to violence and martyrdom. This trend is often facilitated by the counterproductive outcomes of the fight against terrorism. Belonging to a particular ethnic group or religious community has been reconstituted, in itself, into a security threat.[69] This approach has failed to recognize the diversity of Muslims and has obfuscated rather than clarified the distinction between moderate and radical Muslims. It has therefore increased the number of Muslims who feel alienated while fueling the anti-Western agenda of the supporters of Islamic extremism. Paradoxically, resentment against the West is sometimes the result of what Robert Leiken calls "adversarial assimilation"—"integration into the host country's adversarial culture . . . a sort of anti-West westernization."[70] According to Olivier Roy, a significant pattern in Euro-Islamist radicalization "is the blending of Islamic wording and phraseology with a typically Western anti-imperialism and third-worldist radicalism. For the most part, Euro-Islamist targets are the same ones than the Western ultra-leftist movements of the 1970s identified. The Islamists target 'US imperialism' and 'Zionism' in support of the *ummah* [community of believers] that, like the world proletariat, is an abstract universal."[71]

Resentment can be fueled by the negative perception of Islam and/or Muslims through media coverage. As noted by Jocelyne Cesari et al., "Most mainstream media are not openly Islamophobic in Europe. [However,] in these sensationalist news stories especially, but also across the media overall, there is a tendency to mix foreign and domestic Islam together, thus extending the entire trope of politically radical Islam to immigrant Muslim populations."[72] A number of detailed media studies have been done in various European countries. In France, for instance, Pierre Tévanian shows how the media helped construct the "problem of the hijab" by deciding which voices would be included in the public debate: "social scientists, feminists, teachers, and civil actors not opposed to the hijab were excluded, helping to construct a narrative in which bearded foreign religious men defended the Muslim head scarf against women who had rejected the hijab, supported by native or emancipated male intellectuals."[73] This same narrative is also supported by some European intellectuals. In the Netherlands the prominent philosophy professor Herman Philipse has made numerous appearances claiming that Islam is a violent tribal culture incompatible with modernity and democracy. In the same vein, media coverage about Islam in Germany is dominated by controversies about mosque constructions, forced marriage, honor killings, and the ban of the veil. These controversies have been recently reignited by the large popular impact of a book on the "threats posed by Muslims to Germany" written by Thilo Sarrazin, a Social Democratic politician and a former member of the executive board of the Bundesbank.[74]

In addition, political disaffection is often increased by a sense of political impotence, such as that which emerged in the wake of demonstrations in Europe that failed to stop the war in Iraq. The feeling of being unable to exert meaningful political influence is exacerbated by a lack of civic and political integration. Enfranchisement is indeed a persistent problem. In France about 50 percent of the Muslim population, mostly of Maghrebian origin, is French. The large majority, however, is under eighteen years of age and for this reason cannot vote. In Germany, where there are about three million Muslims, 80 percent of them do not have German citizenship and are therefore excluded from the right to vote. In the United Kingdom and the Netherlands, 50 percent of the Muslim population cannot vote either. More to the point, 70 percent of British Muslims believe that Muslims are politically underrepresented.[75] There are, characteristically, thirty Muslims elected to Western European parliaments, out of an estimated population of ten to fifteen million. At the EU level, in the 2009 elections for the European Parliament, eleven candidates with a Muslim family background were elected. Altogether, they represent only six countries, while the remaining twenty-one member states have no Muslim members of the European Parliament (MEPs). If the EU parliament proportionally represented the population of the twenty-seven member states, more than 3 percent (or about 24 of the 785 MEPs) would come from a Muslim background.

In contrast, in the United States, Muslims responded to discrimination and suspicion by increasing their political participation. The post-9/11 policies of the Bush administration perpetuated a feeling of betrayal among Muslims who voted for Bush in 2000.[76] Indeed, the 2004 presidential election strengthened the unity of the Muslim voting bloc. A dozen U.S. Muslim organizations and the American-Muslim Taskforce on Civil Rights and Elections endorsed John Kerry, the Democratic candidate. An exit poll commissioned by CAIR indicated that more than 90 percent of Muslim voters cast their ballots for Kerry. Other surveys confirmed this shift in partisan affiliation, as well as the role of both external and domestic policy.[77] U.S. Muslim political involvement continued to attain a higher level of national visibility during the 2006 congressional elections, which were characterized by an overwhelming turnout of U.S. Muslim voters and the election of the first Muslim member of the U.S. Congress, Minnesota Democrat Keith Ellison. This trend was confirmed by the 2008 presidential elections, when nearly 90 percent of U.S. Muslims supported Democrat Barack Obama, and only 3 percent voted for the Republican candidate, John McCain. Turnout among Muslim voters reached 95 percent, according to the American-Muslim Taskforce findings.[78] In addition to Keith Ellison, a second Muslim, André Carson, was elected to the 110th Congress in a special election in March 2008.

U.S. Muslims, however, remain underrepresented in state politics. By 2010 there were no Muslim governors or lieutenant governors, and only five state legislators were Muslims. According to political scientists Eileen Braman and Abdulkader H. Sinno, "Observed and latent anti-Muslim sentiment in the electorate makes it more difficult for Muslims to win the electoral support they need to win office and also dissuades qualified candidates from running if they fear they will be harshly judged or discriminated against because of their religion."[79] Indeed, there is a good deal of data suggesting that Muslims suffer from discrimination in politics, as illustrated by the study published by Braman and Sinno, based on polls conducted between 1999 and 2007 by Gallup, Fox News, the Los Angeles Times, Rasmussen, and Pew. They find that between 31 percent and 61 percent of respondents claim that they would not vote for a Muslim candidate for president.[80] Other variables have to be taken into account for explaining this underrepresentation, such as the impact of ethnicity, gender, age, and education, foreign-born status, and political affiliation. Yet prejudice clearly plays a major role. Given the current scrutiny Muslims face, they are hesitant to participate. Furthermore, young Muslim Americans are much less likely than older people to be registered to vote. In 2007 only 48 percent of eligible Muslims under the age of thirty were registered to vote (20 percentage points lower than among Muslims older than thirty).[81]

Cultural and Religious Factors

The relationship between the religion Islam and radicalization in the current context of securitization is complex and controversial. A common assumption, strengthened in the aftermath of 9/11, is that Islam (viewed as a monolithic entity) is a concern in itself. In Europe Islam is overwhelmingly viewed as both a threat to Western liberal values and a barrier to the integration of immigrant minorities. This image of Islam is mainly characterized by a profile of fanaticism, medieval backwardness, subordination of women, and other practices that abrogate human rights (such as polygamy and forced marriages). Yet the vast majority of Muslims living in Europe express concerns about religious extremism. In 2005 Professor Jytte Klausen interviewed more than three hundred leading Muslims in six countries (Britain, Denmark, France, Germany, the Netherlands, and Sweden). She found that the majority of them were overwhelmingly secular and supportive of liberal values.[82] Subsequent studies and surveys reach a similar conclusion.[83] In terms of political values, Muslim Americans hold liberal political views on questions about the size and scope of government. At the same time, however, they are socially conservative and supportive of a strong role for government in protecting morality. A solid majority (61 percent) say that homosexuality is a way of life that should be discouraged by society. Just 27 percent say homosexuality should be accepted, compared with 51 percent of the general public. Similarly, 59 percent of Muslim Americans believe that the government should do more to protect morality in society.[84] Yet they strongly reject religious extremism.

On both sides of the Atlantic, there are concerns about increased religious consciousness among a tiny fraction of the members of the younger generation. For some experts, this "re-Islamization" is neither detrimental to their integration nor a sign of Islamic radicalization. For others, it has created a pool of potential radicals who may be recruited by terrorist groups. In this case there is weak evidence that religion in itself is an explanation of radicalization. According to the Club of Madrid (an independent organization comprising world leaders, former heads of state and government, and policy specialists), political and economic grievances are primary causes, and religion has become a means to legitimate violence and mobilize recruits.[85] In terms of Islam itself, religion only contributes to a culture of violence when it is focused on polarized themes (such as concepts of truth, "just cause," and other moral absolutes) in order to provide a "defining issue" in the identity of activist groups.

The crucial question is therefore how and why a particular interpretation of Islam provides an "oppositional identity" for young Muslims.[86] Jihadism is sometimes perceived by them as a way to reassert their identity. Young Muslims are caught between the beliefs and traditions of their parents and Western secularism. This can lead to a gradual lack of identification with both minority and majority cultures. The loss of minority culture is illustrated by the "Western profile" of radicals in their studies, languages, and in matrimonial affairs (many of them marrying or dating European women). The adoption of secular Western lifestyles prior to radicalization is often the result of the rejection of overbearing family control, as well as an attempt to fit the expectations of the host society. Yet when the incorporation into majority culture proves to be ineffective in preventing alienation and discrimination, Muslim youth face something of a quandary. "In the absence of an appealing cultural paradigm from either group," the British expert on contemporary Islam Akil Awan argues, "the individual simply resorts to a cultural entrenchment that assumes a religious hue by default (due to a lack of viable alternatives)."[87] Religious radicalization becomes a way of constructing a legitimate identity outside both minority and majority cultures. Identification and loyalty are transferred to the *ummah* exclusively, while radicals are rejected by both "ordinary civilian fellow Muslims" and the host society.[88] It is worth noting that, in most cases, the jihadization phase of the radicalization process involves a withdrawal from the mosque. In their report on the homegrown threat commissioned by the New York City Police Department, Mitchell D. Silber and Arvin Bhatt analyzed the behavioral dynamics of homegrown terrorists in Europe, Canada, Australia, and the United States. They underlined that "as individuals begin to conceive militant Jihad as an objective, they retreat from the mosque. . . . This withdrawal is sometimes provoked by the fact that the mosque no longer serves the individual's radicalization needs. In other words, the individual's level of extremism surpasses that of the mosque."[89] During this indoctrination phase, the Internet becomes a virtual "echo chamber"—acting as a radicalization accelerant while providing radical clerics with a worldwide audience. Among the most influential of them was Anwar al-Awlaki, who was a U.S. citizen based in Yemen. Two of the 9/11 hijackers attended his sermons, and Awlaki was also linked to Nidal Hasan, the U.S. Army major at Fort Hood, as well as Farouk Abdulmutallab, the Nigerian man accused of trying to blow up a plane on Christmas Day.

Finally, the phase of political and "religious" seeking generally includes a personal crisis, such as the death of a family member, a divorce, or losing a job. This identity crisis is admittedly correlated with personal factors, such as a particular psychological predisposition (often a narcissistic desire to reconstruct the self through action), and previous delinquent activities. It is worth noting in this regard that radicals such as "shoe bomber" Richard Reid and Theo van Gogh's assassin, Mohammed Bouyeri, converted to jihadism while in prison. Prison conversion raises new concerns in terms of vulnerability to radicalization, concerns that are inextricably tied to alienation. In the United States, for example, some 30 percent of the incarcerated African American population converted to Islam while in prison. With the highest incarceration rate in the world, the United States faces the growing issue of the radicalization of even a small faction of that population. Since 2007 the Federal Bureau of Prisons has tried to address this issue by ensuring that providers of Muslim religious services more rigorously screen volunteers who enter prisons, in order to prevent the propagation of radical propaganda. So far the Bureau of Prisons has relied on just ten Muslim chaplains to serve the entire federal prison system.[90] Prison plays a critical role in the radicalization process in Europe as well. Two of the Madrid bombers, Jamal Ahmidan and Alleka Lamari, were radicalized in prison, where they were in contact with veterans of the Afghan jihad.

The Weak Prevention of Further Islamic Radicalization

Both the U.S. and European governments have become increasingly aware of the necessity to prevent further Islamist radicalization. At the EU level, this led to the adoption by the European Commission of the 2005 Communication Concerning Terrorist Recruitment. This document suggested addressing various factors contributing to violent radicalization, such as terrorist propaganda in the broadcast media and the Internet, religious and cultural prejudice, and socioeconomic alienation.[91] Various European programs were initiated: the Socrates Program, the Youth Program, and the 2007 Culture Program. They all aimed at promoting active European citizenship and enhancing mutual understanding by respecting and celebrating cultural diversity. In Great Britain, Jacqui Smith, then home secretary, unveiled in 2009 a new UK strategy, called CONTEST Two, to tackle terrorism. Aiming at enlisting the widest possible degree of support, it included training six thousand shop and hotel workers in vigilance for terrorist activity, tackling antidemocratic extremist voices in the Muslim community, and supporting mainstream pro-democratic Muslim leaders. One of the most striking differences between CONTEST One (2006) and CONTEST Two relates to the presentation of the nature of the terrorist threat. CONTEST One described the principal threat as coming "from radicalised individuals." In contrast, CONTEST Two refers to four sources of threat: (1) the al-Qaeda leadership and its inner associates; (2) the affiliated groups in North Africa, the Arabian Peninsula, Iraq, and Yemen; (3) self-starting individuals (the London and Glasgow car bombers); and (4) lone individuals (the Exeter café bomber).[92]

The wave of arrests and thwarted plots recently seen in the United States has severely undermined the long-held assumption that American Muslims, unlike their European counterparts, are virtually immune to radicalization. According to data collected by the New York University Center on Law and Security, for example, more than five hundred individuals have been convicted by authorities in the United States for terrorism-related charges since 9/11.[93] While making a numerically accurate comparison is not easy, it is fair to say that the proportion of U.S. Muslims involved in violent activities is either equal to or only slightly lower than that of any European country with a comparable Muslim population. Yet despite this evidence, for a long time the American authorities and commentators seemed unwilling to acknowledge the existence of radicalization among small segments of the American Muslim population. In the FBI's parlance, for example, until 2005, the term "homegrown terrorism" was still reserved for domestic organizations, such as antigovernment militias, white supremacists, and ecoterrorist groups such as the Earth Liberation Front. According to Lorenzo Vidino, security expert at the RAND Corporation, "such groups were termed 'homegrown' to distinguish them from jihadist terrorist networks, even though some of the latter possessed some of the very same characteristics (membership born and raised in the US and a focus on US targets). Since the cause of the *jihadists* was perceived to be foreign, the US government did not label them as 'homegrown,' despite the typically homegrown characteristics of many of them."[94]

Both the authorities and public were shocked by the Times Square incident of May 2010. Janet Napolitano, the homeland security secretary, subsequently publicly acknowledged that "home-based terrorism is here. And, like violent extremism abroad, it will be part of the threat picture we must now confront."[95] The new National Security Strategy includes homegrown terrorism among the major threats to the United States. The "Counter Radicalization" section states that

> several recent incidences of violent extremists in the United States who are committed to fighting here and abroad have underscored the threat to the United States and our interests posed by

individuals radicalized at home. Our best defenses against this threat are well informed and equipped families, local communities, and institutions. The Federal Government will invest in intelligence to understand this threat and expand community engagement and development programs to empower local communities. And the Federal Government, drawing on the expertise and resources from all relevant agencies, will clearly communicate our policies and intentions, listening to local concerns, tailoring policies to address regional concerns, and making clear that our diversity is part of our strength—not a source of division or insecurity.[96]

Western political leaders commonly refer to a dividing line between two categories of Muslims: the "moderates" and the "radicals." The key goal is explicitly to get the support of the former in order to fight the latter. Illustrating this point, President Bush's visit to a Washington, D.C., mosque shortly after 9/11 was designed to reassure the Muslim and Arab communities in the United States. Tony Blair, then British prime minister, declared in October 2001: "We do not act against Islam. The true followers of Islam are our brothers and sisters in this struggle."[97] Several new Muslim organizations have been created, and some existing ones have been invigorated, in an attempt to address the challenge of Muslim radicalism. In the United States, for example, the National Fiqh Council of North America, an American Muslim group concerned with Islamic jurisprudence, issued an extraordinary fatwa in July 2005 condemning all forms of extremism. It asserted that all acts of terrorism targeting civilians are forbidden in Islam; it is forbidden for a Muslim to cooperate with any individual or group involved in any act of terrorism or violence; and it is the civic and religious duty of Muslims to cooperate with law enforcement authorities. One of the supporters of the fatwa was the Muslim Public Affairs Council, which initiated a "National Grassroots Campaign to Fight Terrorism" stressing a zero-tolerance policy on terrorism. Identifying and preventing radicalization within the Muslim community have been made a priority by several other organizations, such as the Islamic Society of North American (the national Sunni association of Muslim organizations), the North American Shia Ithna-asheri Muslim Communities, the American Society for Muslim Advancement, the American Muslim Alliance, and Muslims against Terrorism. They have initiated programs to raise awareness on issues of radical ideologies and terrorist propaganda. Yet they walked a fine line between reassuring the American public about Islam while avoiding alienating their constituents, who faced a complex set of issues.

European governments implemented a similar strategy. In the Nether-lands, the Ministry for Aliens and Integration published two policy memo-randa in 2005 on the issue of the fight against radicalism. In Great Brit-ain, collaboration with Muslim organizations became a key component of CONTEST. The Muslim Council of Britain is the primary representative organization for Muslims in the UK, with a network of at least 380 smaller organizations. It was founded in 1997, after a meeting of a number of Mus-lim organizations, and is associated with about 70 percent of Muslims in Great Britain. There are several more academic and elite organizations that also play important roles in the UK. The Forum against Islamophobia and Racism, for example, was founded after 9/11 and works in lobbying and on research. The Muslim Public Affairs Committee works to empower Mus-lims at the grassroots level. The Islamic Cultural Centre, which includes the London Central Mosque, was established in 1944 and maintains a board of trustees of prominent Muslims, local and international. The Federation of Student Islamic Societies in the UK and Eire organizes student groups, and the Islamic Mission pursues education and other charity work across the UK. In recent years (particularly in the wake of the July 7, 2005, London bomb-ings) the government has sought to engage "representative" Muslim organi-zations, such as the Muslim Council of Britain. Following 7/7, a "Muslim Task Force" was created in an attempt to seek collaboration with Muslims to prevent extremism. Questions have been raised, however, about the extent to which such organizations are in fact representative of the UK's incredibly diverse Muslim community.

French authorities face a similar issue. In 2003 the Conseil français du culte musulman (CFCM) was formed with the encouragement of the state, in the hope that a centralized representational body for the Muslim com-munity would help remedy its long-term underrepresentation and prevent radicalization. Yet the CFCM has drawn criticisms about state interfer-ence and complaints that the organization does not adequately represent the diverse makeup of French Muslims. Meanwhile, Interior Minister Giuseppe Pisanu of Italy proposed the creation of a council of Muslims—similar to the French model. The Consulta Islamic (Islamic Consultation) was set up in September 2005 to facilitate dialogue with local Muslim leaders on pressing issues. In 2005 an Islamic Anti-Defamation League was created in Italy by a diverse group consisting of intellectuals, workers, parents, professionals, and students—most of them Italian citizens or those who had lived in Italy for years, all of them Muslims. In Germany the Bundeszentrale für politische Bildung (Federal Office for Political Education) established the Muslimische Akademie (Muslim Academy) in 2004 to encourage Muslims to participate in German politics. The aim of the organizers (most of them Muslims) was to establish a forum for discussion. The project, however, has been criticized by some Muslim organizations, who objected that they were not asked to participate.

Meanwhile, Western governments strengthened their efforts against radical Muslims. The British government enacted laws in 2003 allowing the government to strip dual nationals of their British citizenship and to deport them if they threatened the national interest. The following year the home secretary withdrew the citizenship of militant preacher Abu Hamza al-Masri in preparation for his deportation. It also charged two implicated Muslim clerics with incitement to violence. One of the two was Abu Qatada, reportedly the "spiritual counselor" of the 9/11 ringleader Mohamed Atta. In 2007 Sheikh Abdullah al-Faisal (who is thought to have had an influence on one of the four London bombers) was deported from the UK for seeking to incite racial hatred. About thirty religious leaders were likewise deported from France between 2001 and April 2004. The German government implemented a law in 2005 making it easier to expel "spiritual inciters to disorder." The same year, the Dutch Immigration Ministry moved to expel four imams accused of radicalism.[98] In June 2004 the Danish parliament passed the so-called Imam Law, which would require religious leaders to speak Danish and respect "Western values," such as democracy and the equality of women. Further legislation gave the Danish government the right to reject "foreign missionaries" who espouse radical views. In 2007 Italian police investigated several imams in a terror probe. Most notable of these was the case of Mohamed Kohaila, an imam in Turin who was expelled and sent back to his native Morocco after his sermons were secretly filmed and deemed a threat to public security. Kohaila had been living in Italy for several years, but investigations by antiterrorism authorities showed that he incited violent and anti-Western behavior.[99]

Attempts to secure the support of moderate Muslims and to address the issue of radicalization have been part of a much larger strategy aimed at improving the cultural and religious accommodation of Islam in Western societies. In Europe, where the issue of the institutional recognition of Islam was already seen as problematic prior to 9/11, the prevention of radicalization was extended to specific actions dealing with the relationship between the state and religious organizations; the establishment and functioning of mosques; the funding of faith schools; the training of imams; and the professionalization of Muslim chaplaincies. What was at stake beyond combating extremism was the promotion of an Islamic-Western dialogue about democratic rules and values. Forms and degrees of accommodation have varied from one country to another. Yet there has been a noticeable convergence toward the institutionalization of Islam. This "Europeanization" of Islam included a series of initiatives: the creation of new centralized representative bodies (such as the French Council of the Muslim Religion); further possibilities for establishing Muslim faith-based educational institutions (such as Islamic schools in Great Britain, and the Lycée Averroès, the first publicly funded French Muslim school); and a greater recognition of Muslim practices in schools (such as the provision of halal meals and the allowance of absenteeism for religious reasons). Many European governments have decided to contribute to the costs of establishing mosques in order to obstruct the influx of foreign money and thus limit the potential disruptive influence of radical Muslim countries or transnational Muslim organizations. A similar rationale explains the new training of imams. In France, for example, support for the emergence of an "Islam of France" (as opposed to the controversial issue of Islam *in* France) led to the establishment in 2008 of a "republican training"—taught at the Institut Catholique de Paris—for Muslim religious workers.

In Italy a major interfaith dialogue event called "Architects of a Plural Community" brought together several youth groups with different religious affiliations in 2004. The groups involved included the Italian Muslim Youth, the Union of Italian Jewish Youth, Federazione Universitaria Cattolica Italiana, and the youth section of the Association of Italian Catholic Workers. In October 2007 Interior Minister Giuliano Amato visited Rome's mosque to present a Charter of Values for Citizenship and Integration. It was the first public presentation of the symbolic document, seeking to bridge the divide between Muslim and Catholic communities in Italy, and is aimed at the harmonious integration of Italy's growing immigrant communities. More than three thousand Muslims gathered in Milan's Palaldo stadium that year in an effort to send a message of love and fraternity. Muslim and Jewish youth groups engaged in an interfaith initiative in Milan in early 2008. The meeting took place at an exhibition called "The Fairness of Islam" at the Center of Culture and Missionary Activity, with representatives from two organizations, Young Jews of Italy and Young Muslims of Italy.

In Germany efforts to engage the Muslim community led to the creation of the Islam Forum, an initiative supported by several politicians, including the former president of the Bundestag Rita Süssmuth, and Chancellor Angela Merkel. The German government also initiated the Deutsche Islamkonferenz (German Islam Conference) in September 2006. Today it remains the only national initiative to recognize interlocutors for Islam. Fifteen representatives of Islam in Germany (from each federal state) take part, along with five major Muslim organizations. In the summer of 2009, the Alliance for Peace and Fairness was launched as "the first Muslim party" in Germany. The German parliament elected in September 2009 had twenty members with a migrant background. Nine of them had a Muslim family background, of which three explicitly identity themselves as Muslims on the official website of the Bundestag.

Efforts to promote a positive image of Islam, however, have been undermined by a heightened level of public suspicion, targeted government policies and behavior, negative media portrayals, and—in turn—an increasing feeling of alienation on a community-wide level. In the Netherlands, for example, a Moroccan-born Muslim politician named Ahmed Aboutaleb was elected mayor of Rotterdam in October 2008. The event was hailed in media and political circles as a significant historical turning point for the Netherlands, a country still somewhat mired in the grips of the anti-Islam, anti-immigrant backlash prompted by Theo van Gogh's murder. Yet Aboutaleb's appointment was met with criticism from two right-wing Dutch political parties, Leefbar Rotterdam and the Party for Freedom. Geert Wilders publicly stated that "appointing a Moroccan as mayor of the second largest Dutch city is just as ridiculous as appointing a Dutchman as mayor of Mecca. Instead, he should become mayor of Rabat in Morocco. With him as mayor, Rotterdam will be Rabat on the banks of the river Maas. Soon we may even have an imam serving as archbishop. This is madness."[100] In Italy the minister of reforms and a member of the Northern League Party was quoted as saying, "For every day the hostages are kept prisoners in Iraq, each EU country should revoke the residence permit of 1000 Muslim migrants from so-called rogue-states and expel them. Lex taglionis [law of retaliation] may be a cruel law, but it is the only one these criminal brutes are capable of understanding."[101] In May 2008, members of the Islamic community in and around the southern Italian city of Naples protested against the new security measures proposed by Prime Minister Silvio Berlusconi. These measures made illegal immigration a crime and replaced single police officers with security personnel—including soldiers—to patrol the streets. "We Muslims will also march to condemn what happened to the Roma Gypsy community in the region. Among them there are many Muslims from Bosnia with whom we sympathise," declared the imam of Salerno.[102]

In addition to the counterproductive effect of discrimination, both the European and U.S. strategies to prevent radicalization do little to tackle the root causes of extremism. The European Commission has emphasized the need to step up the regeneration of deprived neighborhoods, to improve housing conditions, to encourage access to education, and to protect against social exclusion.[103]

Yet the EU's antidiscrimination framework suffers from drastic limitations, while crucial policy areas (such as housing and education) remain largely the preserve of the EU member states. Western governments are rightly fearful that Islamic extremism may become more influential. Yet they use the actual threat of radical minorities to justify indiscriminate measures against the majority of Muslims whose greater concern is not to plot terrorist attacks but to integrate into their host societies. Furthermore, Western governments seem unable to appreciate the relationship between domestic radicalization and foreign issues rationally. On the European side, the EU emphasizes the need for "a dialogue with and, where appropriate, technical assistance to third countries and regional partners" as "an integral part of the approach to addressing violent radicalisation and terrorist recruitment." To this end,

> the Community will step up its assistance to support partner countries' and regional organisations' efforts to strengthen early warning systems, governance/institutional capacity building and promotion of human rights protection to enable them to engage effectively in a preventive approach. It will also improve its ability to recognize early signs of state fragility through improved joint analysis, joint monitoring and assessments of difficult, fragile and failing states with other donors.[104]

Yet, critically, it is worth noting that none of the actual foreign policy issues related to radicalization—such as Iraq, Afghanistan, and the Israeli-Palestinian conflict—are mentioned.

The change in American leadership no doubt raised hopes among Muslims. President Obama introduced significant changes in style, tone, and strategy. "To the Muslim world, we seek a new way forward, based on mutual interest and mutual respect" the new president said in his inaugural address. This statement was highly welcomed, as were Obama's remarks to the Turkish parliament (April 2009) and his speech in Cairo (June 2009). In addition to repeatedly pointing out the contribution of Muslims to America ("Islam has always been part of America's history," and "the United States has been enriched by Muslim Americans"), Obama tried to address the most urgent concerns expressed by Muslims both in the United States and abroad. Muslim and Arab American advocates have participated in policy discussions with senior White House adviser Valerie Jarret, DHS secretary Janet Napolitano, and Attorney General Eric H. Holder Jr., discussing civil liberties concerns and counterterrorism strategies. "For the first time in eight years, we have the opportunity to meet, engage, discuss, disagree, but have an impact on policy," said James Zogby, president of the Arab American Institute.[105]

The Obama administration appointed special envoys for the Middle East, Afghanistan and Pakistan, Southwest Asia, the Gulf, and Sudan. Obama also condemned the excesses of the war on terror, such as racial profiling and discrimination against Muslims. Closing the Guantanamo Bay camp was part of his first set of executive orders in January 2009—a decision overwhelmingly approved by Muslims in the United States and abroad.[106] Furthermore, the 2010 National Security Strategy lists a series of foreign issues that need to be addressed in order to secure the homeland. This includes completing a "responsible transition as we end the war in Iraq," pursuing "Arab-Israeli peace," and "succeeding in Afghanistan," as well as "promoting universal values abroad by living them at home."

However, the new administration still faces a set of crucial, urgent, and seemingly intractable challenges. In regard to Iraq, in February 2009 Obama announced a drawdown plan that saw U.S. forces reduced to about fifty thousand by August 2010 and resulted in the end of American combat operations. Regarding Afghanistan, Pakistan, and the federally administered tribal areas spanning the two nations, Obama reaffirmed his commitment to pursue al-Qaeda and the Taliban with the support of an international coalition of forty-six countries. He also planned to invest $1.5 billion each year between 2010 and 2015 to partner with Pakistanis in building schools and hospitals. However, the substantial increase in the use of unmanned aerial vehicles or "attack drones," and the collateral damage that has inevitably resulted from their deployment, has been the central point of outrage over the administration's approach to prosecuting the war against the Taliban, al-Qaeda, and their extremist allies in the region. Nonetheless, achieving a breakthrough to comprehensive Arab-Israeli peace has been described as the cornerstone of the Obama administration's strategy in the Middle East. The failure so far to achieve progress on this issue, combined with the troop surge in Afghanistan and the continued delay in closing Guantanamo Bay, has frustrated the Muslim community. Abdulbari Atwan, editor of *al-Quds al-Arabi*, has expressed skepticism about Obama's true ability and desire to transform relations with the Muslim world, warning that "the U.S. legacy, which is hated in the Muslim world, cannot be redressed with rhetorical words and phrases [. . .] The Arabs are fed up with false promises that were made by former administrations. We have a feeling that the Muslims' honeymoon with Obama will not be long and that his rhetorical language will not produce an effective result."[107] Notably, global perceptions of U.S. leadership improved in 2009, except in many Muslim countries, where favorable dispositions toward America remain extremely scarce. Pakistan registered the most dismal approval rating (9 percent), followed by Iraq (14 percent),

Syria (15 percent), Egypt (37 percent), Tunisia (37 percent), and Morocco (38 percent).[108]

The radicalization process described in this chapter illustrates the most dramatic counterproductive effect of the excesses of securitization. All the measures adopted, to date, do not address the vicious circle of discrimination and resentment. Muslims are considered a threat, being treated as potential terrorists since 9/11. This has generated more discrimination, more suspicion, less integration, and more potential for radicalization. The rise in anti-Muslim hatred does not reduce the threat of terrorism. Instead, it maximizes the influence of the most radical members of that community, who can, as a result, more easily recruit followers at the expense of moderates. Thus, by targeting Muslim communities in the name of security, both U.S. and European policies make Western societies more vulnerable to terrorism.

When combined with the negative effects of the securitization of immigration policy, this trend fuels the security/insecurity escalation. As Mikhail Alexseev argues, "responses rooted in the perpetual logic of the security dilemma are more likely to spread rather than to solve security-related problems arising from migration."[109] This situation raises one crucial question I address in the next chapter: How do we explain why states are unable (or unwilling) to escape from the dynamics of policy failure?

PART III

Why Do Failed Policies Persist?

I have demonstrated in the previous chapters that restrictive security-driven immigration policies have not only proven ineffective in achieving their prescribed goals but in fact aggravated the problems they were intended to solve. I discuss in the following chapters three factors that explain why states persist in implementing inadequate policies. First, I argue that Western states do not properly address the "push factors" that motivate people to emigrate. Although the motives for individual migration are more complex than pure socioeconomic gaps between the country of origin and the host country,[1] migration is mainly perceived as a response to growing global differences between areas. These differences relate to demographic growth, economic opportunity, income disparities, and the protection of human rights. In 2005, for example, the less-developed countries accounted for 81 percent of the world population (6.5 billion). The population of these countries is projected to rise steadily, from 5.3 billion people to 7.8 billion people by 2050, and to account by then for 97 percent of the world's population.[2] Levels of poverty in most of the less-developed countries are high: over 20 percent of their overall population live on less than $1 a day. This means that, on average, individuals moving from a poorer to a higher-income country can increase their income by 2,200 percent. The distance between the country of origin and the destination country also has a substantial impact on the costs of migration: the greater the distance to the country of destination, the higher the expense of moving. Geographical proximity, by contrast, highlights economic differences between sending and receiving countries. The border between Spain and Morocco, for example, constitutes the highest development gap in the world between adjacent countries. According to the 2005 UN Development Report, the wealth gap in average annual per capita income between Spain ($22,391) and Morocco ($4,004) was 25 percent larger than the one between the United States ($37,562) and Mexico ($9,168). The pressures generated by the North-South divide tend to erode the foundations of "Fortress Europe" and to dig big holes under the fences along the U.S.-Mexico border. The dominant assumption is, therefore, that the improvement of conditions in sending countries (through long-term development programs) is as crucial as acting on pull factors (through immigration control policies) to halt migration between countries. Yet there is evidence that neither the United States nor the European Union effectively addresses the gap between North and South in terms of economic prosperity, security, and human rights. In addition, the increasing securitization of Official Development Aid (ODA) does nothing to alleviate poverty. Rather, it increases instability and insecurity while ignoring the root causes of immigration, and radicalization abroad.

Second, Western states do not properly address the major "pull factors" either. The idea that it is possible on one side to channel legal labor immigration—to meet the needs of Western economies—and yet on the other side to combat irregular migration and the informal labor market is based on the assumption that public policies are able to identify (and manage) the forms of labor often demanded by the market.[3] There is evidence, however, that this assumption suffers from major flaws, as illustrated by the issues that skills-based immigration policies face in many Western countries. I demonstrate that a "selective immigration" approach often fails to match the labor market needs, resulting in both high-skilled migrant shortages and illegal low-skilled migrant increases. Illegal immigration, initiated by recruitment on the part of employers in the United States and European countries, fills a demand for cheap labor. This explains the existence of a "hidden agenda" whereby Western governments do not fully implement sanctions against employers.

Third, and finally, in order to explain why states persist in doing "more of the same," it is crucial to recognize the impact of the politicization of immigration issues. These issues provide political opportunities to both pro- and anti-migrant groups. The post-9/11 process of securitization has changed the electoral dynamics driving policymaking in this policy area, by limiting the influence of ethnic voters, facilitating the growth of anti-immigrant propaganda, accentuating the pressure from anti-migrant groups on mainstream parties, and damaging the prospects for a more comprehensive and balanced immigration policy.

Clearly, these findings are troubling, as are their implications for the future of both safety and democracy in the West. In the concluding chapter, I argue that the volatile balance between liberty and security, respect of civil rights and the need to control security threats, has been seriously damaged on both sides of the Atlantic. These controversial issues have been studied extensively since 9/11. My point here is not to examine all the challenges democratic governments face, but rather to focus on three aspects that are crucial for Western democracy.

The first relates to what advocates refer to as a "lesser evil" argument. Concerns about long-term adverse effects on civil rights and liberties have been consistently dismissed by U.S. and European governments. They legitimize this trend by arguing that to diminish civil liberties is an unfortunate but inevitable necessity in order to provide more security. Actually, the fight against terrorism has been too often used as an excuse for compromising and eroding civil liberties, as illustrated by secret detentions, detentions without charge or trial, expedited removal processes, extrajudicial prosecution, the use of "secret evidence," and invasion of privacy. Not only has the oversecuritization of U.S. and European agendas been developed at the expense of democratic rights and values, but it has also enhanced insecurity by providing new incentives for radicalization and civil unrest.

Second, the securitization of immigration policy raises concerns about its adverse effects on human rights, as illustrated by the conditions of detention and processes of deportation of illegal immigrants, the violation of the rights of asylum seekers, and the rising death toll of people attempting to reach Europe or the United States. These issues raise the question of the degree to which human rights should be sacrificed in the name of security.

Finally, the actual outcomes of the tradeoff between liberty and security raise questions about the policy priorities of democratic states. The tendency to overestimate the immigration-related security threats contrasts with a relative lack of policy coherence when it comes to addressing a new constellation of integration issues. Western governments focus more on a "law and order" approach than trying to improve their integration policy; and when they do attempt to deal with some integration issues that generate actual insecurity (such as civil unrest or racial riots), security concerns tend to limit the opportunities for immigrants and their children to integrate.

CHAPTER 7

Emigration, Development, and (In)security

Since their unanimous adoption by United Nations member states in 2000, the Millennium Declaration and the Millennium Development Goals (MDGs) have become a universal framework for development.[1] One of their main objectives is to increase development aid in order to eradicate poverty in a sustainable way. To this end the U.S. strategy has been revised in order to achieve seven priority goals, including promoting economic growth, poverty reduction, and providing humanitarian assistance. Most Official Development Aid (ODA) programs are managed by the U.S. Agency for International Development (USAID) and are designed to "advance freedom for the benefit of the American people and the international community by helping to build and sustain a more democratic, secure, and prosperous world ... reduce widespread poverty, and act responsibly within the international system."[2] According to the principle that "growth in developing countries is in the U.S. interest," the goal is to address the issues raised by poor countries: "Countries that stagnate are less able and sometimes less willing to help address transnational issues, many of which originate within their borders, including illegal migration; trafficking in narcotics, weapons, and persons; health threats such as HIV/AIDS and avian flu; and environmental concerns such as loss of biodiversity."[3]

As in the United States, European states have included the MDGs in their foreign aid initiatives. In 2000 the EU member states signed new development cooperation agreements with the ACP (Africa-Caribbean-Pacific) countries, notably the Cotonou Agreement. The European Development Fund, the main instrument for providing EU development aid to ACP countries, was allocated €13.8 billion for 2000–2007.[4] Furthermore, the EU Energy Initiative for Poverty Eradication and Sustainable Development was launched in 2002 as a joint commitment by the EU member states and the European Commission to give priority to the important role of energy in poverty alleviation. The ACP-EU Energy Facility was established in 2005 in order to support projects on increasing access to sustainable and affordable energy services for the poor living in rural and peripheral-urban areas in ACP countries. The overall framework for EU cooperation with Africa was defined by the EU Strategy for Africa, adopted in December 2005. An Africa-EU strategy partnership, founded in 2007, marked a tightening of relations and further efforts to promote MDGs in Africa. Dialogue with North African countries developed within the framework of the European Neighborhood Policy and in the context of Euromed.[5] The European Commission proposed a new instrument, the Aeneas program, which was endowed with a budget of €250 million to cover the period 2004–8.[6] This was followed by the adoption of the Thematic Program on Migration and Asylum (up to €205 million for the period 2007–10), designed to foster the link between development and migration, as well as to strengthen the fight against illegal immigration. In the context of the global economic and financial crisis, the EU Council further reaffirmed its commitment to achieving its own ODA targets according to the MDGs.[7] The council welcomed the European Commission's intention to reinforce and reshape the EU-Africa Infrastructure Trust Fund and to allocate €200 million for that purpose in 2009–10. It also invited the commission to strengthen the Facility for Euro-Mediterranean Investment and Partnership, as well as the Neighborhood Investment Facility. All these initiatives illustrated the EU notion of "enlightened self-interest." According to the European Commission, "The EU acts out of enlightened self-interest just as much as global solidarity. On an increasingly interconnected planet, supporting economic development and political stability in the wider world is an investment in one's future. By helping others, the EU helps to make life safer within its frontiers for its own citizens."[8]

The Poverty-Immigration Nexus

Both the U.S. and European governments have been very active in their efforts to promote development—and therefore to address the issues related to poverty such as illegal immigration and global instability. According to the OECD Development Assistance Committee, U.S. ODA to the developing world has increased dramatically between 2001 and 2005, from $11.4 billion to $27.5 billion. Furthermore, President Bush, in March 2002, unveiled a new development program, the Millennium Challenge Account (MCA). He promised to increase the U.S. foreign aid budget by 50 percent over the fiscal year 2000 budget. Bush also claimed that aid for the MCA would be "above and beyond" conventional aid requests, which were expected to increase to $5 billion by fiscal 2007. The EU and its member states provided over 56 percent of all official development assistance delivered by the major industrialized countries in 2006. The total value was €47 billion, which translates to nearly €100 per citizen (compared to €53 per citizen from the United States and €69 from Japan).[9]

Yet despite all these initiatives—and a long series of declarations on the need for a comprehensive policy addressing the absence of socioeconomic prospects in third world countries—efforts made by Europe and the United States to reduce the gap between North and South in economic prosperity, security, and human rights remained limited. According to the UN *Millennium Development Goals Report*, published in 2010, "unmet commitments, inadequate resources, lack of focus and accountability, and insufficient dedication to sustainable development have created shortfalls in many areas. Some of these shortfalls were aggravated by the global food and economic and financial crises."[10] As illustrated by figure 5, aid remains well below the UN target of 0.7 percent of gross national income for most donors. In 2009 the only countries to reach or exceed the target were Denmark, Luxembourg, the Netherlands, Norway, and Sweden. The largest donors by volume were the United States, followed by France, Germany, the United Kingdom, and Japan—none of whom approached the targeted threshold.

Net disbursements of ODA amounted in 2009 to $119.6 billion, or 0.31 percent of the combined national income of developed countries. In real terms this was a slight increase (of 0.7 percent) compared with 2008, even though, measured in current U.S. dollars, actual ODA fell by over 2 percent—from $122.3 billion in 2008. The EU official development assistance corresponded to 0.42 percent of the EU's gross national income. To date, the EU is still behind schedule to reach the collective EU intermediate target of 0.56 percent of GNI, making it very unlikely to reach 0.7 percent by 2015.[11] In the current financial and economic crisis, there is thus no reason to believe that the EU will play its full part in ensuring that the MDGs are achieved. This shortfall in aid particularly affects Africa. Data for 2009 showed that bilateral ODA to Africa as a whole rose by only 3 percent in real

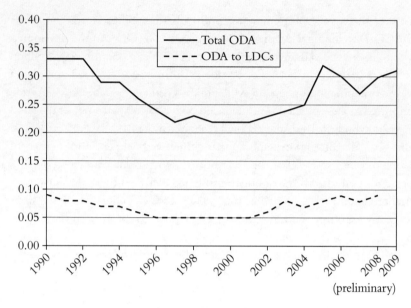

(preliminary)

FIGURE 5.   Net official development assistance (ODA) from OECD-DAC (DAC = Development Assistance Committee) countries as a proportion of donors' gross national income, 1990–2009 (percent).

terms. Sub-Saharan Africa fared only slightly better: bilateral aid increased by 5.1 percent in real terms over 2008. It is estimated that Africa will have received in 2010 only about $11 billion out of the $25 billion increase envisaged at the 2005 Gleneagles Summit, mainly due to the underperformance of some European donors who earmark large shares of their aid to Africa.[12] Meanwhile, sub-Saharan Africa is the worst-performing region in terms of poverty alleviation, with the poverty rate rising from 46.7 percent in 1990 to 49.7 percent in 2000, the absolute number of poor people increasing by a third. Over half of those employed in this region are "working poor," meaning that although they have a job, they live in a household where each member earns less than $1.25 a day.

In addition, although the EU initiatives regarding the MDGs were designed to foster prosperity, European states outlined their priorities (such as illegal immigration, drug trafficking, and terrorism), while the provisions related to economic cooperation were more limited. Cooperation was actually understood as an obligation by the sending countries to improve border management, not as an incentive for EU member states to address the existing socioeconomic disparities between Europe and its neighbors.[13] The Hague Program stated that the EU should aim at assisting third countries, in full partnership, using existing Community funds where appropriate, in their efforts to improve their capacity for migration management and refugee protection, prevent and combat illegal immigration, inform on legal channels for migration, resolve refugee situations by providing better access to durable solutions, build border-control capacity, enhance document security and tackle the problem of return.

The European Commission stated that "the prime challenge is to tackle the main push factors for migration: poverty and the lack of job opportunities."[14] Yet this "comprehensive migration policy" hinged on "responsibility-sharing" between EU member states and sending countries, remaining more focused on border controls than on the economic development of countries of origin and transit. Cooperation with the sending countries therefore emphasized return procedures for asylum seekers whose applications are rejected, reinforcing the fight against illegal immigration and improving procedures for the return of illegal immigrants, as well as prefrontier measures (such as cooperation between consular services of the EU member states and local authorities).

U.S. attempts to achieve the MDGs also produced mixed results. The original vision of $5 billion in aid increases for countries eligible for the Millennium Challenge Account never came to fruition during the Bush administration. For fiscal 2007, Bush requested $3 billion and Congress appropriated only $2 billion to the MCA, the highest allocation to date at that time but still far below the original target. Meanwhile, requests for certain core development accounts declined, and despite Bush's promise, the MCA funding came at the expense of existing development programs.[15] Another problem was raised by the allocation of various funds. Only MCA-eligible countries in South and Central Asia and the Near East saw increases in core development aid. In contrast, in Africa's twelve MCA-eligible countries, average core development aid appropriations declined by 10 percent between 2002 and 2006.[16] This shift partly reflects the greater emphasis put on specific target sectors, such as those linked to energy security, trade, and investment—to the detriment of assistance aimed at poverty reduction and sustainable economic growth. In 2005, for example, the U.S. government spent over $1.4 billion on food aid to Africa but only $134 million on agriculture programs to enable Africans to grow their own crops and end recurring food crises.

Furthermore, the Millennium Challenge Account was characterized by major inconsistencies. It was expected to be politically neutral, providing aid to countries with low income (equal to or less than the ceiling set by the International Development Association) and to countries eligible for assistance from the International Development Association. The actual allocation of funds, however, was based on the implementation by poor countries of "good policies," with a high level of conditionality. Failed states such as Somalia and Sudan were therefore excluded because they had a "poor policy environment."

The Obama administration significantly improved the management and financial capabilities of the State Department and USAID. Secretary of State Clinton announced in July 2009 the creation of the Quadrennial Diplomacy and Development Review, designed to address the issues of accountability and efficiency. The Department of State reported budgetary resources of $50.1 billion as of September 30, 2009, an increase of 29 percent from the prior fiscal year, and USAID reported $19.0 billion in budgetary resources, up 24 percent from the previous fiscal year. The fiscal 2010 requests put the United States on a path to double U.S. foreign assistance by 2015 (up to $53.9 billion, an increase of 9 percent over fiscal 2009).[17] Obama also announced his intention to provide at least $35 billion over the next three year (fiscal years 2010 to 2012) as the U.S. contribution to address the issue of global hunger, including assistance for agricultural development and nutrition. Funding for various programs, conversely, decreased, such as those for the protection of vulnerable populations (from $1 billion in 2009 to $575 million in 2010).[18]

If the rationale of ODA is that acute conditions in the country of origin tend to be a key trigger for migration, push factors remain quite strong—despite the U.S. and European measures implemented since 2000. The 2009 MDG Gap Task Force Report showed that the Global Partnership for Development has recently suffered important setbacks, most of which have arisen from the global financial and economic crisis. About 1.4 billion people worldwide still suffer from extreme poverty. The World Bank estimates that the crisis could have pushed around 55 million more people into extreme poverty in 2009, with the figure rising to 64 million people by the end of 2010. These figures are in addition to the 130–155 million people who were already pushed into poverty in 2008 as a result of the food crisis. The pace of poverty reduction has already significantly slowed because of the succession of food and financial/economic crises. The number of poor people is expected to rise in more than half of all developing countries, two-thirds of low-income countries, and three-quarters of sub-Saharan African countries. Many of the world's poorest countries can be described as "fragile," the majority of them located in sub-Saharan Africa.[19]

It is unlikely in this context that emigration pressures will decrease, for various reasons. First, ODA does not adequately address the root causes of migration. Widening disparities in income and opportunities among countries admittedly add to the pressures for people to move. Yet the dynamics of the relationship between development and migration are more complex than commonly assumed. According to the International Organization for Migration, "development is not simply economic growth," and "migration is not merely a movement of people from one place to another." Furthermore, "migration cannot be a substitute for development, and development is not necessarily dependent on migration."[20] Population movements are closely related to a variety of socioeconomic, demographic, and political dimensions. Poverty is thus one factor among many others. As pointed out by the UN General Assembly,

> Continued political instability and violations of human rights in some parts of the world have led to the forced movements of people, often on a large scale. Technological transformations and economic globalization in particular have generated new demands for skills and labor in many parts of the world, demands that are often being satisfied by migrant workers. As a result, a growing number of countries are involved in international migration, whether as countries of origin, transit or destination for migrants.[21]

Second, although international mobility has been increased by reductions in the cost of transportation and the creation and maintenance of transnational networks of people, those who migrate to developed countries are not the poorest. This explains why the vast majority of international population movement is in fact South–South and not South–North migration. As noted by the UN Observatory on Migration,

> Growing discrepancies between richer and poorer countries have contributed to an increase in migration to developed countries, yet most people who move do so within the borders of their own country or within the region. Three out of four migrants in the world are internal migrants and nearly 70 per cent of international migrants in sub-Saharan Africa move within the region. In 2010, only one in three international migrants moved from a developing to a developed country and almost as many migrants from developing countries resided in another developing country.[22]

Third, migration may have a positive impact on development for countries of origin. Migrant remittances, for example, continue to provide an additional income to the families and households left behind. Estimated remittances sent by migrants to developing countries have increased exponentially, reaching $307 billion in 2009 (up from $83 billion in 2000). Recorded remittances are therefore more than twice as large as ODA. And in addition, nearly two-thirds of foreign direct investment flows to developing countries.[23] Furthermore, background research for the United Nations Development Program's Human Development Report of 2009 found that, in general, migrants are more likely to improve their health and education levels than those who stay in the origin country. Moreover, "human mobility often leads to transfer of considerable human and social capital and a flow of ideas and values that can impact on the cultural and political development of origin societies."[24]

Finally, ODA does not address the root causes of emigration related to insecurity. As Myron Weiner demonstrated, international migration works within a "security/stability framework" in which noneconomic considerations play a key role.[25] While immigration is perceived as a threat to security by developed countries, emigration is often the result of actual threats in the countries of origin, such as civil wars, political violence, and social instability. Regarding forced migration, refugees accounted for 7 percent of the migrant stock in 2005. They constituted almost 18 percent of all international migrants in Africa and 15 percent of those in Asia. Particularly large populations of refugees were present in western Asia (4.7 million) and in south-central Asia (2.3 million). In 2009 the number of forcibly displaced persons reached 43.3 million, the highest level since the mid-1990s. Of these, 15.2 million were refugees. As a side effect of the war on terror, Afghanistan and Iraq were the two major source countries of refugees—and Pakistan the first recipient country.

The Poverty-Terrorism Nexus

The use of development programs to combat insecurity is commonly based on two interrelated assumptions. First, insecurity is perceived as the result of poverty-related issues, along a continuum from socioeconomic depravation to political instability, bad governance, illicit drug production, weapons proliferation, interstate conflicts, and civil wars. Thus, promoting development is supposed to increase security—both in developing and developed countries. According to the European Commission, "security and development are interdependent and mutually reinforcing. No sustainable development is possible in a country threatened by internal insecurity, crisis and conflicts. At the same time, there cannot be sustainable peace without development. Moreover, insecurity, crisis and conflicts can impede the efficient use of aid."[26]

Second, ODA is conceived as being part of a broader foreign-policy agenda that includes not only economic aid but also military assistance, humanitarian concerns, and commercial interests. These overlapping objectives have an impact on the allocation of resources, as illustrated by the distinction between traditional foreign aid (USAID and EuropeAid) and nontraditional foreign aid (through other foreign-policy agencies such as the U.S. Department of Defense, National Institutes of Health, and Centers for Disease Control). These overlapping objectives also explain the strong relationship between aid and national interests. For example, during the cold war, U.S. assistance programs were designed as a way to prevent the expansion of Communist influence and to promote U.S. exports. After the cold war, the focus shifted from an anticommunist containment policy to a series of regional issues (such as the Middle East peace initiatives) and specific concerns (such as international drug trafficking). For decades EU countries used development assistance to preserve their sphere of influence in their former colonies and to promote their trade and financial interests.

Since 9/11, both U.S. and European governments have increasingly associated foreign aid with the fight against terrorism. The focus of foreign aid policy has been transformed according to the common belief that terrorism was the main source of insecurity. This belief also suggested a straightforward correlation between poverty and terrorism. The Millennium Challenge Account, for example, was presented as a tool for fighting global poverty not only for its own good but also as part of the fight against terrorism. In introducing this new program, President Bush declared, "We also work for prosperity and opportunity because they help defeat terror. Yet, persistent poverty and oppression can lead to hopelessness and despair. And when governments fail to meet the most basic needs of the people, these failed states can become havens for terror."[27] The poverty-terrorism linkage was also stressed in the 2002 National Security Strategy, redefining the global orientation of U.S. foreign aid policy. This strategy established global development as a third pillar of U.S. national security, along with defense and diplomacy. Also in 2002, the justifications for foreign budgetary assistance presented by the White House began to emphasize the war on terrorism as the top foreign-aid priority, highlighting U.S. assistance to thirty "front-line" states in the fight against terrorism, including Iraq, Afghanistan, and Pakistan. The substantial reconstruction programs in Afghanistan and Iraq—which accounted for more in fiscal 2004 than the combined budgets of all other aid programs—were also part of the emphasis on the use of foreign aid as a tool against terror.[28] The Framework for U.S. Assistance, adopted in 2006, reflected the priorities listed by the National Security Strategy (as revised the same year), both emphasizing that "development reinforces diplomacy and defense, reducing long-term threats to our national security by helping to build stable, prosperous, and peaceful societies." The Policy Framework underlined that "USAID will support U.S. foreign policy goals with special emphasis on Iraq, Afghanistan, Pakistan and other front-line states in the War on Terror in the Asia and the Near East and Africa regions."[29] In the same vein the fiscal 2007 budget request fully supported "U.S. foreign policy goals and national security interests. The request responds to President Bush's priorities, including support for the Global War on Terrorism."[30] A basic premise of the president's fiscal year 2008 foreign operations budget was that the "security of the American people depends on global stability and prosperity."[31]

The Obama administration subscribed to a similar viewpoint. The U.S. strategy for meeting the MDGs, adopted in 2010, stressed that "the successful pursuit of development is essential to advancing our national security objectives... . Therefore, we are elevating development as a key pillar of our foreign policy and making it central to our engagement with the world."[32] The White House justified the fiscal 2009 Department of State USAID budget by arguing that "the United States directly confronts threats to national and international security from terrorism, weapons proliferation, failed or failing states, and political violence... . It is a tenet of U.S. policy that the security of U.S. citizens at home and abroad is best guaranteed when countries and societies are secure, free, prosperous, and at peace."[33]

A similar notable securitarian orientation was evident in Europe. Through a "multi-functional approach" outlined in the 2003 European Security Strategy, the EU promoted a holistic approach wherein security, economic development, and democracy were seen as crucial for the political stability of the EU's international environment. In 2006 the EU adopted a new external aid concept of security system reform aimed at "preventing and resolving violent conflict, combating terrorism and addressing state fragility [as] part of the EU's efforts to reduce insecurity and eradicate poverty."[34] The twelve-point EU action plan, adopted in 2010, stated that "no development is possible without security and no long term security can be ensured without investing in development."[35] The securitization of foreign aid was notably illustrated by the evolution of the relationship with Africa. EU member states were increasingly convinced of the importance of Africa to European security, resulting in EU military interventions, such as Operation Artemis in the Democratic Republic of Congo in 2003. This trend illustrated the convergence between ODA and the new European Security and Defense Policy framework. The rather impressive list of EU member states contributing to the multinational force in the Democratic Republic of Congo and to other civilian-military operations in Africa (such as in Chad) confirmed this trend. Following the 2005 midterm revision of the Cotonou Agreement, the assistance provided to African partner countries became increasingly linked to political measures of "good governance" rather than purely defined by economic criteria. Meanwhile, terrorism (article 11.a), migration (article 13), and drugs and organized crime (article 30) were identified as the main common concerns. The New Partnership for Africa's Development, launched in 2001, was revised according the same concerns as the Joint Africa-EU Strategy adopted in December 2007.[36]

The emphasis on security concerns informed the allocation of ODA. In 2004 the U.S. Congress appropriated $5.4 billion (26 percent of total assistance) to programs supporting U.S. political and security objectives, and $4.8 billion (23 percent) to military assistance programs—compared with $2.5 billion for humanitarian assistance (12 percent). In 2006 the Policy Framework for Bilateral Foreign Aid budgeted USAID's programs according to five core strategic goals: supporting strategic states (33 percent of the total foreign aid); promoting transformational development (24 percent); providing humanitarian relief (19 percent); addressing global issues and special concerns (18 percent); and strengthening fragile states (6 percent). The Strategic Plan for fiscal years 2007–12 listed seven strategic goals as laid out in table 15. The first was "achieving peace and security" by promoting counterterrorism abroad; detecting weapons of mass destruction; developing robust political-military operations, and fighting transnational crime.[37] The Department of State and USAID allocated $14.1 billion toward this goal in fiscal 2009, constituting 29 percent of the total State-USAID budget (compared with 9 percent for humanitarian aid).

The Peace and security objective remained a priority in 2010. It was funded at $10.4 billion by USAID (up 42 percent from $7.3 billion in 2006), to which the Department of Defense added $10.2 billion for training and equipping Iraqi and Afghan security forces. Two-thirds of the budget ($3.6 billion) allocated to the Strategic Goal 2 (governing justly and democratically) went to five countries of special strategic interest: Afghanistan (40 percent alone), Iraq, Mexico, Pakistan, and Haiti. Humanitarian assistance slightly increased (up to $5.0 billion).

Both the war on terror and subsequent security concerns framed the geographical distribution of aid. In 2000 Afghanistan, Iraq, and Pakistan did not appear on the list of the top recipients of U.S. foreign assistance. In 2010 these three countries were among the top six recipient countries. As noted by Curt Tarnoff and Marian Leonardo Lawson in their report for

Table 15.   Department of State/USAID Strategic Plan (2007–2012), fiscal year 2009 budget

Strategic goal	Strategic area of focus	Budget allocation
1. Peace and security	• Counterterrorism • WMD and destabilizing conventional weapons • Security cooperation and security sector reform • Conflict prevention, mitigation, and response • Transnational crime • Homeland security	$14.1 billion (29%)
2. Governing justly and democratically	• Rule of law and human rights • Good governance • Political competition and consensus building • Civil society	$3.4 billion (7%)
3. Investing in people	• Health • Education • Social services and protection for especially vulnerable populations	$10.7 billion (22%)
4. Promoting economic growth and prosperity	• Private markets • Trade and investment • Energy security • Environment • Agriculture	$4.7 billion (10%)
5. Providing humanitarian assistance	• Protection, assistance, and solutions • Disaster prevention and mitigation • Orderly and humane means for migration management	$4.5 billion (9%)
6. Promoting international understanding	• Offer a positive vision • Marginalize extremism • Nurture common interests and values	$1.2 billion (2%)
7. Strengthening consular and management capabilities	• Consular services • Major management functions	$10.08 billion (20%)

Source: Adapted from Department of State / USAID, *Joint Summary of Performance and Financial Information*, fiscal year 2009.

Congress, reconstruction assistance to Iraq and Afghanistan from all U.S. sources accounted between 2002 and 2010 for $104 billion and "has disproportionately shaped the portrait of the US foreign aid program."[38] In addition, most of Foreign Military Financing went to U.S. friends and allies, such as Israel and Egypt, and about 90 percent of the funds provided through the Economic Support Fund went to support the Middle East peace process, as well as countries of importance in the war on terrorism. In 2010 about $5.0 billion went to Iraq, Afghanistan, and Pakistan through the Economic

Table 16. U.S. Foreign Operations Budgeting for Strategic Goal 1, peace and security, by region ($ in thousands)

Region	FY 2008	FY 2009	FY 2010 request
Africa	250,619	399,470	388,982
East Asia and the Pacific	106,359	153,000	114,507
Near East	4,374,050	4,886,825	4,863,760

Source: Adapted from Department of State / USAID, Congressional Budget Justifications, Foreign Operation, fiscal year (FY) 2010.

Support Fund. As illustrated by table 16, the Near East received the lion's share of U.S. funding to prevent the spread of terrorism in various regions.

The United States backed African efforts to carry out peace-support operations and to fight terrorism, including the Trans-Sahara Counter-Terrorism Partnership and the East Africa Regional Security Initiative, as well as stabilization operations and security sector reform efforts in countries such as Liberia, Somalia, Ethiopia, and the Democratic Republic of Congo. U.S. resources were also used to enhance coordination with partnership countries (Mali, Niger, Chad, Senegal, Nigeria, and Mauritania) and bolster regional activities to resist "attempts by Al Qaeda and others to impose their radical ideology on traditionally moderate and tolerant Muslim populations in the region."[39] In the East Asia and Pacific region, U.S. priorities were to protect vital national security interests and promote regional stability. This included supporting counterterrorism and law enforcement programs in the Philippines and Indonesia, enhancing maritime security cooperation in strategic waterways such as the Strait of Malacca and the currently poorly monitored Sulawesi Sea, and developing the capacity of countries to participate in peace-support operations. The strategic objectives were to defeat terrorist organizations, support peaceful resolution of internal conflicts, enhance maritime security, strengthen nonproliferation efforts, and support stabilization operations and security-sector reform.[40]

The emphasis on security concerns also informed the allocation of European aid. At the EU level, security is not a "sector" for external aid in the traditional sense. Instead, a "security sensitive approach" is found in all external assistance programs, including the Euro-Mediterranean Partnership, the European Neighborhood Policy, the EU Initiative for Democracy and Human Rights, the Instrument for Stability (created in 2006), and the Development Cooperation Instrument (created in 2007). Aimed at helping Mediterranean countries to reform their economic and social structures, the Euro-Mediterranean Partnership focused its funding (up to €5.3 billion) on three key priorities for the 2000–2006 period: stability, security, and sustainable development. Its strategic partners included countries playing a key role in EU security policy, such as Algeria, Egypt, Israel, Jordan, Lebanon, the Palestinian Authority, Syria, Tunisia, and Turkey (Libya having observer status since 1999). The European Neighborhood Policy, which replaced the Euro-Mediterranean Partnership in 2007, explicitly asked partner countries to cooperate on key EU foreign policy objectives such as counterterrorism and nonproliferation of weapons of mass destruction. A number of security provisions were included in the action plans with sixteen neighbors (and in the negotiations with Libya, which started in 2009), while funding increased by 32 percent (up to €12 billion for the period 2007–13). The promotion of democracy and human rights through the EU Initiative for Democracy and Human Rights, as well as DG ECHO (the Humanitarian Aid Department), also related to security concerns by linking democratization and the fight against terrorism. Middle Eastern countries (Jordan, Egypt, Morocco, Algeria, and Yemen) were among the major recipients of aid. A specific priority was also given to Iraq and Afghanistan in order to strengthen the role of civil society in political reform and the fight against corruption. The EU mobilized €350 million between 2006 and 2009 for the Instrument for Stability, aimed at targeting the needs of each conflict/post-conflict situation. A total of €139 million was devoted to address transregional security threats, such as maritime trafficking, international organized crime, money laundering, and terrorism. The Instrument for Stability was used to finance a large number of crisis response projects, notably in Somalia, Sudan, and Afghanistan. The Development Cooperation Instrument also paid special attention to Afghanistan (with €65 million for rural governance in 2009), as well as Pakistan, Iraq, and Yemen. In addition, the EU's Africa-Caribbean-Pacific partnership increasingly reflected the shift from development aid to security concerns. EU investments in infrastructure in Africa, for example, amounted to €308.7 million in 2009.[41] Approximately €560 million was spent on food assistance, and €121 million was allocated to health research. That same year EU funding to support the African Peace and Security Agenda mobilized €1 billion.[42] The EU mission in Somalia received in 2010 an additional allocation of €80 million to maintain security in Mogadishu.

Yet there are concerns that this shift may divert attention from poverty while not addressing the root causes of both poverty and terrorism. The poverty and terrorism relationship is complex and often controversial. There is clear evidence that poor countries such as Afghanistan, Sudan, and Yemen provide safe heavens for al-Qaeda operatives. "Although some perpetrators of terrorism may not themselves be poor," Francis Y. Owusu argues, "terrorists often come from societies that are poor. Thus, one cannot look at the characteristics of individual terrorists and conclude that there is no relationship between poverty and terrorism; rather we need to look at the characteristics of societies in which terrorism thrives."[43] On the other hand, terrorism is fueled by many other factors, and the majority of poor people around the world are not terrorists. Moreover, insecurity and instability in conflict and post-conflict countries make long-term development efforts extremely difficult. In turn, a failure to achieve any progress toward sustainable development can further heighten the risk of instability and conflict.

A detailed review of the actual outcomes of the poverty-terrorism strategy provides mixed results. Both the U.S. and European antiterrorist development strategies suffer from similar flaws. First, the combined goals to alleviate poverty and to fight terrorism have not been achieved, as illustrated by the situations in Algeria and Yemen. The EU increased its financial assistance to Algeria after the end of the civil war in 2002.[44] The average annual commitment under the Euro-Mediterranean Partnership (MEDA II) for 2000–2006 was estimated to be €48.4 million (compared with €33 million under MEDA I for the period 1995–99). The strategic framework for EU cooperation with Algeria under the European Neighborhood and Partnership Instrument requested a further €220 million over the period 2007–13. Since 1980 the European Investment Bank has granted almost €2.243 billion in loans to Algeria. This financial assistance has been complemented by bilateral aid from EU members such as France, the first bilateral partner of Algeria and the strongest donor (€205 million for public development aid in 2008). Algeria's financial and economic indicators slightly improved between 2000 and 2008, but weak global hydrocarbon prices in 2009 contributed to a 40 percent drop in government revenue. About 23 percent of the population remained below poverty level in 2009.

Yemen, the ancestral homeland of Osama bin Laden and the site of the 2000 USS *Cole* bombing that killed seventeen American sailors, has long grappled with the presence of extremists on its soil. Although Western officials have argued for years that Yemen's instability poses a terrorism threat, government records show that annual U.S. military and development aid to Yemen in the past decade has been less than $50 million, a fraction of the sums sent to its regional neighbors (for example, up to $1 billion a year to Pakistan). U.S. assistance increased from $17.7 million in 2008 to $30.3 million in 2009. In addition, Yemen received €90 million from the EU for the period 2007–10 through various programs. Under the Development Cooperation Instrument, the objective was to prevent Yemen from state failure (raising the planned allocation for 2011 by 20 percent). President Ali Abdullah

Saleh, in exchange, was supposed to improve security and counterterrorist policies, as well as to push forward a political and social reform agenda. Yet Yemen remains one of the poorest nations and one of the most unstable states in the world. It ranks 153 out of the 177 countries in the United Nations Development Program Human Index for development: nearly 45 percent of the population lives on less than $2 a day. President Obama signed a measure in January 2010 that more than doubles annual civilian development aid to Yemen, after increasing military aid the prior year. According to Christopher Boucek, a Yemen expert at the Carnegie Endowment for International Peace, "at issue is whether the new aid, still comparatively modest, is enough to help prevent that poor, strife-torn, loosely governed country from remaining a staging ground for Islamic extremists."[45] In addition, the U.S. Central Command proposed in September 2010 to supply Yemen with $1.2 billion in military equipment and training over the next six years. This initiative raised two concerns: first, U.S. weapons might be used against political enemies of President Saleh and thus provoke a backlash that would further destabilize the country; second, countering extremism in Yemen must involve the development of sustainable institutions that can deliver real economic and social progress. To date, the Yemen quandary reflects the uncertainty Western governments face as they try to promote development *and* security.

This relates to a second, and more crucial, limitation to the antiterrorist development strategy. The poverty-terrorism nexus is based on the assumption that ODA can be used as a tool against terrorist radicalization abroad by linking development, democratization, and security. Both the United States and European countries have committed themselves to expand democratic governance in the developing countries. Under Strategic Goal 2 (governing justly and democratically), USAID programs aim at strengthening the performance and accountability of government institutions, combating corruption, and supporting elections. Funding levels for good governance and the rule of law have grown significantly in recent years (from $1.7 billion in 2006 to $3.6 billion in 2010). The "Freedom Agenda" also includes specific programs such as the Middle East Partnership Initiative and the Broader Middle East and North Africa Initiative—both illustrating the intensification of U.S. democracy-promotion efforts in the region. On the European side, the European Neighborhood Policy is allegedly designed to build upon a commitment between the EU and partner countries to common values (such as democracy, rule of law, human rights, and good governance). The Union for the Mediterranean also promotes democratic reforms across Southern Europe, North Africa, and the Middle East—as well as other EU instruments such as the Conflict Prevention Partnership and the EU Initiative for Democracy and Human Rights. National plans for human rights and democracy have been adopted by EU member states since 2005, notably for the modernization of the judicial system in Tunisia and the support of civil society in Egypt and Jordan.

Yet there is little conclusive evidence of an effective relationship between foreign aid and democratization in target states. Most studies of ODA conclude that such assistance does not actually affect democratization[46]—and may even have a negative impact when aid conditionality does not address the political particularities of recipient countries (especially in the Arab world).[47] Thomas Carothers, for example, underlines the often inappropriate efforts of the U.S. administration to export a "democracy template" that emphasizes elections to the detriment of other, more effective components (such as freedom of expression, an independent legislature and judiciary, and a civilian-controlled military). One result of this approach is that U.S. policymakers are often prone to portray even significantly flawed election results, especially in allied countries, as nonetheless constituting "important starting points" in the transition to democracy.[48] Peter J. Schraeder reaches a similar conclusion, noting that "it is precisely for this reason that critics have often criticized US democracy promotion as placing too much faith in the election process, in essence favoring a 'top-down' approach to democratization that is too elite centered."[49] The less-skeptical studies on the contribution of ODA to the dynamics of democratization point out the role of internal factors, such as economic growth, effective good governance, education, and free press, as key correlates to democracy. Targeted democracy assistance can eventually work when national actors (such as empowered voters, political parties, human rights groups, and labor unions) have the ability—and are willing—to contribute to democratization, as illustrated by the cases of Guatemala and Malawi.[50] A smooth "democratic diffusion" is therefore more likely to happen in countries where there is a "democratic environment" already achieved. This excludes the most authoritarian regimes, as well as the "illiberal democracies" that have flourished since the end of the cold war.[51]

Furthermore, as Peter Schraeder argues,

Democracy promotion is typically compromised when the normative goal of democracy clashes with other foreign policy interests. Especially in the wake of the events of 11 September 2001, several northern industrialized democracies are clearly willing to adopt a *realpolitik* approach to international politics that compromises democratic values

in favor of national security interests, as witnessed by the Bush administration's strong support for undemocratic allies where convenient as
part of Washington's global war on terrorism.[52]

All of North Africa's leaders, Libya's Muammar Qaddafi included, have
been regarded as strong partners in the global war on terror. In turn, the
status of "partner states" in the antiterrorism coalition has allowed these
authoritarian leaders to oppose any democratic reform by invoking the threat
of an Islamist takeover. In this context, the tendency of U.S. and European
governments to call for greater democratization while supporting authoritarian leaders has been patently counterproductive. First, it has caused Western standing in the region to plummet over the last decade. According to
Claire Spencer, expert at Chatham House (home of the British Royal Institute of International Affairs), "the downside has been a retreat by the US
and European governments from raising concerns about human rights and
extra-judicial detentions that featured large in their previous policy initiatives towards the region." Furthermore, "allegations of Western complicity in
extra-judicial investigations of terror suspects have weakened the credibility
of US and EU positions that urge reforms in these areas."[53] Also, it has fueled
the resentment of many political and civil society groups who complain that
Western powers turn a blind eye when democratic rights are violated. In
Algeria, elected political parties have rarely represented more than a rubber
stamp for the presidency since the 1990s, despite the initiation of officially
sanctioned democratic processes.[54] A growing political discontent, coupled
with socioeconomic frustration, fuels both civil unrest and radicalization.
A similar process is taking place in many other countries, such as Jordan and
Syria.

Both the U.S. and European governments can (and actually do) pretend—
to some extent—that the recent revolutions in Tunisia and Egypt are the
result of their support for democratization. However, funding for democracy
and governance-related reforms has remained a small portion of their development aid in these countries. U.S. aid to Egypt, for example, went mainly to
the military for more than thirty years (up to $1.3 billion in annual defense
aid), while funding for democracy initiatives declined from 1999 to 2009.
Furthermore, Western policymakers have displayed a strong reluctance to
engage with Islamist groups such as the Muslim Brotherhood (banned from
all political activities in 2007 by the Mubarak regime). As noted by Alex
Glennie in a report for the Institute for Public Policy Research (a leading
British think tank), "economic and security interests in the Middle East
and North Africa have led western governments to place a high premium

on regional stability, which has meant offering fairly uncritical support to autocratic regimes and failing to build strategic relationships with other potential reform actors, including non-violent Islamist movements."[55] Both U.S. and European governments now face a quandary: to display greater consistency in promoting democracy supposes a dialogue with these movements, while reform of undemocratic political structures in the region may well benefit Islamist movements and therefore "involve significant risks and tradeoffs for North American and European policymakers."[56] As for Libya, the key objectives of the European support have been the stability of the region and the prevention of new immigration flows. To date, European countries face more instability and a dramatic increase of refugees.

CHAPTER 8

Immigration, Economic Interests, and Politics

Rather than addressing the root causes of immigration, both the U.S. and European governments have prioritized their security concerns in the allocation of development aid—affecting in turn both prosperity and security, and thus increasing the incentives for emigration to the West. Meanwhile, both the United States and European countries believe that immigration policy should include control of the "pull factors," such as job opportunities, access to social benefits, and civic integration. This belief is currently the basis of the "selective immigration" policy—a system inspired by the Canadian and Australian policies, providing "points" for education, skills in demand, and working experience. Mainly designed to attract highly skilled immigrants and to protect the national labor market, this option is increasingly popular on both sides of the Atlantic. Yet the dual objectives of limiting the number of the "unwanted" immigrants *and* attracting the most "wanted" ones faces serious obstacles, such as the impossibility of identifying (and managing) the forms of labor often sought by the market.

A better understanding of the consequences of public policy choices, as well as the main motivations of the receiving states, also requires paying attention to their hidden agendas. What states profess as their goals, and what they tend to do, are often inconsistent. Stephen Castles, for example, notes that "the state tries to balance competing interests, or at least to convince certain groups that their wishes are being considered. . . . This can mean that politicians are content to provide anti-immigration rhetoric while actually pursuing policies that lead to more immigration, because this meets important economic or labor market objectives."[1] In this case, the gap between official rhetoric (which professes the will to manage flows) and the actual outcomes may not be understood as a policy failure, but alternatively as the result of the competition between various pro- and anti-immigrant factions.

Finally, a policy failure can provide political opportunities. Anti-immigrant groups or parties become more influential as U.S. and European policymakers are unable to achieve an effective and comprehensive immigration reform. This deep politicization, in turn, impairs the opportunities for addressing the problems commonly associated with immigration—which fuels a further polarization of the politics of immigration. In turn, the inability of U.S. and European governments to tackle the main problems fuels a growing political distrust, which provides fertile ground for xenophobic feelings. Mainstream parties, in response, tend to do "more of the same" by implementing tougher immigration measures in order to compete with extremist parties and to secure their electorate.

"Selective Immigration" and False Assumptions about the Migration Phenomenon

In the United States, attempts to achieve a more selective—and thus more effective—immigration recruitment have been undertaken since the mid 1980s. This was illustrated, for example, by bill S 2104 passed by the Senate in 1988 that allowed a limited number of admissions (independently from the family visa allocation program) based on criteria of age, education, and skills. A similar point system was part of a bill adopted in 1989, providing a "flexible ceiling" of 630,000 admissions for independent visas and families. The 1990 Immigration act introduced a new H-1B visa (capped at sixty-five thousand) that enabled employers to offer permanent jobs to migrants in "specialty occupations" on a three-year, onetime renewable visa, after which immigrants could apply to adjust their status to permanent residency. Subsequent legislation was passed in 1998 and 2000, expanding the H-1B visa program. Currently, the annual cap stands at sixty-five thousand applications, with an additional twenty thousand visas for workers with at least a master's degree. In addition to the admission of highly skilled "nonimmigrants," the employment-based preferences policy includes legal permanent residents or "green card" recipients who have needed skills—especially professionals with advanced degrees or aliens of exceptional ability, priority workers, skilled workers, special immigrants (for example, ministers, religious workers, and employees of the U.S. government abroad), needed unskilled workers, and investors. In 2009 the employment-based preferences limit was equal to 140,000 (plus any unused family preferences from the previous year).

In Europe the implementation of "selective immigration" policy is of a more recent vintage. In 2000, for example, Germany proposed granting temporary work permits to Indian computer specialists. The results were mixed. Not only did this proposal meet with the opposition of anti-immigrant groups, but it failed to attract enough workers to fill even its meager visa quota. In 2001 the German government attempted to expand the program to include other temporary workers, but this initiative was deferred after 9/11. Finally, in 2004, the German parliament enacted a new Immigration Act allowing highly skilled workers to be granted permanent residency on arriving in the country. The act also provided permanent resident permits for the "self-employed" if they invested at least €1 million and generated at least ten new jobs in Germany.

The German initiative was mirrored by other European countries. In 2001 the Czech government introduced a preferential access to the national labor market to highly skilled immigrants—those from European non-EU countries, Canada, and India. In 2005 the British government proposed a new points system designed to attract workers with special skills and experience. Beginning in early 2008 the new system, with five categories, or tiers, replaced the former eighty work permit and entry schemes. The more skill an applicant has, and the more those skills are in demand, the more points the applicant gains, increasing the likelihood of entry to the UK. The first level (Tier 1) is designed to attract entrepreneurs, top scientists, and business people who will automatically have enough points to come without a job offer. All applicants have to pass an English test, unless they have £1 million or more to invest. Tier 2, launched later in 2008, covers people with qualifications or important work-related skills in various sectors, such as health services, white-collar jobs, and trades. People in this category will be allowed into the UK if they have a job offer in a "shortage area," such as nursing. Tier 3, covering temporary low-skilled workers, was to be introduced at a later date. Until now, the government has reduced permissions in this tier in favor of EU workers. Finally, Tier 4 (students) and Tier 5 (youth mobility, including professional sports people and musicians) came into force in 2009. France has also moved toward a "selective immigration" approach, while limiting family reunification and rights of residency for less-skilled immigrants. Under the Immigration and Integration Act of July 2006, those selected for their needed "skills and talents" are offered three-year resident permits. In January 2007 Ireland introduced a green-card scheme offering two-year temporary visas for highly skilled workers from non-EU countries. Candidates must find a job paying at least €60,000 or more to obtain a permit.

At the EU level, concerns that highly skilled immigrants prefer to move to the United States prompted Commissioner Franco Frattini in 2005 to propose a "job seekers" permit, which would have allowed skilled immigrants to enter the EU territory and search for work in any of the twenty-seven EU member states. The objective was to enhance Europe's attractiveness as a whole by offering more opportunities to highly skilled workers and reducing structural barriers to mobility (such as national differences in taxation, salaries, access to services, and pension schemes). After two years of negotiations, the European Commission proposed, in October 2007, a blue-card system— similar in theory to the U.S. green card.[2] Applicants must have secured a job in the EU and have at least three years' experience in the sector concerned, or a university qualification recognized by the member state. Once admitted in one EU state, blue-card holders could seek and gain employment in any other EU states without going through additional immigration processes, at least after a probationary period of two years. They could benefit from immediate family reunification, and their spouses would have the right to work. They could also have a three-month grace period if employment is lost. However, the proposed system does not replace the twenty-seven national systems, as EU member states retain full control over immigration flows.

Consequently, as senior advisers to the Transatlantic Council on Migration Elizabeth Collett and Fabian Zuleeg note, "a degree that one member state recognizes as qualifying for a Blue Card may be rejected by another member state. Such differing national standards may cause friction once Blue Card holders have the right to move across the continent."[3] The newer member states, for example, argue that a common immigration system for highly skilled workers is inappropriate when their own citizens still face the impediment of labor-market safeguards imposed by the EU-15 states. Furthermore, in January 2008 the United Kingdom decided not to participate in the adoption and application of the Legal Migration Directives, including the blue card.

From a Western perspective, the ideal goal remains to admit only high-skilled immigrants. Yet, paradoxically, skills-based immigration policies do not always make sense. As British economist Philippe Legrain argues, "if countries admit only highly-skilled workers, they will exacerbate the shortage of low-skilled workers. . . . More generally, are governments capable of correctly picking the people that an economy needs?"[4] In Great Britain, for example, under the new system, skilled workers in occupations where there is a shortage will be able to enter, provided they have a job offer.

The government is confident the system will be flexible enough to rapidly address the economy's needs. Some experts, however, express reservations about the flexibility of this policy. According to shadow immigration minister Damian Green, there are already "real strains in some areas on housing, on police, on hospitals and on school places and the new system makes no attempt to address that at all. You still don't know whether you're getting the right number of people that the social services, the public services, can absorb." Tom Brake, speaking for the Liberal Democrats, expresses similar concerns: "This is going to discriminate against people perhaps working in the care sector because they are unlikely to get a high number of points, or, for instance, people working in the restaurant trade. These jobs are unlikely to be filled by people from other EU countries."[5] Actually, as many Eastern European workers decided to return to their home countries after working a few months, it became common in Great Britain to joke about the difficulty of finding a Polish plumber.

Attracting high-skilled workers is not an easy task, either. Much has been made of the limited success of the German attempt in 2000–2001 to recruit Indian IT specialists. The current system for the highly skilled sets a minimum annual salary threshold for needed IT workers at €85,000—which is apparently not enough to persuade these specialists to move to Germany, and which is also too costly for German businesses to hire them. Despite the attempts of IT industries to get the threshold lowered, the government refuses to do so, in order to privilege native workers.

According to the Institute for Public Policy Research (IPPR), a center-left think tank, more than 190,000 migrants left the UK in 2007. Short-stay migration is a growing phenomenon, and those most likely to leave are highly skilled: "As global competition for highly skilled migrants increases in future years, schemes to retain migrants may become as important as attracting them in the first place."[6] The IPPR suggested that new incentives should be offered to keep these "super mobile" immigrants, such as a simpler visa extension and tax breaks. Yet in December 2010 the government announced a cap on skilled workers from outside the EU and is planning to curb the number of foreign students. According to IPPR director Nick Pearce, "this could hurt the economic recovery. Hasty measures to reduce numbers artificially would be even more damaging. Bringing down the level of immigration is a legitimate policy goal, but this should be done by making long-term and sustainable reforms to the structure of our economy and labor market."[7]

Skills-based immigration policies can therefore make sense, but only under two conditions: a better assessment of the needs of the labor market and, even more important, a more accurate perception of what is "highly skilled."

Given shifts in economic conditions, a global approach requires examining the labor dynamics, inputs, and local agents or markets involved in both sending and receiving countries—including the costs of intermediaries (such as recruiters, travel and visa services, and placement agents). Characteristically, European countries wish to attract highly skilled immigrants on the grounds that they boost economic growth, but at the same time these countries underutilize the qualifications of foreign workers. According to a report from the German Marshall Fund, "In many cases, migrants who have been selected by point system–based selective migration policies fail to find or maintain employment in their profession or, if so, at a level that takes full advantage of their skills."[8] Consequently, immigrants tend to be overqualified for the jobs they perform, as illustrated by the proverbial taxi driver with a PhD. In Europe one-quarter of immigrants have higher education (university level), compared with one-fifth of all workers in OECD countries. In some countries, such as Spain, Italy, and Sweden, the proportion of immigrants working at jobs below their qualifications is twice as high as for native workers.

Europe's skills-based immigration policy is admittedly influenced by other models, such as the Australian and North American systems. It is perhaps premature to evaluate the effect of the British points system and the EU blue card. Yet the Australian and North American systems show that governments do not always have the capacity to know exactly which type of workers the economy needs at any given time. Economic trends are forever changing, as much as the demand for particular skills. A report published by the Immigration Policy Center found that nearly all the visa preference categories that do exist in the United States for less-skilled workers are subject to numerical caps that fall short of meeting the demands of the U.S. economy. Of the five categories of visas for permanent immigration status, the only employment-based avenue for less-skilled workers is the "third preference," designated for "other workers," which allots only five thousand visas each year. A similar bottleneck exists for less-skilled workers who seek employment-based visas for temporary immigrant status. Of the sixteen categories of temporary immigrant visas available for employment and training, only two are available for less-skilled workers: H-2A (restricted to agricultural workers) and H-2B (limited to "seasonal" or otherwise "temporary" work). The number of H-2A visas declined from 2001 (27,695) to 2004 (14,094).[9] In 2006 the total number reached 46,432—a cap that many experts considered as too low to meet the labor demand in the U.S. agricultural sector. With regard to the H-2B visas, the cap of 66,000 was reached in 2004 halfway through the fiscal year, and in 2005 the last week of January.[10] Entries of seasonal non-agricultural workers recently declined further—48 percent from 109,621 in

2008 to 56,543 in 2009. The number of seasonal agricultural workers also decreased (from 173,103 in 2008 to 149,763 in 2009).[11] The result, according to experts at the Migration Policy Institute, is that "a large number of prospective employment-based immigrants are crowded into a small number of highly limited visa categories, or are forced to pursue immigration opportunities through an already overburdened family-based system."[12]

An increasing number of immigrants applied through a qualifying relative as a way to overcome the deficiencies of the employment-based system. In 2005, for example, the allotment of visas through this kind of adjustment of status represented 89 percent of the total number of employment-based visas. As a result, the family-based system is overwhelmed by applications, and undermined by excessively long delays. According to the Immigration Policy Center, this "not only undermines the family-reunification goal of the family-based immigration system, but also renders that system an ineffective means of responding to U.S. labor demand. The rise of undocumented migration is a predictable result."[13]

Finally, what is also predictable is that the global competition to attract highly skilled workers is going to impact the prosperity of both the United States and European countries. They have to compete with other countries that are actively seeking to recruit highly skilled immigrants, such as Canada and Australia; and they are direct competitors in the race for talent. To date, the United States is still far ahead of the EU: foreign highly skilled workers make up 3 percent of the U.S. labor force but only 1.7 percent of the employed population in Europe.[14] The United States accounts for 40 percent of the world's total spending on scientific research and development—based on R&D spending—employs 70 percent of the world's Nobel Prize winners, and is home to three-quarters of the world's top forty universities.[15] Yet many U.S. experts express concerns about highly skilled workers opting to go to Europe instead of moving to the United States. About 70 percent of foreign scientists and engineers who received PhDs from U.S. universities remain in the country after receiving their degrees, but that situation could change as salaries and research opportunities improve overseas—notably in Europe with the project of developing an European Institute for Innovation and Technology. Furthermore, Europe and China are both graduating more university-educated engineers on a yearly basis than the United States. As a result, the United States faces an increasing reliance on foreign-born workers and students. An inflow of foreign students has helped the country build and maintain its leadership. For example, foreign students earn nearly 60 percent of engineering doctoral degrees awarded by U.S. universities. Continuing this flow is crucial to the United States in maintaining a worldwide lead.

Various recent reports have urged the U.S. government to attract more workers in science and technology and to make it easier for foreigners who have graduated from U.S. universities with degrees in these fields to remain indefinitely. Both the RAND Corporation and the Heritage Foundation, for example, recommend an emergency increase in H-1B visas. James Sherk and Diem Nguyen estimate that the United States will take an extra $69 billion in new tax revenue if 195,000 additional H-1B visa holders are allowed to work each year for the next eight years.[16] Currently, the annual cap represents far fewer people than needed in the country. U.S. Citizenship and Immigration Services received 163,000 applications in 2008 for these visas within a week of accepting applications for fiscal 2009 and is no longer accepting new applications; in 2007 the agency reached the cap within hours of accepting applications for fiscal 2008. Because of political considerations, both Republicans and Democrats are unable to reach an agreement on raising the annual H-1B cap. The vocal lobbying of the Federation for American Reform, which supports more-restrictive immigration measures, does not help to clarify the terms of the debate. Meanwhile, H-1B admissions decreased 17 percent, from 409,619 in 2008 to 339,243 in 2009.

The Hidden Agenda

The issue of employer sanctions illustrates the tension between the need to address labor shortages in some sectors (partly connected to the buoyancy of the informal economy) and the stated objective to curb the number of illegal immigrants. In Europe, illegal immigration persists because it is a source of cheap labor, which helps to alleviate labor shortages—especially in low-skilled positions for which it remains difficult to attract nationals or EU nationals. Pressure from business groups and industries that are dependent on illegal immigrant labor partially explains the weak enforcement of employer sanctions. When policymakers are determined to forcefully deter illegal immigration, it often increases political discontent. In the eastern part of Germany, for example, where growers traditionally rely heavily on Polish workers (who were mainly illegal before the admission of Poland into the EU), the asparagus season of 2006 was spoiled by a clash of conflicting interests. The government ruled that national farmers must hire at least 20 percent of their pickers from among Germany's unemployed, who showed no enthusiasm for the arduous task of harvesting. As a result, the shortage of migrant workers became critical, and German consumers complained about the effects of immigration policy on the availability and price of asparagus. More important, this episode gave the local agricultural industry the opportunity to vehemently criticize the federal authorities.[17] We can assume that German asparagus producers would agree with the American economist Alan Greenspan, who declared that "undocumented foreigners are keeping our strong economy afloat."[18]

In May 2007 Vice President Franco Frattini, EU commissioner responsible for Justice, Freedom and Security, declared that "experience has shown that existing sanctions have failed to achieve full compliance with bans on employers."[19] Actually, checks on staff records in European firms are rare—just over 2 percent of the twenty-two million lawfully established firms were checked in 2006. While 7 percent to 16 percent of EU's GDP is estimated to come from the shadow economy, the European Commission introduced stringent new measures on illegal immigrants and required that member states inspect at least 10 percent of their companies every year.[20] Interestingly, in a Communication on Immigration, Integration and Employment, the European Commission also acknowledged that illegal immigration could confer significant economic benefits. The commission noted that "public authority frequently refers to the temporary and even seasonal nature of the immigration they are willing to allow. Past experiences of immigration have demonstrated that it is extremely difficult to sustain temporary immigration schemes, because people who want to stay generally find ways of doing so."[21] In Italy, for example, the Berlusconi administration enacted a new anti-immigration law in July 2009. Under this legislation, illegal immigrants are liable to pay a fine of $14,200 and can be detained for up to six months. People who knowingly house illegal immigrants can face up to three years in prison. The new law also permits the formation of unarmed citizen patrol groups to help police keep order. Yet, interestingly, there is no provision dealing with employer sanctions. The fact that illegal immigration in the agricultural sector accounts today for 17.6 percent of Italy's GDP may explain this omission.

In the United States the 1986 Immigration Reform and Control Act attempted to reduce illegal immigration by imposing sanctions on employers who hired illegal aliens, in addition to increasing Border Patrol and other enforcement activities. However, only 27 percent of the supplemental funds for the act's implementation targeted sanctions enforcement in 1987, compared with 57 percent for border enforcement.[22] In 1993 President Clinton responded to the growing anti-immigrant hostility by enacting new measures that focused on controls along the U.S.-Mexico border. This strategy was based on the assumption that all illegal workers were illegal immigrants. Yet unauthorized employment also includes those in the country legally who nevertheless are not authorized to work. Furthermore, only 2 percent of the INS budget was devoted to enforcing employer sanctions. Yet, as noted by

Peter Andreas, the reliance of California's agricultural industry on illegal aliens has increased as border controls have tightened: illegal workers represented 40 percent of the labor force in 1997, compared with 10 percent in 1990.[23] Under the George W. Bush administration, workplace raids by Immigration and Customs Enforcement agents were highly publicized, but their efficacy was hotly debated. Recruitment of illegal workers has continued in spite of these raids and the implementation of civil fines. An estimated 7.2 million unauthorized workers were among the U.S. civilian labor force in March 2005 (representing about 5 percent of the total labor force).[24] This population grew at an average annual rate of more than five hundred thousand between 2000 and 2005. Table 17 shows that, in some sectors, their share of the labor force represented between 10 and 20 percent.

The attempt of the Bush administration to curb the hiring of illegal workers faced the opposition of an unusual coalition, which included the AFL-CIO, the American Civil Liberties Union, and the U.S. Chamber of Commerce. The government intended to mail Social Security "no-match" letters to approximately 140,000 employers warning them that they had to check their employees' identities or fire them within ninety days. Opponents of this initiative argued that the Social Security Administration database includes so many errors that no fewer than 8.7 million workers would be threatened, with a staggering impact on both legal workers and their employers who might be victims of clerical mistakes. According to the president of the AFL-CIO, more than 70 percent of Social Security Administration discrepancies apply to U.S. citizens. Major American labor unions,

Table 17.   Estimates of unauthorized employment in selected industries in the U.S. (2005)

Industry group	Unauthorized workers (in industry) (%)
Private households	21
Food manufacturing	14
Agriculture	13
Furniture manufacturing	13
Construction	12
Textile, apparel, and leather manufacturing	12
Food services	12
Administrative and support services	11
Accommodation	10

Source: Jeffrey Passel, *Size and Characteristics of the Unauthorized Migrant Population in the U.S.*, Pew Hispanic Center, March 2006.

businesses, and farm organizations reaffirmed their intent to block what they considered to be an "unlawful rule."[25]

When he was running for presidency, Barack Obama stated that his objectives regarding employer sanctions were the use by all employers of a new electronic system (E-Verify) to verify whether newly hired employees were eligible to work; the implementation of stiff penalties on employers who knowingly hire or exploit illegal workers; and the end of disruptive, high-profile work-site raids. These objectives were reaffirmed by Janet Napolitano when she was appointed secretary of the Department of Homeland Security. According to the new "comprehensive worksite enforcement strategy" designed in 2009, an effective policy "must address both employers who knowingly hire illegal workers as well as the workers themselves." Therefore, Immigration and Customs Enforcement "will continue to arrest and process for removal any illegal workers who are found in the course of these worksite enforcement actions in a manner consistent with immigration law and DHS priorities." But ICE will also "focus its resources in the worksite enforcement program on the criminal prosecution of employers who knowingly hire illegal workers in order to target the root cause of illegal immigration."[26]

Nevertheless, the issue of employer sanctions has remained controversial. In 2009, of more than 1,100 criminal arrests tied to work-site enforcement investigations, only 135 were employers facing charges, including harboring or knowingly hiring illegal immigrants. According to ICE, the low number of employers can be explained by the fact that "white-collar crime investigations take years to bear fruit" while arresting—and deporting—an increasing number of immigrants is immediate (and supposedly effective). Federal immigration authorities deported about four hundred thousand in each of the last two years—the highest numbers in the country's history, according to DHS officials. Some experts, however, argue that the high numbers of illegal immigrants are confounding enforcement efforts by the Obama administration. According to Jeffrey Passel, co-author of a report for the Pew Hispanic Center, "we just don't see indications that enforcement is pushing people to leave the U.S." Despite record deportations, the number of illegal immigrants in the workforce (about eight million, or 5 percent of the U.S. workforce) has remained unchanged.[27] Others argue that the current administration is too soft in its enforcement strategy. According to Jessica Vaughan, director of policy studies at the Center for Immigration Studies, "it could be that the shift away from work-site enforcement is making it more attractive for illegal immigrants to stay here, since they do not feel as threatened at work."[28] Others claim that the current strategy pretends to punish employers but in reality punishes workers. According to journalist

David Bacon and law professor Bill Ong Hing, work-site raids should stop, and a true reform that recognizes the rights of all workers should be enacted: "The rise of employer sanctions enforcement causes hardship for our fellow human travelers who only seek an opportunity to work to feed their family at an honest day's wage."[29] Meanwhile, the Obama administration is sending conflicting messages: first, by appointing to the National Labor Relations Board a labor lawyer, Craig Becker, who opposes employer sanctions for hiring illegal immigrants; second, by asking the Supreme Court to prevent Arizona from enforcing a law that punishes businesses that employ illegal immigrants (notably by suspending or revoking the business license), arguing that federal immigration law trumps state initiatives; and third, by increasing the number of audits on employee files and collecting a record $3 million in civil fines in the first six months of 2010.

Political Opportunities and Electoral Competition

"When we refer to the 'politicization' of immigration issues, New York University professor Martin Schain argues, "we mean that immigration issues have become part of a public discourse, or are important for electoral purposes; have become issues in political party competition more generally or that they are the subject of proposed or considered legislation about which there is political conflict."[30] This process is often fueled by concerns over the nation-state, as illustrated by debates about state sovereignty and national identity. It involves various actors, such as political and administrative institutions, political parties, interest groups, public opinion, and the media. These actors influence the agenda's formation according to the political salience of a given immigration issue, as measured by the level of attention paid to it through references in newspapers and electoral campaigns, political debates, social campaigns, and the ranking of this issue in public opinion surveys. The level and scope of its salience have an impact on the content of immigration policy. If the salience is low, restricted to a narrow group of policymakers and interest groups (such as businesses), "client politics" is the normal state of affairs in immigration policy. Immigration policy tends to be more open "because businesses standing to gain from free movement of cheap labor face great incentives to lobby for such a policy."[31] By contrast, as the scope of salience of immigration grows, policy tends to become more restrictive. Not only does the public become more involved in an issue, but political parties also become increasingly involved. The low-conflict mode of client politics is therefore replaced by a high-conflict mode of policymaking, leading to long-term shifts in immigration policy toward more-restrictive measures.

The question, then, is how do immigration issues become salient for policymakers, interest groups, the media, and public opinion? I argue that the securitization of immigration in the aftermath of 9/11 has affected the nature of the politicization process in two ways. First, it has dramatically increased the intensity of the debate over immigration policy, expanding the controversy beyond border controls to issues related to migrant integration, such as civic enfranchisement, ethnic identity, and freedom of religion. Second, the security-driven politicization of immigration has provided further opportunities for restrictionists and security lobbies, eroding support for a more open immigration policy. Although the forces that drive the politics of immigration remain different in the United States and Europe (as well as within Europe), there are signs of convergence in terms of policy proposals designed to achieve electoral gain.

Comparative studies of U.S. and European immigration policies commonly emphasize the fact that opposition to immigration, as illustrated by nativist ideology and anti-migrant groups, has been consistently balanced in the United States by attempts to mobilize immigrants as potential voters by political parties.[32] As a result, immigration policy has remained more open in the United States than in Europe, where a growing number of ethnic voters has not been translated into significant strategies by political parties intended to capture immigrant voters. In Great Britain, for example, immigrant/ethnic voters are concentrated in only a few constituencies and do not weigh heavily in major party decisions on immigration policy.[33] In the United States, by contrast, in 2000 more than a third of the states (35 percent) and more than a third of the congressional districts (35 percent) had immigrant populations of 10 percent or more.[34] The mobilization of immigrant citizens and ethnic voters has become central to the strategies of U.S. parties since the 1990s, as illustrated by the controversial Proposition 187 in California, which attempted to deny social benefits, health care, and public education for illegal immigrants. While it secured the reelection of Governor Pete Wilson, the Republican candidate, in 1994, this restrictive legislation also highlighted the capacity of ethnic groups to organize and lobby against anti-immigrant initiatives. Opposition came mainly from the Hispanic community. But other groups, such as Asians, joined the campaign against the implementation of this legislation.[35] The 1996 presidential elections confirmed the electoral potential of immigrant populations. More than one million people were naturalized in 1996 alone, voter registration among Latinos having grown by 1.3 million (or 28.7 percent) between 1992 and 1996. In California, where Latinos increased from 8 percent of the state's electorate to 10 percent, Latino voter turnout percentages exceeded non–Latino voter turnout. According to political scientist Daniel Tichenor, these increases reflected "new interest in politics among Latinos angered by anti-immigrant measures."[36] Democrats were the immediate beneficiaries of these trends. The 1998 state and midterm congressional elections were the "Republicans' Waterloo":[37] in California, for example, the new congressional delegation included five Hispanic Democrats but not a single Republican one. Both Democrats and Republicans distanced themselves from immigration issues after these elections, and no significant anti-immigration proposals were brought to the U.S. House or the Senate.

Although immigration was not considered a top priority during the 2000 presidential elections, attracting the Latino vote was a priority of both Democrats and Republicans. George Bush proved to be more talented than Al Gore in seducing the Hispanic community and reassuring the interest groups. Furthermore, the Republican Party financed an unprecedented commercial campaign in Spanish. George Bush was elected with one-third of the Latino vote and with the support of economic interest groups. Following the elections, the Republican shift away from previous restrictionism was confirmed by a series of initiatives designed to appeal to Hispanic Americans and address the issue of labor shortages in agriculture. Congress approved a measure allowing the legalization of immigrants who entered the country before 1982. About two hundred thousand green-card applicants, upon payment of a fine, would be able to wait in the United States for their visas to be approved. Negotiations started with labor unions and farmers' organizations about opportunities for guest workers to gradually earn legal residence.

Yet the events of 9/11 complicated the Bush administration's agenda. The main challenge was to deal with three conflicting priorities: business interests, ethnic courtship, and securitization. The rapprochement with the Hispanic community was still actively pursued by President Bush. It took various forms, from the celebration of the Mexican national holiday (Cinco de Mayo) at the White House to meetings with U.S. Hispanic leaders and the Mexican president, Vicente Fox. As the 2004 presidential elections approached, this strategy proved to be successful. Bush's support among Hispanic men grew from 35 percent in 2000 to 41 percent in 2004, while it remained stable among women (about 35 percent).[38] However, nativist conservatism and a commitment to a "law and order" approach increasingly informed immigration proposals after 9/11. The Bush administration relented in its support of legalization and other measures that were considered essential by the Hispanic community and other ethnic groups.

What happened after 2004 confirmed the importance of the immigrant/ethnic vote. The 2006 midterm elections resulted in a sweeping victory for the Democratic Party, which captured the House of Representative, the Senate, and a majority of governorships and state legislatures from the Republicans. The war in Iraq was considered the most important issue by a large segment of the electorate. However, opposition to security and restrictive immigration measures played a key role in the mobilization of immigrant citizens and ethnic voters. The immigration debate was indeed central to the Latino vote, and it hurt the Republican Party. The 2006 national exit polls showed that in elections for the U.S. House of Representatives, 69 percent of Latinos voted for Democrats and only 30 percent for Republicans. In California, which is home to more than a quarter of all Latino voters in the country, Democrat Dianne Feinstein easily won reelection to the Senate, receiving 71 percent of the Latino vote.[39] Some 57 percent of Hispanic registered voters in 2007 called themselves Democrats or said they leaned to the Democratic Party, while just 23 percent aligned with the Republican Party. A Pew Hispanic Center national survey found that many more Latinos (41 percent) believed that the policies of the Bush administration had been harmful to Latinos than said they had been helpful (16 percent). Some 79 percent of Hispanic registered voters said immigration was an "extremely" or "very" important issue in the upcoming presidential race (compared with 63 percent in 2004).[40] By the 2008 presidential election, Hispanics voted for Democrats Barack Obama and Joe Biden over Republicans John McCain and Sarah Palin by a margin of more than two-to-one. Obama won 57 percent of the Latino vote in Florida, a state where Latinos have historically supported Republican presidential candidates. He carried 78 percent of the Latino vote in New Jersey, 76 percent in Nevada, and 74 percent in California.

Do these trends suggest that the electoral importance of immigrant voters is likely to balance the pressure from anti-migrant groups, thus creating strong electoral incentives for national political leaders to adopt expansive policies toward future arrivals? I argue that the securitization of immigration issues has broken down this political dynamic. My point is not to deny the potential of the new generation of enfranchised immigrants to use their democratic rights in order to oppose restrictive—and often discriminatory—immigration measures, as illustrated by the intensity of the mobilization over Arizona's initiative. Yet the issues of border controls, family reunification, illegal immigration, and citizenship have been reframed since 2001 in such a way that the Obama administration has little leverage in trying to reform the immigration system. During his presidential campaign, Obama said that comprehensive immigration legislation would be a priority in his first year in office. In May 2009 he reaffirmed his intention to convene working groups and to begin discussing possible legislation, while acknowledging that the economic crisis has made this goal more difficult to achieve. Obama made his first major speech on immigration in July 2010, urging Congress to fix the "broken" immigration system, reiterating his support for an approach proposed by Senators Charles E. Schumer, Democrat of New York, and Lindsey Graham, Republican of South Carolina. Under their plan, illegal immigrants who wish to remain in the country would be required to admit they broke the law and pay fines and back taxes, pass background checks, and prove that they can speak English before going to the back of the line of those seeking permanent legal residency. The proposal would also strengthen border security and interior enforcement, create a process for temporary workers, and require Social Security cards with biometric data like fingerprints or retinal patterns to help ensure that illegal workers cannot get jobs.

In his July 2010 address, Obama tried to navigate between the two extremes of oversecuritization and laissez-faire. He rejected the most-dramatic solutions to illegal migration: mass deportations would be "logistically impossible and wildly expensive," he said; but blanket amnesty was "unwise and unfair" to those who played by the rules. The United States "has the right and obligation to control its borders," he added, but sealing off that vast space with troops and fences alone is a "fantasy"—and no amount of security at the border does anything about the undocumented eleven million people who have already crossed it.[41] Obama framed the debate for the approaching midterm election to appeal to Hispanic voters who could be critical in several states, as well as other middle-class voters put off by the anti-immigrant discourse. Many details of the current administration's approach remain to be debated, but actually, broad similarities are evident with the reforms suggested by the Bush administration. As *Washington Post* staff writer Spencer S. Hu notes, "although President Obama has spent much of his time in office moving away from the policies of his predecessor, on immigration enforcement, he has embraced several Bush administration initiatives, and the changes he has promised to make are couched in nuance."[42] More important, most of the actual initiatives of the new administration remain security-driven. According to figures from Immigration and Customs Enforcement, the Obama administration has accelerated the pace of deportations overall. In 2009 the authorities deported 389,834 people, about 20,000 more than in 2008, the final year of the Bush administration. In August 2010 Obama signed into law a $600 million measure designed to put more agents and equipment along the Mexican border. The funds will pay for the hiring of one thousand new Border Patrol agents to be deployed at critical areas along the border, as well as more Immigration and Customs Enforcement agents. Meanwhile, Hispanics have become increasingly disenchanted with President Obama, with their approval of his job performance slipping to 57 percent in May 2010, compared with 69 percent in January and 64 percent in February.[43]

The current administration has actually had little opportunity to move away from the security-driven dependency inherited from the previous administration. Obama's attempt to define a balanced approach to immigration issues is facing a virulent backlash from anti-migrant groups, who refer to every aspect of the immigration debate in terms of national security. The immigration debate is no longer about the potential economic contribution of immigrants or the impact of immigration on national identity, but rather juxtaposes the proponents of the immigration-security nexus with those who reject the excesses of securitization. Yet the only chance for congressional passage of a bill on immigration depends on an emphasis on security measures. Congressional Republicans and some Democrats argue that the government should focus on better law enforcement before moving on to citizenship issues or guest worker programs. This two-step approach is supported by a large part of U.S. public opinion. A CNN / Opinion Research Corporation national poll, conducted in late May 2010, indicated, for example, that public support for increasing security along the U.S. border with Mexico had grown significantly. According to the survey, nearly 90 percent of Americans want to beef up U.S. law enforcement along the Mexican border.[44]

The scope of the controversy about immigration has moved beyond the issue of border control. It now includes access to citizenship through *jus soli* for children born in the United States to illegal aliens, as illustrated by the polarizing rhetoric referring to "anchor babies" posing a threat.[45] Restrictionist organizations, such as the Federation for American Immigration Reform, argue that immigrants take advantage of the Fourteenth Amendment in order to abuse the education system and welfare benefits, as well as family reunification.[46] They demand a revision of the Constitution—a position supported by several leading GOP senators, including Minority Leader Mitch McConnell and 2008 presidential nominee John McCain. According to a CNN / Opinion Research Corporation poll conducted in August 2010, 49 percent of Americans are in favor of changing that portion of the Fourteenth Amendment.[47]

Another controversy relates to the principle of freedom of religion, as illustrated by the debate about the construction of mosques in various states. The proposal to build an Islamic center in lower Manhattan, near Ground Zero, received most of the attention, but controversies over proposed mosques have arisen in Tennessee, California, Georgia, Kentucky, Wisconsin, and Illinois, as well as in Sheepshead Bay, Brooklyn, and Midland Beach, Staten

Island, in New York City. Those opposing the construction of the center in Manhattan focus on security concerns.[48] According to Rick A. Lazio, a former Republican candidate for governor and former member of the House of Representatives, "with over 100 mosques in New York City, this is not an issue of religion, but one of safety and security."[49] In California, those opposed to mosque construction in the city of Temecula express their concerns about "sleeper cells," while in Tennessee, Lou Ann Zelenik, a Republican congressional candidate, denounced the project near Ground Zero and characterized its proponents as foreign agents with a "radical agenda."[50] A majority of Republican leaders opposed the Manhattan Islamic center, as well as 68 percent of the respondents to a CNN / Opinion Research Corporation national poll conducted in August 2010.[51] Democrats were divided. Those who felt insecure about their election or reelection in conservative states opposed the project, such as Representative Charlie Melancon of Louisiana and Senate Majority Leader Harry M. Reid of Nevada. By contrast, the supporters of the project represented safe Democratic districts, with the expectation of being re-elected, such as Representatives Keith Ellison of Minnesota and Jerrold Nadler of New York.

These examples suggest that the forces driving U.S. politics have changed. Security concerns have taken precedence over the attempts to attract ethnic voters and dominate the debate over immigration issues and ethnic diversity in the United States. This trend has affected the Obama administration's efforts to balance the exclusive effects of securitization and a more liberal approach. Obama is himself trapped in a catch-22 situation. During a White House dinner celebrating Ramadan, he claimed that "Muslims have the same right to practice their religion as anyone in the country." The day after those remarks, he said that although he supports the right of Muslims to build a community center and mosque near Ground Zero, he would not comment on the wisdom of doing so. American Muslims were disappointed by his attitude, while his opponents reignited rumors about his "secret" affiliation to Islam. The president's religion, like his place of birth, has been the subject of Internet-spread rumors since before he began his presidential campaign, and the polls indicate that those rumors have gained currency since he took office. The number of people who correctly identified Obama as a Christian dropped to 34 percent by August 2010, down from nearly half when he took office. The number of Americans who believe—wrongly—that he is a Muslim increased significantly since his inauguration, accounting for nearly 20 percent of the population (compared with 10 percent in 2008).[52] Those who said he is a Muslim also overwhelmingly disapprove of his job performance. Some even suspect him of posing a threat to national security because of his religion. The belief that "Muslim" is synonymous with "un-American" or "anti-American" is actually widespread in U.S. politics today. Twenty-eight percent of voters, for example, do not believe Muslims should be eligible to sit on the U.S. Supreme Court. Nearly one-third of the country thinks adherents of Islam should be barred from running for president.

In terms of partisan competition and the immigrant vote, the forces that drive the politics of immigration are quite different in Europe, but the spill-over effect of securitization on electoral politics is notably similar to the trend in the United States: security concerns tend to benefit the most-restrictive immigration agenda, leaving few options for a more balanced policy. In many European countries, including those with a large number of immi-grants, both leftist and rightist parties had not been disposed before 9/11 to regarding immigrant and ethnic voters as a political resource. Martin Schain, in his comparative study of France, Great Britain, and the United States, con-vincingly demonstrates that "the politics of immigration in both France and Great Britain was built around the mobilization of sentiment against immi-grants," while the votes of immigrants were crucial in the United States.[53] Factors explaining the lack of influence of immigrants in Europe include the weak organization of immigrant groups, the ability of political parties to ignore their interests even at the local level, and an upsurge of anti-immigrant public opinion. Political polarization surrounding immigration issues was initiated prior to 9/11, as illustrated by the controversy surrounding the author Salman Rushdie in Great Britain and the head-scarf controversy in France. Mainstream parties, either leftist or rightist, converged toward restric-tionist policy during the late 1980s and early 1990s. France's Socialist Party, for example, introduced restrictive proposals in its agenda by the mid-1980s. As Schain pointed out, "it was a Minister of Justice of the Left who in 1983 proposed and passed legislation that gave the police the right to use skin and hair color to decide which people to stop for identity checks; and it was the Left that first established rules in 1984 that made family reunification far more difficult."[54] These rules were further tightened by three leftist govern-ments (between 1988 and 1993) and codified in the so-called Pasqua laws (after Gaullist politician Charles Pasqua) passed by the right in 1993–94.

A similar pattern of convergence occurred in other European countries. In Great Britain the Conservative and Labour parties' bipartisan consensus over restrictive immigration measures was built around the issues of British identity (leading to the adoption of the 1981 British Nationality Act) and integration of immigrants and ethnic communities. "The consensus was based," Schain argues, "on a compromise through which Labour accepted exclusionary policies, while the Conservatives accepted that integration was based on legislation that prohibited racial discrimination."[55] The implementation of immigration restrictions by Conservative governments during the 1980s and early 1990s was followed by the Blair government's restrictive policies, as illustrated by the provisions of the 1999 Immigration and Asylum Act.

Two interrelated factors played a key role in the politics of immigration and electoral strategy in Europe before 9/11: the upsurge of anti-immigrant groups and a growing opposition among the public in general to immigrants (and asylum seekers). Extreme-right-wing parties (ERPs) proliferated across Western Europe during the 1980s and 1990, exploiting the fears and diffuse resentment of native citizens. ERPs asserted that immigration increased crime, removed jobs from natives, placed an undue burden on the welfare state, and threatened national culture and identity. Connection between immigration and unemployment, for instance, was made by ERPs in their electoral strategies. The National Front in France used the slogan "Two million immigrants are the cause of two million French people out of work" during the 1984 European elections. The Republicans in Germany campaigned under a similar slogan: "Eliminate Unemployment: Stop Immigration." Austria's Freedom Party developed the notion of "Austria First," while France's Jean-Marie Le Pen stated his *"préférence nationale"* in advocating the repatriation of immigrants, with job-market preference being given to French citizens. The issue of immigration also energized the German People's Union party, as well as ERPs in other countries, such as the British National Party, the Flemish Bloc in Belgium, and the Italian Northern League (Lega Nord).

Electoral results during the 1980s and 1990s provided evidence that this strategy benefited the ERPs. Their consolidation obviously had different causes within different countries—not to mention variations in electoral success over time. Yet anti-immigrant discourse provided new political opportunities and mobilized voters with the development of "niches" in the electoral arena. In Denmark electoral support for the Progress Party increased during the 1980s when the party capitalized upon rising anti-immigrant sentiment. Its national parliamentary delegation expanded from nine in 1987 to sixteen in 1988, while its national vote almost doubled (from 4.8 percent to 9 percent). The National Front, in France, achieved its electoral breakthrough in the 1984 European elections, attracting 11 percent of the vote. At that time 39 percent of its supporters stated that immigration was the main reason for their vote, this figure reaching 46 percent in the 1986 legislative elections. By 1988 Jean-Marie Le Pen garnered 14.4 percent of the vote in the first round of the presidential election. His party secured its electoral basis during the 1990s, receiving 12.5 percent of the vote in the legislative election in 1993 and 14.9 percent in 1997. Although the National Front did not benefit from parliamentary representation (due to the majority vote system), the party continued its steady advance. In the first round of the presidential election in 1995, Le Pen received 15.5 percent of the vote, and in 2002 he received 17.8 percent. The Flemish Bloc enjoyed a similar progression in Belgium. It increased its parliamentary representation from two to twelve seats after the 1991 general election, reflecting a rise of 400 percent in its electoral support. About two-thirds of those who voted for the Flemish Bloc that year cited immigration as the primary motivation for their support.[56] In a similar pattern, after the electoral success of Italy's Casa delle Libertà (comprising Forza Italia, the Alleanza Nazionale, and the Lega Nord), 42.8 percent of Italians responded in 2001 that immigration increased crime and 32.3 percent felt it represented a threat to employment.

The impact of the ERPs on the politics of immigration in European countries was twofold. First, mainstream parties co-opted immigration-related issues in order to challenge the ERPs' electoral success. In France, for example, former Socialist prime minister Laurent Fabius declared in 1985 that "the [National Front] poses some real questions." Jacques Chirac, then running for the presidency, declared in 1991 that the threshold of tolerance had been passed, and commented that the "French worker goes nuts having to live next to the noise and odor of immigrants." Jean-Marie Le Pen, for his part, responded that "Chirac talks like Le Pen," accusing the RPR (Gaullists) of stealing his political agenda. In France, as in other Western European countries, the objective was to undercut the electoral support of the ERPs by addressing anti-immigrant feelings of the electorate, leading to the adoption of restrictive immigration measures. This was illustrated by a series of initiatives targeting illegal immigrants and "delinquent families" (a French euphemism for immigrant families) in the aftermath of the 1995 presidential election. The move toward exclusionary policies accelerated in Austria and Italy, where the ERPs became part of government coalitions. Austria's Freedom Party got four Cabinet posts in the government in 1999. Legislation was subsequently passed that reflected the most salient aspects of the party's anti-immigrant platform by reducing immigration quotas, fingerprinting asylum seekers, and focusing on integration. All immigrants who could not demonstrate an adequate command of German were forced to take integration courses. In 2001 the Italian Northern League joined a governing coalition led by Silvio Berlusconi. The result was the Bossi-Fini Law, adopted in February 2002, which made family reunification more difficult and increased penalties for illegal immigrants.

The second effect of ERPs on immigration politics was an increasing support for xenophobic feelings in most European countries, as reflected in public opinion surveys conducted by the EU. In 1992 approximately 50 percent of European respondents believed that there were "too many" non-EU nationals living in their country.[57] In 1997—the "European Year against Racism"—the Eurobarometer opinion poll revealed that 33 percent of the respondents declared themselves as being "quite racist" or "very racist."[58] These survey results demonstrated the complexity of the relationship between racism, anti-migrant feelings, and xenophobia. These feelings targeted third-country nationals, as well as unemployed immigrants and illegal immigrants. The presence of non-European immigrants was negatively perceived by 48 percent of those interviewed. Anti-immigrant feelings during this period were fueled by frictions between natives and immigrants in various European countries, as well as a series of controversies related to migrant integration (including, for example, the construction of mosques in France and Germany). Anti-immigrant feelings were also fanned by the attitude of established political leaders, who in their attempts to capture the ERPs' electoral base pandered to illiberal popular sentiment and endorsed claims made by their extremist competitors. This attitude in turn gave legitimacy to the immigration-security linkage exploited by ERPs and made the expression of xenophobic feelings more acceptable.

The events of 9/11, followed by the 2004 Madrid bombings and the 2005 London bombings, accelerated the securitization of immigration by providing further opportunities to mainstream parties to radicalize their discourse, as well as driving the implementation of more-restrictive policies. Anxieties about immigration as a security risk allowed mainstream parties to further co-opt the ERPs' agenda, as illustrated by the evolution of the politics and policies of immigration in France and Italy. The French government between 2002 and 2007 made a series of moves designed to prove that the National Front did not have a monopoly in addressing immigration issues. This led to more-restrictive rules for family reunification and marriage, increased levels of expulsion of illegal immigrants, and new restrictions on asylum seekers and naturalization. Most of these measures were initiated by Nicolas Sarkozy, then minister of the interior, who periodically employed an extreme-right discourse. In his 2007 presidential campaign, Sarkozy emphasized the issues of immigration and security. "France is exasperated by the dispute about national identity, by uncontrolled immigration, by fraud, by waste," he argued, adding that there was "an obvious link between 30 or 40 years of a policy of uncontrolled immigration and the social explosion in French cities."[59] Once elected, he created a new ministry to deal with questions of immigration and integration (ominously entitled the Ministry for Immigration, Integration, and National Identity), designed to implement his approach on *"immigration choisie"* (selective/wanted immigration), as opposed to *"immigration subie"* (unregulated/unwanted immigration). He pushed for a controversial measure to ban Muslim veils in both private and public places and planned the policy of deporting illegal immigrants from France (about twenty-five thousand each year). In the aftermath of the July 2010 riots, and with an eye on the 2012 elections, Sarkozy announced plans to strip French citizenship from naturalized immigrants convicted of attacking police or other authorities.[60] He also ordered the removal of Roma undocumented immigrants and the dismantling of their camps, arguing that "illegal Gypsy camps are sources of trafficking, exploitation, and prostitution" and "will be systematically evacuated."[61] Prime Minister Silvio Berlusconi of Italy supported Sarkozy's initiatives while applying a similar strict law-and-order policy.[62] Berlusconi's conservative government initiated a series of restrictive measures in 2008 regarding legal immigration, and making illegal immigration punishable by prison. The same year he endorsed a package of tough measures aimed at Roma, making their deportation easier despite the fact that they are EU nationals. In 2009 Interior Minister Roberto Maroni announced a plan to create a national registry of the country's Roma population. All Roma, regardless of whether they are immigrants or Italian nationals, are now being registered as members of their ethnic group, as well as being fingerprinted. In August 2010 Berlusconi's government suggested a new policy intended to turn back would-be immigrants from Libya before they arrived on Italian shores.

The situation in France and Italy illustrates the dramatic intertwined impact of both security concerns and ERPs' pressure on immigration policy. Mainstream parties co-opted immigration-related issues in order to challenge the ERPs' electoral success—a tactic that neither reduces the pressure from ERPs nor address the anxieties of natives about immigration. Sarkozy was given credit for the relative decline of the National Front in 2004 (with 9.8 percent of the vote for the European elections). In the first round of the 2007 presidential election, Jean-Marie Le Pen was eliminated after receiving only 10.4 percent of the vote, a 6.49 percent decline from his 2002 vote. Clearly, the *"politique sécuritaire"* implemented by Sarkozy largely explains this trend. It is less clear that the National Front is less influential, for at least two reasons. First, its agenda on immigration is now implemented by the government, which enhances the National Front's credibility. Second, although anti-immigration claims constitute the core of its propaganda, the party has broadened its ideological and issue bases by developing a platform about unemployment, corruption, the environment, and the EU. As Anthony Messina argues, "the FN [National Front] is likely to maintain its special influence in French politics and society into the indefinite future."[63] Similarly, in Italy, anti-immigrant groups and parties, notably the Northern League, are flourishing.[64] This trend encourages Berlusconi to pursue his restrictive immigration policy while xenophobic feelings increase in the country.

In other European countries the securitization of immigration issues has increased the societal support for right-wing extremism. During the 2004 European elections, the Union of Europe of the Nations, which grouped together the most influential ERPs across Europe, took twenty-seven seats. The extreme-right Popular Orthodox Rally made its first electoral breakthrough (4.12 percent of the vote), with one seat in the European Parliament. The framing of immigration as a security problem also helped ERPs increase their share of the vote in Poland, Latvia, Germany, and Belgium. In the UK, the British National Party got 4.9 percent of the total vote, while the Independence Party won twelve seats in the European Parliament by promoting extreme-right-wing views on immigration. These parties were able to mobilize citizens who expressed xenophobic feelings and a more general dissatisfaction. In Eastern Europe the combination of ethnic exclusionism, security concerns, and virulent anti-immigrant propaganda has been extremely beneficial to ERPs. In Hungary, for example, the openly anti-Semitic and anti-Roma party Jobbik (or Movement for a Better Hungary) won 17 percent of the vote in the 2010 general election (compared with 2.2 percent in 2006), becoming the third-largest party.[65] Jobbik's platform included issues such as unemployment, corruption, and disillusion with the EU—some of its supporters described it as "the tea party of Hungary." Yet it was the party's proposals for dealing with the "Roma problem" that attracted most of those who voted for it. Gábor Vona, the head of Jobbik, has actually pledged to "eradicate Gypsy crime."[66] A similar xenophobic attitude largely explains the progression of the Attack Coalition in Bulgaria. Composed of several extremist movements, with a program advocating a "mono-ethnic" Bulgaria, in 2009 it attracted approximately 9.4 percent of the vote in the general election and 12 percent in the European election.

It appears that, as Anthony Messina argues, "there is no single best strategy that the mainstream parties can pursue to undercut the popular support for anti-immigrant groups, although neglecting immigration-related issues appears to be the worst possible approach."[67] I believe, however, that mainstream parties have shifted from one extreme (failing to address the concerns raised by immigration) to another (focusing on immigration issues almost exclusively in terms of security threat) in less than two decades.

What this analysis of the impact of securitization on European politics also suggests is that pro-migrant groups have fewer opportunities to push for a more open immigration policy while ethnic political mobilization remains weak (and much weaker than in the United States). Ethnic minorities in Europe are far less inclined than natives to vote in both local and national elections.[68] During the British general election of 2001, for example, voter turnout among whites (59.4 percent) was approximately thirteen percentage points higher than that of ethnic minorities taken together (47 percent). According to the Electoral Commission, a sense of alienation played a role in this political disaffection, as well as social exclusion and community segregation.[69] A similar trend is noticeable in other European countries, although there are variations both among various ethnic minorities and from one country to another. Ethnic mobilization is low in Great Britain and Germany, yet still higher in both those countries than in Latvia, where non-Latvian citizens are excluded from political participation.[70] Ethnic minorities are also underrepresented at all levels of politics and government, despite a few brighter spots. In France, for example, the number of *Beurs* (North African–born citizens) serving as local councilors increased from 13 in 1983 to 390 in 1989; in Belgium the number of ethnic minority councilors rose from 13 in 1994 to 92 in 2000. In most countries, however, the number of immigrant citizens elected at the local level is between 2 and 4 percent of all officeholders (that is, about half or less of the percentage of ethnic voters within the electorate).[71] As a result ethnic minority populations are not very visible politically, with no effective representational option and little influence on immigration policy.

This underrepresentation has been traditionally compensated for by the support of leftist parties. There is evidence, however, that this special affinity is challenged by the effects of the securitization of immigration (and integration) issues, as illustrated by the evolution of Britain's Labour Party after 9/11 and the subsequent restrictive legislation on immigration and counterterrorism implemented by Blair's government. Leftist parties tend to distance themselves from "ethnic politics" for political and electoral reasons. In France, for example, the most controversial discriminatory measures are quite popular. The 2004 ban on "conspicuous religious symbols in schools" targeting Muslim veils was supported by 69 percent of the population.[72] The 2010 ban on "burqa-like veils" in public spaces was approved of by 82 percent of French voters. About 75 percent of those who declared themselves as being leftist agreed with the ban.[73] The Socialist Party was divided over this issue: most of its representatives in the National Assembly did not take part in the vote in July 2010, but twenty legislators from the left voted for the bill. By opposing the dominant security-immigration nexus, leftist parties risk alienating a large part of their electorate, especially white working-class voters who are increasingly attracted by the ERPs. Le Pen's share of the vote in the first round of the 2002 presidential election was 15 percent nation-wide, but exit polls indicated that 27 percent of working-class voters and unemployed people supported him. The results of the 2009 parliamentary election in Great Britain showed that the British National Party gained votes not from the Conservatives, whose share of the vote had remained virtually unchanged since 2004, but from Labour. Similarly, the 2009 European elec-tions showed that in many countries (such as Hungary, Denmark, Greece, and the Netherlands), a significant portion of the leftist electorate defected to ERPs. Given the electoral pressure from this right-wing populism, it could be reasonably argued that the commitment of leftist political parties to the immigrant interests is likely to decline, subsequently diminishing the chances for a more open immigration policy.

Conclusion

Threats to Western Democracy

We have met the enemy and he is us.

Pogo

          Liberal democracies are ideally required to provide efficient law enforcement while upholding civil rights and liberties in times of national emergency. In times of war this challenge has historically created a tension between protecting the state and protecting civil liberties. President Lincoln, for example, suspended the writ of habeas corpus during the Civil War without congressional approval. Likewise, during World War II the Supreme Court upheld the constitutionality of the detention of Japanese Americans in its *Korematsu* decision by arguing that "the military urgency of the situation demanded that all citizens of Japanese ancestry be segregated from the West Coast temporarily."[1] Comparable exceptions to, and derogations from, constitutional principles and civil liberties have also been made in other democracies, allowing the detention of persons suspected of being of "hostile origin" (as illustrated by Defense Regulation 18B in the United Kingdom), while also increasing the powers of the executive branch with a corresponding narrowing of the scope of legislative and judicial review. Such political decisions have often been fairly easy ones. As David Cole argues, "no one has ever been voted out of office for targeting foreign nationals in times of crisis; to the contrary, crises often inspire the demonization of 'aliens' as the nation seeks unity by emphasizing difference between 'us' and 'them.'"[2]

The current securitization of immigration policies on both sides of the Atlantic thus inspires a disturbing feeling of déjà vu in terms of the retrenchment of civil liberties for distinct groups among the general population, as well as in terms of the arguments commonly used to legitimize these practices. The first argument focuses on the notion of the "lesser evil": policies justified by the nature and the extent of the threat are still less evil than those taken by the enemies of democracy. It is therefore legitimate, in the name of the majority's security interests, to sacrifice the rights of a minority group posing a threat. The forfeiture of *their* liberties for *our* security is justified by the prospect of democracy's enemies exploiting the opportunities provided by an open society. "In a war on terror," Michael Ignatieff argues, "the issue is not whether we can avoid evil acts altogether, but whether we can succeed in choosing lesser evils and keep them from becoming greater ones."[3] The second argument is that emergency measures take effect temporarily, only in times of crisis, and therefore normal legal processes will be restored in peacetime, a policy justified by international law. The International Covenant on Civil and Political Rights, for example, recognizes that states may take measures to derogate from certain rights "in time of public emergency which threatens the life of the nation and the existence of which is officially proclaimed."[4] Conditional provisions, however, aim to ensure the transparency, proportionality, and necessity of the measures taken. One fundamental requirement, for example, is that such measures must be of an exceptional and temporary nature and relate to the duration, geographical coverage and material scope of the state of emergency.

Western democracies have relied on these arguments since 9/11 to justify policies that have diminished individual civil liberties, limited basic rights and freedoms, and strengthened executive power. Emergency alterations to constitutional principles and habeas corpus may be necessary, but "there is a price to pay when you do."[5] The fight against terrorism has deeply affected the exercise of fundamental democratic principles, notably the rule of law, the separation of powers, the independence of judicial authority, and the openness and accountability of government.

I argue that these policy changes since 9/11 have been far more damaging to democracy than earlier emergency measures for at least two reasons. First, the definition of the "others" who have been subject to the curtailment of civil liberties keeps expanding. In the aftermath of 9/11, it was largely confined to Muslims and those who look like Muslims from the Middle East (including Sikhs, with tragic consequences). Now, however, the "other" has incorporated a variety of other potential and actual immigrants and their children. In the United States, in addition to Muslims from any part of the globe, Mexicans have been increasingly associated with insecurity and subject to deportation and profiling: the children of immigrants have been characterized as "anchor babies," and those children as embryonic terrorists by sections of a frustrated public egged on by politicians desperate to gain or maintain office. In some European countries, such as France and Italy, the same kind of linkage to anyone who potentially threatens civil unrest has been extended to Bulgarian and Romanian Roma, a number of whom have been "voluntarily" repatriated, justified by the dubious claim that doing so is consistent with EU law.

Second, unlike prior wars, one characteristic of this global war against terrorism is that it is a conflict without an end—and without limits. The prospects of the restoration of civil liberties to those who have been deprived therefore tend to dim, with no time horizon. Japanese Americans eventually had their civil liberties restored, if only at the cessation of hostilities. The U.S. Presidential Commission on the Wartime Relocation and Internment of Civilians even concluded in 1983 that internment "was not justified by military necessity, and the decisions which followed from it—detention, ending detention and ending exclusion—were not driven by analysis of military conditions. The broad historical causes which shaped these decisions were race prejudice, war hysteria and a failure of political leadership."[6] The war on terror offers no comparable prospect of victory, no conclusion, and no prospect of the comparable restoration of rights. Former British prime minister Tony Blair has gone as far as to describe it as "a generational-long struggle."[7] If Blair is correct, then the clear implication is that the deprivation of civil liberties for immigrants, and the racial stereotyping I have detailed in this book, will not abate.

Politicians easily justify the violation of the rights of immigrants, and the abridgement of the civil liberties of a particular suspected group, in a context of widespread public fear. Yet these practices not only endanger democracy but undermine the legal and moral foundations of democracy: emergency alterations are difficult to reverse in the context of an unending war; and even when a partial restoration occurs, the core principles of liberal democracies are perceived as revocable, malleable, and susceptible to a series of political pressures. This begs the ultimate question of the degree to which threats are in fact constructed by politicians and implemented by states seeking to target caricatured "villains." Is it a strategy to reassure mass publics of their governments' own vigilance, as these governments simultaneously make promises about border control and public safety that they cannot deliver? The answers I have offered here have dire consequences for public safety, public discourse, and the future of democracy in America and Europe.

Collateral Damages to Vulnerable Populations

The most controversial policies relate to the violation of immigrant rights involved in the abuse of deportation processes, conditions of detention, and measures against asylum seekers. In 2001 the U.S. Supreme Court stated, for example, that the indefinite detention of immigrants could raise "a serious constitutional problem."[8] The Court found that six months was a reasonable period for the government to enforce an alien's removal. After that, the alien was entitled to release under "conditions that may not be violated." The American Civil Liberties Union (ACLU) reported in 2006, however, that the U.S. government increased its reliance on immigration detention by using "mandatory and categorical detention rather than detention based on individualized determinations that an individual poses a danger or flight risk." Moreover, "given that immigrants have no right to appointed counsel in their immigration proceedings, and the fact that so many of them are indigent and unable to afford counsel, immigrant detainees can be locked up for years without the ability to mount any challenge to what is often unlawful detention."[9]

The regulations promulgated by the U.S. government to implement the Court's ruling thus clearly violated the decision, as documented by the ACLU report. First, the U.S. government argued that this decision could not be applied to aliens who "are dangerous to national security or who pose threats to public safety." Second, it authorized indefinite detention of aliens whose removal is impossible, based on a number of "special circumstances," such as mental illness. Finally, it maintained that detention was not "indefinite" as long as the removal proceedings—which can last for years—were still pending.[10]

To compound the problem, evidence compiled by NGOs and advocacy groups raises serious concerns about the conditions of detention. These included overcrowded facilities; the lack of availability of personal hygiene products and of social workers to identify special religious-dietary needs or medical problems; the refusal to release detainees for medical treatment; and the abuse or mistreatment of detainees by prison officials. Language differences and fear of retaliation have often effectively deprived immigrant detainees of access to internal complaint procedures. Further, there is evidence of the abrogation of due process. Immigrants have been discouraged from pursuing their legal claims, and an increasing number of detainees have been insufficiently represented in court proceedings.[11]

Data on immigrants who actually died in U.S. custody are often unreliable because the U.S. system consists of a patchwork of federal agencies, county jails, and privately run prisons. In January 2008 the U.S. House of Representatives did pass a bill requiring states receiving federal funding to report deaths in custody to their attorneys general. The effect was far from conclusive. The *New York Times* subsequently reported in May 2008 that, according to the incomplete listing compiled by Immigration and Customs Enforcement, sixty-six detainees died in custody from January 2004 to November 2007. Yet this list neither included all detention facilities, nor did it provide sufficient information. The causes of death were "undetermined" in the majority of cases, the victim's nationality was unlisted, and some names or birth dates were unclear.

There is also evidence that the Department of Homeland Security has extensively used a variety of procedures to rapidly remove certain aliens from the United States, notably asylum seekers and refugees, without due process being observed. These aliens are often subject to immediate removal based solely on the judgment of a low-level immigration officer. Asylum seekers thus increasingly face summary return to their last port of embarkation due to the extensive application of administrative discretion. New requirements dealing with application materials submitted to the overseas processing entities, as well as the introduction of new security checks, reduce the number of eligible cases for adjudication. The broader treatment of asylum seekers has also become an issue. In 2003, for example, all arriving asylum seekers from countries that harbor al-Qaeda operatives were detained, including nonterrorist Somali nationals. The REAL ID Act required asylum seekers to demonstrate that their race, religion, nationality, membership in a social group, or political opinion represented a "central reason" for the persecution they fear in their countries of origin. This provision required asylum seekers to prove the motive of their persecutor, and made it more difficult to substantiate an asylum claim without corroborative evidence. It also made it easier to deny a claim based on a "negative credibility" determination.[12]

Detention of migrants and asylum seekers is also an issue in Europe, where camps (or "removal centers" in Great Britain and "*zones d'attente*" in France) have flourished in many countries. By 2009 there were 224 detention camps scattered across the European Union, including 45 facilities in Germany, 20 in France, 16 in Italy, 13 in Spain, 12 in Great Britain, and 10 in Greece. They have mushroomed in the new EU member states over the past decade, especially in Poland (24 detention centers), the Czech Republic (8), Hungary (8), and Slovenia (4). Although the average length of detention is twelve to eighteen months, in a number of EU countries (such as Germany) there is no upper limit. A visit to Malta by members of the European Parliament in March 2006 found that some illegal immigrants and asylum seekers had been in detention for more than five years. Furthermore, detention camps have also spread outside of the EU to places like the Russian Federation, Ukraine, Morocco, Tunisia, Turkey, and Libya—sponsored by the EU and member states.

Reports from various NGOs provided strong evidence that many of those detained were not "criminals." Indeed, individuals were often detained on arrival, some before they had the opportunity to claim asylum, or "after initial rejection and before appeal." This situation raises major concerns. For example,

> people who have not committed crimes (entering a country with-
> out documentation or overstaying a visa is a migration offence, not a
> crime) are deprived of their liberty, usually for an unspecified period of
> time, without charges being pressed, without trial, without a right to an
> automatic bail hearing, usually without adequate legal representation,
> without being informed of their rights or even of what is happening
> to them in a language they understand.[13]

With little oversight, conditions in the camps often fall far below pre-scribed international norms. The Independent Asylum Commission in 2007 conducted a nationwide review of the UK asylum system. It found that Britain's treatment of asylum seekers "falls seriously below the standards to be expected of a humane and civilized society." The report detailed the overuse of detention—including to lock up children, pregnant women, and torture victims—along with a lack of access to legal advice, a "culture of disbelief" among decision makers resulting in judicial neglect, and the brutal removal of asylum seekers and refugees by private security firms. Further-more, a report published in 2007 on the conditions of detention in the ten newest EU states listed violation of many human rights, such as the rights of minors, the right to physical integrity, the right to medical care, and the right to family life.[14]

Concerns about long-term adverse effects on civil rights and liberties have been dismissed by U.S. and European governments. These govern-ments consistently argue that only foreigners posing a threat are subjected to selective security measures. The distinction between citizens and noncitizens has led to the introduction of harsh discretionary measures, on the assump-tion that citizens would be made safer by sacrificing the rights and liberties of a minority group—especially Muslim noncitizens—in the name of the majority's security interests. Yet this justification has been undermined by the fact that provisions directed at noncitizens actually target citizens, while the notion of guilt by association has dramatically increased the scope of coun-terterrorist legislation. Thousands of people were interviewed and detained in the United States in the aftermath of 9/11 on the flimsiest of pretexts—because, Attorney General Ashcroft explained, they "fit criteria designed to identify persons who might have knowledge of foreign-based terrorists."[15] Comparably, the EU has also undertaken a number of explorations of terrorist profiling explicitly based on ethnic criteria. In October 2002 the Council of the European Union recommended that terrorist profiles be based on a "set of physical, psychological or behavioral variables" such as place of birth, nationality, age, sex, physical distinguishing features, family situation, education, methods of communication, and use of techniques to prevent discovery or counter questioning techniques.[16] In Germany, data-mining efforts, conducted between the end of 2001 and early 2003, targeted 8.3 million people, mainly on the basis of their ethnic origin and religious practice. They were not all foreign, but *they were all wrongly suspected*: This operation did not yield a single arrest of a terrorist. In Great Britain it has been a criminal offense since April 2006 to "indirectly encourage" terrorism, with those convicted facing up to seven years' imprisonment. Yet the notion of indirect encouragement is vague, elastic, and therefore politically malleable. Offenses such as "encouragement of terrorism" and "dissemination of terrorist publications" are very broadly defined and do not even require the "intent" that criminal acts will occur as a result of any statement made or material disseminated. Furthermore, in November 2007 the European Commission presented a proposal to amend the 2002 Framework Decision on combating terrorism. The proposal advocated that three new crimes be legislated and introduced: public provocation to commit terrorist offenses; recruitment for terrorist purposes; and training for terrorism. The most contentious issue of the three is the definition of "public provocation," which is far from clear. Indeed, the proposal specified that "for an act to punishable, it shall not be necessary that a terrorist offense actually be committed. Provocation is sufficient."[17] As David Cole argues, "in the long run, the rights of all of us are in the balance when the government selectively sacrifices foreign nationals' liberties."[18] The same is true when the liberties sacrificed are those of selected domestic citizens.

Less Liberty, with No More Security

In its 2004 report, the 9/11 Commission stressed that "we must find ways of reconciling security with liberty, since the success of one helps the other." It added that "the choice between security and liberty is a false choice. . . . Our history has shown us that insecurity threatens liberty. Yet if our liberties are curtailed, we lose the values that we are struggling to defend."[19] In the same vein the 2007 EU annual Report on Human Rights stated that "the EU attaches great importance to guaranteeing the full and effective protection of human rights and fundamental freedoms in Europe and in the wider world in the context of the fight against terrorism. Effective counter-terrorism measures and the protection of human rights are not conflicting but complementary and mutually reinforcing goals."[20]

To date, the fragile balance between the respect of civil and human rights and the need to protect the public from security threats has been seriously damaged on both sides of the Atlantic. In 2006 the ACLU listed the violations of the International Covenant on Civil and Political Rights. These violations included acts of torture and inhumane or degrading treatment and punishment, both within the United States and abroad; a lack of independent investigations and accountability for abuse; unlawful renditions involving clandestine abduction and detention of persons suspected of terrorist activities; the indefinite detention and expulsion of aliens without due process; indefinite detention under material witness legislation; violation of the right to counsel; excessive government secrecy (as illustrated by secret detention centers with "ghost detainees" and secret proceedings); and the violation of freedom of religion, thought, and conscience.[21] In its 2007 Report on the State of Human Rights and Democracy in Europe, the Parliamentary Assembly of the Council of Europe likewise stated that

> the gap between standards on paper and the actual situation in Europe is striking. Human rights violations, enforced disappearances, extrajudicial killings, secret detentions, torture and inhuman treatment, still take place on our continent. The rule of law is still not fully respected. Moreover, the fight against terrorism is often a pretext to undermine or reduce the scope of fundamental rights. It is now time to end hypocrisy and turn words into deeds.[22]

The fight against terrorism has deeply affected the exercise of fundamental democratic principles, such as the constitutional norms of accountability and transparency, and the independence of judicial authority. The Bush administration, for example, used the war on terror as a justification for increasing government secrecy—invoking the vague notion of "sensitive Homeland security information." All federal departments and agencies were instructed not to disclose "information that could be misused to harm the security of our Nation."[23] Secrecy also involved the nondisclosure of names of detainees, closure of immigration hearings, and the secret incarceration of hundreds of people as "material witnesses." European governments subscribed to a similar "wartime" doctrine and thus adopted emergency security measures that had an impact on civil liberties and human rights. In Great Britain the 2001 Anti-Terrorism, Crime and Security Emergency Bill was enacted into law after a stormy passage through Parliament. Both chambers had little opportunity to debate its 129 sections, including section 33, which allowed the British government to circumvent the European Convention on Human Rights. After only brief deliberation, the French parliament also adopted security measures proposed by the government that infringed upon several constitutional rights. As noted by John Finn, professor of government at Wesleyan University, "both the sense of urgency surrounding the adoption of security legislation and the subsequent breakdown of the ordinary processes of democratic dialogue have undermined basic constitutional norms of transparency and deliberation."[24]

Such measures have also affected the constitutional norm of accountability, by which governmental action is subject to review by other actors, notably judicial authorities. The European Court of Justice, for example, was excluded from reviewing the lawfulness of the EU's intergovernmental decisions taken in the field of the Common Foreign and Security Policy. The European Parliament was excluded from negotiations over the security legislation. Europol activities were not subject to control by either the European Court of Justice or the European Parliament. Nor did the adoption of a "common position" by the European Council require member governments to consult the European Parliament or national parliaments.

In the United States, counterterrorism legislation allowed the extension of the powers of the president, thus providing for executive authority over both the legislative and judicial branches. George W. Bush, for example, invoked his presidential authority to sidestep a law requiring the executive branch to provide Congress with written notice of U.S. intelligence activities. Similarly, the Department of Justice consistently refused to provide any detailed information on the use of the Patriot Act, either to the Congress or the public; and the designation of "enemy combatants" removed suspected terrorists from the regular criminal justice process. When Yaser Hamdi and José Padilla, both American citizens, petitioned for a writ of habeas corpus, the government successfully appealed to the president's war powers in arguing that the judiciary should defer to the executive on military matters.

The Supreme Court did rule against the Bush administration in five major cases. Each time, however, the government circumvented the Court's rulings. In *Rasul v. Bush* (2004), the Court challenged the government's authority over "enemy combatants," including the use of indefinite detention and refusal to allow them access to federal courts. The Court declared that the executive branch could not hold foreign-born prisoners at

Guantanamo Bay indefinitely without access to the judicial system and the rights of due process, and therefore held that detainees at Guantanamo should file habeas petitions in a federal court.[25] The government responded with the Detainee Treatment Act of 2005, which omitted the fundamental protection of habeas corpus. In *Hamdi v. Rumsfeld* (2004) and *Rumsfeld v. Padilla* (2004), the Court ordered a lower federal court to begin new proceedings. In the Hamdi case, it ruled that the government could not deny legal rights to a U.S. citizen it declared to be an "enemy combatant."[26] The Court decided that Padilla, an American citizen arrested on a flight from Pakistan to Chicago and held incommunicado in military custody without ever being charged, should be allowed to sue the commander of the naval brigade in Charleston, South Carolina. The Bush administration responded by creating a "combatant status review tribunal," giving no other option to potential plaintiffs than to challenge their status in a military court. In *Hamdan v. Rumsfeld* (2006), the Court ruled that the military commissions created to try detainees at Guantanamo did not have the power to proceed because those procedures violated the Geneva Convention. Yet a provision of the Military Commissions Act of 2006 stripped the federal courts of jurisdiction to hear habeas corpus petitions from detainees seeking to challenge their designation as enemy combatants. These initiatives were challenged by thirty-seven prisoners who appealed to the Supreme Court. In June 2008 the Court delivered another rebuff to the Bush administration's handling of the detainees in Guantanamo Bay, ruling five-to-four in *Boumediene v. Bush* that the prisoners had a constitutional right to appeal to a federal court in challenging their continued detention.[27] Justice Kennedy, in his majority opinion, argued that judicial involvement did not "undermine the Executive's power," adding that the writ of habeas corpus did not apply to the detainees at Guantanamo. Following the Court's decision, a lower federal court ordered the release of Boumediene. When Bush left the White House, however, some two hundred habeas corpus petitions were still awaiting adjudication in district courts.

The infringements upon civil liberties and the violations of constitutional norms in the name of security do not work in isolation. They also affect the values upon which democracy is based, as well as the implementation of civil rights. The Government Accountability Office, for example, in 2009 published a report showing a significant drop in the enforcement of several major antidiscrimination and voting rights laws during the Bush administration. The report noted that the attorney general had realigned resources to reflect the Department of Justice's counterterrorism efforts as its top strategic priority. As a result, lawsuits by the division to enforce laws prohibiting race or sex discrimination in employment fell, from about eleven per year under the Clinton administration to about six per year under President Bush. The study also found a sharp decline in the enforcement of the section of the Voting Rights Act that prohibits electoral rules with discriminatory effects (from sixty-two cases in 2001 to thirty-seven in 2007), although the number of cases actually increased (up to a total of 442 between 2001 and 2007).[28]

Again, consistent with developments in the United States, in its 2007 report the Parliamentary Assembly of the Council of Europe expressed its concerns over the increasing number of democratic deficiencies observable in European states. In addition to human rights violations, the report pointed out that

> basic principles of democracy such as separation of powers, political freedoms, transparency and accountability are widely perceived, and sometimes rightly so, as being insufficiently implemented or not implemented at all. . . . There have been worrying reports of restrictions of freedom of expression, attempts to limit freedom of association, of distortions concerning representative, participatory and inclusive democracy. Likewise, there is evidence of insufficient implementation of other basic democratic principles, including separation of powers, checks and balance and the rule of law. . . . In some countries, certain professional or ethnic groups do not have the right to organize or form a political party.[29]

If, as mentioned, there is a price to pay when liberties are curtailed in the name of security, some may find the bill too expensive, especially if we consider that supporters of the "lesser evil" perspective are still justifying their position by arguing that we are still not safe—despite the retrenchment of civil liberties and human rights for a decade. This paradoxical position is illustrated, for example, by the recent debate in the UK over the official review of counterterrorism laws implemented since 9/11. In response to rulings from the European Court of Human Rights related to deportations, detentions without charge, and control orders, Lord Carlile, a Liberal Democrat member of the House of Lords and independent reviewer of terrorism legislation, has suggested in his annual report that "the UK is a safe haven for some individuals whose determination is to damage the UK and its citizens." He therefore argued that the government should pursue controversial practices, such as deporting people to countries where a risk of torture exists, because "the risk of ill-treatment faced by a detainee in his home country had to be balanced with the threat posed to the UK's national security."[30] In a speech on civil liberties, Deputy Prime Minister Nick Clegg explained that control orders remained the best way of monitoring suspects who could neither be deported nor tried for an offense.[31] In the United States the recent debate about the extension of three controversial provisions of the Patriot Act (which was set to expire in February 2011) provides another illustration of the "less liberty, less security" spiral. Senate Republican leader Mitch McConnell suggested making the three provisions permanent, notably the one allowing a roving wiretap on a terror suspect to monitor his conversations as he moves from phone to phone.[32] Considered by its critics as a violation of the Fourth Amendment's prohibition of unreasonable searches, this provision was supported by McConnell on the basis that "you don't have to be Jack Bauer [a fictional TV-show antiterrorist fighter] to know that today's terrorists are wise at evasion tactics."[33] He thus introduced a bill in February 2011 to repeal the so-called sunset stipulations on the Patriot Act, in order to make the three provisions permanent. One of the cosponsors of the bill, House Judiciary Committee chairman Lamar Smith, a Texas Republican, argued that "the ongoing threat by al-Qaeda and other terrorist groups continues. To let these [three] provisions expire would leave every American less safe."[34] Other legislators, including Senator Dianne Feinstein, a California Democrat, expressed concerns about restoring the civil liberties missing from the original Patriot Act—although they suggested extending the controversial provisions for only three more years. In February 2011 President Obama signed a three-month extension of these provisions.

The Permanent "State of Exception"

An unending war produces enduring changes that seemingly cannot be reversed, even when their effects are judged harmful to democracy. Counterterrorist measures diminishing civil liberties and altering democratic governance were previously justified as expedient, with a limited time horizon. Yet in most Western countries, security measures are today legislated, enacted, and implemented as permanent national legislation. This leads to a set of "permanent emergency" practices, with systematic constitutional and legislative effects, such as the "normalization" of extraordinary measures impinging on the administration of justice and, more generally, the rule of law. This sense of emergency is fueled by both actual terrorist plots and fears of terrorist attacks. In turn, the transformation of provisional and exceptional measures into a conventional technique of governance is altering the distinction between a "real state of exception" and a "fictitious state of emergency" (or "fancied emergency").[35] Within this expanding insecurity domain, going back to a "normal" political process is difficult, if not impossible; and the probabilities of achieving an effective "desecuritization" are limited.[36] It seems likely that any attempt to unravel the tangled effects of securitization will encounter serious obstacles, such as the current routinization of rights infringement, the widespread culture of insecurity, the lack of political will, and—as the ultimate paradox—legal and political constraints limiting judicial and governmental efforts to undo what has been done.

Some controversial aspects of the securitization trend have been challenged by NGOs and advocacy groups on both sides of the Atlantic, with uneven results. In the United States, for example, human rights organizations demonstrated against the rules published in the Presidential Military Order of November 2001. As a result, these rules were amended in March 2002. The ACLU and other law associations crossed swords with the Bush administration, acting as an effective brake against some disproportionate invasions of civil liberties. The U.S. Supreme Court, as mentioned, also ruled against various aspects of the war on terror. Likewise, among EU institutions, the European Parliament has been quite active in criticizing the most blatant violations of civil liberties and human rights. The Council of Europe hopes that these concerns regarding the future of democracy in Europe will generate "a reaction among previously apathetic groups of citizens that will resuscitate pre-existing parties, associations and (especially) movements in defense of threatened freedoms."[37] This hope, however, has to contend with increased public support for security measures that erode civil liberties. In Great Britain, for example, an opinion poll carried out for the BBC in April 2004 indicated that 69 percent of respondents supported police powers to stop and search anyone at any time. Subsequent opinion polls carried out between August 2005 and July 2006 showed that 70 percent of the respondents were in favor of extending the precharge detention of "terror suspects" to ninety days.[38]

The Obama administration explicitly distanced itself from the practices of its predecessor, notably preventive detention, executive secrecy powers, and "enhanced interrogation techniques." In September 2009 Attorney General Holder issued a new state-secrets privilege policy instructing officials to avoid the abuse of secrecy with a motive of hiding lawbreaking. To date, however, not a single victim of the Bush administration's torture program has had the opportunity to seek justice. In September 2010 a federal appeals court ruled that prisoners of the CIA could not sue over their alleged torture in overseas prisons because such a lawsuit might expose secret government information.[39] This decision was hailed by the Justice Department, arguing that the need to protect national security concerns trumped any plaintiff's rights. Furthermore, the Obama administration has also blocked efforts by detainees in Afghanistan to bring habeas corpus lawsuits challenging the basis for their imprisonment without trial, and has continued the CIA's extraordinary rendition program of prisoner transfers.

This trend of continuity is also evidently demonstrated by the persistence of detention centers, despite promises to the contrary. It is symbolized by the case of the Guantanamo camp, still in operation (despite the best of intentions) three years after President Obama signed an executive order for its closure on his first day in office, and well beyond the deadline he specified. The question of how to prosecute detainees who had been subjected to the Bush administration's counterterrorist policies remains a major issue, as illustrated by the case of Ahmed Khalfan Ghailani, the first former Guantanamo detainee tried in a civilian court. His trial was regarded as a way to test the Obama administration's resolve on using civilian courts. His acquittal on all but one of more than 280 charges of conspiracy and murder in the 1998 terrorist bombings of the U.S. embassies in Nairobi, Kenya, and Dar es Salaam, Tanzania, has reignited a fierce debate between those who advocate the use of civilian courts and those who claim that military trials are the only solution in handling terrorism prosecutions.[40] Attorney General Holder decided in November 2010 to prosecute Khalid Sheikh Mohammed and four other accused 9/11 conspirators in a federal courthouse in Manhattan. At the same time he sent five other detainee cases to the military commissions system. The question of where Khalid Sheikh Mohammed will be prosecuted remains in limbo, however, as Congress has blocked the transfer of prisoners from Guantanamo Bay to the United States for trial.

This decision forced President Obama in March 2011 to reverse his previous order halting new military charges against detainees, permitting military trials to resume and thus implicitly confirming the failure to close the prison camp. The issue of detainees assessed as dangerous but who for legal reasons cannot be prosecuted in U.S. courts remains unresolved. A new legal system of continued detention for these prisoners in limbo has been under consideration despite the unconstitutionality of the practice of indefinite detention. A presidential executive order signed in March 2011 requires a review of the status of these detainees within a year and every three years after that to determine whether they remain a threat, whether they should be scheduled for a military trial, or whether they should be released. Yet recent revelations from Wikileaks about how "unlawful combatants" have been captured, detained, interrogated, and qualified as a "major threat" cast a shadow over the entire process of prosecuting these detainees.

The "state of exception" is likely to remain permanent due to both the effects of the security-insecurity spiral and the controversial outcomes of the "lesser evil" approach. In the context of an apparently unending war, the evidence suggests that every time a liberty is curtailed, only a portion of it—at most—is restored for immigrants or citizens, despite court rulings that challenge the provisions, and despite changes in governments. Furthermore, the only way for Western democracies to justify the undemocratic aspects of security measures is to adopt a basic Schmittian distinction between friends and enemies. That is, the enemy is whoever is "in a specially intense way, existentially something different and alien, so that in the extreme case conflicts with him are possible."[41] The actual targets of state policy and public discontent move in cycles, often manipulated by politicians seeking to stir popular discontent for electoral purposes or to distract voters from other pressing issues. Violence on the Mexican border has been extensive since 2007. Yet it was only in 2009, when Arizona was mired in the worst housing crisis since the Great Depression, that local Republican politicians chose to focus on the curtailment of civil liberties for Hispanics as an issue. Likewise, in Europe, President Sarkozy of France only chose to prosecute the very popular campaign against Roma as a "law and order" issue in the period leading up to French elections, with his personal popularity ratings standing at 15 percent. In the same period Sarkozy also raised the simmering issue over Islam's compatibility with European values by launching debates in France about *laïcité* and national identity while enacting a new law against the wearing of the burqa. Such a populist anti-Islam initiative was designed to capture the National Front's share of the electorate. Yet, to date, this strategy has failed: this extreme-right-wing party is increasingly influential, while civil liberties have once again eroded. Other European leaders follow the same populist strategy and therefore may face similar results: prejudicial policies enhancing a sense of alienation; an increased distrust among targeted minorities (with the potential radicalization of some of them); public disenchantment fueled by the failure to stem the flow of immigrants; a pervasive sense of insecurity fueled by real and perceived threats—and yet less democracy at home.

None of these issues will disappear. No one can foresee the end of the "war on terror," whatever title it is given. The death of Osama bin Laden does not end al-Qaeda and will probably have little effect on AQIM and other terrorist organizations that are largely independent of al-Qaeda. Likewise, immigration pressures are unlikely to abate, and will continue to induce significant changes in the composition of the population. The 2010 U.S. Census counted 50.5 million Hispanics, making up 16.3 percent of the U.S. population. The number of Latino children has grown by 39 percent over the last decade. Recent surveys estimate that Muslim minorities in Europe will increase from 6 percent at present to 8 percent of the total population over the next twenty years. The majority of these Muslims will be native citizens, able to mobilize, vote, and express their demands. These trends on both side of the Atlantic can fuel populist fears about the future of national identity and national security. They can also provide new opportunities for those in government to tackle the immigration/security nexus in a more efficient way by acknowledging, for example, that immigration is not a pathological result of negative globalization but the result of complex pull and push factors that need to be addressed without reference to obsessive security concerns; by recognizing that the vast majority of immigrants (notably refugees and asylum seekers) do not deserve to be treated as criminals and potential terrorists; by conceding that repressive border-enforcement policies simply aggravate the issues of border management, without solving the main concerns related to the integration of minorities; and accepting that terrorists are sometimes among "us."

● ● ● ABBREVIATIONS

ACLU	American Civil Liberties Union
AEDPA	Antiterrorism and Effective Death Penalty Act
AFSJ	Area of Freedom, Security and Justice
AQIM	al-Qaeda in Maghreb
CAIR	Council of American-Islamic Relations
CBP	Customs and Border Protection
DHS	Department of Homeland Security
ENP	European Neighborhood Policy
ESS	European Security Strategy
ETA	Euskadi Ta Askatasuna
EU	European Union
EUMC	European Monitoring Center on Racism and Xenophobia
Eurodac	European Dactyloscopy
Eurojust	EU Judicial Cooperation Unit
Europol	European Police office
Eurosur	European External Border Surveillance System
FAIR	Forum against Islamophobia and Racism (UK)
FAIR	Federation for American Immigration Reform
Frontex	European Agency for the Management of Operational Cooperation at the External Borders
ICE	Immigration and Customs Enforcement
IIRIRA	Illegal Immigration Reform and Individual Responsibility Act
INA	Immigration and Nationality Act
INS	Immigration and Naturalization Service
JHA	Justice and Home Affairs
MCA	Millennium Challenge Account
MDGs	Millennium Development Goals
MEDA	Euro-Mediterranean Partnership
MPAC	Muslim Public Affairs Council
NAFTA	North American Free Trade Agreement
NGO	nongovernmental organization

NSEERS	National Security Entry-Exit Registration System
NSS	National Strategy for Homeland Security
ODA	official development aid
OECD	Organization for Economic Cooperation and Development
SEA	Single European Act
SIS	Schengen Information System
TCN	third-country national
TFEU	Treaty on the Functioning of the EU (Lisbon Treaty)
TIDE	Terrorist Identities Datamart Environment
Trevi	Terrorisme, Radicalisme, Extrémisme, Violence Internationale
TSA	Transportation Security Administration
USAID	U.S. Agency for International Development
USA Patriot	Uniting and Strengthening America by Providing Appropriate Tools Required to Intercept and Obstruct Terrorism
USCIS	U.S. Citizenship and Immigration Services
US-VISIT	U.S. Visitor and Immigrant Status Indicator Technology
VIS	Visa Information System

Notes

Introduction

1. 66 Fed. Reg. 48334–35, amending 8.C.F.R §287.3(d), September 20, 2001.

2. Mikhail Alexseev, *Immigration Phobia and the Security Dilemma* (Cambridge: Cambridge University Press, 2006), 57.

3. Conclusions adopted by the Council of the European Union (Justice and Home Affairs), September 20, 2001, Council Document SN 3926/6/01.

4. European Council, Council Common Position of December 27, 2001, on Combating Terrorism, 2001/930/CFSP.

5. Council Directive 2004/83, OJ L/304/12 (article 14).

6. According to the Immigration and Naturalization Service, immigrants are aliens who have been granted lawful permanent residence in the United States. They are commonly referred to as "green card" recipients. Temporary admissions refer to arrivals of aliens who are authorized to stay in the United States for a limited period. These aliens are also known as nonimmigrants. Temporary admissions include aliens arriving in the United States with nonimmigrant visas, aliens arriving without visas from countries eligible for the Visa Waiver Program, and aliens paroled into the United States for humanitarian and other reasons. Although most nonimmigrants enter the United States as tourists, some come to work, study, or engage in cultural exchange programs. Certain aliens admitted for temporary residence are eligible for adjustment of status to permanent residence.

7. Findings of the Final Report of the Senate Select Committee on Intelligence and the House Permanent Select Committee on Intelligence Joint Inquiry into the Terrorist Attacks of September 11, 2001 (S.HRG 107–1086, December 2002), 6. Available at http://intelligence.senate.gov/pdfs/1071086v2.pdf.

8. Majid Tehranian, "Global Terrorism: Searching for Appropriate Responses," *Pacifica Review* 14 (2003): 57–65; U.S. Department of State, *Patterns of Global Terrorism 2001* (Washington, D.C.: U.S. Department of State, 2002); Strobe Talbott and Nayan Chanda, *The Age of Terror: America and the World after September 11* (New York: Basic Books, 2002); François Heisbourg, *L'Hyperterrorisme* (Paris: Odile Jacob, 2002); Richard L. Garwin, "The Technology of Megaterror," *Technology Review* (September 2002).

9. Didier Bigo, "The Emergence of a Consensus: Global Terrorism, Global Insecurity, and Global Security," in *Immigration, Integration and Security: America and Europe in Comparative Perspective*, ed. Ariane Chebel d'Appollonia and Simon Reich (Pittsburgh: University of Pittsburgh Press, 2008), 68.

10. Richard Jackson, *Writing the War on Terror: Language, Politics and Counter-Terrorism* (Manchester: Manchester University Press, 2005).

11. Ian Loader and Neil Walker, *Civilizing Security* (Cambridge: Cambridge University Press, 2007).

12. Buzan et al. call this a "securitizing move." See Barry Buzan, Ole Waever, and Jaap de Wilde, *Security: A New Framework for Analysis* (Boulder, Colo.: Lynne Rienner, 1998).

13. Didier Bigo et al., *The Changing Landscape of European Liberty and Security: Mid-Term Report on the Results of the CHALLENGE Project* (CHALLENGE, February 2007), 7. Available at http://www.libertysecurity.org/IMG/pdf_Challenge MidReport.pdf.

14. Quoted by Donald Kerwin, "The Use and Misuse of 'National Security' Rationale in Crafting US Refugee and Immigration Policies," *International Journal of Refugee Law* 17 (2005): 2.

15. Regarding the role of implementation structure that explains policy failure or success, see Benny Hjern and David O. Porter, "Implementing Structures: A New Unit of Administrative Analysis," *Organization Studies* 2, no. 3 (1981): 211–27; and Larry O'Toole, "Research on Policy Implementation: Assessment and Prospects," *Journal of Public Administration Research and Theory* 10, no. 2 (2000): 263–88. Regarding the role of actors in the assessment of achievements, see Susan M. Barrett, "Implementation Studies: Time for a Revival? Personal Reflections on 20 years of Implementation Studies," *Public Administration* 82, no. 2 (2004): 249–62.

16. The notion of policy failure is therefore used in an analytical sense: policy failure occurs when policies do not achieve their stated objectives. See Christina Boswell, "Theorizing Migration Policy: Is There a Third Way?" *International Migration Review* 41, no. 1 (March 2007): 75–100; Stephen Castles, "Why Migration Policies Fail?" *Ethnic and Racial Studies* 27, no. 2 (March 2004): 205–27.

17. Quoted by David Luban, "Eight Fallacies about Liberty and Security," in *Human Rights and the War on Terror*, ed. Richard Ashby (New York: Cambridge University Press, 2005), 242.

18. Prime Minister's Press Conference, August 5, 2005 (*BBC News*, August 6, 2005).

19. For example, section 56 of the British Immigration, Asylum and Nationality Act of 2006. See http://www.legislation.gov.uk/ukpga/2006/13/section/56.

20. Peter Chalk, "The Liberal Democratic Responses to Terrorism," *Terrorism and Political Violence* 7 (1995): 10–44; Joseph V. Montville, *Conflict and Peacemaking in Multiethnic Societies* (Lexington, Mass.: Lexington Books, 1991); G. K. Robertson, "Intelligence, Terrorism and Civil Liberties," in *Contemporary Research on Terrorism*, ed. Paul Wilkinson and Alastair M. Stewart (Aberdeen: Aberdeen University Press, 1987); Paul Wilkinson, *Terrorism and the Liberal State* (London: Macmillan, 1986); Christopher Hewitt, *The Effectiveness of Anti-Terrorist Policies* (New York: University Press of America, 1984); Irving Horowitz, "The Routinization of Terrorism and Its Unanticipated Consequences," in *Terrorism, Legitimacy and Power: The Consequences of Political Violence*, ed. Martha Crenshaw (Middletown, Conn.: Wesleyan University Press, 1983).

21. David Cole, *Enemy Aliens: Double Standards and Constitutional Freedoms in the War on Terror* (New York: Free Press, 2003).

Part I The Framing of Immigration as a Security Issue

1. Steven Camarota, "The High Cost of Cheap Labor: Illegal Immigration and the Federal Budget," *Center for Immigration Studies Backgrounder* (August 2004): 1–48; Donald Huddle, *The Cost of Immigration* (Washington, D.C.: Carrying Capacity Network, 1993); Vernon Briggs, *Mass Immigration and National Interest* (Armonk, N.Y.: M. E. Sharpe, 1992).

2. George Borjas, "The Labor Demand Curve Is Downward Sloping: Reexamining the Impact of Immigration on the Labor Market," *Quarterly Journal of Economics* (November 2003): 1335–74; George Borjas, Richard B. Freeman, and Lawrence Katz, "How Much Do Immigration and Trade Affect Labor Market Outcomes?" *Brookings Paper on Economic Activity* 1 (1997): 1–90; Claudia Goldin, "The Political Economy of Immigration Restriction in the United States, 1890 to 1921," in *The Regulated Economy: A Historical Approach to Political Economy*, ed. Claudia Goldin and Gary Libecap (Chicago: University of Chicago Press, 1994), 223–58; Joseph G. Altonji and David Card, "The Effect of Immigration on the Labor Market Outcomes of Less-Skilled Natives," in *Immigration, Trade, and the Labor Market*, ed. John M. Abowd and Richard B. Freeman (Chicago: University of Chicago Press, 1991).

3. Steven Camarota, "A Snapshot of America's Foreign-Born Population, 2000–2004," *Center of Immigration Studies Backgrounder* (December 2005): 1–32; Steven Camarota and Leon F. Bouvier, "The Impact of New Americans: A Review and Analysis of the National Council's *The New Americans*," *Center for Migration Studies Backgrounder* (November 1999): 1–16.

4. Pew Research Center, *America's Immigration Quandary: No Consensus on Immigration Problem or Proposed Fixes*, Survey Report, March 30, 2006, 5–6.

5. European Commission, "Public Opinion in the European Union," *Standard Eurobarometer* 66 (December 2006): 19.

6. Samuel P. Huntington, *Who Are We? The Challenges to America's National Identity* (New York: Simon & Schuster, 2005); Patrick J. Buchanan, *The Death of the West: How Dying Populations and Immigrant Invasions Threaten Our Culture and Civilization* (New York: St. Martin's Press, 2002).

7. Pew Research Center, *No Consensus on Immigration Problem*, 7.

8. Gary Richardson, "The Origins of Anti-Immigrant Sentiments: Evidence from the Heartland in the Age of Mass Migration," *Topics in Economic Analysis & Policy* 5, no. 1 (2005): 1–46; Andreas Zick et al., "Acculturation and Prejudice in Germany: Majority and Minority Perspective," *Journal of Social Issues* 57 (Fall 2001): 541–57; Jan Pieter Van Oudenhoven et al., "Attitudes of Minority and Majority Members towards Adaptation of Immigrants," *European Journal of Social Psychology* 28 (1998): 995–1013.

9. European Social Survey, Round 1, 2003. See FRA (EUMC), *Majorities' Attitudes towards Migrants and Minorities. Key Findings from the Eurobarometer and the European Social Survey* (Wien: Manz Crossmedia, 2005), 1–44.

10. "Immigration Has Damaged Culture, Say Britons," *Angus Reid Global Monitor*, April 11, 2008. Available at http://www.angus-reid.com/polls/31678/country_changed_by_immigration_say_britons/.

11. "Italians Think Muslims Shun Integration," *Angus Reid Global Monitor*, January 6, 2007. Available at http://www.angus-reid.com/polls/5600/italians_think_muslims_shun_integration/.

12. Cited by Georgios Antonopoulos, "The Limitations of Official Statistics in Relation to the Criminality of Migrants in Greece," *Policy Practice and Research* 6 (July 2005): 252.

13. Evan Schofer and Ann Hironaka, "The Effects of World Society on Environmental Protection Outcomes," *Social Force* 84, no. 1 (September 2005): 25–47; Paul Stubbs, International Non-State Actors and Social Development Policy," *Global Social Policy* 3 (2003): 319–48; Daphne Josselin and William Wallace, eds., *Non-State Actors in Global Politics* (London: Palgrave Macmillan, 2002); Richard Higgott, Geoffrey Underhill, and Andreas Bieler, *Non-State Actors and Authority in the Global System* (London: Routledge, 2000); Margaret E. Keck and Kathryn Sikkink, *Activists beyond Borders: Advocacy Networks in International Relations* (Ithaca, N.Y.: Cornell University Press, 1998); John Meyer et al., "World Society and the Nation-State," *American Journal of Sociology* 103 (1997): 144–81; Jackie Smith, Ron Pagnucco, and Charles Chatfield, *Transnational Social Movements and Global Politics* (Syracuse, N.Y.: Syracuse University Press, 1997); Thomas Risse-Kappen, *Bringing Transnational Relations Back In: Non-State Actors, Domestic Structures, and International Institutions* (Cambridge: Cambridge University Press, 1995).

14. Ronald Skeldon, *Migration and Development* (Harlow, Essex: Addison Wesley Longman, 1997); Ethan Kapstein, "Workers and the World Economy," *Foreign Affairs*, January/February 1996, 16–37; Robin Cohen, *Sociology of Migration* (Cheltenham: Edward Edgard Publishing, 1996); Fred Block, *The Vampire State and Other Stories* (New York: New Press, 1996); Manuel Castells, *The Information Age: Economy, Society and Culture* (Oxford: Blackwells, 1996); Vincent Cable, "The Diminished Nation-State: A Study in the Loss of Economic Power," *Daedalus* 124 (Spring 1995): 1–31; Alejandro Portes and J. Walton, *Labor, Class, and the International System* (New York: Academic Press, 1981); Stephen Castles and Godula Kosack, *Immigrant Workers and Class Structure in Western Europe* (London: Oxford University Press, 1973); Albert O. Hirschman, *Exit, Voice, and Loyalty: Responses to Decline in Firms, Organizations, and States* (Cambridge, Mass: Harvard University Press, 1970).

15. John Boli and George M. Thomas, *Constructing World Culture: International Nongovernmental Organizations since 1875* (Stanford, Calif.: Stanford University Press, 1999); Robert Cox, "Civil Society at the Turn of the Millennium," *Review of International Studies* 25, no. 1 (1999): 3–28.

16. Saskia Sassen, *Losing Control? Sovereignty in an Age of Globalization* (New York: Columbia University Press, 1996), 95. See also David Jacobson, *Rights across Borders: Immigration and the Decline of Citizenship* (Baltimore: Johns Hopkins University Press, 1996).

17. Wayne Cornelius, Philip Martin, and James Hollifield, *Controlling Immigration* (Stanford, Calif.: Stanford University Press, 1994).

18. Alexseev, *Immigration Phobia*, 21.

19. Jack Citrin and John Sides, "European Immigration in the People's Court," in *Immigration and the Transformation of Europe*, ed. Craig Parsons and Timothy Smeeding (Cambridge: Cambridge University Press, 2006), 352.

20. European Union Agency for Fundamental Rights, *EU-MIDIS Main Results Report* (FRA, 2009), 1–276. Available at http://fra.europa.eu/fraWebsite/attachments/eumidis_mainreport_conference-edition_en_.pdf.

21. Clifford D. Shearing and Lee Johnston, *Governing Security: Explorations in Policing and Justice* (London: Routledge, 2003).

22. Ian Loader and Neil Walker, *Civilizing Security* (Cambridge: Cambridge University Press, 2007), 20.

23. Gallya Lahav, "The Rise of Non-State Actors in Migration Regulation in the United States and Europe," in *Immigration Research for a New Century: Multidisciplinary Perspectives*, ed. Nancy Foner, Ruben Rumbault, and Steven J. Golds (New York: Russell Sage Foundation, 2000), 215–42; Virginie Guiraudon and Gallya Lahav, "A Reappraisal of the State Sovereignty Debate: The Case of Migration Control," *Comparative Political Studies* 33, no. 2 (March 2000): 163–95.

1. Newcomers, Old Threats, and Current Concerns

1. The number of 18.7 million was reported by Eurostat's Chronos database. The OECD's SOPEMI network put the number of foreign nationals in the EU 15 at 20.1 million people. The European Labor Force Survey raised the estimates to 22.7 million. See International Organization for Migration, *World Migration Report*, 2005, 142–43.

2. U.S. Census Bureau, *The Foreign-Born Population in the United States: Current Population Survey* (2005). Available at http://www.census.gov/.

3. American Community Survey, October 2010. Available at http://www.census.gov/acs/www/.

4. Jeffrey Passel, *Unauthorized Migrants: Numbers and Characteristics*, Pew Hispanic Center Survey Research Report, March 7, 2006, 1–23.

5. The International Labor Office assumed that illegal immigrants constituted 15 percent of the foreign population in Western Europe. But these figures were largely unsubstantiated.

6. Samuel Huntington, *Who Are We?* (2005); Peter Brimelow, *Alien Nation: Common Sense about America's Immigration Disaster* (New York: Random House, 1995).

7. Huntington, *Who Are We?* 18–19.

8. Former editor of *Forbes*, Peter Brimelow created in 1999 the Center for American Unity, dedicated to preserving the "historical unity" of Americans by addressing emerging threats such as "mass immigration, multiculturalism, and affirmative action." See http://www.vdare.com/.

9. Peter Brimelow, "America's Assisted Suicide," *National Review*, November 25, 1996, 45.

10. Lawrence Auster, *The Path to National Suicide: An Essay on Immigration and Multiculturalism* (Monterey, Va.: American Immigration Control Foundation, 1990).

11. Patrick Buchanan, a conservative political commentator and politician, sought the Republican presidential nomination in 1992 and 1996. He ran on a Reform Party ticket in the 2000 presidential election (he got 0.4 percent of the popular vote).

12. Patrick Buchanan, *State of Emergency: The Third World Invasion and Conquest of America* (New York: St. Martin's Press, 2006).

13. Oriana Fallaci, *La forza della ragione* (Milano: Rizzoli, 2004). A former partisan during World War II, Fallaci received much public attention for her controversial anti-Muslim writings. An Italian judge ordered her to stand trial on charges of defaming Islam, but she died before the trial, in December 2006. Fallaci's arguments have been supported in the United States by Daniel Pipes (www.danielpipes.org/art/1796).

14. Pim Fortuyn, *Tegen de islamisering van onze cultuur* (Utrecht: A. W. Bruna, 1997). Fortuyn was assassinated in May 2002. His party won 17 percent of the seats in the parliament shortly after his death but declined rapidly in electoral popularity afterward.

15. American Community Survey, October 2010. Available at http://factfinder. census.gov/servlet/STSelectServlet?_ts=327403890666.

16. U.S. Census Bureau, *U.S. Interim Projections by Age, Sex, Race and Hispanic Origin* (2004). Available at http://www.census.gov/ipc/www/usinterimproj/.

17. Eurostat, "Population in Europe in 2007," *Statistics in Focus* 81 (2008): 2. Available at http://epp.eurostat.ec.europa.eu/cache/ITY_OFFPUB/KS-SF-08–081/EN/KS-SF-08–081-EN.PDF.

18. David Coleman, "Immigration and Ethnic Changes in Low-Fertility Countries: A Third Demographic Transition," *Population and Development Review* 32, no. 3 (September 2006): 401–46. See also http://www.migrationwatchuk.org/.

19. The foreign-born population represented 14.7 percent of the total population in 1890 and 1910 and 13.2 percent in 1920.

20. The total number of foreigners in EU statistics includes citizens of other EU member states (EU nationals) and non-EU citizens (TCNs). The high rate in Luxembourg is due to a large number of EU nationals living in this country, mainly "Eurocrats" working for the EU institutions.

21. Eurostat, "Population of Foreign Citizens in the EU 27 in 2008," *News Release* 184 (December 16, 2009): 1–13. Available at http://epp.eurostat.ec.europa.eu/cache/ITY_PUBLIC/3–16122009-BP/EN/3–16122009-BP-EN.PDF.

22. John Sides and Jack Citrin, "European Opinion about Immigration: The Role of Identities, Interests and Formation," *B. J. Pol. S* 37 (2007): 477–504. Accessed March 13, 2008. doi: 10.1017/S0007123407000257; Lee Sigelman and Richard G. Niemi, "Innumeracy about Minority Populations: African Americans and Whites Compared," *Public Opinion Quarterly* 65 (Spring 2001): 86–94.

23. James Glaser, "Social Context and Inter-Group Political Attitudes: Experiments in Group Conflict Theory," *British Journal of Political Science* 33 (2003): 607–20.

24. Pew Research Center, *America's Immigration Quandary*,, 29.

25. Cara Wong, "'Little' and 'Big' Pictures in Our Heads: Race, Local Context and Innumeracy about Racial Groups in the U.S.," *Public Opinion Quarterly* 71, no. 3 (Fall 2007): 392–412.

26. *Guardian* (UK), April 11, 2005.

27. Hajo G. Boomgaarden and Rens Vliegenhart, "Explaining the Rise of Anti-Immigrant Parties: The Role of News Media Content," *Electoral Studies* 26 (2007): 404–17; Johanna Dunaway, Marisa Abrajano, and Regina Branton, "Agenda Setting, Public Opinion, and the Issue of Immigration Reform," *Social Science Research*

Network (2007). Available at http://papers.ssrn.com/sol3/papers.cfm?abstract_id=1017846; Alessandra Buonfino, "Between Unity and Plurality: The Politicization of the Discourse of Immigration in Europe," *New Political Science* 26, no. 1 (March 2004): 23–49; William E. Saris and Paul M. Sniderman, *Studies in Public Opinion: Attitudes, Nonattitudes, Measurement Error, and Change* (Princeton, N.J.: Princeton University Press, 2004); Paul Sniderman et al., *The Outsider: Prejudice and Politics in Italy* (Princeton, N.J.: Princeton University Press, 2002); Thomas Meyer and Lew Hinchman, *Mass Media: How the Media Colonize Politics* (Cambridge: Polity Press, 2002); John Street, *Mass Media, Politics and Democracy* (London: Palgrave Macmillan, 2001); Giovanna Campini, "Migrants and the Media: The Italian Case," in *Media and Migration: Constructions of Mobility and Difference*, ed. Russell King and Nancy Wood (London: Routledge, 2001), 38–52.

28. *Sun*, January 19, 2004; *Daily Express*, January 20, 2004.

29. Home Office, *Accession Monitoring Report*, Border and Immigration Agency, September 2007, 1–38.

30. The convergence between media coverage and policy agenda is facilitated in Italy by the fact that the most influential national newspapers are all dependent upon large financial groups that are all in turn involved in politics. See Campini, "Migrants and the Media." To date, Silvio Berlusconi, the prime minister, retains control of about 90 percent of all national television broadcasting, in addition to newspapers and the largest Italian publishing house.

31. OECD, *International Migration Outlook* (Paris: SOPEMI, 2006), 1–6.

32. EU enlargements have led to a de facto transformation of "immigrants" from the EU 12 into "EU nationals" within the EU 27.

33. Valsamis Mitsilegas, "Measuring Irregular Migration," in *Irregular Migration and Human Rights: Theoretical, European and International Perspectives*, ed. Barbara Bogusz et al. (Leiden: Martinus Nijhoff, 2004), 29–40.

34. Passel, *Unauthorized Migrants*, 1–23.

35. Aristide Zolberg, *A Nation by Design: Immigration Policy in the Fashioning of America* (Cambridge, Mass.: Harvard University Press, 2006), 421.

36. U.S. Immigration and Naturalization Service, 2003. Regarding the reform of the INS by President George W. Bush and its absorption by the Department of Homeland Security (DHS) see chapter 4.

37. Lauren McLaren and Mark Johnson, "Resources, Group Conflict and Symbols: Explaining Anti-Immigration Hostility in Great Britain," *Political Studies* (2007): 1–24; Lawrence Bobo and V. L. Hutchings, "Perceptions of Racial Group Competition: Extending Blumer's Theory of Group Position to a Multiracial Social Context," *American Sociological Review* 61, no. 6 (1996): 951–72; Lawrence Bobo, "Group Conflict, Prejudice, and the Paradox of Contemporary Racial Attitudes," in *Eliminating Racism: Profiles in Controversy*, ed. P. Katz and D. Taylor (New York: Plenum Press, 1988), 85–109; Susan Olsak, *The Dynamics of Ethnic Competition and Conflict* (Palo Alto, Calif.: Stanford University Press, 1992).

38. M. Semyonov, R. Rijman, and A. Gorodzeisky, "The Rise of Anti-Foreigner Sentiment in European Societies," *American Sociological Review* 71 (2006): 426–49; Silke L. Schneider, "Anti-Immigrant Attitudes in Europe: Outgroup Size and Perceived Ethnic Threat," *European Sociological Review* 24, no. 1 (2008): 53–67.

39. Bart Meuleman, Eldad Davidov, and Jacques Billiet, "Changing Attitudes toward Immigration in Europe, 2002–2007: A Dynamic Group Conflict Theory Approach," *Social Science Research* 38, no. 2 (2009): 352–65; Zan Strabac and Ola Listhaug, "Anti-Muslim Prejudice in Europe: A Multilevel Analysis of Survey Data from 30 Countries," *Social Science Research* 37, no. 1 (2008): 268–86.

40. Lincoln Quillian, "Prejudice as a Response to Perceived Group Threat: Population Composition and Anti-Immigrant and Racial Prejudice in Europe," *American Sociological Review* 60, no. 4 (1995): 586–611.

41. Lauren McLaren, "Immigration and the New Politics of Inclusion and Exclusion in the European Union: The Effect of Elites and the EU on Individual-Level Opinions Regarding European and Non-European Immigrants," *European Journal of Political Research* 39, no. 1 (January 2001): 81–108.

42. Marcel Coenders et al., "Majority Populations' Attitudes towards Migrants and Minorities," *EUMC Report* 4 (2005): 51.

43. M. V. (Trey) Hood III and I. L. Morris, "Amigo o Enemigo? Context, Attitudes and Anglo Public Opinion toward Immigration," *Social Science Quarterly* 78, no. 2 (1997): 309–23.

44. Eric Olivier and Tali Mendelberg, "Reconsidering the Environmental Determinants of White Racial Attitudes," *American Journal of Political Science* 44 (2000): 574–89.

45. Kenneth Scheve and Matthew Slaughter, "Labor Market Competition and Individual Preferences over Immigration Policy," *Review of Economics and Statistics* 83, no. 1 (2001): 142.

46. Regina Branton, Gavin Dillingham, Johanna Dunaway, and Beth Miller, "Anglo Voting on Nativist Ballot Initiatives: The Partisan Impact of Spatial Proximity to the U.S.-Mexico Border," *Social Sciences Quarterly* 88, no. 3 (September 2007): 882–97.

47. Aristide Zolberg and Long Litt Woon, "Why Islam Is Like Spanish: Cultural Incorporation in Europe and the United States," *Politics & Society* 27, no. 1 (March 1999), 5.

48. Ibid., 7.

49. Charles Hirschman, "The Impact of Immigration on American Society: Looking Backward to the Future," *Working Paper* (2006), Center for Studies in Demography and Ecology, University of Washington, Seattle, 3.

50. Richard Alba and Victor Nee, "Rethinking Assimilation for a New Era of Immigration," *International Migration Review* 31 (1997): 845.

51. Quoted by Zolberg, *Nation by Design*, 54.

52. Ellis Cose, *A Nation of Strangers: Prejudice, Politics, and the Populating of America* (New York: Morrow, 1992); David Bennett, *The Party of Fear: From Nativist Movements to the New Right in American History* (Chapel Hill: University of North Carolina Press, 1988).

53. Quoted by Graham Otis, *Unguarded Gates: A History of America's Immigration Crisis* (Lanham, Md.: Rowman & Littlefield, 2004), 24.

54. Eugen Weber, *Peasants into Frenchmen: The Modernization of Rural France, 1870–1914* (Stanford, Calif.: Stanford University Press, 1976).

55. Hirschman, "Impact of Immigration," 7.

56. Oscar Handlin, *The Uprooted: The Epic Story of the Great Migration That Made the American People* (Boston: Little Brown, 1951), 2.

57. Richard Alba, "Cohorts and the Dynamics of Ethnic Change," in *Social Structures and Human Lives*, ed. Mathilda Riley, Bettina Huber, and Beth Hess (Newbury Park, Calif.: Sage, 1988); Paul Buhle, *From the Lower East Side to Hollywood* (London: Verso, 2004).

58. Richard Alba and Victor Nee, *Remaking the American Mainstream: Assimilation and Contemporary Immigration* (Cambridge: Cambridge University Press, 2003); Richard Alba, "Assimilation's Quiet Tide," *Public Interest* 119 (1995): 1–18; Mary C. Waters, *Ethnic Options: Choosing Identities in America* (Berkeley and Los Angeles: University of California Press, 1990); Herbert Gans, "Symbolic Ethnicity: The Future of Ethnic Groups and Cultures in America," *Ethnic and Racial Studies* 2 (1979): 1–20.

59. Yves Lequin, ed., *La mosaïque France: Histoire des étrangers et de l'immigration* (Paris: Larousse, 1988); Gérard Noiriel, *Le creuset français: Histoire de l'immigration, XIX–XXè siècle* (Paris: Le Seuil, 1988).

60. Nancy Green, "Le Melting-Pot: Made in America, Produced in France," *Journal of American History* 86, no. 3 (1999): 1203.

61. Adrian Favell, "Integration Nations: The Nation-State and Research on Immigrants in Western Europe," *Comparative Social Research* 22 (2003): 13–42.

62. Quoted by Christian Joppke, "Multiculturalism and Immigration: A Comparison of the United States, Germany, and Great Britain," *Theory and Society* 25 (1996): 480.

63. Frank D. Bean, Susan K. Brown, and James Bachmeier, "Comparative Integration Contexts and Mexican Immigrant Group Incorporation in the United States," in *Managing Ethnic Diversity after 9/11: Integration, Security, and Civil Liberties in Transatlantic Perspective*, ed. Ariane Chebel d'Appollonia and Simon Reich (New Brunswick, N.J.: Rutgers University Press, 2010), 262.

64. Pew Hispanic Center, *The American Community: Hispanics 2004*, Survey Report, February 2007, 1–26.

65. Pew Hispanic Center, *Latino Children: A Majority Are U.S. Born Offspring of Immigrants*, Survey Report, May 2009, 1–17. During this same period the unemployment rate for all persons in the labor market increased from 4.6 percent to 6.6 percent.

66. United States Department of Labor, Bureau of Labor Statistics. Available at http://www.bls.gov/news.release/empsit.t03.htm.

67. Dominique Meurs, Ariane Pailhé, and Patrick Simon, "Mobilité entre générations d'immigration et persistance des inégalités: L'accès à l'emploi des immigrés et de leurs descendants en France, *Population* 5, no. 6 (2006): 763–801.

68. OECD, Programme for International Student Assessment, *When Immigrants Succeed: A Comparative Review of Performance and Engagement in PISA 2003*, 2006.

69. Victoria M. Esses, John F. Dovidio, and Gordon Hodson, "Public Attitudes toward Immigration in the United States as a Response to the September 11, 2001 'Attack on America,'" *Analyses of Social Issues and Public Policy* 2, no. 1 (December 2002): 74.

70. Mexicans accounted for 64 percent of the Hispanic population.

71. Pew Hispanic Center, *American Community: Hispanics 2004*, 7.

72. U.S. Census Report, *The Foreign-Born Population in the United States*, 2005.

73. Pew Hispanic Center, *National Survey of Latinos, Survey Report*, August 2006, 15.

74. Ibid., 13.

75. Pew Hispanic Center, *Between Here and There: How Attached Are Latino Immigrants to Their Native Country?* Survey Report, October 2007, 1–29.

76. Bean, Brown, and Bachmeier, "Comparative Integration Contexts," 253–75.

77. Pew Hispanic Center, *Latino Children*, 2.

78. Ibid., 3.

79. Sylvain Brouard and Vincent Tiberj, *Français comme les autres? Enquête sur les citoyens d'origine maghrébine, africaine et turque* (Paris: Presses de Sciences Po, 2005).

80. Rahsaan Maxwell, "Muslims, South Asians and the British Mainstream? A National Identity Crisis," *West European Politics* 29, no. 4 (2006): 736–56.

81. Commission for Racial Equality, "Citizenship and Belonging: What Is Britishness?" *ETHNOS Research* (2005): 39.

82. Dalia Mogahed and Zsolt Nyiri, "Reinventing Integration: Muslims in the West," *Harvard International Review* 29, no. 2 (Summer 2007). Available at http://hir.harvard.edu/courting-africa/reinventing-integration. See also Zsolt Nyiri, "The Clash of Perceptions: Comparison of Views among Muslims in Paris, London, and Berlin with Those of the General Public," in Chebel d'Appollonia and Reich, *Managing Ethnic Diversity after 9/11*, 98–113.

83. Ankica Kosic and Karen Phalet, "Ethnic Categorization of Immigrants: The Role of Prejudice, Perceived Acculturation Strategies and Group Size," *International Journal of Intercultural Relations* 30 (2006): 769–82; Ankica Kosic et al., "The Role of Majority Attitudes towards Out-Group in the Perception of the Acculturation Strategies of Immigrants," *International Journal of Intercultural Relations* 29 (2005): 273–88.

84. R. M. Kunovich, "Social Structural Position and Prejudice: An Exploration of Cross-National Differences in Regression Slopes," *Social Science Research* 33 (2004): 20–44; Peer Scheepers, M. Gijsbert, and Marcel Coenders, "Ethnic Exclusionism in European Countries: Public Opposition to Civil Rights for Legal Migrants as a Response to Perceived Ethnic Threat," *European Sociological Review* 18, no. 1 (2002): 17–34; Joel Fetzer, "Economic Self-Interest or Cultural Marginality? Anti-Immigration Sentiment and Nativist Political Movement in France, Germany and the United States," *Journal of Ethnic and Migration Studies* 26, no. 1 (January 2000): 5–23; Jeannette Money, *Fences and Neighbors: The Political Geography of Immigration Control* (Ithaca, N.Y.: Cornell University Press, 1999); Lawrence Bobo and James R. Kluegel, "Opposition to Race-Targeting: Self-Interest, Stratification Ideology, or Racial Attitudes?" *American Sociological Review* 58 (1993): 443–64; Lawrence Bobo, "Whites' Opposing to Busing: Symbolic Racism or Realistic Group Conflict?" *Journal of Personality and Social Psychology* 45 (1983): 1196–1210; Herbert Blumer, "Race Prejudice as a Sense of Group Position," *Pacific Sociological Review* 1 (1958): 3–7.

85. Carolyn L. Funk, "The Dual Influence of Self-Interest and Societal Interest in Public Opinion," *Political Research Quarterly* 53, no. 1 (2000): 37–62; Victoria Esses et al., "Intergroup Competition and Attitudes toward Immigrants and Immigration," *Journal of Social Issues* 54, no. 4 (1998): 699–724; Jack Citrin et al., "Public Opinion toward Immigration Reform: The Role of Economic Motivations," *Journal of Politics* 59 (1997): 858–81.

86. Lauren McLaren and Mark Johnson, "Resources, Group Conflict and Symbols: Explaining Anti-Immigration Hostility in Great Britain," *Political Studies* (2007): 6.

87. Jason E. Kehrberg, "Public Opinion on Immigration in Western Europe: Economics, Tolerance, and Exposure," *Comparative European Politics* 5 (2007): 264–81.

88. Coenders et al., "Majority Populations' Attitudes," 4, 5.

89. Sides and Citrin, "European Opinion about Immigration," 477–504.

90. Peter Burns and James G. Gimpel, "Economic Insecurity, Prejudicial Stereotypes, and Public Opinion on Immigration Policy," *Political Science Quarterly* 115, no. 2 (Summer 2000): 201–25.

91. Wayne Cornelius, "Controlling Unwanted Immigration: Lessons from the United States, 1993–2004," *Journal of Ethnic and Migration Studies* 31, no. 4 (July 2005): 775–94.

92. Anna Maria Mayda, "Who Is against Immigration? A Cross-Country Investigation of Individual Attitudes toward Immigrants," *Review of Economics and Statistics* 88, no. 3 (August 2006): 510–30; J. Hainmueller and M. Hiscok, "Educated Preferences: Explaining Attitudes toward Immigration," paper presented at the annual meeting for the APSA, Chicago, September 2004.

93. Gallya Lahav, "Public Opinion toward Immigration in the European Union: Does It Matter?" *Comparative Political Studies* 37 (2004): 1151–83.

94. McLaren and Johnson, "Resources, Group Conflict and Symbols," 13–14.

95. Thomas J. Espenshade and Katherine Hempstead, "Contemporary American Attitudes toward U.S. Immigration," *International Migration Review* 5 (1996): 547.

96. Thomas J. Espenshade and C. Calhoun, "An Analysis of Public Opinion toward Undocumented Immigration," *Population Research and Policy Review* 12, no. 3 (1993): 189–224; Myron Weiner, "Ethics, National Sovereignty and the Control of Immigration," *International Migration Review* 30, no. 1 (Spring 1996): 171–97.

97. Chang-Hoong Leong and Collen Ward, "Cultural Values and Attitudes toward Immigrants and Multiculturalism: The Case of the Eurobarometer Survey on Racism and Xenophobia," *International Journal of Intercultural Relations* 30 (2006): 799–810; Victoria Esses et al., "The Immigration Dilemma: The Role of Perceived Group Competition, Ethnic Prejudice, and National Identity, *Journal of Social Issues* 57, no. 3 (Fall 2001): 389–412.

98. Pew Research Center, *2006 Immigration*, Survey Report, March 7, 2006, 1–14.

99. Paul Snidermann, L. Hagendoorn, and M. Prior, "Predisposing Factors and Situational Triggers: Exclusionary Reactions to Immigrant Minorities, *American Political Sciences Review* 98, no. 1 (2004): 35–94.

100. Alexseev, *Immigration Phobia*, 227.

101. Will Jennings, "Responsive Risk Regulation? Immigration and Asylum," *Risk and Regulation Magazine* 9 (Summer 2005): 10–11.

2. Securitization before 9/11

1. Senate Joint Resolution 23, September 14, 2001. Available at http://www.law.cornell.edu/background/warpower/sj23.pdf. See also Public Law 107–40, 115 Stat. 224 (September 18, 2001).

2. *BBC News*, March 5, 2004.

3. Deborah W. Meyers, "U.S. Border Enforcement: From Horseback to High-Tech," *MIP Insight* 7 (November 2005): 18.

4. Giorgio Agamben, *State of Exception* (Chicago: University of Chicago Press, 2003).

5. Mae Ngai, "The Strange Career of the Illegal Alien: Immigration Restriction and Deportation Policy in the United States," *Law and History Review* 21, no. 1 (Spring 2003): 81.

6. Judith Ann Warner, "The Social Construction of the Criminal Alien in Immigration Law Enforcement Practice and Statistical Enumeration: Consequences for Immigrant Stereotyping," *Journal of Social and Ecological Boundaries* 1, no. 2 (Winter 2005–6): 61.

7. Martin Schain, *The Politics of Immigration in France, Britain, and the United States* (New York: Palgrave Macmillan, 2008), 47.

8. Anthony M. Messina, *The Logics and Politics of Post-WWII Migration to Western Europe* (Cambridge: Cambridge University Press, 2007), 48–51.

9. Derek Lutterbeck, "Blurring the Dividing Line: The Convergence of Internal and External Security in Western Europe," *European Security* 14, no. 2 (June 2005): 231.

10. President Reagan signed a National Security Decision Directive in 1986 that described drug trafficking as a "threat to national security" and authorized military involvement in antidrug activities.

11. Public Law 208, 104th Cong., 2nd sess. (September 30, 1996), Illegal Immigration Reform and Immigrant Responsibility Act. Available at http://uscis.gov/lpBin/lpext.dll/inserts/publaw/.

12. Kenneth J. Franzblau, *Immigration's Impact on U.S. National Security and Foreign Policy*, Research Paper, U.S. Commission on Immigration Reform, October 1997, 2.

13. See *Reno v. American Arab Anti-Discrimination Commission* (97–1252) 525 U.S. 471 (1999).

14. Schengen Agreements, 1985, article 7. Available at http://europa.eu/legislation_summaries/justice_freedom_security/free_movement_of_persons_asylum_immigration/l33020_en.htm. The Schengen Agreements were signed between 1985 and 1990. The Schengen area was gradually extended to include every member state. Ireland and the United Kingdom are part of Schengenland, but they have not ended border controls.

15. The Maastricht Treaty reorganized the EU policy structures into three pillars. The first pillar (European Community) included the pre-existing European Economic Community (in which the Commission, the Parliament, and the Court of Justice had supra-national powers). The second pillar was devoted to the Common Foreign and Security Policy. The third pillar on Justice and Home Affairs extended cooperation in the fields of law enforcement, criminal justice, asylum, and immigration.

16. The acquis communautaire includes the EU legislation, legal acts, treaties, and court decisions—all having binding force.

17. Reflection Group Report (Brussels, December 1995). Available at http://www.europarl.europa.eu/enlargement/cu/agreements/reflex2_en.htm.

18. This attack was perpetuated by two American citizens, Timothy McVeigh and Terry Nichols, who were driven by antigovernment and antitax beliefs. The FBI subverted other right-wing plots during the 1990s—but it failed to prevent the

July 1996 bombing of the Centennial Park during the summer Olympic Games in Atlanta.

19. The most spectacular incident abroad during the Carter administration was the November 1979 seizure of the U.S. embassy in Tehran. During the Reagan administration, Hezbollah planned the suicide car-bombing of the U.S. embassy in Beirut in April 1983 and the suicide truck-bombing of the U.S. Marine headquarters in Beirut (causing the death of 241 marines). It also carried out the bombing of the U.S. embassy in Kuwait in 1983.

20. Laura K. Donohue, "In the Name of National Security: U.S. Counter-terrorism Measures, 1960–2000," *Terrorism and Political Violence* 13, no. 3 (Autumn 2001): 16.

21. White House Commission on Aviation Safety and Security. Final Report to President Clinton, February 1997, p. 21. See http://www.fas.org/irp/threat/212fin~1.html.

22. Yonah Alexander, "Introduction," in *Counterterrorism Strategies: Successes and Failures in Six Nations*, ed. Yonah Alexander (Washington, D.C.: Potomac Books, 2006), 1–8.

23. Other measures included Council Joint Action 96/610/JHA of October 15, 1996, concerning the creation and maintenance of a directory of specialized counterterrorist competences, skills, and expertise to facilitate counterterrorism co-operation between the member states of the European Union; Council Joint Action 98/428/JHA of June 29, 1998, on the creation of a European Judicial Network, with responsibilities in terrorist offenses, in particular article 2; Council Joint Action 98/733/JHA of December 21, 1998, on making it a criminal offense to participate in a criminal organization in the member states of the European Union; and the Council Recommendation of December 9, 1999, on cooperation in combating the financing of terrorist groups.

24. Quoted by Guillaume Parmentier in Alexander, *Counterterrorism Strategies*, 63.

25. Council of Europe, La Gomera Declaration, 1995. See http://www.europarl.europa.eu/summits/mad2_en.htm#annex3.

26. EP Report on the Role of the EU in Combating Terrorism, 2001/2016 (INI). See http://www.europarl.europa.eu/sides/getDoc.do?pubRef=-//EP//NONSGML+REPORT+A5–2001–0273+0+DOC+PDF+V0//EN&language=EN.

27. Jef Huysmans, "The European Union and the Securitization of Immigration," *Journal of Common Market Studies* 38, no. 5 (December 2000): 759.

28. Peter Andreas, *Border Games: Policing the U.S.-Mexico Divide* (Ithaca, N.Y.: Cornell University Press, 2000); T. Dunn, *The Militarization of the U.S.-Mexico Border, 1978–1992* (Austin: Press of the University of Texas, 1996).

29. Jason Ackleson, "Directions in Border Security Research," *Social Science Journal* 40 (2003): 574.

30. Wayne Cornelius, "Death at the Border: Efficacy and Unintended Consequences of U.S. Immigration Control Policy," *Population and Development Review* 27, no. 4 (December 2001): 661–85; Peter Andreas and T. Snyder, eds., *The Wall around the West: State Borders and Immigration Controls in North America and Europe* (Lanham, Md.: Rowman & Littlefield, 2000).

31. U.S. Commission on Immigration Reform, *Final Report* (1997), 42. See http://www.utexas.edu/lbj/uscir/becoming/ex-summary.pdf.

32. The IIRIRA repealed the old judicial-review scheme in the Immigration and Nationality Act, 8 *U.S. Code* §1105a, and instituted a new provision, 8 *U.S. Code* §1252(g), which restricts judicial review of the attorney general's "decision or action" to "commence proceedings, adjudicate cases, or execute removal orders against any alien under this Act."

33. To obtain asylum through the affirmative process, applicants must be physically present in the United States and apply within one year of the date of their arrival. A defensive application for asylum occurs when an applicant requests asylum as a defense against removal from the United States.

34. Department of Homeland Security, Office of Immigration Statistics, August 2007, 2. Available at http://www.dhs.gov/files/statistics/immigration.shtm.

35. Han Nicolaas and Arno Sprangers, "Immigrants Come and Go," *CBS Web Magazine* (October 11, 2004). Available at http://www.cbs.nl/en-GB/menu/the mas/bevolking/publicaties/artikelen/archief/2004/2004–1552-wm.htm.

36. Gil Loescher, "State Responses to Refugees and Asylum Seekers in Europe," in *West European Immigration and Immigrant Policy in the New Century*, ed. Anthony Messina (London: Praeger, 2002), 39.

37. Derek Lutterbeck, "Policing Migration in the Mediterranean," *Mediterranean Politics* 11, no. 1 (March 2006): 59–82.

38. Meyers, "U.S. Border Enforcement," 8.

39. U.S. Department of Justice, INS Budget Authority and Authorized Positions. Available at http://www.usdoj.gov.

40. Lutterbeck, "Blurring the Dividing Line," 239.

41. Ibid., 249.

42. Richard Clarke, *Against All Enemies* (New York: Free Press, 2004), 190.

43. Donohue, "In the Name of National Security," 18.

44. Huysmans, "European Union and the Securitization of Migration," 751–77. See "Migrants as a Security Problem: Dangers of 'Securitizing' Societal Issues," in *Migration and European Integration: The Dynamics of Inclusion and Exclusion*, ed. R. Miles and D. Thänhardt (London: Pinter, 1995), 53–72.

45. Didier Bigo, "Frontiers and Security in Europe," in *The Frontiers of Europe*, ed. Malcolm Anderson (London: Pinter, Cassel Academic), 199, 130.

46. Didier Bigo, "The European International Security Field: Stakes and Rivalries in the Newly Developing Area of Police Intervention," in *Policing across National Boundaries*, ed. Malcolm Anderson and Monica den Boer (London: Pinter, 1994), 164.

47. Liza Schuster, "Common Sense or Racism? The Treatment of Asylum Seekers in Europe," *Patterns of Prejudice* 37, no. 3 (2003): 244.

48. Ruben G. Rumbaut and Walter A. Ewing, *The Myth of Immigrant Criminality and the Paradox of Assimilation: Incarceration Rates among Native and Foreign-Born Men*, report for the American Immigration Law Foundation, Immigration Policy Center, Spring 2007, 1–16; Rubén G. Rumbaut et al., *Debunking the Myth of Immigrant Criminality: Imprisonment among First- and Second-Generation Young Men*, Report published by the Migration Policy Institute, June 2006, 1–14; Daniel Mears, "The Immigration-Crime Nexus: Toward an Analytical Framework for Assessing and Guiding Theory, Research, and Policy," *Sociological Perspective* 44, no. 1 (2001):

1–19; Matthew Lee, Ramiro Martinez Jr., and Richard Rosenfeld, "Does Immigration Increase Homicide? Negative Evidence from Three Border Cities," *Sociological Quarterly* 42 (2001): 56–68; Matthew Lee, Ramiro Martinez Jr., and S. Fernando Rodriguez, "Contrasting Latinos in Homicide Research: The Victim and the Offender Relationship in El Paso and Miami," *Social Science Quarterly* 81, no. 1 (2000): 375–88; Kristin F. Butcher and Ann Morrison Piehl, "Cross City Evidence on the Relationship between Immigration and Crime," *Journal of Policy Analysis and Management* 17, no. 3 (1998): 457–93; John Hagan and Alberto Palloni, "Sociological Criminology and the Mythology of Hispanic Immigration and Crime," *Social Problems* 46, no. 4 (1999): 617–32; Michael Tonry, "Ethnicity, Crime, and Immigration," *Crime and Justice* 21 (1997): 1–29; Alejandro Portes and Alex Stepick, *City on the Edge: The Transformation of Miami* (Berkeley: University of California Press, 1993); Martin Killias, "Criminality among Second-Generation Immigrants in Western Europe," *Criminal Justice Review* 14, no. 1 (1989): 13–42.

49. Warner, "Social Construction of the Criminal Alien," 56–80.

50. Meyers, "U.S. Border Enforcement," 12.

51. Jason Ackleson, *Fencing in Failure: Effective Border Control Is Not Achieved by Building More Fences*, Report for the Immigration Policy Center (2006), 1–10.

52. Walter Ewing, *Border Insecurity: U.S. Border Enforcement Policies and National Security*, Report for the Immigration Policy Center (2006), 1–16.

53. Cornelius, "Death at the Border," 668.

54. Ibid., 669.

55. Gemma Marotta, "The Illegal Immigration in Italy: Some Qualitative and Quantitative Aspects," *International Review of Sociology* 14, no. 1 (2004): 31–50.

56. Janice Kephart, "Immigration and Terrorism: Moving beyond the 9/11 Staff Report on Terrorist Travel," *Center Paper* 24 (Center for Immigration Studies, September 2005): 1–36.

57. Bill Ong Hing, "Misusing Immigration Policies in the Name of Homeland Security," *New Centennial Review* 6, no. 1 (2006): 208.

58. Zolberg, *Nation by Design*, 442–43.

59. Muzaffar A. Chishti et al., *America's Challenge: Domestic Security, Civil Liberties and National Unity after September 11*, report for the Migration Policy Institute (2003), 12.

60. Ewing, *Border Insecurity*, 2.

61. Ong Hing, "Misusing Immigration Policies," 219.

62. EO 12947 on Prohibiting Transactions with Terrorists who Threaten to Disrupt the Middle East Process referred to "an unusual and extraordinary threat to the national security, foreign policy, and economy of the United States." Available at http://nodis3.gsfc.nasa.gov/displayEO.cfm?id=EO_12947.

63. Findings of the Final Report of the Senate Select Committee on Intelligence and the House Permanent Select Committee on Intelligence Joint Inquiry into the Terrorist Attacks of September 11, 2001 (S.HRG 107–1086, December 2002), 6. Available at http://intelligence.senate.gov/pdfs/1071086v2.pdf.

64. Home Office, *Report into the London Terrorist Attacks on July 7, 2005* (Intelligence and Security Committee, May 2006), 17.

65. Donohue, "In the Name of National Security," 15–60.

66. According to the 1951 Geneva convention and its 1967 protocol, the non refoulement principle concerns the protection of refuges from being returned to places where their rights or lives could be threatened.

67. In December 1996, for example, a wreck between Malta and Sicily caused the deaths of 283 Asian immigrants and was one of the worst Mediterranean maritime disasters since World War II. See Maurizio Albahari, "Death and the Modern State: Making Borders and Sovereignty at the Southern Edges of Europe," *Working Paper* 137 (Center for Comparative Immigration Studies, May 2006): 1–39.

68. Christian Joppke, "Why Liberal States Accept Unwanted Immigration," *World Politics* 50 (January 1998): 272.

69. Quoted by Roger Daniels, *Coming to America: A History of Immigration and Ethnicity in American Life* (New York: Harper Perennial, 1991), 303.

70. A noncitizen may be deported for conduct that was not a deportable offense when it occurred. See Daniel Kanstroom, *Deportation Nation: Outsiders in American History* (Cambridge: Cambridge University Press, 2007).

71. Available at http://www.tribunalconstitucional.es/Lists/constPDF/Consti tucionINGLES.pdf.

3. Securitization after 9/11

1. Office of Homeland Security, July 2002. Available at http://www.dhs.gov/ xlibrary/assets/nat_strat_hls.pdf.

2. Council of the EU, *A Secure Europe in a Better World*, December 2003. Available at http://www.consilium.europa.eu/uedocs/cmsUpload/78367.pdf.

3. Office of the Press Secretary, October 20, 2001. See http://www.whitehouse .gov/news/releases/2001/10/20011030–2.html.

4. The list of countries was further expanded to nationals from Saudi Arabia, Pakistan, Bangladesh, Egypt, Indonesia, Jordan, and Kuwait.

5. S 1927, Public Law 110–55, August 5, 2007.

6. J. M. Colombani, "Nous sommes tous Américains," *Le Monde*, September 13, 2001.

7. Council Common Position 2001/931/CFSP of December 27, 2001.

8. Council Framework Decision 2002/475/JHA of June 13, 2002.

9. Council Regulation (EC) no. 871/2004 of April 29, 2004; Council Decision 2005/211/JHA of February 24, 2005.

10. European Commission, COM (2005) 600 final (Brussels 24.11.2005). Available at http://eur-lex.europa.eu/.

11. European Commission, COM (2005) 184 final (Brussels 10.5.2005). Available at http://eur-lex.europa.eu/.

12. Council Decision 2007/124/EC of February 12, 2007.

13. It should be noted that these powers were repealed and replaced by a system of control orders under the Prevention of Terrorism Act 2005.

14. Available at http://ec.europa.eu/budget/budget_detail/last_year_en.htm.

15. Available at http://ec.europa.eu/budget/budget_detail/current_year_en.htm.

16. Available at http://www.whitehouse.gov/omb/rewrite/budget/fy2008/jus tice.html.

17. National Strategy for Homeland Security, October 2007, 23. Available at http://www.dhs.gov/xlibrary/assets/nat_strat_homelandsecurity_2007.pdf.

18. 66 Fed. Reg. 57 833 (November 16, 2001).

19. Council of the European Union, 144469/4/05, November 30, 2005, 6.

20. A. J. Bacevich, *American Empire: The Realities and Consequences of U.S. Diplomacy* (Cambridge, Mass.: Harvard University Press, 2002), 59.

21. Gilles Andreani, "The 'War on Terror': Good Cause, Wrong Concept," *Survival* 46, no. 2 (2004): 31–50.

22. Amnesty International, *Report 2005: The State of the World's Human Rights* (2005), 35. Available at http://www.amnesty.org/en/library/info/POL10/001/2005.

23. Council of Europe, *Report on Secret Detentions and Illegal Transfers of Detainees Involving Council of Europe Member States* (2006). Available at http://www.coe.int/ASP.

24. Monica den Boer, *9/11 and the Europeanisation of Anti-Terrorism Policy: A Critical Assessment*, Policy Paper 6, Groupement d'Études et de Recherches (September 2003), 16.

25. INA §212(a)(3)(F). See CRS Report for Congress, *Immigration Legislation and Issues in the 109th Congress* (October 2005), 1–17.

26. Michael Welch, *Scapegoats of September 11th: Hate Crimes & State Crimes in the War on Terror* (New Brunswick, N.J.: Rutgers University Press, 2006), 60.

27. *Demore v. Kim*, 538 U.S. 510 (2003).

28. Susan Coutin, "Contesting Criminality: Illegal Immigration and the Spatialization of Legality," *Theoretical Criminology* 9, no. 1 (2005): 5–33.

29. Office of the Press Secretary, May 16, 2006. Available at http://www.white house.gov/news/releases/2006/6/2006.

30. See www.cbp.gov.

31. *Washington Post*, May 21, 2007.

32. FoxNews.com, January 7, 2004.

33. *Washington Post*, June 17, 2007.

34. Ibid., June 18, 2007.

35. Ibid., August 8, 2007.

36. *New York Times*, May 30, 2007.

37. Ibid., November 18, 2001.

38. Conclusions adopted by the Council (JHA), September 20, 2001, Council Document SN 3926/6/01.

39. European Council, Council Common Position of December 27, 2001, on Combating Terrorism, 2001/930/CFSP.

40. Seville European Council, Presidency Conclusions, June 21–22, 2002, Council of Ministers, SN 200/02.

41. Council Decision 2007/801/EC of December 6, 2007.

42. COM (2006) 257 final, and Regulation (EC) no. 863/2007.

43. CCI, *Instructions on Visas* (2005/C 326/02), 15.

44. See http://www.frontex.europa.eu/origin_and_tasks/tasks/.

45. Convention between Belgium, Germany, Spain, France, Luxembourg, the Netherlands, and Austria on the stepping up of cross-border cooperation, particularly in combating terrorism, cross-border crime, and illegal migration, signed in

Prüm, Germany, May 27, 2005 (See Council Document 10900/05 of July 7, 2005). Most provision of the treaty have now been incorporated in EU law by Council Decision 2008/615/JHA, on the stepping up of cross-border cooperation, particularly in combating terrorism and cross-border crime, *OJ* 2008, L210/1 and Framework Decision 2008/616 on the implementation of Decision 2008/615/JHA, *OJ* 2008, L210/12.

46. European Council Conclusions, Laeken, December 14 and 15, 2001, point 42.

47. European Council Declaration on combating terrorism, Brussels, March 25, 2004, point 6.

48. Council Document 14469/4/05.

49. European Commission, Preparing the next steps in border management in the European Union (2008), 2–3.

50. European Commission, COM (2008) 68 final.

51. European Council, 1999, paragraph 11.

52. The Tampere programme, October 1999. Available at http://www.europarl.europa.eu/summits/tam_en.htm#c.

53. The Hague Programme: Strengthening Freedom, Security and Justice in the European Union (COM [2005] 184 final—Official Journal C 236 of 24.9.2005) and the Council and Commission Action Plan Implementing the Hague Programme (OJ C 198, 12.8.2005, p. 1).

54. Articles 79(1) and (2), TFEU.

55. Article 79(5), TFEU.

56. As regards legal migration, for example, article 63(3)(a) and (4) EC remains subject to unanimity. Only one directive has been adopted so far within the framework of the commission's policy plan on legal migration (Council Directive 2009/50/EC on the conditions of entry and residence of third-country nationals for the purposes of highly qualified employment), *OJ* 2009, L155/17.

57. European Commission, COM (2007) 301 final.

58. Council Directive 2003/86/EC of September 22, 2003; and Council Directive 2003/109/EC of November 25, 2003. The directive on the right to family reunification determines the conditions under which family reunification is granted to third-country nationals (TCNs) residing lawfully in the EU, whether the family relationship arose before or after the resident's entry, as well as the rights of the family members concerned. The second directive advocates a long-term status for TCNs who have legally resided for five years in the territory of a member state. This status enables TCNs to enjoy a legal status comparable to that of EU and national citizens. TCNs may acquire this status if they have been legally resident for an uninterrupted period of five years, are in possession of a sufficient level of stable and regular resources, have sickness insurance, and, where required by the member states, if they comply with integration conditions. This status thus allows TCNs to enjoy equal treatment to nationals in a number of socioeconomic areas, such as access to employment, education and vocational training, and social protection and assistance.

59. Directive 2004/38. It came into force in April 2006.

60. Commission of the European Communities, Fifth Report on Citizenship of the Union, SEC (2008) 197, COM (2008) 85 final, Brussels, 15.2.2008.

61. Communication from the Commission: An Evaluation of the Hague Program and Action Plan, COM (2009) 263 final, Brussels, 10.6.2009, 13

62. Adam Luedtke, "Fortifying Fortress Europe? The Effects of September 11 on EU Immigration Policy," in *Immigration Policy and Security*, ed. Terri E. Givens, Gary P. Freeman, and David L. Leal (London: Routledge, 2006), 144.

63. Council Document 13440/08, Brussels, September 24, 2008.

64. Sergio Carrera and Elspeth Guild, *The French Presidency's European Pact on Immigration and Asylum: Intergovernmentalism vs. Europeanisation? Security vs. Rights?* Policy Brief no. 170 (Center for European Policy Studies), 1–10. Available at http://www.ceps.eu.

Part II The Dynamics of Policy Failure

1. Marc Rosenblum, *US Immigration Reform: Can the System Be Repaired?* Working Paper 132 (Center for Comparative Immigration Studies, January 2006), 18.

2. *New York Times*, July 11, 2009.

3. Fidel Sendagorta, "Jihad in Europe: The Wider Context," *Survival* 47, no. 3 (Autumn 2005): 64.

4. Border Escalation as a Policy Failure

1. Andreas, *Border Games*, 85.

2. Andrew Geddes, *Immigration and European Integration: Towards Fortress Europe?* (Manchester: Manchester University Press, 2000), 16.

3. Renato Rosaldo, "Cultural Citizenship, Inequality, and Multiculturalism," in *Latino Cultural Studies: Claiming Identity, Space, and Rights*, ed. William V. Flores and Rina Benmayor (Boston: Beacon Press, 1997), 27–38.

4. Alexseev, *Immigration Phobia*, 25.

5. Gary Freeman, "Winners and Losers: Politics and the Costs and Benefits of Migration," in *West European Immigration and Immigrant Policy in the New Century*, ed. Anthony Messina (London: Praeger, 2002), 78.

6. U.S. Customs and Border Protection, *Protecting America: U.S. Customs and Border Protection 2005–2010* (May 2005), 20–21.

7. *New York Times*, June 30, 2008.

8. Office of Immigration Statistics, *Annual Report* (U.S. Department of Homeland Security, July 2009), 1.

9. *New York Times*, July 18, 2009.

10. Any alien present in the United States or at a port of entry may apply for asylum regardless of his or her immigration status. Asylum may be obtained in two ways: affirmatively through a USCIS asylum officer or defensively in removal proceedings before an immigration judge of the Executive Office for Immigration Review of the Department of Justice.

11. Quoted by Liz Fekete, "Death at the Border: Who Is to Blame?" *European Race Bulletin* 44 (July 2003): 4.

12. Lutterbeck, "Policing Migration in the Mediterranean," 75.

13. *BBC News*, August 4, 2006.

14. *Telegraph* (UK), April 5, 2009.

15. International Center for Migration Policy Development, *Irregular Transit Migration in the Mediterranean: Some Facts, Futures and Insights* (Vienna: ICMPD, 2004), 8.

See also P. Futo and M. Jandl, *2006 Year Book on Illegal Migration, Human Smuggling and Trafficking in Central and Eastern Europe—A Survey and Analysis of Border Management and Border Apprehension Data from 20 States* (Vienna: ICMPD, 2007), 20–21.

16. Eurostat, *Asylum in the EU in 2008, 8 May 2009.* Available at http://epp.eurostat.ec.europa.eu/cache/ITY_PUBLIC/3–08052009-AP/EN/3–08052009-AP-EN.PDF.

17. Ibid.

18. Net migration is defined as the difference between immigration into and emigration from the territory considered. Net migration is often estimated on the basis of the difference between population change and natural increase. This assumes that any movement of population not attributable to natural change (births and deaths) is attributable to migration. See Eurostat, *Key Figures on Europe* (2009), 54.

19. Organization for Economic Cooperation and Development, *Trends in International Migration Report,* 2003.

20. Ibid., 2006.

21. Eurostat, *News Release* 184/2009 (December 16, 2009).

22. *New York Times,* May 15, 2009. Michael Clemens, Claudio Montenegro, and Lant Pritchett estimate that the average annual wage gain to a thirty-five-year-old male with nine to twelve years of education moving from a developing country to the United States is $10,000 to $15,000 in additional annual income. Filipinos experience a 250 percent increase just by stepping into the United States. Haitian immigrants experience a 680 percent increase. See Michael Clemens, Claudio Montenegro, and Lant Pritchett, *The Place Premium: Wage Differences for Identical Workers across the U.S. Border,* Working Paper 148 (Center for Global Development, 2008), 10.

23. Peter Andreas and Timothy Snyder, eds., *The Wall around the West: State Borders and Immigration Controls in North America and Europe* (Lanham, Md.: Rowman & Littlefield, 2000), 1–10.

24. Deepa Fernandes, *Targeted: Homeland Security and the Business of Immigration* (New York: Seven Stories Press, 2007), 67.

25. Ibid., 174.

26. *New York Times,* June 18, 2006.

27. U.S. Government Accountability Office, *Secure Border Initiative* (GAO-09–894, September 2009), pp. 1–47. Available at http://www.gao.gov/new.items/d09896.pdf.

28. *New York Times,* January 14, 2011.

29. Frontex, *Annual Accounts for 2007,* May 2008. Available at www.frontex.europa.eu/finance.

30. *Guardian* (UK), July 6, 2005.

31. *BBC News,* June 14, 2006.

32. *Corriere della Sera,* May 27, 2005.

33. *Le Monde,* October 3, 2008.

34. CBS News Poll, November 3, 2005.

35. Pew Research Center, *America's Image Slips, But Allies Share US Concerns over Iran, Hamas,* Survey Report, June 2006, 1–12.

36. TNS / *Washington Post* / ABC News, April 25, 2007.

37. The MORI Social Research Institute, "IPSOS-MORI Survey on Attitudes toward Immigration," *International Social Trends Monitor* (November 2006).

38. Arnaldo Ferrari Nasi, in *Angus Reid Global Monitor*, November 17, 2007.

39. Ipsos-MORI/*Observer* (UK), November 12, 2007.

40. European Commission, "The Role of the European Union in Justice, Freedom, and Security Policy Areas," *Eurobarometer Standard* 266 (February 2007): 4.

41. Alexseev, *Immigration Phobia*, 38.

42. This index measures and compares people's predisposition to far-right-wing politics in thirty-two countries using data from the European Social Survey. DEREX's data is culled from people's responses to twenty-nine questions in the European Social Survey's database beginning in 2003. These questions are divided into four categories: Prejudice and Welfare Chauvinism; Anti-Establishment Attitudes; Right-Wing Value Orientation; and Fear, Distrust, and Pessimism. See http://www.riskan dforecast.com/post/in-depth-analysis/back-by-popular-demand_411.html.

43. The higher a country's score, the lower its public morale.

44. Bart Meuleman, Eldad Davidov, and Jaak Billiet, "Changing Attitudes toward Immigration in Europe, 2002–2007: A Dynamic Group Conflict Theory Approach," *Social Science Research* 38, no. 2 (2009): 360.

45. Council of the EU, "External Border Controls, Removal and Readmission: Best Practices and Recommendations," *EU Schengen Catalogue* (February 2002): 13.

46. Algeria, Armenia, Azerbaijan, Belarus, Egypt, Georgia, Israel, Jordan, Lebanon, Libya, Moldova, Morocco, Occupied Palestinian Territory, Syria, Tunisia, and Ukraine.

47. European Commission, *Strategy Paper on the ENP*, COM (2004) 373 final, Brussels, 12.5.2004, 3.

48. Ibid., 17.

49. European Commission, *Sectoral Report Progress*, SEC (2010) 513, Brussels, 12.05.2010, 5.

50. Ruben Zaiotti, "Of Friends and Fences: Europe's Neighborhood Policy and the Gated Community Syndrome," *European Integration* 29, no. 2 (May 2007): 9.

51. Mark P. Sullivan and June S. Beittel, "Mexico-U.S. Relations: Issues for Congress," 7–5700, RL32274, Congressional Research Service, May 13, 2009 (www.crs.gov).

52. In 2008 more than 5,600 people in Mexico were killed in drug-trafficking violence, a 110 percent increase over 2007.

53. Sullivan and Beittel, "Mexico-U.S. Relations," 2.

54. Shannon O'Neil, "Moving beyond Mérida in U.S.-Mexico Security Cooperation," Council on Foreign Relations, statement before Committee on Foreign Affairs: Subcommittee on the Western Hemisphere; and Committee on Homeland Security: Subcommittee on Border, Maritime, and Global Counterterrorism (U.S. House of Representatives, 111th Cong., 2nd sess., May 27, 2010), 3.

55. *Washington Post*, May 17, 2010.

56. Ibid., May 25, 2010.

57. Ibid., April 27, 2010.

5. The Security/Insecurity Spiral

1. As regards the British strategy, CONTEST, it was based around four counterterrorism objectives, the four *P*s: pursue, prevent, protect, and prepare.

2. European Commission, COM (2005) 491 final (Brussels, 12.10.2005).

3. Department of Homeland Security, *National Strategy for Homeland Security* (October 2007), 5.

4. New American Foundation and Syracuse University's Maxwell School of Public Policy, "Post 9/11 Jihadist Terrorism Cases Involving U.S. Citizens and Residents," March 11, 2011. See http://homegrown.newamerica.net/.

5. Home Office Statistical Bulletin, *Operation of Police Powers under the Terrorism Act 2000 nd Subsequent Legislation: Arrests, Outcomes and Stops & Searches* (Great Britain, 200809).

6. Europol, *EU Terrorism Situation and Trend Report*, Te-Sat, 2008, 11–12.

7. Ibid., 2010, 11.

8. Todd Sandler and Daniel G. Arce, *Terrorism*, Copenhagen Consensus Paper 2008 (February 2008), 27. Available at http://www.copenhagenconsensus.com/The%2010%20challenges/Terrorism.aspx.

9. Europol, *EU Terrorism Situation and Trend Report*, Te-Sat, 2010, 13.

10. Organization for Economic Cooperation and Development, "Security, Risk Perception and Cost-Benefit Analysis," *Discussion Paper no. 2009–4* (Joint Transport Research Center, March 2009): 7. Available at http://www.internationaltransport forum.org/jtrc/DiscussionPapers/DP200906.pdf.

11. A recent study shows that since 9/11 there has been a clear geographical transference of attacks against U.S. interests to the Middle East and Asia. See W. Enders and T. Sandler, "Distribution of Transnational Terrorism among Countries by Income Class and Geography after 9/11," *International Studies Quarterly* 50, no. 2 (2006): 367–93.

12. *Washington Post*, May 1, 2005.

13. *Washington Times*, May 8, 2006.

14. *New York Times*, February 4, 2009.

15. *Washington Times*, December 11, 2003.

16. *New York Times*, April 12, 2008.

17. Statement before the U.S. Senate, Committee on the Judiciary, Subcommittee on Immigration, Border Security, and Citizenship, and Subcommittee on Terrorism, Technology, and Homeland Security, regarding "The Need for Comprehensive Immigration Reform: Strengthening Our National Security," May 17, 2005.

18. Department of Homeland Security, *National Strategy for Homeland Security* (October 2007), 31.

19. Ibid., 33.

20. *New York Times*, October 12, 2009.

21. Department of Homeland Security, *National Strategy for Homeland Security*, 38.

22. Migration Policy Institute, *Behind the Naturalization Backlog: Causes, Context, and Concerns*, Immigration Facts (February 2008), 3.

23. Department of Homeland Security, ICE's Compliance with Detention Limits for Aliens with a Final Order of Removal from the United States (Office of Inspector General: OIG-07–28, February 2007), 54.

24. Ibid., 1.

25. Walter Laqueur, *A History of Terrorism* (New Brunswick, N.J.: Transaction, 2001).

26. David Cole, "Terrorizing Immigrants in the Name of Fighting Terrorism," *Human Rights Magazine*, Winter 2002, 3.

27. OJ L 164.06.2002, art. 1(1)(d).

28. Jörg Monar, "Common Threat and Common Responses: The European Union's Counter-Terrorism Strategy and Its Problems," *Government and Opposition* 42, no. 3 (Summer 2007): 298–99.

29. Dirk Haubrich, "September 11, Anti-Terror Laws and Civil Liberties: Britain, France, and Germany," *Government and Opposition* 33, no. 1 (2003): 14.

30. Thomas Gimesi et al., *National Threat Perception: Survey Result from Germany*, Garnet Working Paper 18.6, Garnet Project JERP 5.3.2 (May 2007), 1–37. Available at http://www.garneteu.org/fileadmin/documents/working_papers/1807/6%20 Germany.pdf.

31. See COM (2008) 69 final, February 13, 2008. This proposal does not detail under what circumstances nonborder searches would be permitted.

32. Peter Hustinx, "Third Opinion of the European Protection Supervisor on the Proposal for a Council Framework Decision on the Protection of Personal Data Processed in the Framework of Police and Judicial Cooperation in Criminal Matters," (Brussels: European Data Protection Supervisor, August 2007), 17.

33. *Washington Post*, March 25, 2007.

34. Congressional Research Service, "European Approaches to Homeland Security and Counterterrorism," *Report for Congress* (Washington, D.C.: Library of Congress, July 2006), 1–47.

35. Davide Casale, "EU Institutional and Legal Counterterrorism Framework," *Defense against Terrorism Review* 1, no. 1 (Spring 2008): 57.

36. Den Boer, *9/11 and the Europeanisation of Anti-Terrorism Policy*, 15.

37. Doron Zimmermann, "The European Union and Post-9/11 Counterterrorism: A Reappraisal," *Studies in Conflicts & Terrorism* 20 (2006): 124.

38. Sandler and Arce, *Terrorism*, 3.

39. Ibid., 23.

40. *BBC News*, February 28, 2008.

41. Ronald Crelinsten, "The Discourse and Practice of Counter-Terrorism in Liberal Democracies," *Australian Journal of Politics and History* 44, no. 1 (1998): 407.

42. Individuals from thirty-five countries (notably in the Middle East, North Africa, and South Asia).

43. Jan C. Ting, "Immigration and National Security," *Orbis* (Winter 2006): 42 and 48.

44. *New York Times*, March 14, 2005.

45. Robert S. Leiken and Steven Brooke, "The Quantitative Analysis of Terrorism and Immigration: An Initial Exploration," *Terrorism and Political Violence* 18 (2006): 503–21.

46. Robert S. Leiken, "Europe's Angry Muslims," *Foreign Affairs*, July/August 2005, 11. Jan C. Ting reached a similar conclusion by arguing that some terrorists came from Morocco, "where Spanish is widely spoken" [sic], 45.

47. Rachel Swarns, "Program's Value in Dispute as a Tool to Fight Terrorism," *New York Times*, December 21, 2004.

48. Ewing, *Border Insecurity*, 1.

49. *Statewatch Bulletin*, November/December 2003.

50. Home Office Statistical Bulletin, *Operation of Police Powers*, 3.

51. Quoted by Jocelyne Cesari et al., "Securitization and Religious Divides in Europe; Muslims in Western Europe after 9/11: Why the Term Islamophobia Is More a Predicament Than an Explanation," *Report on the Changing Landscape of Citizenship and Security* (Brussels: European Commission, June 2006), 119.

52. "Al-Qaeda," *Economist*, May 3, 2007.

53. *La Vanguardia*, January 26, 2003.

54. Liz Fekete, "Anti-Muslims Racism and the European Security-State," *Race Class* 46, no. 1 (2004): 11.

55. Nicole Henderson et al., *Law Enforcement & Arab African Community Relations after September 11, 2001: Engagement in a Time of Uncertainty* (New York: Vera Institute of Justice, 2006), 17.

56. Migration Policy Institute, *America's Challenge*, 7.

57. Brigitte L. Nacos, Taeli Bloch-Elkon, and Robert Y. Shapiro, "Post-9/11 Terrorism Threats, News Coverage and Public Perception in the United States," *International Journal of Conflict and Violence* 1, no. 2 (2007): 118.

58. Fox News / Opinion Poll Dynamics, May 18–19, 2010.

59. Rasmussen Reports national telephone survey, May 24, 2010. Available at http://www.rasmussenreports.com/public_content/politics/mood_of_america/war_on_terror_update).

60. CNN / Opinion Research Corporation Poll, January 8–10, 2010.

61. *Foreign Policy*, September/October 2007, 62.

62. *BBC News*, December 9, 2006.

63. Gallup / CNN / *USA Today*, September 21–22, 2001, and June 15–19, 2008.

64. Fox News / Opinion Dynamics, February 11–12, 2003.

65. Ibid., August 21–22, 2007.

66. *USA Today* / Gallup, May 29–31, 2009.

67. Ibid., January 8–10, 2010.

68. Populus/*Times* (UK), July 25–26, 2007.

69. Metroscopia/ABC, April 16–18, 2007.

70. ABC News / *Washington Post*, October 8–9, 2001, and September 5–7, 2006.

71. CBS News / *New York Times*, March 20–24, 2003, and August 17–21, 2006.

72. COT Institute for Safety, "Security and Crisis Management," *Report on Transnational Terrorism: Theoretical Approaches and Policy Discourse*, November 12, 2008. Available at http://www.transnationalterrorism.eu.

73. Europol, *EU Terrorism Situation and Trend Report*, 5.

74. CBS News Poll, March 29–April 1, 2010.

75. Nacos et al., "Post-9/11 Terrorism Threats," 125.

76. Gallup/CNN/*USA Today*, February 24–25, 2003.

77. CBS News, April 26–27, and August 11–13, 2006.

78. AP/Ipsos, March 3, 2004. The opinion poll survey was conducted before the Madrid bombings (March 11).

79. IFOP / *Le Journal du Dimanche*, July 10–11, 2008.

80. Harris Interactive / *Financial Times*, August 1–13, 2007.

81. Harris Interactive / France 24 Poll Survey (November 30–December 9, 2006), in *Ethics Newsline*, January 8, 2007. Available at http://www.globalethics.org/newsline/2007/01/08/survey-gauges-different-nations-greatest-concerns/.

82. *USA Today* / Gallup Poll Survey, May 24–25, 2010.

83. AP/Ipsos, March 21–23, 2005.

84. Jessica Wolfendale, "Terrorism, Security, and the Threat of Counterterrorism," *Studies in Conflict & Terrorism* 30 (2007): 77.

85. Richard Jackson, *Writing the War on Terror: Language, Politics, and Counterterrorism* (Manchester: Manchester University Press, 2005), 92–93.

86. Sandler and Arce, *Terrorism*, 3.

6. Radicalization in the West

1. New America Foundation and Syracuse University's Maxwell School of Public Policy, "Post 9/11 Jihadists," 1.

2. Peter Bergen and Bruce Hoffman, *Assessing the Terrorist Threat: A Report of the Bipartisan Policy Center's National Security Preparedness Group* (Bipartisan Policy Center, September 10, 2010). Available at http://bipartisanpolicy.org/sites/default/files/NSPG%20Final%20Threat%20Assessment.pdf.

3. One of its members, Mohammed Bouyeri, was sentenced to life in prison for murdering Dutch film director Theo van Gogh. Another member, Samir Azzouz, was suspected of planning terrorist attacks on the Dutch parliament and several strategic targets such as the national airport and a nuclear reactor.

4. See www.homeoffice.gov.uk/about-us/news/ct-speech-08.

5. Europol, *EU Terrorism and Trend Report* (2010), 20.

6. Tore Bjørgo, *Root Causes of Terrorism: Myths, Reality and Ways Forward* (London: Routledge, 2005).

7. Maha Azzam, "The Radicalization of Muslim Communities in Europe: Local and Global Dimensions," *Brown Journal of World Affairs* 13, no. 2 (Spring/Summer 2007): 123–34; Jessica Wolfendale, "Terrorism," 75–96; Richard Jackson, "Constructing Enemies: 'Islamic Terrorism' in Political and Academic Discourse," *Government and Opposition* 42, no. 3 (2007): 394–426.

8. Bruce Hoffman et al., *The Radicalization of Diasporas and Terrorism: A Joint Conference by the RAND Corporation and the Center for Security Studies, ETH Zurich* (Santa Monica, Calif.: RAND, 2007), 1–55.

9. Europol, *EU Terrorism and Trend Report* (2010), 20.

10. *New York Times*, March 10, 2011.

11. New America Foundation and Syracuse University's Maxwell School of Public Affairs, "Post 9/11 Jihadists," 2.

12. Department of Homeland Security, *National Strategy for Homeland Security* (2007), 9.

13. COM (2005) 313 final.

14. European Monitoring Center on Racism and Xenophobia, *Summary Report on Islamophobia in the European Union after 9/11* (Vienna: EUMC, May 2002), 7.

15. European Monitoring Center on Racism and Xenophobia, *Muslims in the European Union: Discrimination and Xenophobia* (Vienna: EUMC, 2006), 1–118.

16. *BBC News*, January 20, 2011.

17. Yasemin Karakasoglu et al., "Islamophobia in Germany," in Cesari et al., *Securitization and Religious Divides in Europe*, 155.

18. European Monitoring Center on Racism and Xenophobia, *Muslims in the European Union*, 37.

19. http://www.euro-islam.info/2010/02/27/islam-in-Netherlands.

20. Javier Noya, "Los españoles y el islam," *ARI* 47 (Real Instituto Elcano, 2007): 13–17.

21. Council of American-Islamic Relations, *The Statute of Muslim Rights in the United States: The Struggle for Equality* (2006), 4–5. Available at http://www.cair.com/AmericanMuslims/ReportsandSurveys.aspx.

22. Marcel Maussen, "Islamophobia in the Netherlands," in Cesari et al., *Securitization and Religious Divides in Europe*, 123.

23. Council of American-Islamic Relations, *Survey Reports* (2002, 2003, 2004, 2005, 2006, 2007). Available at http://www.cair.com/AmericanMuslims/ReportsandSurveys.aspx.

24. See http://publicintelligence.info/FBI-Burn-A-Quran-Day.pdf. Actually, at least eight people (including UN staff) were killed in Afghanistan in April 2011 during a protest over the burning of the Koran in a church in Florida by pastor Wayne Sapp (in the presence of pastor Terry Jones).

25. Henderson et al., *Law Enforcement & Arab African Community*, 18.

26. Wayne Baker et al., "Preliminary Findings from the Detroit Arab American Study," University of Michigan, 2003, 1–35. Available at http://ns.umich.edu/Releases/2004/Jul04/daas.pdf.

27. Pew Research Center, *Muslim Americans: Middle Class and Mostly Mainstream*, Survey Report, May 22, 2007, 1.

28. Quoted by Lisa Miller, "American Dreamers," *Newsweek*, July 30, 2007, 20.

29. Pew Research Center, *Muslim Americans*, 3.

30. Pew Research Center, *Support for Terror Wanes among Muslim Publics. Islamic Extremism: Common Concern for Muslim and Western Publics*, 17-Nation Pew Global Attitudes Survey, July 2006, 3.

31. Azzam, "Radicalization of Muslim Communities," 128.

32. Pew Research Center, *Support for Terror Wanes*, 4.

33. European Monitoring Center on Racism and Xenophobia, *Muslims in the European Union: Discrimination and Islamophobia*," EUMC Report (2006), 11

34. Open Society Institute, *Aspirations and Realities: British Muslims and the Labour Market* (London: Open Society Institute, 2004).

35. Netherlands Social and Cultural Planning Office (Sociaal en Cultureel Planbureau, SCP), "Unemployment among Immigrants Has Doubled since the Netherlands Experienced a Recession in 2002," 2006. See also Open Society Institute, Muslims in the EU. Cities Report. The Netherlands (2007). Available online: http://www.eumap.org.

36. European Monitoring Center on Racism and Xenophobia, *Muslims in the European Union*, 45.

37. Ibid., 46.

38. Olivier Roy, *Globalized Islam: The Search for a New Ummah* (New York: Columbia University Press, 2005), 361.

39. While over one million persons claimed "Arab first" ancestry on the 2000 U.S. Census, various sources suggest that the number of Arab Americans and Muslims (both categories combined) is higher—close to three million people. Other American Muslim organizations believe that there are 6 million to 7.5 million Muslims in the U.S., this community consisting of immigrants and second- and third-

generation Arab, Latino, Asian, European, African, and African American Muslims.

40. Henderson et al, *Law Enforcement & Arab African Community*, 35–36.

41. *Washington Post*, May 23, 2007.

42. These estimates are based on a 2001 Georgetown University poll. See Abdus Sattar Ghazali, "American Muslims in Politics—Elections 1996–2006," *American Muslim Perspective*, <http://ampolitics.ghazali.net/index.html>. See Kevin Mooney, "Almost 90 Percent of Muslims Voted for Obama despite Differences on Abortion, Marriage," *CNS News*, November 10, 2008, http://www.cnsnews.com/news/article/39031.

43. Philippa Strum, ed., *American Arabs and Political Participation* (Washington, D.C.: Woodrow Wilson International Center for Scholars, 2006), 3.

44. Paul Findley, *Silent No More: Confronting America's False Images of Islam* (Beltsville, Md.: Amama Publications, 2001).

45. See Farida Jalalzai, "The Politics of Muslims in America," *Politics and Religion* 2 (2009): 163–99.

46. Pew Research Center, *Muslim Americans*, 3.

47. Karen Leonard, "American Muslim Politics: Discourses and Practices," *Ethnicities* 3, no. 2 (2003): 166.

48. Council of American-Islamic Relations, American Muslim Voters: A Demographic Profile (Washington, D.C.: October 2006).

49. Mohamed Nimer, "American Muslim Organizations: Before and after 9/11," in *Muslims in the United States: Identity, Influence, Innovation*, ed. Philippa Strum (Washington, D.C.: Woodrow Wilson International Center for Scholars, 2003), 12.

50. Pew Research Center, *American Muslims*, 54

51. Ibid., 55.

52. Ibid., 32.

53. New America Foundation and Syracuse University's Maxwell School of Public Policy, "Post 9/11 Jihadists," 2.

54. *International Herald Tribune*, January 15–16, 2004; M. Danner, *Torture and Truth: America, Abu Ghraib and the War on Terror* (London: Granta Books, 2004).

55. See Mark Mazzetti and David Rhode, "Amid US Policy Disputes, Qaeda Grows in Pakistan," *New York Times*, June 30, 2008.

56. *New York Times*, June 6, 2010.

57. Bergen and Hoffman, *Assessing the Terrorist Threat*, 15. Al-Awlaki was killed in October 2011.

58. See *International Herald Tribune*, "In Algeria, Insurgents Gain a Lifeline from al Qaeda," July 1, 2008. According to Gilles de Kerchove, the head of counterterrorism for Europe, the ambition of the North Africa branch of al-Qaeda is also to attack European countries.

59. Pew Research Center, *America's Image Slips*, 3.

60. Pew Research Center, *Support for Terror Wanes*, 9.

61. Pew Research Center, *Global Opinion Trends 2002–2007: A Rising Tide Lifts Mood in the Developing World; Sharp Decline in Support for Suicide Bombing in Muslim Countries*," 47-Nation Pew Global Attitudes Survey, July 24, 2007, 46.

62. Jerald Post and Gabriel Sheffer, "The Risk of Radicalization and Terrorism in US Muslim Communities," *Brown Journal of World Affairs* 13, no. 2 (Spring/Summer 2007): 108.

63. Richard Jackson, "Constructing Enemies," 424.

64. Robert Pape, *Dying to Win: The Strategic Logic of Suicide Terrorism* (New York: Random House, 2005).

65. Scott Atran, "Soft Power and the Psychology of Suicide Bombing," *Global Terrorism Analysis* 2, no. 11 (2004): 1–3.

66. Brendan O'Duffy, "Radical Atmosphere: Explaining Jihadist Radicalization in the UK," PSOnline (January 2008), 39.

67. Marc Sageman, *Understanding Terror Networks* (Philadelphia: University of Pennsylvania Press, 2004).

68. Akil N. Awan, "Virtual Jihadist Media: Function, Legitimacy, and Radicalizing Effect," *European Journal of Cultural Studies* 10, no. 3 (2007).

69. David Cole, "The New McCarthyism: Repeating History in the War on Terrorism," *Harvard Civil Rights–Civil Liberties Law Review* 38, no. 1 (2003): 1–30.

70. Robert S. Leiken, "Europe's Angry Muslims," *Foreign Affairs*, July/August 2005, 13.

71. Roy, *Globalized Islam*, 361.

72. Cesari et al., *Securitization and Religious Divides in Europe*, 78.

73. Pierre Tévanian, *Le voile médiatique—un faux débat: L'affaire du foulard islamique* (Paris: Éditions Raison d'Agir, 2005), 45.

74. Thilo Sarrazin, *Deutschland schafft sich ab* (Germany Does Away with Itself), (Deutsche Verlags-Anstalt, 2010).

75. Adam Kirby, "The London Bombers as 'Self-Starters': A Case Study in Indigenous Radicalization and the Emergence of Autonomous Cliques," *Studies in Conflict & Terrorism* 30 (2007).

76. Nimer, "American Muslim Organizations, 5–19.

77. The Zogby 2004 survey found 76 percent in support of Kerry and only 7 percent in support of Bush. The Pew 2007 survey found that 71 percent voted for Kerry, 14 percent voted for Bush, and 15 percent voted for another candidate or refused to answer.

78. These findings are similar to those of the survey results published by Muslim Voters USA (94 percent for Obama and 3 percent for McCain). See http://www.muslimvotersusa.com/UsefulLinks/surveyresults.aspx.

79. Eileen Braman and Abdulkader H. Sinno, "An Experimental Investigation of Causal Attributions for the Political Behavior of Muslim Candidates: Can a Muslim Represent You?" *Politics and Religion* 2 (2009): 250.

80. Ibid., 251.

81. Pew Research Center, *Muslim Americans*, 47.

82. Jytte Klausen, *The Islamic Challenge: Politics and Religion in Western Europe* (Oxford: Oxford University Press, 2005).

83. Charles Hirschman, "The Role of Religion in the Origins and Adaptation of Immigrant Groups in the United States," *International Migration Review* 39 (2004): 1206–33; Jocelyne Cesari, *When Islam and Democracy Meet: Muslims in Europe and the United States* (New York: Palgrave Macmillan, 2004); Diana L. Eck, *A New Religious America* (New York: HarperCollins, 2001).

84. Pew Research Center, *Muslim Americans*, 46.

85. Club of Madrid, *Addressing the Causes of Terrorism* (Madrid: Club of Madrid Series on Democracy and Terrorism, 2005).

86. Nancy Foner and Richard Alba, "Immigrant Religion in the US and Western Europe: Bridge or Barrier to Inclusion?" *International Migration Review* 42, no. 2 (Summer 2008): 360–92.

87. Akil N. Awan, "Antecedents of Islamic Political Radicalism among Muslim Communities in Europe," *Political Science & Politics* 41, no. 1 (2008), 15.

88. Roy, *Globalized Islam*, 361.

89. Mitchell D. Silber and Arvin Bhatt, *Radicalization in the West: The Homegrown Threat* (New York: New York City Police Department, 2007), 36.

90. Frank Cilluffo, Sharon Cardash, and Andrew Whitehead, "Radicalization: Behind Bars and beyond Borders," *Brown Journal of World Affairs* 13, no. 2 (Spring/ Summer 2007): 113–22.

91. COM (2005) 313 final.

92. Her Majesty Government, "Countering International Terrorism: The United Kingdom's Strategy," Cm. 6888, July 2006; and "Pursue Prevent Protect Prepare: The United Kingdom's Strategy for Countering International Terrorism,' Cm. 7547, March 2009. Available at http://www.official-documents.gov.uk/docu ment/cm68/6888/6888.pdf.

93. See http://www.lawandsecurity.org/publications/TTRCHighlightsSept25th. pdf.

94. Lorenzo Vidino, "The Homegrown Terrorist Threat to the US Homeland," Real Instituto Elcano, ARI 171/2009, 18/12/2009. See http://www.realinstitutoel cano.org/wps/portal/rielcano_eng/Content?WCM_GLOBAL_CONTEXT=/elcano/ elcano_in/zonas_in/international+terrorism/ari171–2009.

95. See http://www.securitymanagement.com.

96. U.S. National Security Strategy, May 2010. See http://www.whitehouse. gov/sites/default/files/rss_viewer/national_security_strategy.pdf.

97. Address to the Labour Party Conference, October 2, 2001.

98. Erik Bleich, "State Responses to 'Muslim' Violence: A Comparison of Six Western European Countries," *Journal of Ethnic and Migration Studies* 35 (2009): 366.

99. The U.S. authorities also deported a few radical Muslim clerics. Furthermore, in May 2010 they authorized operations to capture or kill Anwar al-Awlaki.

100. "Wilders Slams Appointment of Moroccan Mayor," Expatica.com, October 17, 2008. http://www.expatica.com/nl/articles/news/Wilders-slams-appointment- of-Moroccan-mayor.html. See also http://www.euro-islam.info/country-profiles/ the-netherlands/.

101. European Monitoring Center on Racism and Xenophobia, *Muslims in the EU*. 2006.

102. *La Repubblica*, May 5, 2008.

103. COM (2005), 313 final.

104. Ibid.

105. Quoted by Andrea Elliott, "White House Quietly Courts Muslims in U.S.," *New York Times*, April 18, 2010.

106. According to a survey conducted in July 2009 by the Pew Global Attitudes Project, this decision was approved by 91 percent of the respondents in Lebanon, 93 percent in the Palestinian Territories, 73 percent in Jordan, and 66 percent in Egypt.

107. Scott MacLeod, Andrew Lee Butters, and Nahid Siamdoust, "Muslims Like Obama's Words but Want to See Action," *Time*, June 5, 2009. http://www.time.com/time/world/article/0,8599,1902892,00.html.

108. Cynthia English, "Global Perceptions of U.S. Leadership Improve in 2009," *Gallup, Muslim West Facts Project*, February 10, 2010. Available at http://www.gallup.com/poll/125720/global-perceptions-leadership-improve-2009.aspx.

109. Alexseev, *Migration Phobia*, 230–31.

Part III. Why Do Failed Policies Persist?

1. There are other psychological, social, and political factors fueling migration patterns, such as cultural proximity, the desire to reunite families, and interpersonal ties and network connections constituting a form of social capital upon which individuals draw. Political instability, violation of human rights, and environmental crises also play a key role. Policies designed to address the root causes of immigration try, however, to manage the complexity of circulation patterns by making a distinction between "pull" and "push" factors. Factors that tend to "pull" immigrants into wealthier countries include socioeconomic conditions such as job opportunities and anticipated higher wages in developed countries. Push factors, by contrast, relate to a set of difficult conditions in the country of origin such as poverty, war, natural disaster, and insecurity.

2. United Nations, *Demographic Yearbook* (UN: Department of Economic and Social Affairs, 2005), 5. These estimates are based on a medium variant (contingent on ensuring that couples have access to family planning and that efforts to limit the spread of the HIV/AIDS epidemic are successful).

3. Richard M. Fischl, Joanne Conaghen, and Karl E. Klare, *Labour Law in an Era of Globalization: Transformative Practices and Possibilities* (Oxford: Oxford University Press, 2002).

7. Emigration, Development, and (In)security

1. United Nations, *The Millennium Development Goals Report* (UN: 2000), 1–80. Available at http://www.un.org/millenniumgoals/pdf. The MDGs constitute a set of eight goals, eighteen quantifiable and time-bound targets, and forty-eight indicators to be achieved (mostly) by 2015. Goals one to seven address different dimensions of poverty, such as hunger, disease, lack of education, and inadequate access to clean water and sanitation. Goal eight sets out the global responsibility of the international community to support the achievement of the other goals, particularly in the areas of aid, debt, trade, and access to information and communication technologies and essential drugs.

2. U.S. Department of State / USAID, *Strategic Plan Fiscal Years 2007–2012* (May 7, 2007), 1.

3. U.S. Agency for International Development, *Securing the Future: A Strategy for Economic Growth* (USAID, April 2008), 3. Available at http://www.usaid.gov/our_work/economic_growth_and_trade/eg/eg_strategy/eg_strategy_v4_final.pdf.

4. The European Development Fund consists of grants managed by the European Commission and loans managed by the European Investment Bank.

5. Launched in 1995 with the Barcelona declaration, the Euro-Mediterranean partnership aims to establish a common area of peace, stability, and shared prosperity in the region. The key objective of this trade agreement is the creation of a Euro-Mediterranean Free Trade Area. See http://ec.europa.eu/trade/creating-opportunities/bilateral-relations/regions/euromed/.

6. COM (2006), 26 final.

7. EU Council, *Conclusions on Supporting Developing Countries in Coping with the Crisis* (Brussels, May 2009). Available at http://ec.europa.eu/development/icenter/repository/COMM_PDF_COM_2009_0160_F_EN_COUNCIL_CONCLUSIONS.PDF.

8. European Commission, *The European Union in the World: The Foreign Policy of the EU* (Brussels, 2007), 4.

9. In 2003, as has been the case since 1993, the United States ranked last, at 0.15 percent of gross national income.

10. United Nations, *The Millennium Development Goals Report*, 4.

11. European Commission, "A Twelve-Point EU Action Plan in Support of the Millennium Development Goals," COM (2010), 156 final, 21.4.2010, p. 7. See http://ec.europa.eu/development/icenter/files/europa_only/12point_eu_action_point_en.pdf.

12. Ibid.

13. COM (2004), 373 final.

14. COM (2006) 735 final, p. 5.

15. Kaysie Brown, Bilal Siddiqi, and Myra Sessions, *US Development Aid and the Millennium Challenge Account: Emerging Trends in Appropriations*, Report for the Center for Global Development (October 2006), 1–10.

16. Ibid.

17. U.S. Department of State/USAID, *Joint Summary of Performance and Financial Information*, fiscal year 2009 (2009), 56. Available at http://www.usaid.gov/policy/summary09/StateUSAID_JointSummary_FY2009r.pdf.

18. U.S. Department of State/USAID, *Fiscal Year 2009 Foreign Operation Report & Fiscal Year 2011 Performance Plan*, 257.

19. United Nations, *The Millennium Development Goals Report 2009*. Available at http://www.un.org/millenniumgoals/pdf/MDG_Report_2009_ENG.pdf; World Bank, *Global Monitoring Report 2009*. Available at www.worldbank.org/gmr2009.

20. International Organization for Migration, "Migration and Development." Available at http://www.iom.int/jahia/Jahia/about-migration/developing-migration-policy/migration-dvlpment/cache/offonce/.

21. United Nations General Assembly, *International Migration and Development: Report of the Secretary-General*, A/58/98, 3. See http://www.un.org/esa/population/publications/ittmigdev2002/SG_REPORT_58_98.pdf.

22. African, Caribbean and Pacific (ACP) Observatory on Migration, *Fostering Research on South-South Migration and Human Development*, UN Population Division, UN/POP/MIG-9CM/2011/06 (February 11, 2011), 3. Available at http://www.un.org/esa/population/meetings/ninthcoord2011/p06-obsmig.pdf.

23. World Bank, *Migration and Remittances Factbook 2011*, Brief 13 (November 8, 2010), 2.

24. Ibid., 4.

25. Myron Weiner, "Security, Instability and International Migration," *International Security* 17, no. 3 (Winter 1992/93): 95.

26. European Commission, "EuropeAid Development and Cooperation." Available at http://ec.europa.eu/europeaid/what/security-conflict/index_en.htm.

27. George W. Bush, Speech at the Inter-American Development Bank, March 14, 2002. See http://www.whitehouse.gov/news/releases/2002/03/20020314–7.html.

28. Curt Tarnoff and Larry Nowels, *Foreign Aid: An Introductory Overview of U.S. Programs and Policy*, CRS Report for Congress (Congressional Research Service, Library of Congress, April 15, 2004), 2.

29. See http://www.usaid.gov/policy/budget/cbj2007/summary.html.

30. USAID, "Budget Justifications to the Congress," FY 2007. Available at http://www.usaid.gov/policy/budget/cbj2007/.

31. See http://www.usaid.gov/policy/budget/cbj2008/.

32. USAID, *The United States' Strategy for Meeting the Millennium Developments Goals* (September 2010), 5.

33. U.S. Department of State/USAID, *Joint Summary of Performance and Financial Information, Fiscal Year 2009*, p. 276. Available at http://www.usaid.gov/policy/summary09/StateUSAID_ JointSummary_FY2009r.pdf.

34. European Commission, *A Concept for European Community Support for Security Sector System*, COM (2006) 253 final, Brussels, 24.5.2006. Available at http://eur-lex.europa.eu/LexUriServ/site/en/com/2006/com2006_0253en01.pdf.

35. COM (2010), 159 final, 12.

36. First Action Plan for the Implementation of Africa-EU Strategic Partnership (2008–2010). Available at http://ec.europa.eu/development/icenter/repository/EAS2007_action_plan_2008_2010_en.pdf.

37. U.S. Department of State/USAID, *Strategic Plan Fiscal Years 2007–2012* (May 7, 2007), 15.

38. C. Tarnoff and M. Leonardo Lawson, *Foreign Aid: An Introduction to U.S. Programs and Policy*, CRS Report for Congress (Congressional Research Service, 7–5700, R40213, February 10, 2011), 34. See http://www.crs.gov.

39. See http://www.usaid.gov/policy/budget/cbj2010/2010_CBJ_Book_2.pdf.

40. Ibid.

41. Africa-EU Infrastructure Fund, *Annual Report* 2009. Available at http://www.eu-africa-infrastructure-tf.net/attachments/Annual%20Reports/eu_africa_infrastructure_trust_fund_annual_report_2009_en.pdf.

42. First Action Plan for the Implementation of Africa-EU Strategic Partnership (2008–2010), 8. This support included a range of activities such as the Continental Early Warning System, the definition and implementation of counterterrorist policies, and the operationalization of the African Standby Forces.

43. Francis Owusu, "Post-9/11 US Foreign Aid, the Millennium Challenge Account and Africa: How Many Birds Can One Stone Kill?" *Africa Today* 54, no. 1 (Fall 2007): 12.

44. In December 1991 the Islamic Salvation Front won the first round of the country's first multiparty elections. The military then intervened and canceled the second round. It forced then-president Chadli Bendjedid to resign and banned all

political parties based on religion (including the Islamic Salvation Front). A political conflict ensued, leading Algeria into a violent civil war. It is estimated that more than 160,000 people were killed between January 1992 and June 2002.

45. *USA Today*, January 5, 2010. Available at http://www.usatoday.com/news/world/2010–01–05-yemen-aid_N.htm. The United States was sending just a few million dollars a year in development assistance before the 9/11 attacks, according to State Department budget records. In 2003, when the U.S. Agency for International Development reopened its mission in the country after a seven-year absence, civilian aid to the country more than doubled, but remained a paltry $15 million, records show.

46. Stephen D. Collins, "Can America Finance Freedom? Assessing U.S. Democracy Promotion via Economic Statecraft," *Foreign Policy Analysis* 5 (2009): 367–89; Steven Finkel, Anibal Pérez-Liñán, and Mitchell A. Seligson, "The Effects of U.S. Foreign Assistance on Democracy Building, 1990–2003," *World Politics* 59 (2007): 404–39; Steven Knack, "Does Foreign Aid Promote Democracy?" *International Studies Quarterly* 48, (2004): 251–66.

47. Sheila Carapico, "Foreign Aid in Promoting Democracy in the Arab World," *Middle East Journal* 56 (2002): 379–95.

48. T. Carothers, *Aiding Democracy Abroad: The Learning Curve* (Washington, D.C.: Carnegie Endowment for International Peace, 1999).

49. P. J. Schraeder, "The State of the Art in International Democracy Promotion," *Democratization* 10, no. 2 (Summer 2003): 15.

50. James M. Scott and Carie A. Steele, "Sponsoring Democracy: The United States and Democracy Aid to the Developing World, 1998–2001," *International Studies Quarterly* 55 (2011): 47–69.

51. Fareed Zakaria, "The Rise of Illiberal Democracy," *Foreign Affairs*, November/December 1997, 22–43.

52. Schraeder, "State of the Art," 41.

53. Claire Spencer, *North Africa: The Hidden Risks to Regional Stability* (London: Chatham House, MENAP BP 2009/01, 2009), 2.

54. President Abdelaziz Bouteflika (since 1999) was reelected for a third term in 2009 after the adoption of a constitutional amendment separating the position of head of government from that of the prime minister.

55. Alex Glennie, *Building Bridges, Not Walls: Engaging with Political Islamists in the Middle East and North Africa*, Institute for Public Policy Research (September 2009), 35. See also *Changing Course: A New Direction for U.S. Relations with the Muslim World*, Report of the Leadership Group on U.S.-Muslim Engagement (September 2008).

56. Glennie, *Building Bridges, Not Walls*, 6.

8. Immigration, Economic Interests, and Politics

1. Stephen Castles, "Why Migration Policies Fail," *Ethnic and Racial Studies* 27, no. 2 (2004): 214.

2. COM (2007) 637, October 2007.

3. Elizabeth Collett and Fabian Zuleeg, *Soft, Scarce, and Super Skills: Sourcing the Next Generation of Migrant Workers in Europe* (Washington, D.C.: Migration Policy Institute, 2008), 3.

4. Philippe Legrain, *Immigrants: Your Country Needs Them* (Princeton, N.J.: Princeton University Press, 2007), 107.

5. *BBC News*, February 29, 2008.

6. Tim Finch, IPPR's head of migration, *BBC News*, May 5, 2009.

7. *BBC News*, December 29, 2010.

8. Jeroen Doomernik, Rey Koslowski, and Dietrich Thränhardt, *The Battle for the Brains: Why Immigration Policy Is Not Enough to Attract the Highly Skilled* (Washington, D.C.: German Marshall Fund of the United States, 2009), 15.

9. Department of Homeland Security, *Yearbook of Immigration Statistics*, 2006, 68.

10. Immigration Policy Center, *Economic Growth and Immigration: Bridging the Demographic Divide* (Washington, D.C.: Immigration Law Foundation, November 2005), 15. Available at http://www.immigrationpolicy.org/special-reports/economic-growth-immigration-bridging-demographic-divide.

11. Department of Homeland Security, Office of Immigration Statistics, *Annual Flow Report, Nonimmigrant Admissions to the United States: 2009*, April 2010. Available at http://www.dhs.gov/xlibrary/assets/statistics/publications/ni_fr_2009.pdf.

12. Immigration Policy Center, *Economic Growth and Immigration*, 14.

13. Ibid., 15.

14. European Commission, Memo/07/423, October 23, 2007.

15. Titus Galama and James Hosek, *US Competitiveness in Science and Technology* (RAND Corp., 2008), 1–118.

16. James Sherk and Diem Nguyen, *Next Steps for Immigration and Border Security Reform: Restructuring the Work Visa*, Backgrounder 2190 (Heritage Foundation, September 30, 2008), 8. Available at http://www.heritage.org/Research/Reports/2008/09/Next-Steps-for-Immigration-and-Border-Security-Reform-Restructuring-the-Work-Visa.

17. *BBC News*, April 16, 2007.

18. *Denver Post*, January 3, 2000.

19. Europa, Press Releases RAPID, IP/07/678, May 16, 2007. Available at http://europa.eu/rapid/pressReleasesAction.do?reference=IP/07/678.

20. COM (2007), 248 final, April 2007.

21. COM (2003), 336, p. 26.

22. Meyers, "U.S. Border Enforcement," 3.

23. Andreas, *Border Games*, 100.

24. Andorra Bruno, *Unauthorized Employment in the United States: Issues, Options, and Legislation* (Washington, D.C.: Congressional Research Service, 2007), 4. The Illegal Immigration Reform and Individual Responsibility Act (IIRIRA) amended some of the provisions of the Immigration Reform and Control Act by reducing the number of acceptable documents for completion of the Employment Eligibility Verification form (I-9), providing employers with a possibility of a good-faith defense against technical paperwork violations and providing some protection for employers who are part of multi-employer associations.

25. *Washington Post*, October 11, 2007.

26. Department of Homeland Security, "Worksite Enforcement Strategy," *Fact Sheet*, March 30, 2009. Available at http://www.ice.gov/doclib/news/library/factsheets/pdf/worksite-strategy.pdf.

27. Jeffrey Passel and D'Vera Cohn, "Unauthorized Immigrant Population: National and State Trends, 2010," Pew Hispanic Center, February 1, 2011. Available at http://pewhispanic.org/reports/report.php?ReportID=133.

28. *New York Times*, February 1, 2011.

29. David Bacon and Bill Ong Hing, "The Rise and Fall of Employer Sanctions," *Z Net*, January 10, 2011. Available at http://www.zcommunications.org/the-rise-and-fall-of-employer-sanctions-by-david-bacon.

30. Martin Schain, *The Politics of Immigration in France, Britain, and the United States* (New York: Palgrave Macmillan, 2008), 23.

31. Terri Givens and Adam Luedtke, "The Politics of European Union Immigration Policy: Institutions, Salience, and Harmonization," *Policy Studies Journal* 32, no. 1 (2004): 149.

32. Schain, *Politics of Immigration*, 23.

33. According to Schain (*Politics of Immigration*, 177), of the 641 UK constituencies for which census data are available, 128 (20 percent) have nonwhite populations of 10 percent or more. Of these, two-thirds are either in London or the West Midlands.

34. Immigrants and ethnic voters are concentrated in states that are important for presidential elections, such as California and New York.

35. Most of the provisions were finally declared unconstitutional in 1995 by a district judge.

36. Daniel Tichenor, *Dividing Lines: The Politics of Immigration Control in America* (Princeton, N.J.: Princeton University Press, 2002), 285.

37. Zolberg, *Nation by Design*, 389.

38. Ibid., 440.

39. However, Arnold Schwarzenegger, a Republican, won reelection as governor with 39 percent backing from Hispanics.

40. Pew Hispanic Center, *Hispanics and the 2008 Elections* (December 2007). Available at http://pewhispanic.org/files/reports/83.pdf.

41. *New York Times*, July 1, 2010.

42. Spencer H. Su, "Little New in Obama's Immigration Policy," *Washington Post*, May 20, 2009.

43. The two major drops in Hispanics' approval of Obama in 2010—in February and May—coincide with two periods when the president was under fire for not doing enough to promote comprehensive immigration reform in Congress. See Gallup Poll Survey, June 7, 2010. Available at http://www.gallup.com/poll/139379/Hispanics-Approval-Obama-Drops-2010.aspx.

44. CNN, July 2, 2010. Available at http://www.cnn.com/2010/POLITICS/07/01/pol.obama.immigration/index.html.

45. The term "anchor baby" is a misnomer to the extent that it implies that by having a baby in the United States, temporary or illegal immigrants can "anchor" themselves in the country. In fact, a U.S. citizen child cannot file for a U.S. visa for its parents until the child is twenty-one years of age, and upon reaching that age the child must also be earning at least 125 percent of the U.S. poverty threshold to be able to apply. Having a child may help an undocumented parent qualify for relief from deportation, but only four thousand unauthorized immigrants can receive such status per year, and the alien has to have been in the United States for at least ten years.

46. According to the U.S. Constitution's Fourteenth Amendment, ratified in 1868, "All persons born or naturalized in the United States and subject to the jurisdiction thereof, are citizens of the United States."

47. See CNN Opinion Research Poll, August 11, 2010. Available at http://i2.cdn.turner.com/cnn/2010/images/08/11/rel11a1a.pdf.

48. Presented by the media as a mosque, the complex will actually feature an auditorium, spa, basketball court, swimming pool, classrooms, exhibition space, community meeting space, 9/11 memorial, and a prayer space for Muslims.

49. *New York Times*, August 13, 2010.

50. Ibid., August 10, 2010.

51. See CNN / Opinion Research Poll, August 11, 2010. Available at http://i2.cdn.turner.com/cnn/2010/images/08/11/rel11a1a.pdf.

52. Pew Forum on Religion & Public Life, "Growing Number of Americans Say Obama Is a Muslim: Religion, Politics and the President," August 19, 2010. Available at http://pewresearch.org/pubs/1701/poll-obama-muslim-christian-church-out-of-politics-political-leaders-religious.

53. Schain, *Politics of Immigration*, 270.

54. Ibid., 102.

55. Ibid., 31.

56. Hans G. Betz, *Radical Right-Wing Populism in Western Europe* (New York: St. Martin's Press, 1994), 65.

57. Messina, *Logics and Politics of Post-WWII Migration*, 77.

58. As defined and measured by the EU in 1997, racism was in fact confused with anti-immigrant feelings.

59. *BBC News*, April 2, 2007.

60. The two riots, although not connected, took place during the national Bastille Day holiday weekend, July 16–18. In the first case, in a suburb of Grenoble in the Alps foothills, a young delinquent of North African descent was killed by police forces in a shootout following an armed robbery of a casino; in the second case, in the small town of Saint-Aignan, a young Gypsy, who had just committed minor theft, was shot dead by the local police after he tried to run a road checkpoint. Ethnic minorities have not been singled out for "denaturalization" since the Vichy regime took such steps against Jews.

61. Forty camps were dismantled in less than two weeks, and seven hundred people were sent back to Bulgaria and Romania on chartered flights.

62. Other Italian leaders expressed their support. Roberto Maroni (a leading figure of the Northern League and interior minister), for example, said in an interview published in *Corriere della Sera* (August 22, 2010) that France is "simply copying Italy" in flying more than two hundred members of the minority to Romania this week.

63. Messina, *Logics and Politics of Post-WWII Migration*, 94.

64. The Northern League took almost 10 percent of the vote across the country in March 2010.

65. Allied with the French National Front and the British National Party in the EU Parliament, Jobbik has created a paramilitary, the Magyar Garda.

66. In a similar pattern the Bulgarian National Union claimed that the Bulgarian society "suffered under Roma terror over the past 17 years." In the Czech Republic

the National Party proposed a "final solution" for the Roma issue, recommending the resettlement of the Roma population to India.

67. Messina, *Logics and Politics of Post-WWII Migration*, 95.

68. Ruud Koopmans and Paul Statham, *Challenging Immigration and Ethnic Relations Politics: Comparative European Perspectives* (Oxford: Oxford University Press, 2000).

69. The Electoral Commission (2002), *Voter Engagement among Black and Minority Ethnic Communities*. Available at http://www.electoralcommission.org.uk/about-us/voterengageblkandeth.cfm.

70. Around a third of the population is defined as ethnically Russian—a category used to include Russian-speakers from all over the former Soviet Union. They cannot vote, cannot work in many state-employed positions, and often have trouble crossing borders. Almost 90 percent of them do not have Russian citizenship either. They are in a limbo between states.

71. Messina, *Logics and Politics of Post-WWII Migration*, 214.

72. CSA/*Le Parisien* survey. See *Economist*, February 5, 2007.

73. Pew Research Center Poll, July 8, 2010. Available at http://pewresearch.org/pubs/1658/widespread-support-for-banning-full-islamic-veil-western-europe-not-in-america.

Conclusion

1. *Korematsu v. United States*, 323 US 214, 223–4, 1944. See Richard Goldstone, "The Tension between Combating Terrorism and Protecting Civil Liberties," in *Human Rights in the War on Terror*, ed. Richard Ashby Wilson, 157–68 (Cambridge, Mass.: Cambridge University Press, 2005).

2. Cole, *Enemy Aliens*, 5.

3. Michael Ignatieff, *The Lesser Evil: Political Ethics in an Age of Terror* (Princeton, N.J.: Princeton University Press, 2004), 18.

4. Article 4 of the ICCPR (1966).

5. Ignatieff, *Lesser Evil*, 33.

6. Quoted by Daniels, *Coming to America*, 303.

7. *ABC News*, September 5, 2010. Available at http://abcnews.go.com/ThisWeek/tony-blair-regrets-mention/story?id=11562892.

8. *Zadvydas v. Davis*, 533 US 678 (2001).

9. American Civil Liberties Union, *Dimming the Beacon of Freedom: U.S. Violations of the International Covenant on Civil and Political Rights*, Report by the ACLU for the United Nations Human Rights Committee, June 2006, 51.

10. The ACLU successfully challenged the government on this point in 2006 in a case that involved a Sri Lankan torture victim, Ahilan Nadarajah, who sought asylum in the United States but was immediately arrested and detained for more than four years. During this period immigration judges twice granted Nadarajah asylum status. Nonetheless, the U.S. government, citing national security concerns, refused to release him, until the Supreme Court found that the detention was an abuse of discretion.

11. See for example Kathleen Glynn and Sarah Bronstein, *Systemic Problems Persist in U.S. ICE Custody Review for "Indefinite" Detainees*, Report for the Catholic Legal Immigration Network Inc. (2005), 1–36. Available at http://www.cliniclegal.org.

International Federation for Human Rights, *United States–Mexico: Walls, Abuses, and Deaths at the Borders; Flagrant Violations of the Rights of Undocumented Migrants on Their Way to the United States*, Report no. 488/2, March 2008.

12. REAL ID Act, §101(a).

13. Schuster, "Common Sense or Racism?" 249.

14. Jesuit Refugee Service, *Detention in the 10 New Member States: A Study of Administrative Detention of Asylum Seekers and Irregularly Staying Third Country Nationals ...*, JRS Europe Report (Brussels, 2007). Available at http://www.jrseurope.org/.

15. Attorney general remarks, May 30, 2002.Available at http://www.fas.org/irp/news/2002/05/ag053002.html. Not one has been convicted of a terrorist crime to date.

16. Council of the European Union, 11858/1/02, REV 1 LIMITE ENFOPOL 117, October 2002.

17. COM (2007) 0650, November 6, 2007.

18. Cole, *Enemy Aliens*, 5.

19. National Commission on Terrorist Attacks upon the United States, *The 9/11 Commission Report* (Washington, D.C.: Government Printing Office, 2004), 395. Available at http://govinfo.library.unt.edu/911/report/911Report.pdf.

20. Council of the European Union, *EU Annual Report on Human Rights* (Luxembourg: Office for Official Publications of the European Communities, 2007), 39. Available at http://www.consilium.europa.eu/uedocs/cmsUpload/2007.5997-EN-EU_annual_report_on_human_rights_2007.pdf.

21. American Civil Liberties Union, *Dimming the Beacon of Freedom: U.S. Violations of the International Covenant on Civil & Political Rights*, June 2006. The United States has been a party of the International Covenant on Civil and Political Rights since 1991.

22. Council of Europe, Doc. 11202, March 28, 2007, p. 1.

23. White House chief of staff, memorandum for the heads of executive departments and agencies, March 19, 2002.

24. John E. Finn, "Counterterrorism Regimes and the Rule of Law: The Effects of Emergency Legislation on Separation of Powers, Civil Liberties, and Other Fundamental Constitutional Norms," in *The Consequences of Counterterrorism*, ed. Martha Crenshaw (New York: Russell Sage Foundation, 2010), 36.

25. This case involved Australians and Kuwaitis captured in Afghanistan.

26. The case involved an American citizen who was allegedly fighting U.S. troops in support of the Taliban regime. The Court stated that "a state of war is not a blank check for the President when it comes to the rights of the Nation's citizens." (*Hamdi v. Rumsfeld*, no. 03–6696 S. Ct. 26 33)

27. Lakhdar Boumediene was a naturalized citizen of Bosnia and Herzegovina who was held at Guantanamo Bay for several years.

28. U.S. Department of Justice, Government Accountability Office, "Information on Employment Litigation, Housing and Civil Enforcement, Voting and Special Litigation Section's Enforcement Efforts from Fiscal Year 2001 through 2007," December 3, 2009, 1–180. Available at http://www.gao.gov/new.items/d1075.pdf.

29. Parliamentary Assembly of the Council of Europe, "State of Democracy in Europe, 2007" (Doc. 11203), 7–8.

30. *BBC News*, February 3, 2011. The UK had deals with countries such as Jordan, Ethiopia, and Libya.

31. Control orders were introduced in 2005 to restrict the freedoms of suspects who could neither be charged nor deported. This process involves relocation far away from home, a sixteen-hour curfew, electronic tag, ban from using phones and Internet, ban from public meetings, and regular reports to the police.

32. The two other provisions include authority to track "lone wolf" suspects who may not be tied to recognized terror organizations, and to obtain records (such as library and bookstore records, tax documents, and gun records) from organizations without being required to show probable cause that the records are related to a terrorist investigation.

33. *CBS News*, October 27, 2007.

34. *Government Executive.Org*, February 9, 2011. Available at http://www.govexec.com/story_page.cfm?articleid=47060&oref=todaysnews.

35. Agamben, *State of Exception*, chap. 1.

36. Paul Roe, "Securitization and Minority Rights: Conditions of Desecuritization," *Security Dialogue* 35, no. 3 (2004): 279–94.

37. Council of Europe, "The Future of Democracy in Europe: Trends, Analyses, Reforms," Green Paper SG/inf (2004) 27, August 31, 2004, p. 8.

38. Home Office, *What Perceptions Do the UK Public Have Concerning the Impact of Counter-Terrorist Legislation Implemented since 2000?* Occasional Paper 88, March 2010, p. 18. Available at http://library.npia.police.uk/docs/homisc/occ88-ctlegislation.pdf. The current limit fixed by the 2006 Terrorist Act is twenty-eight days.

39. This lawsuit involves Jeppesen Dataplan Inc., a Boeing subsidiary accused of arranging flights for the CIA to transfer prisoners to other countries for "interrogation." The ACLU filed the case on behalf on five former prisoners who were tortured in captivity. See *New York Times*, September 8, 2010.

40. This trial has confirmed the fears of those who believe that the protection afforded to defendants in the civilian courts might undermine the attempts to bring terrorists to justice. This trial also failed, incidentally, to fulfil the expectations of the proponents of civilian courts: a ruling by Judge Lewis A. Kaplan ensured that the issue of torture, as well as the conditions of detention by the CIA and the military, would not be addressed. The judge also ruled that the long delay (almost eight years) in bringing Ghailani into court had not violated his right to a speedy trial. Some supporters of the civilian system also admitted that the mixed verdict has damaged their cause because it demonstrates that a jury could acquit a defendant of most of the charges against him (although Ghailani is facing a life sentence). According to Juan C. Zarate, a former member of the Bush administration who argues for using civilian courts, "this complicates the equation with regard to trials of high-level al Qaeda detainees like Khalid Sheikh Mohammed." (*New York Times*, November 8, 2010).

41. Carl Schmitt, *The Concept of the Political*, trans. George D. Schwab (Chicago: University of Chicago Press, 1996), 27.

INDEX

Page numbers followed by letters *f* and *t* refer to figures and tables, respectively.